WITHDRAWN

THE CRISIS OF
ENGLISH LIBERTY

The CRISIS of ENGLISH LIBERTY

A HISTORY OF THE STUART MONARCHY AND THE PURITAN REVOLUTION

BY

Sir JOHN A. R. MARRIOTT

HONORARY FELLOW (FORMERLY FELLOW) OF
WORCESTER COLLEGE, OXFORD ; LATE M.P.
FOR THE CITY OF YORK

' The true end of government is Liberty.

SPINOZA

GREENWOOD PRESS, PUBLISHERS
WESTPORT, CONNECTICUT

Originally published in 1930
by The Clarendon Press, Oxford

Reprinted from an original copy in the collections
of the Brooklyn Public Library

First Greenwood Reprinting 1970

Library of Congress Catalogue Card Number 74-109782

SBN 8371-4272-5

Printed in the United States of America

PREFACE

'ANY such career and character as Cromwell's, like one of the great stock arguments of old-world drama, must still be capable of an almost endless range of presentment and interpretation.' Such was Mr. John Morley's excuse for adding one more to the existing biographies of Cromwell. I adopt it as my own excuse for this book—for retreading such well-trodden paths as those which traverse the seventeenth century. And I will add to it a confession, more intimate and personal. After a protracted immersion in the history of the nineteenth century and the politics of the twentieth, I now return to my historical first love. There are admittedly dangers in that seductive adventure, but I hope my readers will be more slow to discover than I am to confess them. It would be uncandid, however, did I not confess another motive which has impelled me to this enterprise.

History, it has always seemed to me, is something more than a mere record of the past; it must necessarily represent the past as seen through the medium of the present. Consequently, each generation must look at the past from a fresh angle. True of all periods, this is pre-eminently true of the history of the seventeenth century, and of those who look back upon it from the twentieth. For this reason. The seventeenth century was confronted by problems which we thought it had permanently solved. Unexpectedly, they have in these latter days re-emerged; they are still, it seems, living issues; they still stir the blood of those who mingle in public affairs. It is mainly for that reason that I have resumed my study of the constitutional conflicts of the seventeenth century—a study begun half a century ago and, though often interrupted, never wholly laid aside.

I regretfully recognize that this avowal will cost me

the good opinion of some 'orthodox' historians, and that I shall be accused of the deadly sin of 'reading history backwards'. But all history, save contemporary history, must, in a sense, be read backwards.

In any sense inimical to scientific detachment I warmly repudiate any such intention, though I frankly confess that this book has been written from the angle of our own day, and with special reference to problems now insistently confronting us. This indeed constitutes the only claim to originality it may be found to possess.

The book is intended primarily for the 'general reader', for men and women who, being entrusted, as all English adults are, with a share in the government of the Commonwealth, are anxious to discharge their responsibility, and believe, like the author, that they can do their duty to their own generation only if they are familiar with the problems which confronted their forefathers. I hope that the book will also be found useful by those students in Universities and in the highest forms of schools who are making a special study of this period.

Scholars will perceive that I have written largely from the primary sources, though I have made free use of secondary authorities as well. The use of foot-notes has been as far as possible restricted, but a list of authorities, original and secondary, will be found in an appendix. I hope that I have not omitted from the list any work to which I am indebted: but I must here acknowledge a special debt to the works of Dr. Gardiner and Sir Charles Firth. The latter has, indeed, a special claim on my pious gratitude, since it was he who edited the *Clarke Papers*, a collection of papers bequeathed to Worcester College by Dr. George Clarke, a son of the writer, Sir George Clarke, Secretary to the Council of the Army (1647–9) and to General Monk (1651–60). These papers are still in possession of the College to which Dr. Clarke was in this and other ways a generous benefactor. They constitute, I need hardly add, a contribution of incomparable value for the history of the period 1647–60. To renew acquaintance with those papers in the library of my own College has been one of the many pleasures incidental to a return to the studies of my youth.

Some paragraphs from one of those studies, my *Life and Times of Lucius Cary, Lord Falkland*, a book which has been for many years out of print, are incorporated in the present volume.

J. A. R. MARRIOTT.

May 1930.

TABLE OF CONTENTS

CONTENTS

Characteristics of the English Revolution: (a) conservative, (b) parliamentary, (c) short-lived popularity. The Non-Jurors. Toleration Act. Character of William III. Divergence of views between William and the Whigs. Results of the Revolution. The rule of the Aristocracy. Freedom of opinion. Licensing Act lapsed. Independence of the Judiciary.

PROLOGUE

THE EXECUTIVE AND THE LAW

The Problem of Liberty

'WE have a form of government not obtained by imitation of the laws of neighbouring States—nay rather we are a pattern to others than they to us.' Thus proudly did Pericles speak of the Athenian Polity. Englishmen have, in the past, been not less proud of their form of government, not less confident than Pericles that it was for them to show the way, for the less advanced peoples of the world to follow, if they could. 'Let not England', wrote John Milton, 'forget her precedence of teaching others how to live.' *The English Constitution*

Nor did foreign commentators hesitate to concede the precedence which Milton claimed. On the contrary, competent critics in different countries have, with rare unanimity, paid homage to England as the home of liberty and the birth-land of Parliamentary Government. The admiration conceived by Montesquieu, the father of modern Political Science, calls for no illustrative citation; it is writ large over the face of the *Esprit des Lois*. But the less familiar comment of an American writer is worth quoting:— *Montesquieu*

'The British Constitution', wrote Madison in the *Federalist*, was to Montesquieu what Homer was to the didactic writers on Epic poetry. As the latter have considered the word of the immortal bard as the perfect model from which the principles and rules of the epic art were to be drawn, and by which all similar works were to be judged, so this great political critic appears to have viewed the Constitution of England as the standard or, to use his own expression, as the mirror of political liberty; and to have delivered, in the form of elementary truths, the several charactertistic principles of that particular system.'

Madison's observation is as just as it is discerning.

Monta-
lembert

Montalembert, writing just a century later than Montesquieu, was not behind him in admiration for the English
system of government. To him as to other philosophical
writers of that time England seemed to afford the most
perfect example in the modern world of a State in which
liberty was reconciled with order. 'No other form of
Government', he wrote, 'has ever given to man more
opportunities of accomplishing all that is just and reasonable, or more facilities for avoiding error and for correcting
it.' And again: 'To restrain and guide democracy without
debasing it, to regulate and reconcile it with a liberal
monarchy or a conservative republic—such is the problem
of our age; but it is a problem which has been as yet
nowhere solved except in England.' [1]

Milton—
Maine

Englishmen have mingled their praises with those of
foreigners. From Milton to Maine—a space of more than
two centuries—there was hardly a dissentient note. 'There
is no civil Government that hath been known . . . more
divinely and harmoniously toned and more equally balanced,
as it were, by the hand and scale of justice than is the
Commonwealth of England.' So Milton wrote in the
seventeenth century. Burke, writing a hundred years later
declared, perhaps with a touch of pardonable arrogance,
that 'We ought to understand [the admired Constitution
of England] according to our measure; and to venerate
where we are not able presently to comprehend'. Sir
Henry Maine, just a century later than Burke, wrote:
'Many persons in whom familiarity has bred contempt,
may think it a trivial observation that the British Constitution, if not (as some call it) a holy thing, is a thing unique
and remarkable. A series of undesigned changes brought
it to such a condition, that satisfaction and impatience, the
two great sources of political conduct, were both reasonably gratified under it. For this condition it became, not
metaphorically but literally, the envy of the world, and
the world took on all sides to copying it.'

The tone is entirely confident. Nor did any doubt that

[1] *The Political Future of England* (1855), p. 36.

the confidence was justified. Further: most critics would The Critical Period
probably have agreed that while each period of English
History had made its contribution to the imposing structure, as it stands to-day, the critical period in its building was the seventeenth century. Of the salient characteristics of the English Constitution two obviously stand
out pre-eminent: the one is the doctrine of Parliamentary
Sovereignty; the other is the 'Rule of Law'. A great
German commentator [1] characterized England in a single
word as a *Rechtstaat*—a Commonwealth based upon justice
and law. De Lolme, a Swiss commentator, declared the
combination of stability and liberty to be peculiar to
England, and he attributed it to the English system of
Parliamentary Government and to the prevalence of the
Rule of Law. Is it controvertible that these outstanding
features were the result pre-eminently of the constitutional
conflict of the seventeenth century, or that we can clearly
discern them in the Revolution Settlement?

The Revolution of 1688 was for centuries accepted, in
regard to the fundamental bases of our Constitution, as
final and conclusive. 'The battle', as Hallam says in a
notable passage, 'had been fought and gained.'

Are the grave issues then fought out between the Crown
and Parliament, and between the Executive and the
Judiciary, about to be reopened in our own day? Indications seem to point to an affirmative answer. On 30
October 1929 it was announced that the Lord Chancellor [2]
had appointed a Committee 'to consider the powers exercised by or under the direction of (or by persons or bodies
appointed specially by) Ministers of the Crown by way of
(*a*) delegated legislation, and (*b*) judicial or quasi-judicial
decision, and to report what safeguards are desirable or
necessary to secure the constitutional principles of the
supremacy of Parliament and the supremacy of the Law'.
Two days later the Lord Chief Justice of England de-
scended from the forum into the market-place and issued
urbi if not *orbi* his reflections upon the contemporary

[1] Rudolph Von Gneist.   [2] Lord Sankey.

B 2

situation. His work bears the significant title *The New Despotism*,[1] and if the argument of his essay should, on closer investigation, be sustained, his arresting title, and the unusual step he has taken in publication, will be more than justified.

Lord Hewart naturally refers to the earlier crisis in the long struggle for liberty in England.

Lord Hewart on 'The New Despotism' 'It is manifestly easy', he writes, 'to point a superficial contrast between what was done or attempted in the days of our least wise kings, and what is being done or attempted to-day. In those days the method was to defy Parliament—and it failed. In these days the method is to cajole, to coerce, and to use Parliament—and it is strangely successful. The old despotism, which was defeated, offered Parliament a challenge. The new despotism, which is not yet defeated, gives Parliament an anaesthetic. The strategy is different, but the goal is the same. It is to subordinate Parliament, to evade the Courts, and to render the will, or the caprice, of the Executive unfettered and supreme.'[2]

The issue is, *mutatis mutandis*, precisely the same as that which confronted our fathers under the Stuarts. The Stuart kings desired to make 'the will or the caprice of the Executive unfettered and supreme'. They sought to attain their end by exalting the prerogative of the Crown, by curtailing the power of Parliament, and, above all, by subordinating the Judiciary to the Executive, by making the Judges, in Bacon's famous phrase, 'lions under the throne'.

Symptoms The danger against which the Lord Chief Justice has deemed it incumbent on him to utter a grave warning would seem to have arisen from three main sources: the exaltation of the 'expert' in all spheres of activity; the multiplication of the functions of Government and the consequent expansion of the Public Deparments; and, not least, the growing volume of legislation and the increasing preoccupation or heedlessness of the Legislature.

[1] Ernest Benn, Ltd., 1929.   [2] *The New Despotism*, p. 17.

Government to-day is increasingly regarded as the function of experts, as the business of the permanent officials in the great Public Departments, not of a Parliament composed of amateurs, not even of the eminent amateurs who are selected from among the legislators at Westminster to preside temporarily over the Departments in Whitehall. Having decided this point in their own favour (and that there is something to be said for it cannot be denied), ambitious Civil Servants have found an easy road towards autocracy. Much of the complicated legislation submitted to Parliament is necessarily drafted in the Departments which will have to administer it, if and when it finds its way on to the Statute Book. Few modern Statutes carry their meaning on the face of them. The drafts are rendered partially intelligible to legislators only by memoranda issued by the Departments concerned. The Statutes themselves are mere skeletons; the clauses contain constant reference to previous Statutes, in the light of which only can they be understood and interpreted, while all matters of detail are delegated to the Departments which take power, under the Statutes, to issue Rules and Orders. It is these Rules and Orders, far more than the authorizing Statutes, that affect the daily life and conduct of the citizen. In some cases the sanction of Parliament is required to validate them, but the control thus secured to the supreme Legislature is, in effect, wholly illusory. By this means the legislative function has been virtually transferred from Westminster to Whitehall.

Delegated Legislature

Nor does the matter end there. If it did, the Law Courts would still afford a considerable measure of protection to the citizen. But the function of the Courts is confined to interpretation. If the *Rule* is *intra vires*; if the Orders made by a particular Department are within the terms of the Statute enacted by Parliament, the Judges, whether they approve or not, must give effect to them.

Impotence of the Courts

A danger even more insidious has of late years revealed itself. The Departments, not content with invading the domain of the Legislature, have essayed to supersede the functions of the Judiciary. There is, in fact, an increasing tendency to make the official, or his temporary chief, judge in his own case.

The Executive and the Judiciary Thus the citizen is deprived of the elementary safeguards of liberty. Among those safeguards are: the independence of the Judges (secured by the Act of Settlement), publicity, and uniformity. A Civil Servant is not independent, but liable to dismissal, if he be identifiable; but as a fact he is frequently anonymous; he need not take evidence, nor regard it if he takes it; nor is he bound by previous decisions. 'Will anybody at this time of day', asks Lord Hewart, 'deny that it is essential to the administration of justice that the decision should be based on evidence . . . that every party should have an opportunity of being heard . . . that all judicial proceedings should be held in public.' All these essentials are or may be conspicuous by their absence in the Departmental Star Chamber of to-day. It is not too much to say that 'such proceedings are a mere travesty of justice', tolerated only because the victims are relatively few, and because they fear lest public protest should bring a worse thing upon them.

Administrative Law and Administrative Lawlessness Some critics have suggested that in recent tendencies we may discern an approximation to the systems of Administrative Law and Administrative Tribunals which are common in continental countries. That idea is, however, hotly repudiated by some of the most accomplished of contemporary jurists in this country. The system of *droit administratif* is, as we shall see later, fundamentally opposed to the English conception of the 'Rule of Law'; but 'Administrative Law' is, as Lord Hewart observes, 'at any rate a form or branch of law . . . the rules and principles of which it is true differ essentially from the rules and principles of the ordinary law governing the relations of private citizens *inter se*'; but at least it is 'administered by a tribunal which applies judicial methods of procedure', and it is, on that account and others, preferable to the 'Administrative Lawlessness' which is gradually insinuating itself into English procedure.

Other competent critics go further. Continental jurists naturally refuse to admit the inferiority of their system; they maintain that, as regards the liberty of the subject, English citizens are actually in a worse position than the citizens, for example, of France or Germany. Nor does this contention lack a measure of support from English jurists.

'As regards legal remedies against the acts of the Executive and its servants', writes Professor J. H. Morgan, 'the subject is placed in a far better position in Germany than in this country. So much so that a German lawyer would be on strong ground if he retorted that it is not our own country but his which is distinguished by the "Rule of Law"' [1]

The most comprehensive treatment of this subject in English is to be found in a treatise lately published by Dr. Port.[2] The learned author shows that to a large extent the objections urged against 'Administrative Law' by English critics have, in the last half century, been removed. He contends, indeed, that 'in no other country is the ordinary citizen so well protected against the consequences of acts of State servants, as he is in France at the present time'.[3] Dr. Port is, of course, constrained to admit that *tribunaux administratifs* are still distinct from the ordinary courts, but they are distinguished, he maintains, 'on account of the scope of their jurisdiction, and not because the standard of justice is lower or more variable'. Similarly, Professor C. K. Allen, though stoutly protesting against the encroachments of the Bureaucracy in England, is fain to admit that 'the development of French administrative law in the last half century has been very much more in favour of the subject than of the administrator'.[4] Nobody can pretend that this is the case in England. On the contrary, the position of a subject engaged in litigation against the Crown is, in the highest degree, anomalous and unsatisfactory. A Bill drafted in 1927, was in fact, designed to

---

[1] ap. Gleeson Robinson, *Public Authorities and Legal Liabilities*, p. xlix.
[2] *Administrative Law*, Longmans, Green & Co., 1929.
[3] *Op. cit.*, p. 330.   [4] *Quarterly Review*, No. 477, p. 247.

assimilate legal proceedings in which the Crown is involved
to those between subject and subject; to make the Crown
liable for torts or wrongs caused to subjects; and to put
the Crown on the same footing as other litigants in regard
to the payment of costs. Unfortunately, the Bill, though
strongly supported by professional and lay opinion, was
never even introduced.

Black-
stone
    There is, then, a gradual convergence of opinion towards
the view that the present situation in England is becoming
year by year more and more intolerable. The idea that
a remedy may be found in the frank adoption of a system
of administrative law and administrative tribunals is,
nevertheless, exceedingly repugnant to Englishmen trained
in the school of Blackstone and Dicey. Blackstone's
superb vindication of the 'vigour of our free Constitution'
has indeed for generations formed the text of innumerable
commentators. His insistence on the legislative Sovereignty of Parliament; on the safeguards provided by the
English Constitution for the liberty of the citizen, his
personal security and the sanctity of his private property;
on the regular administration and free course of justice in
the Courts of Law; on the delicate equilibrium of the
several forces of the State; on the distribution of powers
between the Executive, the Legislative, and the Judicial
organs of Government—all this has now become the
commonplace of historical criticism. Two short passages
—both classical—may however be cited. The first deals
with the danger arising from the confusion or concentra-
tion of.'powers' and runs thus:

    'In all tyrannical Governments the supreme majesty, or the
right both of making and enforcing laws is vested in the same
man or one and the same body of men; and when these two
powers are united together there is no public liberty.' [1]

    Forms and technicalities apart, these powers have in
some measure been united together in the English Government of to-day. Skeletons of Statutes issue from a Public

[1] *Commentaries*, I. ii. 146.

Department; they are remitted by Parliament to the same Department to be clothed with the flesh and blood of Statutory Rules and Orders; if those Rules appear to be infringed it is, not infrequently, the same Department which deals, without appeal to the Courts, with the delinquent.

Even more famous is the second passage which sets forth the principle of Parliamentary Sovereignty as follows:

The
Sove-
reignty
of Parlia-
ment

'The power and jurisdiction of Parliament', says Sir Edward Coke, ' is so transcendent and absolute, that it cannot be confined, either for causes or persons, within any bounds. And of this high court, he adds, it may be fairly said, " Si antiquitatem spectes, est vetustissima; si dignitatem, est honoratissima; si jurisdictionem, est capacissima." It hath sovereign and uncontrollable authority in the making, confirming, enlarging, restraining, abrogating, repealing, reviving, and expounding of laws, concerning matters of all possible denominations, ecclesiastical or temporal, civil, military, maritime, or criminal; this being the place where that absolute despotic power, which must in all governments reside somewhere, is entrusted by the constitution of these kingdoms.'

The principle of Parliamentary Sovereignty remains indeed theoretically sacrosanct. Can it be contended that the growing practice of delegating legislative power to Public Departments and other subordinate bodies has not very seriously impaired it?

'The action of our Acts of Parliament', writes a careful commentator, 'grows more and more dependent upon subsidiary legislation. More than half our modern Acts are to this extent incomplete statements of law.' [1] Dr. Carr understates the case. Some idea of the extent to which the practice of delegated legislation has developed may be gained from a comparison of the number of Statutory Rules and Orders issued by Departments with the number of Acts of Parliament placed upon the Statute Book. During the years 1926, 1927, and 1928, which are entirely

Depart-
mental
Legisla-
tion

[1] *Delegated Legislation*, p. 1.

typical years, the number of Acts passed averaged 50·6, the average number of Statutory Rules and Orders in the same period issued was 1,408·6. The average number of pages in the official volumes was, in the former case 539, in the latter 1,844, and the volumes of Orders are much more closely printed than the Statute volumes.[1]

Of the disproportion between a Statute as enacted by Parliament and the subsidiary, though not less 'Statutory' Rules and Orders, a conspicuous illustration is afforded by the *Factory and Workshops Amendment Act* (1929). The Act itself consists of two short operative clauses, which cover half a page. Before the ink on that Act was dry the Secretary of State issued, in order to fulfil the intentions of the Act, a White Paper consisting of no fewer than six closely printed *Statutory Rules and Orders*.

Legislative Methods and Forms

The tendency thus illustrated marks a relatively recent departure from the traditional methods and forms of English legislation. Until yesterday Englishmen were said to have an

'instinctive distrust of official discretion, an instinctive scepticism about bureaucratic wisdom. They are ready enough, they are often embarrassingly eager to confer new powers on the executive authority central or local. But they like to determine for themselves how those powers are to be exercised. They like to see in black and white the rules by which their liberty of action is restrained. . . . And they insist on the meaning of those rules being determined, not by any special tribunal but by the ordinary Courts of the country. This is the peculiarity which constitutes the most marked distinction between British and American legislation on the one hand and Continental legislation on the other, and which makes the framework and arrangement of an English Statute such an incomprehensible puzzle to the ordinary continental student of laws.'

Those words sound like an echo from the distant past; the passage is in fact extracted from the classical work on

[1] Reply of Mr. Stanley Baldwin to Sir John Marriott: *Commons' Debates*, vol. 226, cols. 24–5.

Legislative Methods and Forms published in 1901 and written by Sir Courtenay Ilbert, who was for many years Clerk of the House of Commons and had, therefore, exceptional opportunties for close observation of the changing form of English Statutes. The change is also noted and commented upon by an equally acute and somewhat more detached critic of English institutions, President Lowell of Harvard. After a reference to the 'growing practice of delegating legislative power' Dr. Lowell proceeds:

'We have much talk about the need for the devolution of the power of Parliament on subordinate representative bodies, but the tendency is not mainly in that direction. The authority of this kind vested in the county councils is small, too small to affect the question. The real delegation has been in favour of the administrative departments of the central government, and this involves a striking departure from Anglo-Saxon traditions, with a distinct approximation to the practice of continental countries.' [1]

A new and a striking departure from Anglo-Saxon tradition it unquestionably is. Partly owing to the increasing complexity of industrial and social conditions, partly under the subtle and influence of a Civil Service, consciously or unconsciously permeated by the ideas of Fabian Socialism, partly in deference to the prevailing fashion which derides the principle of *laisser-faire* and to the growing demand for governmental guidance and control in all the affairs of life, partly, it may be, from sheer inability to cope with the insistent demand for legislation which shall cover every department of human activity, Parliament has unquestionably manifested a disposition, in these latter days, to give more and more discretion to the administrative Departments. Many modern Statutes are mere *cadres*, giving a very inadequate idea of their ultimate scope. They lay down general principles and leave it to the appropriate Departments to give detailed effect to them.

[1] A. L. Lowell, *Government of England* (1908), i, p. 363.

Recent
Illustra-
tions Among a multitude of illustrations a recent and characteristic one may be cited. Section 67 (1) of the *Rating
and Valuation Act* (1925) ran as follows:

'If any difficulty arises in connexion with the application of
this Act to . . . or otherwise in bringing into operation any of
the provisions of this Act, the Minister may by Order remove
the difficulty or . . . do any other thing which appears to him
necessary or expedient for [then follow certain details] . . . and
*any such Order may modify the provisions of this Act so far as
may appear to the Minister necessary or expedient* for carrying
the Order into effect.'

A clause on the same lines was inserted in the *Local
Government Bill* (1929), but was slightly modified in deference to the strongly expressed fears of the House of
Commons. The Minister sought, indeed, to justify his
original clause by reference to many recent precedents,
but the reference merely proved that the vigilance of
Parliament has been less conspicuous than the arrogance of
the Departments.

Safe-
guards Apologists of the new order argue that we are not so
defenceless as hostile critics allege; that in fact there exist
very ample safeguards for the protection of the individual
in his possible conflict with the State. Is it so? Mr.
Baldwin, in the statement to which reference has already
been made, indicated two safeguards against possible
abuse of the power to make Statutory Rules and Orders'.
The first is the power of the Courts to treat as void any
Rule or Order which is beyond the powers of the Rule—
making Authority; the second is the opportunity open to
any member of Parliament, while such Rules or Orders lie
on the Table of the House to move for their annulment.
But of these safeguards the second is almost wholly illusory,
and the utility of the first is necessarily limited, and, of late
years, has been grievously curtailed by the carelessness of
the Legislature. Any one who is acquainted with the procedure and business methods of the House of Commons
can measure the value of the second of the safeguards on
which Mr. Baldwin elaborately insisted; but it would be

interesting to have a return of the occasions on which,
during the period covered by the figures he quoted, private
members have utilized the opportunity which the 'laying'
of Papers has afforded them.

Far greater importance does unquestionably attach to
the powers of the Judiciary. But on the position of the
Courts in this regard two observations must be made.
First, every one knows that a Court of Law, even that
most powerful of tribunals, the Supreme Court of the
United States, can intervene only when moved thereto by
an aggrieved suitor. Not every citizen is aware of the
rights he possesses against a Government Department, and
of those who are, few care to go to the trouble and expense
of vindicating them. Great corporations can, of course,
look after their own interests, and do; the individual is
apt to prefer the disease, even if he is sufficiently expert
to detect it, to the only remedy which is open to him. This,
however, should be said. If the citizen has a grievance and
can afford to seek redress from the Courts, he will quite
certainly obtain it. The independence of the Judiciary is
above reproach. *The Courts of Law*

In face of the heedlessness of Parliament the Courts are,
however, powerless. If the legislators betray the pass, how
shall the Judges defend it? This is where Mr. Baldwin's
statement betokened misapprehension of the point at
issue. If a Rule or Order is *ultra vires* the Courts will, of
course, treat it as void. The root of the mischief lies much
deeper than that. It lies in the method and form of
legislation. Law-making, as already said, has passed largely
into the hands of the same persons who will have to administer the law when it has received the sanction of
Parliament. *Responsibility of Parliament*

Who can blame the administrator? His inclination,
entirely natural, is to make things as easy as possible for
his own Department. His zeal—nor need one deny its
purity—is for efficient administration. In his eyes Parliamentary interference and judicial interpretation are drags
upon efficiency. If Parliament can be persuaded to abandon

its control, so much the better for the public and so much the easier for the public servant.

In connexion with the position of the Judiciary another point deserves to be noticed. Familiar to students of the seventeenth century as the 'auricular consultation' of the judges, the device was, as we shall presently see, the subject of a vigorous protest by Sir Edward Coke. King James I attempted to obtain the opinion of the Judges beforehand as to the legality of certain proceedings which the Crown was about to take against an individual. A similar device was discovered in Clause iv of the *Rating and Valuation Bill* (1928). The clause as originally drafted empowered the Minister of Health to submit to the High Court. a doubtful point of law in relation to the valuation of hereditaments. The object of this procedure might seem, on the face of it, to be not merely innocent but expressly designed to save time, trouble, and expense to Local Authorities and individual ratepayers. It was hoped, in fact, by this method to obtain beforehand an authoritative opinion from the Court, and thus to secure equality and uniformity in valuation. But the great lawyers in the House of Lords scented the danger involved in the clause, and compelled a reluctant Government to delete it. The case against it was admirably put by Lord Merrivale, an eminent judge who had also held office as Secretary of State. He declared his conviction that the clause in question was mischievous, and added:

'What it would effect, whether it is designed or not, would be to make the Judiciary act in an ancillary and advisory capacity to the Executive, and confound the working of the judicial system with Executive administration. Every student of politics who has considered the matter during the whole of our political history has seen that that is the road to mischief. It was the kind of proposal, the kind of intention, which led to the removal of Lord Coke from his high office, and to his going into opposition against the then Government (which, of course, had an autocratic flavour about it but which he had honestly as an Englishman supported), because, as he said, it established a species of auricular relation between His Majesty's Administration and the Judges, who had to be impartial in all questions affecting the subject . . . a system which puts a public Department in a position to take charge of the question with which it deems itself administratively concerned, to organize the argument of it, to provide payment according to its views for some of the argument, to obtain a decision and then to promulgate or to retain it to regulate its relations with His Majesty's subjects is unheard of. I believe such a system is very unhealthy.'

Then follow words which are among the gravest which have fallen from a constitutional jurist in England since the seventeenth century:

'It is no part of the business of His Majesty's Judges, and never has been part of their business, at any rate since the Act of Settlement, to have any advisory concern in the acts of the Administration or to take any part in advising the Administration. The natural effect of associating them with the Administration and attaching to them the responsibility for conclusions which are put forward by the Administration will be to weaken the authority of the Judiciary. It can have no other effect.[1]

Lord Haldane's opinion coincided with that of Lord Merrivale:

'The clause he said, is an attempt to introduce something quite novel, so far as the law of England is concerned, into our procedure—to introduce the plan of enabling an abstract question, a question not necessarily relating to any concrete case but purely general; to be put before the Judges, and the Judges are to be compelled—the word is "shall"—to give an opinion upon that question. That plan is unknown to our law.'

Lord Hanworth, the Master of the Rolls, and Lord Hewart, the Lord Chief Justice, were not less emphatic in their condemnation of the clause:

'This power,' said the former, 'given to the Minister to take the opinion of the High Court without a sufficient investigation of the facts and without opportunity being given to all those who desire to be heard and ought to be heard, to come before the Court is to my mind a piece of mischievous legislation.'

Lord Hewart went so far as to say that the clause was without exception 'the worst clause of its kind which has ever appeared. . . . This was a proposal to convert his Majesty's Judges into departmental solicitors'.

[1] Lords' Debates, vol. 70, No. 23, pp. 759–62.

The vigilance of these great lawyers was rewarded; their insistence prevailed; and the offending clause was deleted from the Bill.

The fight for freedom   The attempts made by the Government of the day to insert such a clause into an Act of Parliament is, however, another and gravely disquieting symptom of the recrudescence of the mischievous tendencies successfully resisted by our predecessors in the seventeenth century. It may be only another illustration of the famous French proverb, *plus ça change, plus c'est la même chose*; but this much is clear, that, under conditions greatly altered and in forms not always recognizable, devices adopted by the Stuart Kings in their contest with Parliament and in their relations with the Judges are to-day making an unwelcome reappearance.

For that reason, among others, it has seemed worth while to retell an oft-told tale, and to recall, for the benefit of the present generation, the recollection of the battles fought and the victories won by their forefathers. Liberty is a term not easily defined. Many attempts, not here to be recalled, have been made to define it. Two shall suffice for our immediate purpose. In his Second Treatise on Government John Locke wrote:

'The liberty of man in Society is to be under no other legislative power but that established by consent in the Commonwealth, nor under the dominion of any will, or restraint of any law but what that legislative shall enact according to the trust put in it.' [1]

The second definition is from Montesquieu's *Esprit des Lois*:

'La liberté politique dans un citoyen est cette tranquillité d'esprit qui provient de l'opinion que chacun a de sa sûreté; et pour qu'on ait cette liberté, il faut que la gouvernement soit tel, qu'un citoyen ne puisse pas craindre un autre citoyen.'

Definitions are notoriously inadequate, but one thing is certain: the 'price of liberty is eternal vigilance'. English people complacently imagine that having paid that price

[1] iv, § 22. (ii) i. 261.

consistently throughout the ages the appropriate reward
has not been withheld. 'The prize which we now play for
is the liberty of the subject.' So said Nicolas Culpepper in
1649. He never doubted that by the execution of King
Charles the prize had been secured for his own and for
succeeding generations. Nay more: it was the common
belief of Englishmen that to them alone had the prize been
awarded. Liberty is the chief distinction of England from
other European countries.' So John Scott, a publicist of
the day, wrote from Paris in 1816. That conviction was
tenaciously held for at least another century. It was
largely responsible for the contemptuous pity with which
the average Englishman regarded his less fortunate continental neighbour. Educated opinion is, however, no
longer so complacent or so confident as regards our
monopoly or even our pre-eminence.

To desire a monopoly were unfriendly; to abandon the   The
hope of pre-eminence were craven. Not the least powerful   Crown
incentive to renewed endeavour and reawakened vigilance   and the
is to recall the struggles and victories of the past. Parlia-   subject
ment may be more chary of delegating legislative powers
to the Executive to-day, if its members remember the
stand taken by their predecessors against the claims put
forward by the Stuarts to issue Proclamations, having the
force of law, or to suspend or dispense with the Statutes
of the Realm. The Judges may be encouraged to maintain
their resistance to the new despotism by renewed research
into the history of the seventeenth century. Such cases as
those of the Levant merchant Bates, of the Five Knights,
of *Rex* v. *Hampden*, of *Godden* v. *Hales*, and of the Seven
Bishops, may well suggest reflections even to the eminent
judges who have been called upon to decide the many
difficult cases which have come before the Courts since the
close of the Great War. Some of those cases—such as that
of *Attorney-General* v. *De Keyser's Royal Hotel* (1920);
Rex v. *Home Secretary, ex parte O'Brien* (1923); *Rex* v.
Halliday (1917); *Attorney-General* v. *Wilts United Dairies*
(1921), to mention only a few—have made history

not less surely than those cited from the seventeenth century.[1]

They prove, were proof needed, that never in the long history of the Judicial Bench have the Judges been more keenly alive to their responsibilities as the custodians of the liberties of the subject. But it must be repeated with emphasis that if the Legislature be careless, or subservient to the Executive, the Judiciary is powerless.

The final result of the prolonged conflict of the seventeenth century was to confide the key of the position to Parliament. Parliament still retains it. If, however, Parliament should neglect to use it, the battle will have to be fought afresh, under the same flag, on the same field. Our fathers fought against Princes; we have to fight against the Powers which lurk in the darkness of Whitehall and still cover themselves under the Prerogative of the Crown.

Recent tendencies have thus invested the history of the seventeenth century with a new and arresting significance. It may not, then, be amiss to con once more the lessons which that period is pre-eminently calculated to teach.

[1] For particulars of these cases cf. Port, *Administrative Law*.

I. THE PROBLEMS OF THE AGE

The Stuart Theory of Monarchy

CRISIS is a word which rises lightly to the lips of the A critical period orator and runs even more trippingly from the facile pen of the publicist. But unquestionably it may in strictness be applied by the historian to the period of the seventeenth century. In a sense, all periods of history are critical, as they are all transitional; yet some are more critical, and more obviously transitional, than others. Among these none in all English history stands out more definitely than the period of the Puritan Revolution. The age which witnessed the momentous conflicts between Bacon and Coke, between Charles I and John Hampden, between Pym and Strafford, between Cromwell and Fairfax on one side, and, on the other, the Lilburnes and Winstanleys, and not least between the later Stuarts and the small group of enlightened statesmen who achieved the bloodless revolution of 1688—that surely were a period unequivocally and in the strictest sense critical.

These names, moreover, suggest the great issues that were involved in the conflict, succinctly though not exhaustively; for besides a sheaf of constitutional problems there was another not less momentous: it was the problem suggested by such names as those of Laud and Chillingworth, of Baillie, Baxter, and Milton. But with the ecclesiastical problem of the age this book is concerned only in so far as it reacts upon the political problem.

The political position of Roman Catholics and Protes- The points at issue tants, conforming and non-conforming, has now been placed happily beyond the range of controversy. So also, it was hoped, have the political problems. But can this be so confidently affirmed? Broadly speaking, the issues which the seventeenth century had to decide were, on the one hand, between Personal monarchy and Parliamentary democracy, and on the other between the Rule of Law—

and all that the Rule of Law involved for personal liberty —and the principle that the administration of justice should be subordinated to the dictates of public policy.

Were these issues finally decided by the contest of the seventeenth century—even for England? It is evident that the Puritan Revolution definitely and finally involved the defeat of the principle of Personal Monarchy. The Stuart theory of government was decisively rejected: no English King could ever again hope to occupy the position of a Louis XIV of France. Not less clear was it that England was henceforward committed to some form of 'Democracy'. But 'Democracy' has assumed many and widely diverse forms; and in the seventeenth century it was still uncertain which of these forms English Democracy would assume. Would it take the form of Direct Democracy as exemplified in the City-States of the ancient world, advocated in the seventeenth century by the Levellers, and in some degree realized in the modern Federal Republic of Switzerland? Or would it anticipate the Presidential type which approved itself to the fathers of the American Constitution? Or was it destined to enjoy the distinction of evolving a type of government of which the world had as yet no experience—a species known in scientific terminology as Parliamentary Democracy? By Parliamentary Democracy we are to understand a system based upon an extended Electorate, a fully representative Legislature, and an Executive responsible and respondent, in the first place, to the Legislature, and, ultimately, to the Electorate to which the Legislature itself is answerable.

How far solved? This entirely new system of government was gradually evolved in England during the seventeenth, eighteenth, and nineteenth centuries. Foreign countries have widely adopted it, but not with universal success. The United States of America rejected it in favour of a system more conformable to the conditions of a composite state. The Czardom in Russia has yielded place not to Parliamentary Democracy but to an inverted autocracy based upon economic syndicalism. Italy, after a brief and not too happy experience of Parliamentary Democracy on the English model, has abandoned it, whether temporarily or permanently we cannot know, in favour of a popular Dictatorship. Spain has not found it adapted to her historical traditions or to contemporary conditions. It has yet to make good in Germany.

Nor is the prospect entirely reassuring in England itself. England is never likely to run to the extremes either of personal autocracy or the dictatorship of the proletariat. Neither Fascism nor Sovietism has obtained any real grip upon English opinion; nor are they likely to do so. Nevertheless, indications are not lacking of some weakening of the foundations upon which Parliamentary Democracy has hitherto rested in well-balanced equipoise. A vast electorate which cannot be reached by conventional methods of electioneering; the increased and increasing influence of a popular Press; the weakening of Parliamentary control over Publice finance; the delegation of legislative and quasi-judicial powers to the administrative Departments; the multiplication of representative bodies which threaten the exclusive authority of Parliament; the tendency on the part of the Executive to consult less with the Legislature and to deal directly with bodies representative not of national but of sectional interests—all these are indications, perhaps severally insignificant but cumulatively substantial, of the dangers which threaten the political omnipotence if not the legal sovereignty of Parliament.

Nor is political theory quite so confident as it was in the nineteenth century, that Parliamentary Democracy is the last word in the evolution of political liberty. Such treatises as Mill's *Representative Government* recall an atmosphere which is already beginning to seem a trifle old-fashioned. That essay ignores many of the problems with which in the constitutional sphere our own generation is particularly concerned. Even a generation ago discerning publicists like Mr. Lecky had misgivings as to the permanence of Parliamentary Democracy as understood in England. To

Recent Political Theory

them it seemed that the system reached its apex in the period between the Reform Bill of 1832 and those of 1867 and 1884–5. Since Mr. Lecky's time the doubt has deepened and manifests itself to-day in quarters widely apart and indeed definitely antagonistic. Thus Mr. G. D. H. Cole writes:

'Misrepresentation is seen at its worst to-day in that professedly omnicompetent "representative" body Parliament. . . Parliament professes to represent all the citizens in all things, and therefore, as a rule, represents none of them in anything. It is chosen to deal with everything that may turn up quite irrespective of the fact that the different things that do turn up require different types of persons to deal with them . . . there can be only one escape from the futility of our present methods of parliamentary government, and that is to find an association and method of representation for each function, and a function for each association and body of representatives. In other words, real democracy is to be found not in a single omnicompetent representative assembly but in a system of co-ordinated functional representative bodies.' [1]

From the opposite pole of political opinion we have a curious echo in the words of Mr. Harold Cox:

'Our present territorial constituencies have no communal interest of their own in the vast number of problems now coming before Parliament. . . . We have to evolve new forms of government to deal with new problems. If our plans are to be successful they must be based upon the principle of a direct and logical connexion between the purpose aimed at and the character of the agency framed for achieving that purpose. The most urgent of modern-day problems are industrial or commercial; therefore the basis of the agency or agencies for dealing with them must be industrial or commercial and not territorial. The germ of such an organization may be discovered in contemporary industrial movements.' [2]

A quarter of a century ago an acute Belgian philosopher expressed similar doubts as to the adequacy of representation on the basis of locality:

'Il est incontestable que le suffrage universel sans cadres,

[1] G. D. H. Cole, *Social Theory*, p. 207.   [2] *Economic Liberty*, p. 186–7.

sans organisation, sans groupement est une système factice;
il ne donne que l'ombre de la vie politique. Il n'atteint pas le
seul but vraiment politique que l'on doit avoir en vue, et qui
est non de faire voter tout le monde, mais d'arriver à repré-
senter le mieux les intérêts du plus grand nombre. . . . Le
suffrage universel moderne c'est surtout le suffrage des passions,
des courants irréfléchis, des partis extrêmes. Il ne laisse
aucune place aux idées modérées et il écrase les partis modérés.
La victoire est aux exaltés. La représentation des intérêts, qui
contient les passions par les idées qui modèrent l'ardeur des
partis par l'action des facteurs sociaux, donne à la société plus
d'équilibre.'[1]

A final illustration of contemporary opinion may be added
from the pen of an anonymous writer in the *Edinburgh
Review*:

'The Soviet scheme of government embodies a principle
differing fundamentally from the parliamentary system which
it has been our habit to regard both as complete and ideal from
the constitutional standpoint. So much dissatisfaction is,
however, now being manifested towards Parliament that it is
not surprising to find even serious-minded people wondering
whether some merits are not latent in the Soviet system which
might permit of its transfusion—gradual and partial if not
total—into a truly democratic body.'[2]

Those opinions, whatever degree of importance be
attached to them, undoubtedly reflect, to some extent,
contemporary thought. But, if that be so, it is evident
that we cannot approach the problems of the seventeenth
century from the standpoint of the historians even of
a generation ago, still less from that of the great Whig
writers of the first half of the nineteenth century.

They were confident that the seventeenth century had
solved for all time the problem of political liberty, not
merely in outline, but in detail, not merely for England but
for the world. It is not necessary to assume that they were
mistaken. They may still prove to be right. But our stand-

---

[1] Adolphe Prins, *L'Organisation de la Liberté* (Brussels, 1895, quoted
ap-Lecky: *Democracy and Liberty*, i. 219.
[2] *Edinburgh Review*, No. 473, p. 66.

point has been shifted. On the one hand the development of the Science of Comparative Politics has to some extent dispelled our insular complacency. We are no longer certain that the solution reached in England, the peculiar species of Democracy evolved in this country, is necessarily the one which is best adapted to all countries, however much they may differ from ourselves in historical traditions, and whatever the stage of civilization at which they may severally have arrived. On the other hand it is plain that even among ourselves, in this first home of Parliamentary Democracy, there are those who decline to accept that form of Government and its implications as the last word in the development of the idea of political liberty. There are some who go even further and question whether 'liberty' is the last word in human happiness. But these speculations need not be pursued; their existence suffices to prove that the problems of the seventeenth century must be approached by the commentator of to-day, no longer from the angle of complacent confidence, but of respectful interrogation, if not of aggressive scepticism.

The Problem of Personal Liberty   The second of the outstanding problems of the seventeenth century was that of personal liberty, the rights of the individual citizen as against the Executive. A generation ago it would have been rank heresy even to hint a doubt whether the foundations of personal liberty in this country were secure. Had not the conflicts of the seventeenth century solved the problem, as far as England was concerned, for all time? Had not Chief Justice Coke asserted, once for all, the supremacy of the Common Law? Had not the Long Parliament and the Bill of Rights vindicated the independence of the Judicial Bench and thus guaranteed the security of the individual against the encroachments of an autocratic Executive? Had not the disgrace of Lord Chancellor Bacon, coupled with the Petition of Right and the legislation of the Long Parliament on the ship-money judgement, dissipated all danger of the introduction of administrative law and administrative tribunals into this country? Had not Montesquieu pointed to England as the freest country in the world, because (as he supposed) there was the completest separation between the judicial, the legislative, and the executive functions of government? Did not Blackstone emphasize for his generation the lessons taught by Montesquieu? Did not Mr. Dicey follow in the steps of his illustrious predecessor? Did not Rudolph von Gneist, the most profound and discriminating of German commentators on English political institutions, characterize England, in a single word, as a *Rechtsstaat*—a commonwealth based upon justice and law? Did he not regard France, with its system of administrative law and administrative courts, as the antithesis, in this respect, of England? And was not all this noble superstructure built on the foundations so truly laid by the champions of personal liberty in the seventeenth century?

But is the superstructure secure? If any significance is to be attached to debates in Parliament, to the utterances of distinguished judges, to discussions in the Press, and to articles in reviews and journals, lay and technical, these questions can no longer be answered with a confident affirmative. Judges, publicists, and politicians have lately combined to warn the public that they must beware of subtle encroachments upon the domain of individual liberty.

The danger, as already indicated, arises partly from the increasing complexity of our social and economic life demanding, it seems, increasing activity on the part of the State and of Public Authorities; partly from the preoccupation—dare one say the carelessness?—of the Legislature; partly from a subtle change in the actual form of our legislative enactments, and not least from the zeal and ambition of Public Departments and the officials who control them.

We must repeat that the problems which confronted the statesmen of the seventeenth century are still living issues; that political solutions, however apparently complete, are rarely permanent; that the enjoyment of Liberty cannot be purchased by a single transaction; that the price of it is eternal vigilance, and that if we are to enjoy the fruits of victory won by our ancestors we must be prepared to do battle for them afresh and indeed unceasingly.

Aspects of the struggle To return to the crisis of the seventeenth century. That crisis, as already hinted, had several aspects. It may be described in very general terms, as a struggle for liberty, but the fighting took place at many points on an extended front. There was, firstly, the question, raised by the dispute about *Impositions*, as to the precise sphere over which Parliament exercised fiscal jurisdiction. Were Custom Duties *taxation*, or did they represent a species of licence to trade? The same sort of difficulty arose in regard to the collection of *Ship-Money*. Was Ship Money *taxation*, over which the control of Parliament was admittedly absolute, or might it be plausibly represented as naturally incident to the right and duty of the Crown to take all such precautions as seemed to it good for the defence of the realm? Closely parallel in political logic with the question as to the legality of Impositions and Ship Money was that of *Proclamations*. That the Crown had certain rights of a quasi-legislative character was not denied; but how far did those rights extend? If pushed too far their exercise would evidently imperil the liberty of the subject and the sanctity of private property. If *Ship-Money* and *Impositions* raised important questions as to the respective spheres of Crown and Parliament in fiscal matters; if the practice of issuing *Proclamations* tended at once to impair the legislative authority of Parliament and to endanger the rights of the individual citizen, the famous case of Darnel or the *Five Knights* (1626) raised in the most acute form the problem of personal liberty, and the limits, if any, attaching to the rights of *Habeas Corpus*. The Darnel case involved also important questions as to the true relation between the Judicature and the Executive.

Why the crisis arrived in the seventeenth century To all these matters more detailed reference will be made later on. Meanwhile, a question obtrudes itself which demands an immediate answer: Why did the crisis arrive in the seventeenth century? Many of the problems which confronted the statesmen of the seventeenth century were of long standing; they had emerged as soon as an administrative system began to be developed by our Norman and Angevin Kings; they are dealt with, albeit in embryo, in the Great Charter of 1215, and indeed, in the earlier Charter of Henry I; but not until the seventeenth century did they become sufficiently acute to provoke the people of England to actual rebellion.

One potent factor in the provocation of rebellion must be noticed at once. For the first time in English history constitutional and political issues were complicated by a sharp division of opinion on religious matters. Apart from the ecclesiastical problem a political crisis could hardly have been avoided (for reasons to be presently explained) in the seventeenth century; but, had it not been for the Puritan attack upon the episcopal government of the Church, the crisis would have been surmounted without a civil war. For this reason: on the political issue there was substantial agreement among all parties; the courtiers were too few to fight; but the attack on the Bishops created a schism in the ranks of the opposition and gave the King a Party strong enough to face, with some assurance of victory, an appeal to arms. *The religious question*

In this sense the Great Rebellion may in strict accuracy be described as the Puritan Revolution. Reform we must needs have had; that the demand for reform should have led to civil war must be ascribed to the deep feelings aroused by differences in matters of religion.

It remains, then, to inquire what were the causes which, apart from religion, precipitated the crisis.

We must be careful to distinguish, as Aristotle sagely remarked, between the occasion and the causes of revolution. The occasion may be trivial, the causes never are. Lord Macaulay described the attempted arrest of the Five Members 'as undoubtedly the real cause of the war'. The occasion of the outbreak of war it may have been; but to ascribe the civil war to any single cause, still more to ascribe it to a particular incident, is to take a curiously *Occasion and Cause* unphilosophical view of one of the great movements of history.

We must go deeper and further in our quest. The causes which brought about the crisis were, as is invariably the case, both general and particular. Among the more general causes primary importance must be attributed to the fact that the Tudor sovereigns having done their work thoroughly, the necessity for the 'dictatorship' with which Close of they had been entrusted had passed away. The Tudors Tudor had come to the throne at a difficult moment. Lancastrians Dictator- ship and Yorkists had represented something more than dynastic rivalries. They stood for conflicting principles of government. If the Lancastrians were compelled, largely by circumstances, to subscribe to the doctrine of Parliamentary control, the Yorkists stood for strong government. In neither case did success attend the policy. The 'bastard feudalism' deplored by Sir John Fortescue had plunged the England of the fifteenth century into anarchy. The correspondence which passed between the members of the Paston family paints a vivid picture of the evils from which in the middle years of that century the country was suffering: local wars between noble and noble, between county and county; great lords protecting their offending retainers from the weak arm of the law; sheriffs accepting bribes; judges corrupted; juries intimidated; justice perverted.

The From this state of anarchy, intensified by the faction Tudors fights known as the Wars of the Roses, the country was delivered by the Tudors. To enable them to cope with it they were endowed by popular assent and by parliamentary legislation, with dictatorial, though not unlimited, power. Extraordinary tribunals such as the Council of the North, the Council of Wales, the Court of Castle Chamber, and, most famous of all, the Court of the Star Chamber, were set up or furnished with fresh powers; local government was reorganized, and 'stacks of statutes' (as William Lambarde complains) were piled on the backs of the Justices of the Peace. Henry VII, by a variety of expe-

dients, filled up an empty Treasury, and to Henry VIII
was given the right of issuing *Proclamations* having the
force of law. But if the Tudors were dictators, they were
almost invariably careful to clothe their dictatorship with
the forms of law. Thus, Parliament became, for the first
time, a real instrument of government. The basis of representation was widely extended, not only by the inclusion
of the Palatine county of Chester, the counties of Wales
and that of Monmouth in the Parliamentary system, but
by the creation of new Parliamentary boroughs. Many of
the latter were in Cornwall, and, though the fishing towns
in that county were at that time increasing in importance,
it may well be that Cornwall was specially favoured as a
royal Duchy. But among other new constituencies were
towns like Westminster, Preston, Liverpool, Chester, and
Lancaster, to which no exception could be taken. In all,
during the Tudor period no fewer than 166 members were
added to the House of Commons, raising its numbers from
296 to 462.

Parlia-
ment
under the
Tudors

Not only was the House of Commons increased in size;
it grew enormously in political importance. There stands
to its credit a great mass of legislation on a wide variety
of topics—social, commercial, and ecclesiastical, and under
Elizabeth some of the bolder spirits put forward a tentative claim to the control of Executive policy. That claim
the Queen would not concede. Parliament was not to
'meddle with matters of State'. But that a new temper
was developing, even under the Tudors, among members of
Parliament is not to be questioned.

Nor was the new temper of Parliament a thing apart—
an isolated phenomenon. It was due in large measure to
the Reformation, and to the increasing wealth of the
country gentlemen and merchants. The Wars of the Roses
represented the last flicker of the embers of medieval
feudalism, and the Tudors had an easy task in destroying
the remnants of aristocratic independence. A new nobility,
enriched by enclosures, by the new agricultural system, and
not least by the spoils of the monastic houses, gradually

The
Squires
and Mer-
chants

arose. The nobles sat by right in a House of Lords which for the first time became a predominantly lay assembly, and behind the nobles was a new squirearchy, similarly enriched, who sought and found admission to the House of Commons. For nearly three centuries the country squires formed the backbone of that House and provided its leaders. With the squires came a certain proportion of merchants who had taken advantage of the new opportunities opening out to Englishmen by recent geographical discoveries and by the development of trade with the East Indies. Of trade with South America, Spain claimed a monopoly, but that monopoly was seriously infringed by the daring exploits of the Elizabethan seamen.

Local Government

Not only in Parliament, however, were the squires being trained for fresh and larger political responsibilities. The efficiency of parliamentary Government in England has always been, in large measure, due to the vitality of our local institutions and to the excellent school provided by those institutions for aspirants to seats in the national Legislature. Even to-day the best training-grounds for young politicians are the County and Borough Councils. The Tudors reorganized and reinvigorated local government; they made the Parish their administrative unit, and the Justice of the Peace their man-of-all-work. More than 150 statutes affecting the functions of this overburdened official were passed in that period. The process was, in the highest degree, educative, and the results were plainly manifest when, under the Stuarts, the squirearchy threw up such leaders as Eliot and Hampden, Pym and Cromwell; when Parliament as a whole claimed, and ultimately won, an entirely new position in the national Economy.

Dangers from abroad dissipated

Yet Parliament could not have achieved victory had the condition of the realm remained under the Stuarts what it had been under the Tudors. In the sixteenth century there was almost continuous apprehension lest the dynastic rivalries, so fatal to England in the fifteenth century, should revive. The undisputed accession of James I dissipated these apprehensions and settled the dynastic question. Nor did men any longer fear the restoration of Papal authority in England. The defeat of the Armada had settled once for all that England was not to be recalled to the Roman obedience; thereafter Protestants could safely afford to quarrel among themselves.

Rome was not, however, the only menace to English independence. The Armada decided that England was not to be engulfed in the waters of the Counter-Reformation, but at the accession of Elizabeth it had been still uncertain whether she might not be absorbed into the Hapsburg Empire. Elizabeth extricated herself and her country from the perils which threatened them with consummate adroitness and dexterity. As compared with Spain or France England was relatively weak and poor; her population was exiguous (probably under 4,500,000) and her resources scanty. Scotland, in close alliance with France, was an added danger, and Ireland, then as since, was a nest of rebels—a recruiting-ground for the continental enemies of England.

From all these dangers, which in retrospect have lost their imminence, England emerged triumphant. Nor was Parliament, during the last years of Elizabeth, slow to realize that the danger was past; but they realized also that the passing of it was due to the sagacious leadership and the sleepless vigilance of the ageing Queen. Advisedly, therefore, Parliament postponed the assertion of its rights and the claim to an extension of its functions. That the postponement was deliberate is clear from the terms of the *Apology* of 1604:

'In regard of her (Queen Elizabeth's) sex and age, which we had great cause to tender, and much more upon care to avoid all trouble which by wicked practice might have been drawn to impeach the fact of your Majesty's right in the succession, those actions were then passed over which we hoped in succeeding time of freer access to your Highness of renowned grace and justice to restore, redress, and rectify.'

The hint in regard to the succession was a shrewd thrust; for the rest, the Commons plainly told the King that, unlike his predecessor, he was not an old lady who had acquired a strong title to the gratitude of Parliament and people of England.

National Self-consciousness

Evidently, then, the sixteenth century had witnessed in England (as in Spain and France) a wonderful development in national self-consciousness. The results of this self-consciousness are manifest. Not merely was Parliament ready at the close of the century, as it had not been ready at its opening, to take upon itself fresh responsibilities in the sphere of self-government, but it was conscious of its readiness. Unless, therefore, the Stuarts should prove, like their predecessors, to be endowed with political sagacity and personal tact, difficult times were plainly in store for them.

Economics and Politics

Before discussing the personal equation there remains to be noticed another general cause to which insufficient attention has been paid. That the poverty of the Crown under James I was one of the predisposing causes of the crisis is indeed a commonplace of historical criticism. But the real causes of that poverty have commonly been ignored. That James I was extravagant while Elizabeth was thrifty is true; but no thrift on the part of the King could have counteracted the operation of more general economic causes. The experience of recent years (1914–29) has done something to bring home to the present genera-

Currency and Prices

tion the relation between currency and prices. Everybody can realize to-day how much prices have risen since the outbreak of the World War. The phenomenon must be primarily, though not exclusively, ascribed to the large issues of paper currency. In the sixteenth century price levels were affected by two concurrent causes. Under Henry VIII and Edward VI the coinage was persistently debased; not only were the coins reduced in weight but the silver metal contained therein was debased by a large admixture of alloy. It is true that in 1561 Elizabeth restored the silver coinage to its original purity, but the new coins were lighter in weight and smaller in size than the statutory coinage of Plantagenet days—one pound of silver being minted into sixty instead of twenty shillings.

Consequently, though debasement was arrested, depreciation continued, and added much to the suffering and poverty which was so marked a feature of Elizabeth's reign. Economic causes accentuated the effects of government policy. The mines of South America were flooding Europe with silver. No government could cope with that phenomenon, and despite all efforts prices continued to rise. So did rents; as we learn from much contemporary literature; and the rise both of rents and prices was due mainly to the operation of natural causes. In time the tendency worked itself out and equilibrium was restored, but the time was long, the mills of economic reactions grind very slowly, and in the meantime the poor suffered much hardship. Labour was dislocated, wages fell, vagrancy increased, and this at a time when the dissolution of the Abbeys had deprived the vagrants of the casual assistance and temporary shelter to which in preceding times they had become accustomed. In the *Statute of Apprentices*, and in a long series of measures dealing with vagrancy, pauperism, and unemployment, a great effort was made to mitigate the sufferings caused by economic changes and currency disturbances, but the effort was only partially successful, and prices rose steadily until the reign of Charles I, when it was estimated that in the course of a century the price of commodities had risen by some three or four hundred per cent.

Among the sufferers from the fall in the value of money was the Crown, and James I, from the outset of his reign, felt the financial position acutely. Even Queen Elizabeth, parsimonious as she was, had been compelled during the last five years to sell Crown lands to the value of £327,000, and in addition had incurred a debt of £400,000. The new King, even had he been as careful as his predecessor, could not have avoided an annual deficit; but in fact he was as extravagant as Elizabeth was thrifty. Consequently he was compelled to apply to Parliament not only to meet, as had been usual, extraordinary emergences, but to defray the ordinary expenses of government.

Poverty of the Crown

The increasing pugnacity of Parliament rendered it in the highest degree unlikely that Parliament would grant supplies to the Crown without using the opportunity to demand a redress of grievances. Nor, as we shall see presently, was the opportunity slow to present itself. About the right of the Crown to dispose of its own revenues there was no dispute, and as little about the right of Parliament to grant or withhold taxation. But, between the well-defined territory of the Crown on the one side and that of Parliament on the other, there lay a debatable land which offered a tempting opportunity alike for those who desired to encroach and for those who were on the look-out for trespassers. On one such field the battle of *Impositions* was fought; on another that of *Ship-Money*. But these battle-fields we must survey at closer quarters later on.

It is, then, evident that there was plenty of combustible material lying about, and that the hope of avoiding an explosion rested largely upon the prudence and vigilance of those who, on one side and the other, were charged with the responsibility of directing operations.

Charac-
ter of
James I

Unfortunately those who were most conspicuous in place were not most conspicuous for wisdom. James I might, in ordinary times, have taken fair rank among English sovereigns; but the times were not ordinary, and James I was not an Englishman. A contemporary sovereign described him as the 'wisest fool in Christendom'. The description was singularly inept; for James I was no fool, and he was certainly not wise. He was in truth a pedantic doctrinaire; by no means devoid of learning, and not lacking a measure of shrewdness and sagacity, but cursed with fondness for metaphysical speculation, which I hesitate to describe as characteristically Scotch. Moreover, he came to England with a preconceived idea as to the theory of the English Constitution and the practical position of the English Crown. He had seen, no doubt with envious eyes, the popular success achieved by his cousin of England; small blame, therefore, to him if he imagined that the Tudors had bequeathed to him a prerogative almost unlimited. But, in truth, it was the crowning irony of a paradoxical situation that the success of the Tudor monarchs had rendered impossible, because unnecessary, a continuation of the Tudor monarchy.

Well had it been for England and for her Stuart Kings Stuart Theory of Monarchy had they been able to discern this elementary but far from obvious truth. Writ large before the eyes of their subjects, it was unfortunately hidden from theirs. From the outset they propounded a theory of the English monarchy which was historically untenable and politically fraught with mischief and confusion. Alike in his writings and his speeches, James I gave expression to doctrines which must have sounded strange in the ears of statesmen and lawyers trained in the traditions of Bracton, Fortescue, and Hooker.

'As for the absolute prerogative of the Crown, that is no subject for the tongue of a lawyer, nor is it lawful to be disputed. It is atheism and blasphemy to dispute what God can do; good Christians content themselves with His will revealed in His Word, so it is presumptuous and high contempt in a subject to dispute what a King can do, or say that a King cannot do this or that, but rest in that which is the King's will revealed in his law.'

So James spoke in the Star Chamber on 20 June 1616. In similar terms he had written in his *True Law of Free Monarchies*, published anonymously in 1598:

'According to these fundamental laws already alleged, we daily see that in the parliament (which is nothing else but the head court of the King and his vassals) the laws are but craved by his subjects, and only made by him at their rogation and with their advice: for albeit the King make daily statutes and ordinances, enjoining such pains thereto as he thinks meet, without any advice of parliament or estates, yet it lies in the power of no parliament to make any kind of law or statute without his sceptre be to it, for giving it the force of a law. . . . As likewise, although I have said a good King will frame all his actions to be according to the law, yet is he not bound thereto but of his good will, and for good example-giving to his subjects. . . . So, as I have already said, a good King, though he be above the law, will subject and frame his actions thereto for example's sake to his subjects, and of his own free will, but not as subject or bound thereto. . . .

Arminian Preachers

The language of the King found an echo in that of Arminian preachers and legal professors. Dr. Roger Mainwaring, a prominent Arminian clergyman who afterwards (1636) became Bishop of St. David's, wrote: 'The King is not bound to observe the laws of the realm concerning the rights and liberties of his subjects, but his royal will and command doth oblige the subjects' conscience upon pain of eternal damnation.'[1] Another Arminian clergyman, Dr. Robert Sibthorpe, preaching the Assize Sermon before the Judges at Northampton, a few months earlier, held language not less uncompromising: 'If a Prince impose an immoderate yet an unjust tax, yet the subject is bound in conscience to submit.'

Cowell's Inter-preter

Eminent jurists were not far behind the Arminian preachers in their exaltation of the Royal Prerogative. Thus in 1607 Dr. Cowell, Professor of Civil Law at Cambridge, published an encyclopaedia of Constitutional Law, entitled *The Interpreter*. In the article on *Parliament* he wrote:

'The assembly of the King and the three estates of the Realm, videlicet, the Lords Spiritual, the Lords Temporal, and Commons, for the debating of matters touching the Commonwealth, and especially the making and correcting of laws; which assembly or court is of all other the highest and of greatest authority'

So far so good, but then he proceeded:

'Of these two, one must needs be true, that either the King is above the Parliament, that is, the positive laws of his Kingdom, or else that he is not an absolute King. . . . And, therefore, though it be a merciful policy, and also a politic mercy (not alterable without great peril), to make laws by consent of the whole realm, because so no one part shall have cause to complain of a partiality, yet simply to bind a prince to or by those laws were repugnant to the nature and constitution of an absolute Monarchy.'

[1] Sermon on Religion and Allegiance preached before Charles I (July 1627).

Still more objectionable to the Commons was the article on the *King*, in which Dr. Cowell wrote:

'He is above the law by his absolute power (Bracton, i. 8); and though for the better and equal course in making laws he do admit the three estates, that is, Lords Spiritual, Lords Temporal, and the Commons unto council, yet this, in divers learned men's opinions, is not of constraint, but of his own benignity, or by reason of his promise made upon oath at the time of his coronation. For otherwise were he a subject after a sort and subordinate, which may not be thought without breach of duty and loyalty. For then must we deny him to be above the law, and to have no power of dispensing with any positive law, or of granting especial privileges and charters unto any, which is his only and clear right. . . .'

The Commons 'took notice'[1] of this book, which was prudently suppressed by Royal Proclamation. Such doctrines as those propounded by Cowell, though characteristic of the Roman Law, had never found acceptance among English lawyers and publicists. *Quod principi placuit legis vigorem habet* was a precept which had no place in English jurisprudence. So far back as the thirteenth century Bracton, to whose authority Cowell so imprudently appealed, had explicitly denied its validity, and had affirmed the contrary principle:

'Rex autem habet superiorem, Deum scilicet; item legem per quam factus est rex; item curiam suam, videlicet comites, barones, quia comites dicuntur quasi socii regis, et qui habet socium habet magistrum: et ideo si rex fuerit sine fraeno, id est sine lege, debent se fraenum ponere, nisi ipsimet fuerint cum rege sine fraeno.'

Two centuries later Sir John Fortescue, writing for the instruction of a Lancastrian prince, set forth in unequivocal terms the essentially 'limited' and 'constitutional' character of the English monarchy.

'A King of England cannot at his pleasure make any alterations in the laws of the land, for the nature of his government is not only regal but political. . . . He can neither make any alteration or change in the laws of the realm without the

[1] 27 Feb. 1610.

consent of the subjects nor burden them against their wills with strange impositions, so that a people governed by such laws as are made by their own consent and approbation enjoy their properties securely and without the hazard of being deprived of them either by the King or any other. . . . For he is appointed to protect his subjects in their lives, properties, and laws; for this very end and purpose he has the delegation of power from the people and he has no just claim to any other power but this.' (*De Laudibus Legum Angliae.*)

Even at the zenith of the Tudor monarchy the 'judicious' Hooker ventured to re-echo the language of the earlier commentators on the constitution.

'Lex facit regem; the king's grant of any favour made contrary to the law is void; what power the king hath he hath it by law, the bounds and limits of it are known.'

That the constitutional tradition was unbroken we may learn from such a work as Sir John Eliot's *Monarchy of Man*,[1] no less than from the parliamentary utterances of his immediate political associates:

'The law', wrote Eliot, 'is the ground of authority, all authority and rule a dependant of the law. The edict of Gratian was not only an edict for that time but for the genera- tions of succeeding ages, and for all posterity to come. Rightly, therefore, and most worthily, stiled an oracle. And in corre- spondence to this, is the modern practice of these times. Almost in all the states of Europe, princes at the assumption of their crowns assume and take an oath for the maintenance and observation of the laws. So, if we look either into authority or example, the use and practice of all times from the moderne to the ancient, the reason is still cleare, without any difficulty or scruple, *de jure*, in right, that princes are to be regulated by the laws, that the law has an operation on the Sovereign.'

We are thus confronted, at the outset of our inquiry, with two contrasted views as to the character of the English monarchy, and as to the relation of the monarchy to parliament. Philosophers and jurists held, with equal tenacity, directly opposite opinions. To prevent theoretical

[1] First printed in 1879.

differences developing into actual political conflict demanded from both parties a degree of patience and tact to which neither could lay claim. But the differences between such men as Cowell and Eliot, though adapted to statement in philosophical terms, were not merely theoretical. On the contrary they lay at the root of the practical disputes which quickly ensued on such questions as Impositions and Proclamations, on the relations between the Judiciary and the Executive, and between the Executive and Parliament. In a word they raised in an acute form the problem of *Sovereignty*.

Where in the English Constitution did ultimate sovereignty reside? Was it vested, as the Stuart Kings insisted and as Thomas Hobbes of Malmesbury taught, in the King? Or, as Eliot and Pym held, in the King in Parliament? Or, as the Protectorate parliaments contended, in Parliament alone? Or, as the Levellers taught, in the people? This was the central and cardinal issue which the seventeenth century was called to decide. *The Problem of Sovereignty*

Meanwhile, it is only fair to the Stuarts to remember that the circumstances under which they came to the English throne inclined, if they did not actually compel them, to an assertion of the doctrine of Divine Right, and the high views of the Royal Prerogative so closely allied therewith. By the will of Henry VIII, executed under special Parliamentary sanction, the Crown had been settled upon the descendants of his younger sister Mary, Duchess of Suffolk, to the exclusion of, or in preference to, those of his elder sister Margaret, Queen of Scotland. Claims under that will might have been advanced on behalf of the Suffolk line represented in 1603 by William Seymour, Lord Beauchamp, the husband of James's cousin, Arabella Stuart. As a fact they were not. The Statutory claim of the Suffolks was quietly ignored, and no serious question was raised as to the validity of the title of James.

A wiser man would quietly have accepted the accomplished fact; to a pedantic metaphysician the temptation to seek philosophical justification for a political claim was *Divine Right of of Kings* irresistible. James demanded of his new subjects not merely the practical recognition of his right, but the theoretical acceptance of a philosophical dogma. Thus conflict was deliberately provoked not by the fact of his succession but by the doctrine of indefeasible hereditary right by which he foolishly preferred to justify it.

Moreover, the theory of Divine Right, if accepted, was bound to carry both the King and his subjects far beyond the immediate question of succession to the throne. It would be held to justify' the freest use of the Royal Prerogative; it did in fact lie at the root of the almost continuous quarrels in which Crown and Parliament were during this period involved.

Worked out in practical politics the theory of Divine Right meant that the Crown could claim a twofold power: an *Ordinary* power, ascertained and limited by law; and an *Extraordinary* power for the exercise of which the King was answerable only to God. It was reliance on this extraordinary or prerogatival power that James I insisted on levying *Impositions*, on issuing *Proclamations*, on auricular consultation with the judges; that Bacon issued his famous writ *De Non Procedendo Rege Inconsulto*; that Charles I levied his forced loan and imprisoned, without trial, those who refused to pay it; and collected ship-money.

In every political community, and under every form of constitution, some 'reserve power' or 'prerogative' must exist, and some person or body of persons must be entrusted with the exercise of 'discretion' in public affairs. Without it an Executive would be impotent, and the lack of governance would soon be disastrously apparent. How can the existence and the exercise of discretionary power be reconciled with adequate securities for the liberty of the individual citizen; with the maintenance of political freedom in the community at large? How can 'Prerogative' be asserted without derogating from the principle of ultimate popular control? That is the *crux* of the problem presented to every political society, particularly at that stage in its constitutional evolution when it emerges from the shelter of paternal government. That problem lay at the root of the contest between the Stuart Kings and their Puritan Parliaments. Failure to solve it was the essential cause of the Great Rebellion and the Civil War.

To a more searching analysis of that problem and to more detailed discussion of possible methods of solution, the succeeding chapters of this book will be devoted.

II. CROWN AND PARLIAMENT

Parliamentary Privilege

The Constitutional Problem OF the questions at issue in the seventeenth century the most fundamental, in the political sphere, was that of Parliament: its position, powers, and privileges. The struggle between Crown and Parliament is frequently described as one between the principle of Autocracy and that of Democracy; but Democracy is a term which calls, as we have seen, for more precise definition. The seventeenth century decided that the Government of England should take the form of a Parliamentary, not a Presidential, a Direct, or even a Referendal Democracy.[1]

Thus the period was critical, both as regards species and genus. Relatively, it is a detail, though a vastly important one, whether the Executive shall be independent of or dependent on Parliament. That detail the Puritan Revolution decided. But it had to decide the much broader question, whether England was to live under a Personal Monarchy or a Parliamentary Monarchy, to be ruled henceforward by the King or by the King-in-Parliament.

The English Parliament The decision was in favour of the King-in-Parliament. But the English Parliament, with its peculiar structure, its functions, powers, and procedure, is itself the outcome of a long process of evolution. One of the two Chambers into which, after a period of uncertainty, it was ultimately organized was primarily a Court of Law, a part of the King's *Curia* sitting *in banco* at Westminster. Even to-day it is for the 'High Court of Parliament' not less than for the 'Great Council of the Realm' that we habitually pray. To that Great Council King John and his successors, in order to relieve their financial necessities, summoned representative knights from the shires and burgesses from the towns. If, then, the primary function of the Lords was

[1] For fuller discussion of these forms see Marriott, *Mechanism of the State*, cc. ii–v.

judicial, that of the 'Commons' was and is financial, though it was not for long years that the two Houses were finally and definitely differentiated.

Only, indeed, by a slow and gradual degrees did Parliament assume its present form and its present functions. With the administration of Justice and the granting of supplies it was from the first concerned. By the seventeenth century it had also acquired almost exclusive control over the making of laws. But that control was acquired only after a long contest with the King and his Council who continued to issue *Ordinances* or *Proclamations*.

A body which is called into being to grant money is naturally tempted to bargain. Bargaining leads to discussion, and debates upon grievances soon became a regular prelude to the grant of supplies. The discussion of grievances led inevitably to a criticism of those who were supposed to be responsible for their existence. As early as the fourteenth century Parliament attempted not merely to criticize but to control the servants of the Crown. The *Ordinances* of 1311 went so far, indeed, as to provide for the appointment of Ministers in Parliament. Again, in 1341 Edward III, in order to secure a grant of supplies from Parliament, promised that Ministers and Judges should be appointed in Parliament, but the Statute to effect this object was hardly passed before it was annulled. Before the close of the same reign the Commons initiated the process of *impeachment*, a new form of judicial procedure intended to bring powerful offenders to justice. Between 1376 and 1449 this process, which consisted in an accusation preferred by the Commons to the Lords, was frequently adopted: but between 1449 and 1621 this particular weapon was allowed to rust. Under the Tudors the Commons were hardly in a position to impeach the servants of the Crown. Henry VIII adopted a far more dangerous weapon, an Act of Attainder. This was not a judicial but a legislative process, and was the more formidable that it could create, *ex post facto*, the offence which it simultaneously proceeded to punish. Thomas Cromwell,

Legislature and Executive

to whom rumour attributed the sharpening of the new weapon, was one of its most conspicuous victims. Nearly a century later Strafford was, as we shall see, another.

Impeachment and Acts of Attainder were, however, at best but clumsy weapons. How clumsy the seventeenth century was to prove. But by what other method was Parliament to obtain that control over administration which had long been an object of its ambition? To answering that vital question a substantial part of this book will be devoted. Summarily it may be said that the problem was solved not by the invention of a new weapon but by the gradual evolution of a new institution, the perfecting of which has established England's claim to a pre-eminent place in the history of Political Institutions. The development of the *Cabinet* will, therefore, demand detailed investigation later on.

Supply, legislation, deliberation—such were the acknowledged functions of Parliament when James I was called to the English throne. But two questions almost immediately arose: first, what did these general terms cover; what precisely did these functions imply; and, secondly, was Parliament likely to be content with them; was it not certain that the Legislature would renew a claim, already, as we have seen, asserted, to a continuous control over the administration of public affairs? Before answering those questions, a preliminary word must be said as to the general position of Parliament.

Parliament under the Tudors   The first of the Stuarts faced a Parliament which differed vastly from the Parliament which confronted the first of the Tudors. It differed much in composition, to some extent in structure, and above all in temper. Both Houses had been transformed under the Tudors: the House of Lords by the dissolution of the abbeys and the creation of new peerages; the House of Commons, as we have seen, by the extension of the principle of representation. In the first Parliament of Henry VII the House of Lords[1] contained only 76 members, of whom 29 were lay

[1] The abbots had in 1305 numbered as many as 75, but their atten-

peers. The abbots disappeared after the dissolution of the monasteries; the spiritual peers, now consisting only of bishops, dwindled to 26. At this figure they have remained constant ever since, save during the period (1801–69) when four Irish bishops represented the Irish Church in the House of Lords. On the other hand, mainly by the creation of new peerages, the lay element increased to 81. Thus the House of Lords became for the first time a predominantly lay and hereditary assembly.

The House of Commons increased, as we have seen, by more than fifty per cent. (296 to 462), but even more important than the change in its composition was its increase in importance and in self-confidence. This was due partly perhaps to a development in the structure of Parliament. Not until the reign of Henry VIII was the bicameral form finally established. Then for the first time we hear of a 'House of Lords', and then for the first time the Commons appear to have begun to keep their separate Journals.[1] On this ground, if on no other, would a modern writer seem to be justified in saluting Henry VIII with the unfamiliar title of the 'Great Architect of Parliament'.[2]

Another marked feature of that period was the increased frequency with which Parliament met. It did not, of course, meet with the regularity of to-day, but there was nothing in the nature of a constitutional hiatus. During the twenty-four years of Henry VII's reign there were seven Parliaments with ten sessions; during the thirty-eight years of Henry VIII's there were nine distinct Parliaments; and of these one sat for seven years, and two others sat for three.[3] During the short reigns of Edward VI and Queen Mary, Parliament was practically continuous. The

Frequent meetings

dance had by Henry VII shrunk to 27. The archbishops (2) and 19 bishops made up the complement of 47 spiritual peers. Henry VIII created six new bishoprics, but one of them, the bishopric of Westminster, lapsed under Edward VI, and the number of bishops, which temporarily rose to 27, sank again to 26.

[1] For evidence on this controverted point see A. F. Pollard, *Trans. Royal Hist. Soc.*, 3rd series, viii. 26–7.

[2] A. F. Pollard, *Evolution of Parliament*.

[3] Stubbs *Lectures*, p. 269.

first Parliament of Edward VI held four sessions extending over nearly five years; the second had one. In the five years of Mary's reign there were five Parliaments: 'there is one thing, however, greatly commendable in the government of Queen Mary, which was reviving the ancient constitution of annual Parliaments'.[1]

Elizabeth, being far more economical than any of her predecessors, had less need of Parliaments; but she 'summoned ten Parliaments, which held in all thirteen sessions. Parliament met, therefore, on the average about once in every three and a half years'.[2] But though Parliament met irregularly during her reign, Elizabeth, like all the Tudors, gave it plenty to do. Bacon's sagacious advice to James I was really based upon Tudor practice:

'Look on a Parliament as a certain necessity, but not only as a necessity; as also a unique and most precious means for uniting the Crown with the Nation, and proving to the world outside how Englishmen love and honour their King, and their King trusts his subjects. Deal with it frankly and nobly as becomes a king, not suspiciously like a huckster in a bargain. Do not be afraid of Parliament. Be skilful in calling it; but don't attempt to "pack" it. Use all due adroitness and knowledge of human nature, and necessary firmness and majesty, in managing it; keep unruly and mischievous people in their place; but do not be too anxious to meddle, "let nature work"; and above all, though of course you want money from it, do not let that appear as the chief or real cause of calling it. Take the lead in legislation. Be ready with some interesting or imposing points of reform or policy, about which you ask your Parliament to take counsel with you. Take care to "frame and have ready some commonwealth bills, that may add respect to the King's government, and acknowledgement of his care; not *wooing* bills to make the King and his graces cheap; but good matters to set the Parliament on work, that an empty stomach do not feed on humour".'[3]

Legis-
lative
activity

Not less significant than increased frequency of meeting was the extraordinary activity of Parliament in the matter

[1] *Parliamentary History*, iii. 340, but there was no Parliament 1556-7.
[2] Prothero, *Statutes and Documents*, p. lxii.
[3] Dean Church's *Bacon*, p. 122.

of legislation. The additions to the Statute book were, as Dr. Prothero points out, 'more copious and not less weighty than in any previous age'.[1] Professor Maitland is equally emphatic. 'The part,' he writes,[2] 'which the assembled estates of the realm have to play in the great Acts of Henry VIII may in truth be a subservient and an ignoble part, but the Acts are great, and they are all done by the authority of Parliament.' Recall the great mass of social and economic legislation which we owe to the Parliaments of Henry VII: a whole series of Navigation Acts; Acts for the protection of English industry; Acts for securing the purity of the coinage, or for maintaining a standard of weights and measures; Acts for the regulation of wages and the general conditions of labour; Acts for the encouragement of tillage and the suppression of vagrancy. Or we may recall the great series of ecclesiastical statutes passed by Henry VIII, by Somerset, by Northumberland, and by Queen Mary; or the immensely important social legislation of the period; Henry VIII's Statute of Uses, Queen Elizabeth's Statute of Apprentices, and the long series of enactments for the repression of the evils of vagabondage and the relief of the impotent poor—a series which culminated in Elizabeth's great Poor Law of 1601. The Crown cannot indeed be accused of unreadiness to bring forward 'interesting or imposing points of reform', nor can Parliament have had much time to feel the pangs of 'an empty stomach', or to 'feed on humour'. Well had it been if the Stuarts could have taken to heart the wise lessons which Bacon was willing to teach them from the stores of his Tudor experience.

But it was not only upon legislative activity that Bacon laid stress. 'Use all due adroitness and knowledge of human nature, and necessary firmness and majesty in managing it.' The Tudor sovereigns were, by general admission, extraordinarily adroit in the management, if not the manipulation, of Parliament. They never raised, unnecessarily or gratuitously, a point of principle, and

---

[1] *Op. cit.*, p. xxiv.   [2] Ap. *Social England*, ii. 477.

invariably took the line of least resistance. Consequently, actual collisions between Crown and Parliament were as rare under the Tudors as they were frequent under their successors.

The Crown and the Speaker

Apart, however, from the generally accepted conditions of a Dictatorship the Tudors enjoyed, in their dealings with Parliament, certain advantages which it is only fair to the Stuarts to recall. The first was the virtual nomination of the Speaker of the House of Commons. The Speaker's position in the House in the sixteenth century was entirely different from what it is to-day. He was the stipendiary nominee of the Crown, his control of the proceedings was all but absolute, and, until the development of the ministerial system, he was the main channel of communication between the House and the Crown. How great was the importance attached by the Crown to the election of a Speaker well affected towards itself may be inferred from Clarendon's lament over the election of Lenthall, in place of the man designated by Charles I for the office, as Speaker of the Long Parliament. He refers to it as 'an untoward and, in truth, an unheard-of accident, which broke many of the King's measures and infinitely disordered his service beyond a capacity of reparation.'

Privy Councillors in Parliament

If the Speaker was the main agent of the Tudor sovereigns in regulating the business of Parliament, he was not the sole agent. The Privy Council of the sixteenth century contained comparatively few Peers, but the *Act of Precedence* (1539) provided that the Lord Chancellor, Lord Treasurer, Lord President of the King's Council, Lord Privy Seal, and Chief Secretary, even if not peers, should sit in the House of Lords, though only as 'assistants' and without the right to vote.[1] Privy Councillors, however, obtained election with increasing frequency to the House of Commons. From 1560 onwards, as Sir William Anson points out, 'the King's Ministers, the Chancellor of the Exchequer and the Secretaries are active in debate'. The same authority goes so far as to suggest that the multi-

[1] Tanner, *Tudor Constitutional Documents*, p. 205.

plication of parliamentary boroughs and the interference
of the Crown in elections was largely designed to secure
seats for the officials of the Crown.[1] But when all is said,
the felicity which on the whole characterized the relations
between Crown and Parliament in the sixteenth century
must be ascribed mainly to two causes. On the one hand
it was due to the consummate tact, the political insight,
the quick sympathy, and, not least, the firm hand of the
Tudor sovereigns who brought the nation through the
crises of the sixteenth century not merely unscathed but
braced and strengthened, and made it ready to take upon
itself the grave responsibilities of self-government. On the
other hand it was due to the frank recognition on the part
of Parliament of the debt which the country owed to the
sovereigns of the Tudor line, not least to the last of them,
and to the consequent and conscious postponement of
awkward questions to a more fitting occasion. Even
between Queen Elizabeth and her Parliaments there was
on many questions a sharp difference of opinion: on the
need, for instance, for settling the succession; on religion;
on questions of privilege; on monopolies. But on neither
side was there a disposition to carry matters to extremities:
mutual concessions were made, and differences were not
permitted to harden into disputes.

The fitting occasion arrived with the accession of James I.
Hardly was he seated on the throne before the House
of Commons drew up the *Apology* of 1604—a very remarkable document, designed to put before the King, in unequivocal terms, the position, powers, and privileges of the
House of Commons as understood by itself. Mr. S. R.
Gardiner, the highest of all English authorities on the
history of this period, declared with emphasis that

*Parlia-
ment
under
James I*

'to understand this Apology is to understand the cause of the
success of the English Revolution. They (the Commons) did
not ask for anything which was not in accordance with justice.
They did not demand a single privilege which was not necessary
for the good of the nation as well as for their own dignity'.

---

[1] *Law and Custom of the Constitution*, ii. pt. i, p. 75.

That may well be, but though the address was undoubtedly 'manly and outspoken', it is permissible to doubt whether Mr. Gardiner was equally accurate in describing it as 'conservative and monarchical to the core'.

Apology
of 1604

After acknowledging their gratitude to God that he had given them a King 'of such understanding and wisdom as is rare to find in any prince in the world', the Commons proceeded somewhat abruptly to express their 'grief and anguish of mind' that His Majesty had been greatly 'wronged by misinformation' as to the estate of his subjects at large and as to the privileges of the House of Commons to the 'extreme prejudice' of both. There was nothing for it, therefore, but to break silence and tell His Majesty the truth. The King had been misinformed (i) as to the 'cause of the joyful receiving of your Majesty into this your Kingdom'; (ii) concerning the rights and liberties of his English subjects and the privileges of the House; and (iii) 'touching the several actions and speeches in the House'.

In particular they complained that the King had been wrongly informed that the privileges of parliament were not of right but of grace, that the Commons were not a 'Court of Record', and that the return of writs for the election of knights and burgesses was the province not of the House of Commons but of Chancery.

'Contrary wise', they proceeded, 'with all humble and due respect to your majesty our sovereign lord and head, against those misinformations we most truly avouch—first, that our privileges and liberties are our right and due inheritance, no less than our lands and goods; secondly, that they cannot be withheld from us, denied or impaired, but with apparent wrong to the whole state of the realm: thirdly, and that our making of request, in the entrance of Parliament, to enjoy our privilege, is an act only of manners, and doth weaken our right no more than our sueing to the King for our lands by petition, which forms, though new and more decent than the old by *precipe*, yet the subject's right is no less now than of old; fourthly, we avouch also, that our House is a court of record, and so ever esteemed; fifthly, that there is not the highest standing court in this land that ought to enter into competency, either for dignity or authority, with this high court of Parliament, which, with your majesty's royal assent gives laws to other courts but from other courts receives neither laws nor orders; sixthly, and lastly, we avouch that the House of Commons is the sole proper Judge of returns of all such writs, and of the election of all such members as belong unto it, without which the freedom of election were not entire; and that the Chancery, though a standing court under your majesty, be to send out these writs and receive the returns, and to preserve them; yet the same is done only for the use of the Parliament over which, neither the Chancery, nor any other court, ever had, or ought to have, any jurisdiction. From these misinformed positions most gracious sovereign, the greatest part of our troubles, distrusts, and jealousies have risen, having apparently found that in the first Parliament of the happy reign of your majesty, the privileges of our House and therein the liberties and stability of the whole kingdom, have been more universally and dangerously impugned than (as we suppose) since the beginning of Parliaments. . . .'

Complaint is then made of the infringement of the rights of free election, as in the case of Sir F. Goodwin; of freedom from arrest, as in that of Sir Thomas Shirley; of freedom of speech in Parliament, and, not least bitter, of the attacks made from the pulpits upon the ancient and undoubted right of Parliament to 'treat matters for the peace and good order of the Church'.

On the last point the House of Commons, like the people they represented, felt special and profound anxiety. The danger from Rome was wellnigh past, though alarm was revived a year later by discovery of the Gunpowder Plot. The nation as a whole was not prepared to accept the discipline, though it inclined towards the doctrine, of Geneva; but it gravely mistrusted certain tendencies which it discovered in the Anglican, or, as it was then called, the Arminian party. Puritanism had a very large number of adherents not only among those who, like the Presbyterians and Independents (or Brownists), repudiated altogether the Episcopalian Government of the Church, but within the Established Church itself.

It was these 'conforming' Puritans who had at the very
outset of the new reign presented to James I the Millenary
Petition. The petitioners prayed: (1) that certain alterations might be effected in the services of the Church: that
the Sign of the Cross in baptism, the use of the ring in
marriage, the cap and surplice, such terms as 'Priest' and
'absolution' might be omitted and the rite of confirmation
abolished; (2) that none should be admitted into the
Ministry but able and sufficient men; (3) that certain
abuses connected with non-residence, pluralities, and tithe
impropriation should be abolished; and (4) that Church
discipline, more particularly as administered by the ecclesiastical courts and enforced by the oath *ex officio*, should
be reformed.

The position of the 'conforming' Puritans is defined with
precision in the Apology:

'For matter of religion', it ran, 'it will appear by examination of the truth and right, that your Majesty should be
misinformed if any man should deliver that the Kings of
England have any absolute power in themselves either to alter
religion (which God forfend should be in the power of any
mortal man whatsoever) or to make any laws concerning the
same otherwise than in temporal causes by consent of Parliament. We have and shall at all times by our oaths acknowledge
that your Majesty is sovereign lord and supreme governor in
both. Touching our own desires and proceedings therein they
have been not a little misconceived and misinterpreted. We
have not come in any Puritan or Brownist spirit to introduce
their parity, or to work the subversion of the state ecclesiastical
as it now stands . . . we came with another spirit, even with
the spirit of peace; we disputed not of matters of faith and
doctrine, our desire was peace only and our device of unity how
this lamentable and long standing dissension among the ministers might at length be extinguished. . . . Our desire hath been
also to reform certain abuses crept into the ecclesiastical state
even as into the temporal; and lastly that the land might be
furnished with a learned, religious and godly ministry for the
maintenance of whom we would have granted no small contribution if in these (as we trust) just and religious desires

we had found that correspondency from others which was expected.'

These words, temperate and respectful though they were, touched the King on the tenderest spot. It is not indeed certain that the *Apology* was ever formally presented to him. It is headed 'To the King's most Excellent Majesty, from the House of Commons assembled in parliament', and the entry in the *Commons' Journals* runs, under date 20 June 1604: 'The Form of Apology and Satisfaction to be presented to his Majesty . . . was now reported and delivered into the House.' Only a few lines of the document are entered in the Journals, but it was read in the House; there is a copy among the State Papers (Domestic) James I,[1] and it is inconceivable that the King should not have been fully and accurately informed of its contents.

However deferential the language the subsiance of the *Apology* could not have been otherwise than profoundly distasteful to him. In form it may be accurately described as 'conservative and monarchical to the core', but is it possible to imagine such a document being presented, or even drafted for presentation to any of the Tudor Monarchs? There was, indeed, a formal appeal to precedent. That is the English mode. The *Petition of Right* is based on *Magna Carta*; *Magna Carta* is based upon the Charter of Henry I, and the latter in turn recalls the Anglo-Saxon *Customs*. Nevertheless, it is plain, as already indicated, that the Commons had definitely resolved to make a fresh start with the first King of a new dynasty, and to register yet another stage in that evolutionary process by which the Sovereignty of a personal monarch was to give place to the Sovereignty of the King-in-Parliament.

Not, however, until the reign of Charles I was the claim to exercise a control over the Executive specifically asserted by the Commons. It was Eliot and Pym who, provoked by the cases of Buckingham and Strafford respectively, asserted the doctrine of ministerial responsibility. Mean-

Points of Collision

[1] viii. 70.

while, collisions occurred between the Crown and Parliament; feelings on both sides were exacerbated; and the Commons were impelled to discover a new principle the acceptance of which would sweep away the last remnants of the Tudor 'dictatorship', and prepare the way for the Constitutional Monarchy finally established under the Hanoverian dynasty.

The Bucking-ham Election
The first collision occurred on a question of 'privilege'. To whom did the determination of disputed elections properly belong? This question was raised afresh, in the first Parliament of James I, by the return of Sir Francis Goodwin as Knight of the Shire for Bucks. Writs for the election of members of Parliament were issued, then as now, by the Clerk of the Crown. A Statute of Henry IV (1406) had made the returns to such writs returnable into Chancery, but under Elizabeth the Commons claimed the right to examine the returns and entrusted the duty to the standing Committee on Privileges.

In summoning his first Parliament James I issued a Proclamation not only giving precise instructions as to the choice of fit persons (as the Tudors had commonly done), but ordering the returns to be 'brought to the Chancery and there to be filed of record'. If any person were returned 'contrary to this proclamation' both the constituency and the elected member were to be punished. In particular no bankrupt or outlaw was to be returned. Goodwin was an outlaw and the Clerk of the Crown refused the return on that ground. On the issue of a second writ Sir John Fortescue was returned. The Commons took the matter up as a question of privilege, summoned the Clerk and Goodwin to the bar, declared Goodwin *de jure* returned and ordered him to take the oath and his seat, 'which he did accordingly'. The King professing indifference as to which candidate was returned, reminded the House that they 'derived all matters of privilege from him' and maintained that an outlaw was ineligible by law and that all writs were by law returnable into Chancery.

The dispute went on for some weeks. James commanded

as an absolute King' that there should be a conference between the House and the judges. The command was received with some amazement until one member up and spake: 'The prince's command is like a thunderbolt; his command upon our allegiance like the roaring of a lion', but the Commons appointed a Select Committee to confer with the judges in the presence of the King and Council. The King proposed that both elections should be set aside and a third writ be issued. This was accepted and a new member was elected. Two other disputed elections were, however, decided without protest from the Crown, by the Commons, whose right was not afterwards disputed. They thus reaped the fruits of victory.[1]

The *Apology* had also referred to the case of Sir Thomas Shirley. After his election as member for Steyning, Shirley was arrested for debt. Freedom from arrest on civil charges was one of the undisputed privileges of Parliament. In 1543 the Commons sent their sergeant to deliver one of their members, Ferrers, and committed the sheriffs who had arrested him. In the case of Smalley (1575) they extended the privilege to a member's servant. Sir Thomas Shirley was similarly released by order of the House and those responsible for his arrest committed to the Tower. The Warden of the Fleet, who refused to release the prisoner, was also committed, until he confessed and apologized for his error at the Bar. In this case the King backed the Commons in defence of their privilege, but there were the rights of creditors to be considered, as well as those of members, and it was accordingly thought well to pass an Act which, while maintaining the privilege of Parliament, protected the rights of creditors and indemnified against damages those who had released Shirley at the bidding of the Commons. The abuse of this privilege became, however, so monstrous in the course of the century that it was found necessary to restrict it.

Of the four great privileges, freedom from arrest, free

Freedom from arrest

Freedom of Speech

---

[1] Long extracts from the *Commons' Journals* are printed in Prothero, *Documents*, pp. 325-31.

access to the Sovereign, a favourable construction of the proceedings of the House, and freedom of speech, each newly elected Speaker, at the beginning of each new Parliament, still demands recognition from the King. They were first demanded of Queen Mary in 1554, and since 1571 the practice has been regularly established. Of these privileges, certainly not the least important to the conduct of parliamentary business is freedom of speech. But the Tudor Sovereigns were slow to concede it. In 1512 one Strode, a member of the House, was imprisoned by the Stannary Court for having proposed certain bills to regulate the privileges of the tin miners of Cornwall. Parliament accepted the challenge to their liberties and passed a Statute, not only declaring void the proceedings against Strode, but also declaring that any proceedings against any member of the present or any future parliament should be utterly void and of none effect. 'This was a statutory recognition of the freedom of debate.' Elizabeth, as we have seen, interpreted the privilege so narrowly as virtually to deny it, but, despite some collisions, neither she nor the Commons wished to push matters to extremities.

No such considerations restrained James I nor his parliaments. In 1610 the King commanded the Commons to refrain from debating his right to levy impositions. The Commons promptly remonstrated against this infringement of 'the ancient and fundamental right of the liberty of Parliament in point of exact discussing of all matters concerning them and their possessions, goods and rights whatsoever'. The King did not persist in his prohibition, and a great debate on impositions ensued, beginning on 23 June and ending only on 3 July.

The Protest of 1621   The quarrel broke out afresh in the Parliament of 1621. In consequence of the outbreak of the Thirty Years War matters of foreign policy were then much to the fore, and the Commons proceeded to debate them. The King petulantly commanded that no one should 'presume henceforth to meddle with anything concerning our Government or deep matters of State'. The Commons retorted that the King's message seemed to abridge them 'of the ancient liberty of parliament for freedom of speech, jurisdiction and just censure of the House, . . . the same being our undoubted right and an inheritance received from our ancestors, without which we cannot freely debate nor clearly discern of things in question before us nor truly inform your Majesty'. To a request for a confirmation of their privileges the King answered with a lecture on their incompetence to handle high matters of State, *ne sutor supra crepidam*, though he assured them that as long as they 'contained themselves within the limits of their duty', he would be as careful to maintain and preserve their lawful liberties and privileges as any 'of our predecessors were to preverse our own royal prerogative'. He reiterated, however, his original contention that the privileges of the Commons were of grace—'derived from the grace and permission of our ancestors and us'.

It was clear, therefore, that the Commons had made no progress since they had drafted the *Apology* of 1604, and in hot temper they reaffirmed the position which they had taken up from the outset of the reign: 'That the liberties, franchises, privileges, and jurisdictions of Parliament are the ancient and undoubted birthright and inheritance of the subjects of England.' Uncompromisingly and in the plainest language they now demanded the recognition of their right to debate freely and without fear of punishment any subject they pleased.[1]

The King's answer to this Protestation was to dissolve Parliament and with his own hand tear the offensive page from the Journals of the House.[2]

The question of privilege blazed up again after the dissolution of the third Parliament of Charles I (1629). In that Parliament Sir John Eliot had specially distinguished himself. Consequently, after the dissolution he and eight other members were committed to the Tower by the Privy

Case of Sir John Eliot

[1] Printed in Prothero, pp. 313–14.
[2] The original page has since been restored, and may be seen to-day in the House of Commons.

Council. They sued out writs of habeas corpus, but the returns to the writs stated that they had been committed for notable treason and for stirring up sedition. Eliot himself refrained from applying for the habeas corpus. From first to last he took his stand on the privilege of Parliament. Anything he had said or done had been said or done in Parliament, and to no Court would he answer for things said or done in that Great Council of the Realm. The King so far gave way as to allow the case to go before the Court of King's Bench instead of the Star Chamber. To Eliot it made no difference. The matter was one for Parliament and Parliament alone.

His associates were in due course, some sooner, some later, released. On Eliot the King's wrath was concentrated, and in the Tower, unsubmitting, he died.

The ground on which Eliot chose ultimately to stand may seem to have been relatively narrow. To the public at large, questions of parliamentary privilege, especially as they affect individual members and not the body corporate, may appear to be of small moment. Nor can it be denied that they are often raised in the spirit of pedantry, or worse still as a means of self-advertisement. Similarly, the niceties of parliamentary procedure are as tiresome to the public as they are perplexing to inexperienced members. Moreover, it is undeniably true that when, as in the eighteenth century, Parliament itself developed an oligarchical temper, privileges that had been won in the contest with the Crown were perverted to the detriment of the electorate. Nevertheless, questions of procedure are important in their reaction upon the dignity of Parliament, and as contributing to the successful working of the parliamentary machine. Even more is this true of questions of privilege. In its contest with the Stuart Kings Parliament not only strove to maintain its own dignity and that of its members, but made a notable and indeed indispensable contribution to the development of parliamentary Democracy.

Not indeed its most notable contribution ; for, important as were questions of privilege, infinitely more important was its claim to exercise the exclusive right of making laws, of granting of supplies to the Crown, and of imposing charges upon the taxpayer.

To these weightier matters we must now pass.

III. THE PROBLEM OF SOVEREIGNTY

Taxation and Legislation. The Power of the Purse

Parlia-
ment and
Finance
PARLIAMENT was originally called into being to supply the financial necessities of the Crown. That is still the primary function of the House of Commons. Its essential business is to exercise a control over public expenditure. Hostile critics of our political institutions affirm that this function is at present inadequately discharged. It may well be that with the multiplication of administrative departments, each vying with the other to extract from the public purse increasingly large amounts of money for the sustenance of its own particular activities, with the steady increase in the power of the Executive, and with the growth of the spirit of prodigality, public and private, the control of the Legislature over expenditure has weakened. But this may be said. Carelessness there may be; but the system of procedure in the House of Commons has been so devised, or rather developed, as to reduce to a minimum the possibility of fraud or even of irregularity. All sums voted by the House of Commons are now appropriated to specific objects, and it is the function of the Committee on Public Accounts to satisfy themselves that every penny has in fact been expended in accordance with the appropriations, and to report to the House accordingly.

In this as in other matters the period of the seventeenth century was critical: the struggle between Crown and Parliament for the control of the purse strings reached under the Stuart Kings its climax.

The
power of
the purse
The general principle of parliamentary control had been already fully accepted when the Stuarts ascended the throne; but, as we have seen, the system was not in practice entirely watertight. Of several loopholes the most important was the right claimed by the Crown to levy charges, additional to those authorized by the grant of tonnage and poundage, upon commodities entering or

leaving the kingdom. These additional charges were known as Impositions.

The Stuart Kings, be it once more recalled, were driven to employ these questionable devices partly by personal extravagance, but, much more, because the revenue was inadequate to meet the legitimate expenditure of the Government. It is easy to be wise after the event, but, in retrospect, it is obvious that half the troubles which ensued might have been avoided if the King and Parliament had been alive to the fact that the old system was obsolete, and wholly inconsistent with the new position which Parliament desired to occupy. The King could no longer 'live of his own' or keep the machinery of Government in running order on the revenue derived from custom duties, from tenths and fifteenths, subsidies and so forth. But for Parliament to grant a regular and permanent revenue to a Stuart King was to part with an invaluable instrument for obtaining a control over the Executive Government. The solution of the problem was ultimately found in a sharp differentiation between the revenue of the Crown and the revenue of the State: but it took two more centuries to work out the final solution, and it was not until the accession of Queen Victoria that the differentiation was complete. *The Financial Problem*

Meanwhile, the financial problem continued to be a constant source of friction between the Stuart Kings and their Parliaments.

Of taxation in the modern sense the most important item was furnished by import and export duties, which it had become customary to vote to the King for life at the beginning of each reign. *Impositions*

The Tudors set the precedent of imposing additional duties, and in 1534 Henry VIII was authorized by Statute, during his 'life natural', 'to regulate by proclamation the course of trade and to repeal or revive acts relating to the importation and exportation of merchandises'. Mary and Elizabeth ignored the limitation and imposed the additional duties.

Bates's
Case
James I, acting on these precedents, imposed a duty on currants. The matter was complicated by the position of the Levant Company, which had been incorporated towards the end of Elizabeth's reign to regulate the trade between England and the Levant. Difficulties ensued but the Queen confirmed the monopoly of the company in return for a payment of £4,000 a year.

Partly in consequence of the outcry against monopolies, partly because it had incurred trading losses, the Company surrendered its charter in 1603, and James lost the revenue enjoyed by his predecessor. The King thereupon decided himself to impose a duty on currants, though he agreed to forgo considerable arrears to which he might justly have laid claim.

In 1605, however, the Levant Company was revived on a new basis under a patent from the Crown, and shortly afterwards John Bates, one of its members, raised the whole question of the legality of Impositions by refusing to pay the duty imposed by the King on currants. The matter was referred to the Court of Exchequer, but the merchants appealed to the House of Commons, and the House promptly inserted in their Petition of Grievances a request that the Crown would cease to levy impositions on the ground that such duties could not be levied without the consent of Parliament.

Judge-
ment for
the
Crown
The dispute now took on a much wider and more important aspect. The Barons of the Exchequer decided in favour of the Crown:—

'All the ports of the realm', said Baron Clarke, 'belong to the king. . . . So consequently may he prohibit all merchants; and as he may prohibit the persons, so may he the goods of any man, viz. that he shall export or import at his pleasure. And if the king may generally inhibit that such goods shall not be imported, then by the same reason may he prohibit them, upon condition or *sub modo*, viz. that if they import such goods then shall they pay, &c. . . .' Chief Baron Fleming spoke to similar effect, declaring that the ports are the gates of the King, and that 'he hath absolute power by them to include or exclude whom he shall please'. [1]

[1] *State Trials* (ed. 1779), vol. xi, p. 31.

From a legal point of view there can be little doubt that the Judges were right.[1] Sir Edward Coke, the stoutest champion of the Common Law, declared that the Government, in this case, had the law on its side. Hakewill, as we shall see presently, delivered a powerful speech against the Royal Prerogative in the debate on Impositions in 1610, but he confessed that when he listened to the judgements in the Court of Exchequer he had been perfectly satisfied with the arguments adduced in support of them. The House of Commons itself acquiesced in the decision.

Unfortunately, however, the Judges, not content with an exposition of the law, proceeded to enlarge upon the doctrine of the twofold power of the King; his *ordinary* power resting upon and limited by law; and his absolute or extraordinary power to be exercised solely at his own discretion. 'And the wisdom and providence of the King', said the Chief Baron, 'is not to be disputed by the subject'.[2]

Twofold Power of the Crown

For the moment Parliament acquiesced in the judgement without inquiring too closely into the arguments on which it was based. Well had it been if the King had been similarly content to let sleeping dogs lie.

In 1608 a new tariff or *Book of Rates* was published: some of the more burdensome duties were remitted, but new duties were imposed mainly on articles of luxury and on foreign goods which came into competition with the products of English manufactures. Such a policy was in complete accord with the best economic doctrine of the time, and the principles were applied with statesmanlike prudence. Moreover an additional revenue of £70,000 was thus secured.

New Tariff

But James, like his Judges, must needs base his fiscal policy on the 'special power and prerogative . . . inherent in the person of princes'.[3] He went, indeed, still further, and, when Parliament assembled for the Session of 1610, commanded the House of Commons 'not to dispute of the

The Royal Preroga-tive

---

[1] Though Maitland finds it 'difficult to understand the judgement as an exposition of law', p. 258.

[2] *State Trials*, ii. 404. Cited by Gardiner, i. 8.

[3] *Commission to Levy Impositions*, 28 July 1608.

King's power and prerogative in imposing upon merchandise exported or imported'. The Commons, as we have seen, bitterly resented this injunction, not merely on the merits of the proposed tariff, but as an infringement of their right of free debate. They, therefore, petitioned the King that 'according to the undoubted right and liberty of Parliament' they might proceed in their 'contended course of a full examination of these new impositions'.[1]

The King gave way; and in due course the House resolved itself into a committee,[2] in order to consider the question of the Impositions. A debate of the highest significance thereupon ensued.

Debate on Impositions Bacon and others who favoured the Royal Prerogative argued, ingeniously enough, that the King had power to prohibit goods from entering the ports of the Kingdom and that if he might prohibit their entrance he might continue the prohibition until a certain sum was paid.[3] Bates, for example, was told: 'you shall bring in no currants; if you do you shall pay so much'. Such reasoning did not satisfy the Opposition, as we may now begin to describe the popular party in the Stuart Parliaments. They hotly resented the action of the Crown alike as an infraction of the law and as contrary to good policy. But Hakewill,[4] who sat successively for several Cornish boroughs, went to the root of the matter. The question now in debate was, he insisted, whether the King might 'by his prerogative royal, without assent of Parliament, at his own will and pleasure, lay a new charge or imposition upon merchandize'. That by the common law the King was entitled to levy custom duties he admitted; but the right was 'limited and bounded'. 'The common law of England, as all other wise laws in the world, delight in certainty and abandon uncertainty as the mother of all debate and confusion,

[1] *Journals*, i, p. 431.
[2] Thus freeing itself from the control of the Speaker. Cf. Marriott, *Mechanism of the Modern State*, i. 527.
[3] Gardiner, ii. 80.
[4] He published in 1641 *Libertie of the Subject against the pretended Power of Imposition*.

than which nothing is more odious in law'; and it is for Parliament to secure this certainty. The reasons against an unlimited right to levy impositions were 'fortified by many records and statutes in the point'.

Mr. Whitelocke, in the course of the same debate, probed even more deeply into fundamentals than Hakewill: admitting that in every commonwealth there are some rights of Sovereignty which 'regularly and of common right do belong to the Sovereign power of that State', he propounded the vital question, 'where the Sovereign power is in this Kingdom; for there is the right of imposition'. Accidentally or intentionally Whitelocke had put his finger on the vital spot. Where did 'Sovereignty' reside?

That was in truth the supreme issue involved in the many-sided contest between the Stuart Kings and their people, or, more precisely, between the Crown and the other organs of government. *The Problem of Sovereignty*

Sovereignty, argued Whitelocke, was vested ultimately in the King-in-Parliament. That the King in his own person enjoyed a Sovereign power 'sole and singular' outside Parliament, he admitted; but such power was subordinated to that of the King-in-parliament. To argue on grounds of policy or State necessity is all very well, but 'this strain of policy maketh nothing to the point of right. Our rule is in this plain Commonwealth of ours, *oportet neminem esse sapientiorem legibus*. If there be an inconvenience, remove it by due process of law. 'It is more tolerable to suffer an hurt to some few for a short time, than to give way to the breach and violation of the right of the whole nation; for that is the true inconvenience.'

The matter could not have been more plainly stated. Where did 'Sovereignty' reside? On to that fundamental issue every particular dispute pushes us back; and the issue was indeed vital. But let there be no mistake about this: hitherto Sovereignty had resided, beyond question or dispute, in the King. It may well be that the time had come to transfer it to the King-in-parliament: but those who advocated the change could not defend themselves, as Mr. Gardiner defends them, on the plea of conservatism. They demanded a change which, even if it did not actually necessitate an appeal to arms, was nevertheless revolutionary. The Stuarts could have avoided revolution only by surrendering a position which on their own theory of government seemed to them vital. Commentators who look back upon the seventeenth century from the platform of to-day, can perceive much that was hidden from the eyes of contemporaries. We have seen the English Monarchy restored, after a troubled interregnum; we have seen it survive not only the Revolution of 1688 but all the much more far-reaching constitutional changes involved in the Legislation of the last hundred years. We see it to-day standing erect amid the ruins of proud Empires, and despite the overthrow of ancient thrones, stronger, perhaps, in the loyalty and devotion of 400,000,000 subjects, than ever was a monarchy in the history of the world.

Looking back upon the events of the Puritan Revolution it is easy for us to discern where the path of wisdom lay. But it was difficult for a King who came to the English throne as a foreigner, supposing, not unreasonably, that he was called not merely to succeed the Tudor Monarchs, but to inherit the Tudor Monarchy. Clearer vision, more sympathetic insight might have averted disaster; vision and sympathy generally can. But such exceptional qualities were not to be found, perhaps they were not to be looked for, in a King who, though not devoid of brains, was peculiar in temper and habits, and had no exceptional endowment of head or heart.

The Great Contract   Yet the Parliament of 1610 witnessed an attempt to reach a settlement which was not without promise of success. The crux of the difficulty was, be it repeated, finance. When Lord Salisbury, as Lord High Treasurer, laid before Parliament the financial necessity of the Crown, the Commons, as we have seen, demanded priority for the redress of grievances, in particular that of Impositions. The King so far retreated from the position he had originally taken up as to permit the discussion of any matter affecting the rights and interests of the subjects. The atmosphere seemed, therefore, not unfavourable to the conclusion of the bargain known as the 'Great Contract'. Salisbury proposed, and after prolonged discussion it was provisionally agreed, that the King was to receive a permanent revenue of £200,000 a year in exchange for the surrender of all his feudal dues—the rights of wardship, purveyance, and the conversion of all military tenures into free socage. The King also agreed not to impose any further custom duties, and to abandon the unlimited right to issue Proclamations.[1] But the bargain was not finally concluded before fresh disputes arose on other matters, and on 9 February 1611 the King dissolved the Parliament which had been sitting at intervals since 1604. He was with difficulty restrained from committing to the Tower some of the more prominent members of the Opposition.

After a three years' interval, however, the King was compelled to summon another Parliament. Every expedient to raise money without recourse to Parliament had been tried in vain, expenditure largely exceeded revenue, and the Crown plunged deeper and deeper into debt.[2] Great efforts were made to secure a more subservient House, but notwithstanding, or perhaps by reason of those efforts, the new House proved to be more recalcitrant than the last. The King offered some minor concessions, but the Commons brushing them aside as inadequate, went straight to the old question of Impositions, and demanded a conference with the Lords on the subject. The Lords refused, though only by a majority of nine, to confer. To the small majority the Bishops contributed no fewer than sixteen, and one of them, Dr. Neile, Bishop of Lincoln, went out of his way to deliver a most intemperate attack upon the Commons. The Commons took the matter up with warmth, and much of the brief session was spent in bickerings about Bishop Neile's

The Addled Parliament of 1614

---

[1] See *infra*, pp. 92 seq.
[2] Revenue fell short of expenditure by £200,000 a year, and the debt which Salisbury had reduced to £300,000 had mounted again to £680,000.

speech. No useful work was done: no supply was voted; no progress towards an accommodation between the disputants was made, and two months later the 'addled' Parliament, as it was mockingly christened, was dissolved.

Seven years were to elapse before another Parliament met in England, and contemporaries might well have speculated how long it might be before Parliament met again. In retrospect we may recall the interesting fact that the year which saw the dissolution of the 'addled Parliament' in England, saw also the last meeting of the States General in France until the Revolution. Representative institutions in Spain had suffered an even earlier eclipse.

England therefore might well have seemed to afford the one hope for the survival of representative institutions in western Europe. Nor was that hope destined, in the event, to disappointment. As for James I, it is only fair to him to record the fact that little as he may have been disposed to accept Bacon's sage advice and look on Parliament 'not only as a necessity, but as a unique and most precious means of uniting the Crown with the nation', he entertained no settled design for its abolition. He did, however, put forward pretensions on behalf of the Crown which, if acknowledged, might well have led to its extinction.

The examples of France and Spain existed to prove that the control of the purse-strings was vital to the usefulness, if not to the existence of Parliament. The question at issue between James I and the Commons was, therefore, crucial; and if the Commons clung, with conscious purpose or in blind instinct, to certain functions or privileges as 'of right' and not 'of grace', we of a later generation may be grateful for a stubborn obstinacy which, though precipitating a crisis in England, saved the cause of Representative Government in western Europe.

To resume the sequence of events. Fears of a complete supersession of Parliament proved to be groundless, but when, after a seven years' interval, the third Parliament of

the reign met, other questions occupied attention to the
exclusion of that of finance. Moreover, the financial skill
of Lionel Cranfield had for the time being extricated the
King from his difficulties.

Cranfield began life as a London apprentice, married his
master's daughter, and quickly made a reputation in the
city as a financier. Appointed Surveyor-General of the
Customs in 1615, he carried through such drastic reforms
in the Royal Household as to save the King no less than
£23,000 a year. After serving James in a variety of offices
he was raised to the peerage, and in 1621 became Lord
Treasurer, with Sir Richard Weston in the subordinate
office of Chancellor of the Exchequer.

Lionel Cranfield, Earl of Middlesex

Between the new Treasurer and George Villiers, Duke
of Buckingham, friction quickly developed. Buckingham
had become Lord High Admiral in 1619 and was as anxious
to extract money from a reluctant Treasury as any modern
Board of Admiralty. Middlesex was as thrifty as any
Victorian Chancellor of the Exchequer. It can occasion
little surprise, therefore, that friction between the two men
should quickly have hardened into positive antagonism.

When the last Parliament of the reign met in 1624
Buckingham determined to turn against his rival the
recently refurbished weapon of impeachment. Few men
rise to eminence so quickly as Middlesex had risen without
making some enemies; no man who is a jealous custodian
of the nation's finances can avoid making many. That the
conduct of Middlesex afforded some grounds for the charges
of malversation brought against him is certain, but the
real cause of his downfall was the offence he had given to
Buckingham and the young Prince of Wales, by his
adherence to the Spanish alliance, after they had decided
to abandon that policy. Exhorted to marry the Infanta,
'for reason of State and the good that would thence
redound to all Christendom', the Prince curtly bade the
Treasurer to 'judge of his merchandize, if he would, for he
was no arbiter in points of honour'.

Impeachment of Middlesex

The Commons, cordially concurring with Buckingham

and the Prince in their anxiety to see the Spanish marriage
project abandoned, were only too ready to impeach
Middlesex. Coke and Sandys conducted the impeachment,
and after a lengthy trial Middlesex was adjudged guilty by
the Peers. The sentence passed on him was terribly severe.
He was to lose all his offices and was declared incapable of
public employment, or of sitting in Parliament, for the
future; he was imprisoned in the Tower, ordered to pay
a fine of £50,000, and was banished for ever from the
precincts of the Court.

To separate Middlesex from the King had been Buckingham's primary purpose. It was now attained. But the
King saw further than the hot-tempered young men who
had compassed the downfall of a loyal servant and a
brilliantly successful steward. 'By God, Steeny, you are
a fool', said the King to the favourite, 'you are making a
rod with which you will be scourged yourself.' 'You will
live to have your belly full of impeachments.' Such was
the King's sage prediction to his son.

Less than twelve months after the downfall of Middlesex
the old King died and Prince Charles reigned in his stead.

Charles I   James I was neither a great man, nor a great king, but,
despite his pedantic adherence to a theory of kingship
alien to the traditions of his English subjects, he was not
devoid of native shrewdness and wit. Charles I was a
better man than his father, but a worse king; and he was
much less fortunate than his predecessor in his more
intimate counsellors. Worse advisers than Buckingham
and Henrietta Maria no king ever had; to Strafford he
turned too late; to those who like Hyde and Falkland
would have guided him more wisely he would not give his
entire confidence.

As regards finance the new reign started badly. James
had bequeathed to his successor a war, but left him, as
Clarendon says, 'unprovided with money to manage it'.
Nor was Parliament prepared to make good the deficiency.
On the contrary, though the House of Commons had
encouraged, if it had not instigated, the war, it betrayed its

mistrust of the King and his favourite by voting tonnage and poundage, not, as was customary, for life, but only for twelve months. The Lords refused to assent to a vote with this offensive limitation, and the King, despite the lack of parliamentary authority, levied the duties as usual. The suspicions of Parliament may have been justified, but to manifest them so obtrusively at this moment was none the less an unfortunate prelude to the new reign. And if there was suspicion on one side, there was a lack of confidence and candour on the other; the King and Buckingham made no disclosure of the financial necessities of the Government.

Financial mistrust was accentuated by religious fears. Would marriage with a French princess involve concessions to English Roman Catholics? Would the new King, like the old, show favour to the Arminians in return for political support of the Prerogative? The attitude of Charles I was not left long in doubt. The President of the College at Douay had lately (1624) attacked the English Church as Calvinistic in a pamphlet quaintly entitled *The Gag for the New Gospel*. Dr. Montagu, a leading Arminian and a King's chaplain, retorted with *A New Gag for an Old Goose*. Montagu's position was precisely that of the Anglo-Catholic of to-day: the English Church is equally opposed to Rome and to Geneva; it is not Calvinist but Catholic. Admitting the errors of Rome, he refused to speak of the Pope as Anti-Christ; denying the doctrine of Transubstantiation, he asserted that of the Real Presence; images and pictures should not be made objects of worship or veneration, but they were no more objectionable than illustrations in a book. *(The Church, the Crown, and the Commons)*

Violent as was Montagu's language, the main argument of his book was reasonable and moderate. Nevertheless, it sufficed to alarm a Puritan House of Commons which appealed to Archbishop Abbot. Abbot gave the author excellent advice: 'Go home, review over your book.' Do not give occasion for scandal or offence; 'do not wed yourself to your own opinion and remember we must give an *(The Arminians)* account of our ministry to Christ.' It was sound advice, admirably characteristic of Lambeth at its best. But it was resented by Montagu as similar advice, coming from the same quarter, has often been resented.

The King's chaplain appealed to King James. 'If that is to be a Papist', said the King, 'so am I a Papist.' Montagu was accordingly authorized to prepare a sequel, but it was not published until after James's death. *Appello Caesarem* was dedicated to his successor.

Charles's first Parliament liked *Appello Caesarem* as little as James's last Parliament had liked *A New Gag for an Old Goose*, the argument of which was restated and reinforced in the offending sequel. The Commons again appealed to Abbot, who was annoyed by Montagu but impotent to restrain him. The matter was, thereupon, referred to a Committee on Recusancy, which condemned the doctrines maintained by Montagu, but recommended postponement of the issue. The Commons, however, accused Montagu of disturbing Church and State and treating the House of Commons with contempt, though they took no further action except a formal committal of the delinquent to the custody of the serjeant-at-arms. The attack on Montagu was resumed with equally inconclusive results when Parliament reassembled after three weeks' adjournment, at Oxford.

Meanwhile, no further progress had been made in regard to the pressing question of finance, and, when Parliament resumed, relations with the Crown were embittered by the news that the French marriage treaty involved the relaxation of the penal laws against Roman Catholics, and the loan of an English fleet for an attack on the Huguenots in Rochelle.

To the King's request for money the Commons retorted with a demand for information. Who is the enemy? Where is the war and who has advised it? 'In the Government', said Phelips, 'there hath wanted good advice, counsels and powers have been monopolized.' A few days later the question of confidence was more specifically raised and Buckingham was attacked by name: 'Let us lay the fault where it is; the Duke of Buckingham is trusted and it must needs be either in him or in his agents.' Alarmed by the attack on his favourite minister, Charles hastily dissolved his first Parliament (August 12).

But money was sorely needed and a second Parliament met on 6 February 1626. During the six months' interval the situation had changed greatly for the worse. The King himself was distracted between the not unnatural demands of a Roman Catholic Queen and the suspicions, equally natural, of a Puritan Parliament. Foreign relations were in hopeless confusion. Charles was, almost at the same moment, negotiating with the French Huguenots behind the back of their lawful Sovereign, and in alliance with that Sovereign dispatching his fleet to attack Cadiz. The expedition to Cadiz was a disastrous failure, and the mysterious complications of foreign policy intensified the bitterness with which the new House of Commons attacked an incompetent minister. Tempers were still further exacerbated by the futile attempt to ward off attacks in Parliament by pricking as sheriffs some of the more prominent leaders of 'the Opposition'. But if Wentworth, Coke, and Phelips were thus excluded, Sir John Eliot was still there to lead the attack on Buckingham.

Of Eliot's part in the constitutional conflicts of that time much has been said, already, more must be said, hereafter, in another connexion.[1] For the moment it must suffice to point out that on the threshold of the conflict Eliot fixed upon the cardinal doctrine destined to provide a solution of the problem. The ministers of the Crown must be made answerable to Parliament, and primarily to that House which held the purse-strings. The grant of supply must be dependent upon confidence in the discretion of the Executive.

The first step towards the establishment of this doctrine was to employ against an incompetent minister a weapon rapidly becoming obsolete. Buckingham was impeached on a criminal charge because Parliament was opposed to

Second Parliament, 1626

Ministerial responsibility

Impeachment of Buckingham

[1] *Supra*, c. ii.

the policy he had pursued. 'The Laws of England have taught us', said Dudley Digges, 'that Kings cannot command ill or unlawful things, and whatsoever ill event succeeds, the executioner of such designs must answer for them.' 'Little', says Mr. Gardiner who quotes them, 'did the Commons think of all that was implied in these words. By the mouth of Digges they had grasped at the Sovereignty of England.' [1]

With the specific charges against Buckingham we need not concern ourselves. Digges had gone straight to the point: Sir John Eliot drove it home. Even if the policy was really the King's, it was Buckingham's duty to have dissuaded him from the pursuit of it; if without avail, he should have laid the matter before the Council; if the Council had failed to dissuade the King, it should have entered a protest against the Sovereign. Like Sejanus, Buckingham so confounded himself with the King that he is often styled *laborum imperatoris socius*. More aptly perhaps he is compared with Richard the First's famous minister, the Bishop of Ely, of whom it was said: 'Pereat qui perdere cuncta festinat. Opprimatur ne omnes oppromat.'

'My lords,' concluded Eliot, 'you see the man, what have been his actions, what he is like you know. I leave him to your judgements. This only is conceived by us, the knights, citizens, and burgesses of the Commons house of Parliament—that by him come all our evils, in him we find the causes and on him must be the remedies.'

Eliot and Digges paid for their audacity by imprisonment in the Tower, but Digges was released almost immediately, and the Commons, profoundly moved by this attack upon the privileges, resolved to suspend their sittings until Eliot also was restored to liberty. A week later (19 May) he was released, but the Commons refused all supplies until their grievances had been redressed; they bluntly told the King that they could have no confidence that their money would be well spent as long as Bucking-

[1] vi. 99.

ham had the spending of it, and they petitioned for his dismissal as an enemy to State and Church.

The King's reply was another dissolution of Parliament.

Eliot was bidden to pursue the charges against Buckingham in the Court of Star Chamber, but he stedfastly refused on the ground that he was but the mouthpiece of a House of Commons, now no longer in existence, and the Star Chamber proceeded to acquit Buckingham.

The King was now in dire straits for money, and fell back upon the expedient, first of a free gift, and then of a forced loan to be collected by Commissioners in every county. Money came in very slowly: the City refused to lend even on the security of the Crown jewels; some counties excused themselves on the plea of poverty, others refused to contribute except through the constitutional channel of Parliament. Seaboard counties and seaports were called upon to furnish ships. Among the prominent men who refused to subscribe were Eliot, Hampden, and Sir Thomas Wentworth, afterwards Earl of Strafford. The expedition which Buckingham himself led to the Isle of Rhé for the relief of the Huguenots besieged in La Rochelle ended in disaster, and disasters abroad stiffened resistance to the collection of the loan. Nor did the sermons of the Arminian clergy help the King or forward his policy. But the King persisted.

Financial Straits

The matter was carried a stage further by the appeal of five Knights, who had been imprisoned on account of their refusal to subscribe to the loan, for a writ of *habeas corpus*.[1] The judges of the King's Bench refused, as we shall see presently, to admit the prisoners to bail, but equally they refused to put it on record that the Crown might persistently decline to show cause.

Meanwhile, confusion deepened both abroad and at home, until at last the King consented, on the earnest entreaty of Buckingham, who, to do him justice, knew no fear, to call another Parliament.

The third Parliament of the reign met accordingly on

[1] *Infra*, p. 107 seq.

17 March 1628. The mood of Parliament was more conciliatory than that of the King, who broadly hinted that
if Parliament failed in its duty towards the country he
must find other means which God had put in his hands.
This was not a threat, for he 'scorned to threaten any but
his equals'. Notwithstanding this tactless utterance, proceedings against Buckingham were tacitly dropped, and the
Commons proceeded to consider conjointly of grievances
and supply. Meanwhile the Commons passed a series of
Resolutions: there must be no taxation without the assent
of Parliament; no freeman might be committed without
cause shown, and every one, however committed, had a
right to a writ of *habeas corpus*, and if no legal cause of
imprisonment was shown, must be delivered or bailed.
Five subsidies were, however, voted, but they were to be
practically conditional on the redress of grievances. The
best friends of the King and of the country had made
desperate efforts to promote conciliation, but they were
baffled by the King's obstinate insistence on the Stuart
claim to be above the law.

Sir Edward Coke, who had now exchanged the Judicial
Bench for the Senate, came forward with a Petition of
Right. After three weeks' debate it was agreed to by both
Houses (28 May). A long historical preamble or recital led
up to the crucial demands, four in number. For the
moment we are concerned only with the first, which ran as
follows:

'They do therefore pray your Most Excellent Majesty, that
no man hereafter be compelled to make or yield any gift, loan,
benevolence, tax, or such like charge, without common consent
by Act of Parliament; and that none be called to make answer,
or take such oath, or to give attendance, or be confined, or
otherwise molested or disquieted concerning the same, or for
refusal thereof. . . . .

The King's answer to the Petition was evasive; Eliot
proposed a further remonstrance; the King tried to stifle
debate; the Commons were reduced to tears. Speaker
Finch reported to the House that a command had been

laid upon him to 'interrupt any that should go about to lay an aspersion on the ministers of State'. Coke was not dismayed:

'I think the Duke of Buckingham is the cause of all our miseries, and till the King be informed thereof, we shall never go about with honour, or sit with honour here. That man is the grievance of grievances. Let us set down the cause of all our disasters, and they will all reflect upon him.'

The Lords were no less resolved than the Commons to obtain from the King an unambiguous answer to the *Petition of Right*, and at last, on 7 June, it was forthcoming: *Soit droit fait comme est desiré.*

But Buckingham remained at the King's side. The Commons accordingly pressed for the full execution of the penal laws against the Roman Catholics, proceeded with the attacks upon the Arminian clergy, and begged the King to consider whether it consorted with the safety of the King or the Kingdom that Buckingham should continue in his great offices or 'in his place of nearness and counsel' about the sacred person of His Majesty. The King in reply promised to discountenance the Arminians, though a series of appointments to bishoprics seemed to throw doubts upon his sincerity in this matter. He would not raise money by irregular means, but he would not give up Buckingham.

The Commons, despite the King's assent to the *Petition of Right*, proceeded with a remonstrance about tonnage and poundage. The King bitterly resented a move which he regarded as an attempt on the part of the Commons to meet his concessions by further demands. Was his resentment unnatural? He had given statutory sanction to a Petition which definitely shut the door against direct taxation. Did the first clause recited above also prohibit the levying of custom duties? The Court of Exchequer had pronounced in favour of 'Impositions'. James I and Charles I had continued to collect them. Had the Commons intended by the first clause of the *Petition of Right* to prohibit them, would they not have said so?

Remonstrance on Tonnage and Poundage

The framers of the Petition were, as Gardiner has pointed out, the first lawyers of the day,

'and it can hardly have been through inadvertence that they omitted the decisive words necessary to include *Impositions* if they had intended to do so. Nor was it without significance that whilst in the preamble to the *Petition of Right* the Houses refer to the imaginary statute *De Tallagio non Concedendo* as enacting that "no tallage or aid should be taken without consent", they make no reference to the clauses in the *Confirmatio Cartarum* which refer to the duties upon merchandise.'[1]

In the subsequent Remonstrance not only did the Commons attempt to rectify an omission; they pretended that all along Tonnage and Poundage had been included:

'The receiving of Tonnage and Poundage and other impositions not granted by Parliament is a breach of the fundamental liberties of this kingdom, and contrary to your Majesty's royal answer to the said Petition of Right.'

Small wonder that Charles deeply resented this language. Tonnage and Poundage was 'never intended by you to ask, nor meant by me—I am sure to grant'. He therefore refused to receive the offensive Remonstrance and forthwith prorogued Parliament (28 June).

Before Parliament met again Buckingham was removed from the scene by the hand of the assassin and Charles took sole charge of the business of State.

Session of 1629   On reassembling for the Session of 1629 (20 January) the Commons at once appointed a Sub-Committee on religion under the chairmanship of Pym. Alarmed by the continued favour shown to the Arminian section of the Church, by the growing influence of Bishop Laud, and not least by the King's *Declaration Prefixed to the Articles of Religion*[2] issued in the previous November, Pym's Sub-Committee drafted a series of resolutions recommending the exemplary punishment of Papists and Arminians, a stricter censorship of books, the burning of the works of Bishop Montagu and

[1] Introduction to *Statutes*, pp. xxiii–iv.
[2] Commonly printed with the Book of Common Prayer.

Cosin, and the preferment of 'learned, pious and orthodox' clergymen.

This Report, owing to the premature dissolution, was never adopted by Parliament, but there is no doubt that it accurately represented the ecclesiastical views of a large majority of the Commons, if not also of the Lords. It should, therefore, dispose for ever of the extraordinary but traditional idea that the Puritan party stood for toleration in religion. No party at that time had the remotest idea of toleration. All were striving for exclusive supremacy: to make the Church coextensive with the nation, and to mould that national Church after their own pattern. *Parliament and Religion*

The religious question was to the fore during this brief Session, but other matters also were in debate: notably one of those questions of privilege in which the House of Commons always delights. John Rolle, one of the merchants whose goods had been seized by the customs officers, was a member of Parliament. The general question of the legality of Tonnage and Poundage was thus further complicated by that of Parliamentary privilege. The Court of Exchequer denied that privilege covered such a case, and had the temperature in Parliament been normal it is unlikely that so extravagant a claim would ever have been put forward. But the temperature was at fever height and Parliament went in daily fear of dissolution. When, therefore, Speaker Finch informed the House on 2 March that he had it in command from his Majesty to adjourn the House until the 10th, a tumult arose. Eliot loudly claimed for the House the right of self-adjournment: the Speaker attempted to leave the chair: Denzil Holles and Benjamin Valentine rushed forward and held him down. 'God's wounds', cried the former, 'you shall sit till we please to rise.' Further protests from the unfortunate Speaker were unavailing. Hot debate ensued, Black Rod was knocking at the door with a message from the King, in great haste the three famous resolutions were recited; Holles put them to the House and amid a scene of excitement and confusion they were carried. The House then voted to adjourn, and *Dissolution of Parliament*

Resolutions of 1629

Black Rod was at last admitted. The historic resolutions ran as follows:

1. Whosoever shall bring in innovation of religion, or by favour or countenance seem to extend or introduce Popery or Arminianism, or other opinion disagreeing from the true and orthodox Church, shall be reputed a capital enemy to this Kingdom and Commonwealth. 2. Whosoever shall counsel or advise the taking and levying of the subsidies of Tonnage and Poundage, not being granted by Parliament, or shall be an actor or instrument therein, shall be likewise reputed an innovator in the Government, and a capital enemy to the King and Commonwealth. 3. If any merchant or person whatsoever shall voluntarily yield, or pay the said subsidies of Tonnage and Poundage, not being granted by Parliament, he shall likewise be reputed a betrayer of the liberties of England, and an enemy to the same.'

The Sequel   A few days later Charles in person dissolved Parliament. He was so far sensitive to public opinion as to issue a lengthy declaration,[1] exhibiting his dealings with Parliament in a favourable light, and promising to 'maintain his subjects in their just liberties'. He would regard it as presumption for any to prescribe any time for Parliament, but he had abundantly proved, by their frequent meeting, his love for Parliaments, and he hoped to call another, when those who 'had bred this interruption had received their condign punishment' and the people at large 'had come to a better understanding of us and themselves'.

Condign punishment followed swifty. Nine members of the late Parliament were summoned to appear before the Privy Council to answer for their conduct in Parliament and were committed to custody. Six of them were presently released, but Eliot, Holles, and Valentine stoutly refused to make submission; Eliot contracted consumption and died in the Tower in 1632; Holles and Valentine remained in prison until the meeting of the Short Parliament in 1640.

End of Act I   So the curtain falls on the first Act of the drama of the seventeenth century. The first two Stuarts had made a

[1] Gardiner, *Documents*, pp. 17–31.

genuine attempt to rule in the traditional manner of the English monarchy with the aid of Parliament. But their theory of Divine Right was intrinsically incompatible, if not with Parliamentary Government as understood by the Tudors, at least with that larger measure of Parliamentary control claimed by Eliot and Pym.

To condemn the Stuart Kings as reactionary despots carries us no further than to denounce the parliamentary leaders as revolutionaries. The Stuarts stood stubbornly in ways which were undeniably ancient, but were rapidly becoming obsolete. The Commons were advancing to a position which might be justifiable, but was certainly new. A wiser man than Charles I might have perceived that the time had come for registering a further stage in the evolution of self-government. A stronger man than Buckingham might, perhaps, have compelled the Commons, if not to abandon, at least to postpone the assertion of their claims. But Buckingham had not the skill or strength of a Richelieu. King Charles, though an attractive personality, lacked the gifts indispensable to one who aspires to personal rule: he was too obstinate to make a graceful concession to Parliament; he was not strong enough to rule without it. Autocracy is sufferable only when combined with competence. Charles refused to barter away the Prerogative: but had not the strength to maintain it, nor the skill and knowledge of statecraft to justify the use of it. What then could avert impending catastrophe?

IV. THE PROBLEM OF PERSONAL LIBERTY

The Crown, the Judges, and the Law

Property and Liberty
THE sanctity of private property has, throughout the ages, been regarded as an elementary right of the individual citizen and a crucial test of civilized society. Had the Stuart theory of Government been permitted to prevail the goods of the subject would have been at the mercy of the Prince. Parliament in defending its right to control taxation was also championing the rights of individuals. It is true that Parliaments have at times been as ready as Kings to sanction schemes of spoliation, but the spoliation has been effected under legal process. The extortions of absolute princes are subject to no such limitations. The Stuart Parliaments in claiming control of the purse-strings were, therefore, maintaining a principle essential to liberty.

Personal Liberty
Even more important than the sanctity of property is the right to the enjoyment of personal liberty: the right of the citizen to do what he will, to say and think what he will, to go where he will, restricted only by regard for the equal rights of his fellow citizens. Of these rights also Parliament is the appropriate guardian. Yet laws reach but a little way. However vigilant and conscientious the legislator, however equitable the laws, the daily life of the citizen may be rendered utterly miserable, if there be any flaw or weakness in the Executive side of Government, or any lack of impartiality or independence in the administration of justice.

What, then, is the proper relation between these three great organs of government, the Legislature or law-making body, the Executive which controls the day-to-day work of Government, and the judiciary which administers and interprets the law?

The Separation of Powers— Montesquieu
For an answer to this question the modern world has, with rare unanimity, gone to Montesquieu, and not in vain. In the whole literature of Political Science there is probably

no aphorism so often quoted, there is certainly none which has exercised so profound an influence upon modern constitutional theory and practice, as this sentence from the *Esprit des Lois*: 'There is no liberty if the Judicial power be not separated from the Legislative and Executive.' A few years later one of the greatest of Oxford and of English jurists, Sir William Blackstone, emphasized the significance of Montesquieu's doctrine of the separation of powers:

'Were [the Judicial power] joined with the Legislative, the life liberty and property of the subject would be in the hands of arbitrary judges, whose decisions would then be regulated only by their opinions and not by any fundamental principles of law.'[1]

Montesquieu imagined that in enunciating his famous doctrine he was but reducing to theory the practice of the English Constitution. Whether the separation of powers is, or ever has been, so complete in England as Montesquieu imagined is a debatable point. Bagehot in his analysis of the Constitution in mid-Victorian days discovered the characteristic feature of the English Constitution not in the separation, but in the 'close union, the nearly complete fusion' of the Executive and the Legislature.

Be that as it may, the question of the separation of powers, and more particularly that of the dependence of the Judiciary upon the Executive, was a crucial problem in the seventeenth century.

Under the first two Stuarts[2] the line between the Executive and the judicial functions was very indistinct. Every Privy Councillor was entitled to sit in the Court of Star Chamber, and the Lord Treasurer was himself a member of the Court of Exchequer, though he was not entitled to deliver a judicial opinion.[3] This feature of the

The Stuart Kings and the Judges

[1] *Commentaries*, i, c. viii.

[2] Until the Long Parliament (1641) abolished the Court of Star Chamber.

[3] Gardiner, ii. 7, who omits to point out that down to the year 1875 the Chancellor of the Exchequer was entitled to sit as a judge in the Court of Exchequer, and still sits annually in the High Court of Justice (King's Bench Division) for the purpose of nominating sheriffs.

period under review was first emphasized by Dr. A. V. Dicey, one of the greatest of Blackstone's successors at Oxford.

Dicey on 'Administrative Law' — 'There was a time when it must have seemed possible that what we now call administrative law should become a permanent part of English institutions. For from the accession of the Tudors till the final expulsion of the Stuarts the Crown and its servants maintained and put into practice, with more or less success and varying degrees of popular approval, views of government essentially similar to- the theories which under different forms have been accepted by the French people. The personal failings of the Stuarts and the confusion caused by the combination of a religious with a political movement have tended to mask the true character of the legal and constitutional issues raised by the political contests of the seventeenth century. A lawyer who regards the matter from an exclusively legal point of view is tempted to assert that the real subject in dispute between statesmen such as Bacon and Wentworth on the one hand, and Coke and Eliot on the other, was whether a strong administration should or should not be permanently established in England. . . . Advocates of the prerogative . . . wished, in short, to give the government the sort of rights conferred on a foreign executive by the principles of administrative law. Hence for each feature of French *droit administratif* one may find some curious analogy either in the claims put forward or in the institutions favoured by the Crown lawyers of the seventeenth century.' [1]

No apology is needed for this lengthy quotation, for the passage is likely to become classical. Dicey's great work accurately reflected the best opinion, if not the universal opinion, of the time (1885). Administrative Law and Administrative Tribunals were foreign devices from which we happy English folk were fortunately free, and we owed our freedom to the successful vindication by the great lawyers and statesmen of Stuart times of the principle of the rule of law. That view is, as we have already seen, no longer universally or perhaps even generally held by English jurists. It may be that Dicey, in the earlier editions of his

[1] *Law of the Constitution* (2nd ed.), pp. 206–7.

great work, over-emphasized the distinction between the English 'Rule of Law' and the *droit administratif*, and was in consequence inclined to deny to Frenchmen the possession of those guarantees for personal liberty which Englishmen have for centuries enjoyed.

Recent critics have called in question the accuracy of his contrast, and one critic, at least, of great distinction has gone so far as to say: 'The development of French administrative law in the last century has been very much more in favour of the subject than of the administration. The remedies of the subject against the State in France are easier, speedier and infinitely cheaper than they are in England to-day.' [1] That may well be, for in England the remedies are neither easy, speedy, or cheap; and Dicey himself in the last edition of his famous treatise took up a more cautious attitude. He admitted 'a very slight though noticeable approximation *towards one another* of what may be called the official law of England and the *droit administratif* of France'. 'It may not,' he added, 'be an exaggeration to say that in some directions the law of England is being officialized . . . by Statutes passed under the influence of socialistic ideas. It is even more certain that the *droit administratif* of France is year by year becoming more judicialized.' [2] *Later critics*

Be this as it may, two facts remain and alone concern us in the present connexion: first, that in the seventeenth century a critical contest took place between the 'rule of law' and the *droit administratif*; and secondly, that the struggle issued to the infinite advantage of the liberty of the English subject in a victory for the Rule of Law. [3]

At this point it is desirable to explain what precisely is meant by *Droit administratif* and 'Rule of Law' *Administrative Law*

[1] C. K. Allen, *Quarterly Review*, No. 477, p. 247.
[2] Introduction to 8th edition (1915), pp. xliii–iv.
[3] On the whole subject there is now a considerable and rapidly growing literature, e.g. G. E. Robinson, *Public Authorities and Legal Liability* (1925); W. S. Robson, *Justice and Administrative Law* (1928); F. J. Port, *Administrative Law* (1929); and Lord Sankey, *The Principles and Practice of the Law To-day* (1928).

respectively. Aucoc defines Administrative Law as 'the body of rules which regulates the relations of the administration or the administrative authority with private citizens'. It determines, he says: '(1) The Constitution and the relations of those organs of society which are charged with the care of those collective interests which are the object of public administration . . . , (2) the relation of the administrative authorities towards the citizens of the State.' [1]

'Under this system', writes Lord Hewart, 'the ordinary Courts of Justice are regarded as having no jurisdiction to deal with any dispute affecting the Government or its Servants, all such disputes being within the exclusive cognizance of the Administrative Courts, the chief of which in France is the *Conseil d'État*. . . . Where, in the course of a case in an ordinary Judicial Court, it appears that a question of administrative law is involved, the Court is bound to refer the matter to the Council of State for decision. . . . In France, a public official is not answerable in any Court, even an Administrative Court, for what is regarded as an act of State, however unjustifiable his conduct may have been according to the ordinary law of the land. And agents of the Government are exempted from punishment for any act of interference with the liberty or rights of citizens if the act was done in obedience to the orders of a superior. On the other hand damages may be recovered from the State itself, through the Council of State for unlawful acts of agents of the Government.' [2]

Administrative Courts   This system of law is administered by a series of Courts or 'Councils' as they are technically and perhaps more accurately termed. The Council of the Prefecture furnishes the first degree of administrative jurisdiction, and parallel with it are certain special Councils, such as the Educational Council. The series culminates in the Council of State, which, as the *Conseil du roi*, played an important part under the *Ancien Régime* and still functions as one of the most distinctive and influential bodies in modern France.

[1] *Droit administratif*, i, § 6.
[2] Lord Hewart, *The New Despotism*, pp. 37–9.

The 'Rule of Law' was resolved by Dr. Dicey into three distinct propositions:

(1) 'That no man is punishable or can be lawfully made to suffer in body or goods except for a distinct breach of law established in the ordinary legal manner before the ordinary courts of the land';

(2) 'That not only is no man above the law but (what is a different thing) that here every man whatever be his rank or condition is subject to the ordinary law of the realm and amenable to the jurisdiction of the ordinary tribunals'; and

(3) 'That with us the law of the Constitution, the rules which in foreign countries naturally form part of a constitutional code, are not the source but the consequence of the rights of individuals as defined and enforced by the courts.'

For a full explanation and illustration of these important propositions reference must be made to Dicey's work.[1] But no review, however summary, of the leading features of our Constitution could pretend to completeness which did not emphasize these fundamental conceptions.

The first, with which alone we are for the moment concerned, asserts, in the most emphatic manner, the right of the individual citizen to personal liberty. No man is punishable except for a proved offence against the law. Two points should be noted: first, there must be a distinct breach of the law; and secondly, this breach must be proved in the ordinary legal manner before the ordinary courts of the land. To us such a proposition is a commonplace. But if we would understand its full significance, we need only turn to the experience of France under the *Ancien Régime*, or to our own in the first half of the seventeenth century. Charles James Fox, on hearing of the fall of the Bastille (14 July 1789), is said to have exclaimed: 'How much the greatest and best event that ever happened in the history of the world!' We may regard such an exclamation as the outcome of political hysteria. It becomes intelligible, however, and excusable, when we realize that the Bastille was the outward and visible sign of a judicial system which was

[1] *Law of the Constitution*, esp. Lectures V, VI, VII.

the negation of the first proposition of our 'rule of law'. Hundreds of men had under that system suffered loss of liberty, not for distinct and proven breaches of the law, but because they had rendered themselves obnoxious to those *Lettres de* who were powerful enough to procure a *lettre de cachet, Cachet* consigning their enemies to imprisonment, which might be lifelong. The Bastille stood not for the rule of law, but for the rule of privilege. Hence its destruction was hailed, alike by Frenchmen and by sympathizers abroad, with an enthusiasm which to the average Englishman seems hysterical. In proportion, however, as we appreciate the blessings of the 'rule of law', we can sympathize with the destruction of the rule of might.

Preroga-   It is, however, unnecessary to go to France to illustrate
tive the significance of the 'rule of law'. The constitutional
Courts in
England crisis of the seventeenth century in England centred in a struggle not merely for parliamentary liberty, but for personal liberty. Both were threatened by the methods adopted by the Stuart Kings. Many men suffered both in purse and person who had never been proved guilty of any breach of the law established in the ordinary legal manner before the ordinary courts. Various extraordinary tribunals deprived the subjects of those liberties which were thought to be guaranteed by *Magna Carta* and many subsequent enactments. The Court of Star Chamber, the High Commission Court, the Council of the Welsh Marches, the Council of the North, the Castle Chamber in Dublin, and other Prerogative Courts, grievously oppressed the subjects of the King. The 'High Commission grew to such excess of sharpness and severity as was not much less than the Romish Inquisition'; the 'Court of Star Chamber both abounded in extravagant censures . . . whereby His Majesty's subjects have been oppressed by grievous fines, imprisonments, stigmatizings, mutilations, whippings, pillories, gags, confinements, banishments. . . .'[1] So ran the *Grand Remonstrance,* and few Acts of the Long Parliament were passed with such universal acclaim as that

[1] *Grand Remonstrance,* §§ 52, 37.

which provided for the abolition of the Star Chamber and other extraordinary tribunals.

But the mischief was even more deep-seated. The extension of the jurisdiction of the extraordinary courts was bad enough, but royal interference with the course of justice in the ordinary courts was, if anything, worse. Nowadays we have two safeguards: there must be, in the first place, a distinct breach of the law, and, in the second, this breach must be proved in an 'ordinary' court. In the first four decades of the seventeenth century the citizen had neither. He was liable to punishment by an extraordinary tribunal, and he was also liable at the hands of an ordinary tribunal without a proved breach of the law.

To descend to detail. The struggle between the Crown and the law, though perhaps inevitable, was certainly precipitated by the personality of the man who in 1606 became Chief Justice of the Court of Common Pleas. Sir Edward Coke has been described by a great historian of to-day as 'one of the most disagreeable figures in our history', and at the same time as 'one of the most important champions of our liberties'.[1] In both respects the description is strictly accurate. A man of brilliant intellect, of untiring industry, of colossal learning, but coarse in fibre and overbearing and truculent in temper, Coke was irresistibly tempted to combat, and well qualified to expose, the philosophical theories of a James I or a Francis Bacon. Between Coke and Bacon there was indeed keen professional rivalry and bitter personal antagonism. Despite the ardent advocacy of the reigning favourite, the Earl of Essex, Bacon had been passed over in 1593 for the Solicitor Generalship in favour of Coke. The latter was promoted to be Attorney-General in 1594, and, as we have seen, became Chief Justice of the Common Pleas in 1606. So long as the old Queen lived he was the foremost champion of the rights of the Crown; but after the accession of James I, and more particularly after his own promotion to the Bench, his attitude underwent a marked

Sir Edward Coke

---

[1] Trevelyan, *England under the Stuarts*, p. 121.

change. He now stood forward as the champion of the Common Law, alike against the Ecclesiastical Courts and against the Court of Chancery, and most of all against the Prerogative of the Crown.

The Prohibitions His first quarrel was with Archbishop Bancroft, who had complained of the interference of the Lay Courts with the Ecclesiastical Courts. The Common Law Courts were accustomed to issue in the King's name *Prohibitions* forbidding the Ecclesiastical Courts to entertain cases which in the opinion of the common lawyers belonged to the Lay Courts. The clergy were impatient of these claims, and in 1605 Archbishop Bancroft presented to the Crown a series of complaints (*Articuli Cleri*) against the obnoxious proceedings of the judges. Neither party was in fact upon firm ground; and both were aware of the instability of their foothold. Bancroft, therefore, proposed that the power to issue prohibitions should be vested in the Court of Chancery; the judges appealed to Parliament to settle the question by legislation.

Meanwhile, one Fuller, a member of Parliament who had often appeared before the Courts on behalf of Puritan clients, had been fined and imprisoned by the High Commission for an attack upon the jurisdiction of that Court, alleged to have been made while he was pleading the cause of a client before it. The judges claimed that the decision in such a case rested with them. Bancroft appealed to the King. James sent for the judges, told them, truly enough, that all jurisdiction was derived from him and that it was for him to decide to what court particular cases should be assigned. Coke gives the following account of the interview:

'Then the King said that he thought the law was founded upon reason, and that he and others had reason as well as the judges. To which it was answered by me that true it was that God had allowed His Majesty's excellent science and great endowments of nature; but His Majesty was not learned in the laws of his realm of England and causes which concern the life or inheritance or goods or fortunes of his subjects; they are not to be decided by natural reason, but by the artificial reason and

judgment of law, which law is an act which requires long study
and experience before that a man can attain to the cognizance
of it; and that the law was the golden met-wand and measure
to try the causes of the subjects, and which protected His
Majesty in safety and peace. With which the King was greatly
offended, and said that then he should be under the law, which
was treason to affirm, as he said. To which I said that Bracton
saith *quod Rex non debet esse sub homine sed sub deo et lege.*'

The dispute between the great lawyer and the King
raised afresh, it will be observed, the whole question of
Sovereignty. Was the King subject to the law, or above it?
Did his subjects enjoy their rights only by his grace, or
were their rights derived from an authority to which the
King also must defer? The problem, though it had many
facets, fiscal, judicial, legislative, is seen to be essentially
one, obtruding itself again and again upon our notice as
we make our way through the history of this period. Not
until after the Revolution of 1688 had virtually decided
that Sovereignty was vested in the King-in-Parliament was
the problem solved.

Meanwhile, in reference to this particular case, the King
was quick to perceive that his own cause was closely bound
up with that of the Church.

'I pray you', he wrote to Salisbury, 'forget not Fuller's
matter, that the Ecclesiastical Commission may not be suffered
to sink besides the evil deserts of this villain; for this farther I
prophesy unto you that, whensoever the ecclesiastical dignity,
together with the government thereof, shall be turned in
contempt and begin evanish in this Kingdom, the Kings hereof
shall not long after prosper in their government and the
monarchy shall fall to ruin, which I pray God I may never live
to see.'

These words are only an extended commentary on the
old text: 'No Bishop, no King.' The tenacious adherence
of Charles I to that dogma cost him, as we shall see, his
crown and his life.

For the moment, however, the King and the Bishops
won a Pyrrhic victory over the judges. Fuller's case was

a weak one and the judges, while maintaining the right of the Common lawyers to restrain the Ecclesiastical Courts from exceeding their jurisdiction, remitted the case to the High Commission. But the practice of prohibition continued until the whole system of Prerogative Courts were swept away by the Long Parliament.

Procla-
mations Another collision between the Crown and the judges occurred on the question of Proclamations. The general and exclusive right of Parliament to make the laws had been acknowledged theoretically in the fourteenth century, and in the fifteenth by a significant change in procedure had been established in practice. By that change procedure by bill superseded procedure by petition. But the Crown had never parted with the concurrent right of issuing 'Ordinances', and the Tudors had frequent recourse to this expedient. 'Proclamations', as they were then called, formed a useful and indeed indispensable part of the dictatorial machinery of the sixteenth century. In this, as in other matters, Tudor parliaments maintained the theory by gracefully conceding the substance, and in 1539 Parliament actually passed a Statute which formally empowered Henry VIII to legislate by means of Proclamations. That enactment marked, as Dr. Dicey observes, the 'highest point of legal authority ever reached by the Crown'; yet even that Act, passed in the heyday of the Tudor dictatorship, contained a limiting clause, excluding from the ambit of legalized proclamations anything which could be prejudicial to 'any person's inheritance, offices, liberties, goods, chattels or life'. The Statute of 1539 was repealed under Edward VI, and under Mary the judges laid it down that 'the King may make a proclamation *quoad terrorem populi* to put them in mind of his displeasure but not to impose any fine, forfeiture or imprisonment; for no proclamation can make a new law, but only confirm and ratify an old one'. Queen Elizabeth made free use of Proclamations, but only in a constitutional manner, as a means of enjoining obedience to the law—chiefly in ecclesiastical matters.

James I In this, as in other matters, James I perverted the dictatorial machinery of the Tudors into an instrument of absolute monarchy. He issued Proclamations to forbid the election of outlaws to parliament; to withdraw parliamentary representation from decaying towns; to levy new custom duties; to restrain building operations in London, and for various other purposes.

Consequently, in 1610, his 'most humble Commons', perceiving their common and ancient right and liberty to be much declined and infringed in these late years, deemed that the time had come to demand 'justice and due redress'. They pointed out that

amongst many other points of happiness and freedom previously enjoyed by Englishmen there is none which they have accounted more dear and precious than this, to be guided and governed by certain rule of law, which giveth both to the head and members that which of right belongeth to them, and not by any uncertain or arbitrary form of Government. . . . Nevertheless it is apparent, both that proclamations have been of late years much more frequent than heretofore, and that they are extended not only to the liberty, but also to the goods, inheritances, and livelihood of men; some of them tending to alter some points of the law and make them new: other some made shortly after a session of Parliament, for matter directly rejected in the same session: others appointing punishments to be inflicted before lawful trial and conviction: some containing penalties in form of penal statutes: some referring the punishment of offenders to the courts of arbitrary discretion, which have laid heavy and grievous censures upon the delinquents . . . and some vouching former proclamations, to countenance and warrant the latter. . . . By reason whereof there is a general fear conceived and spread amongst your Majesty's people, that proclamations will by degrees grow up and increase to the strength and nature of laws: whereby, not only that ancient happiness, freedom, will be much blemished if not quite taken away, which their ancestors have so long enjoyed, but the same may also in process of time bring a new form of arbitrary government upon the realm.'

The Commons, therefore, humbly besought the King that no pains or penalties might be imposed upon his subjects *unless they shall offend against some law or statute of this realm in force at the time of their offence committed.*[1]

Coke, being appealed to in reference to the legality of certain Proclamations, begged leave to be allowed to consult other judges, with the result that he and three of his colleagues delivered, in the presence of the Privy Council, an opinion of historic significance.

'The King', they declared, 'cannot by his proclamation create any offence which was not an offence before, for then he may alter the law of the land by his proclamation in a 'high point. . . . The King hath no prerogative but that which the law of the land allows him. But the King may by proclamation admonish his subjects that they keep the laws and do not offend them.'

The soundness of the doctrine thus enunciated has never since been theoretically questioned, but the abuse was not in practice stopped until the Long Parliament abolished the extraordinary tribunals by which the Royal Proclamations were enforced.

Dispensing and Suspending power   Even more objectionable than Proclamations, from the point of view of the legislative sovereignty of Parliament, was the practice of suspending or dispensing with Statutes by Royal Prerogative.

The later Stuarts, though barred by the action of the Long Parliament from recourse to Proclamations, negatively infringed the legislative rights of Parliament by the exercise of this power. By 'suspending' the operation of statutes, as by the *Declarations of Indulgence* in 1686 and 1687, or even by 'dispensing' with it in the case of individuals, such as Sir Edward Hales in 1686, the legislative will of Parliament was rendered of no effect. The Bill of Rights dealt with these abuses by declaring:

(1) That the pretended power of suspending of laws or the execution of laws by regal authority, without consent of Parliament, is illegal.

(2) That the pretended power of dispensing with laws or

[1.] Petyt, *Jus Parliamentarium*, pp. 319–20.

the execution of laws by regal authority, as it hath been assumed and exercised of late, is illegal.

The language of the Bill of Rights was, it will be noted, definite as regards the suspending power, it was more cautious, not to say ambiguous, as regards the dispensing power. The words 'of late' limit the operation of the Statute in one direction, and no jurist has ever questioned the prerogative of pardon, or the right of the Crown to stop a criminal prosecution by entering a *nolle prosequi*. Such matters are still within the competence of the Crown, though nowadays the Crown acts through a minister responsible to Parliament.

An old controversy, as we have seen, has recently been revived in a new form. Parliament has of late years, as we have already indicated, shown itself increasingly prone to delegate quasi-legislative powers to subordinate bodies and in particular to the great Administrative Departments. Delegated legislation

Whether this tendency is healthy or the reverse is a question outside the scope of this book. Reference is only made to the matter because it illustrates the main thesis of the present work: that the problems which confronted the politicians of the seventeenth century were solved only for the time being, and are apt again to emerge, in different guise and under altered conditions, and again to call for consideration, and if it may be for solution, at the hands of this later generation.

To return to the seventeenth century. The question of the relation between the Executive, represented by the King, and the Judiciary was raised in an acute form during the years which immediately followed the dissolution of the 'addled' Parliament in 1614. How long it might be before Parliament met again no one could at the moment foretell. Representative Institutions in England might share the fate they had encountered in Spain and France. Who could say? James I and the Judges

Under these circumstances the Judges in England might well deem it their duty to attempt to impose some check upon the autocracy of the Crown. A similar attempt on Coke and Bacon the part of the Great Central Law Court of France, known (misleadingly to Englishmen) as the Parliament of Paris, contributed, a few years later, to the outbreak of the *Wars of the Fronde*. The Common Law Bench was at that time completely dominated, as we have seen, by Sir Edward Coke. Coke had long held an exalted, perhaps an exaggerated, view as to the place of the Judiciary in the Constitution. An outstanding personality, a very great lawyer, ardently devoted to the cause of liberty, Coke lacked some of the more obvious qualifications of a statesman. As Burke might have said of him, 'he generally viewed his objects in lights that were somewhat too detached'. In other words, though his instincts were sound, his political perspective was distorted.

Moreover, to political indignation there was now added a personal grievance. For a quarter of a century he had been the rival, and the invariably successful rival, of Francis Bacon. But of late years the star of Bacon had been steadily rising. In 1607 the latter had at the age of fifty-two become Solicitor-General, an office which Lord Essex had vainly endeavoured to procure for him exactly twenty years earlier. In 1613 Bacon became Attorney-General, and in the same year Coke was promoted from the Chief Justiceship of the Common Pleas to that of the King's Bench. Technically it was 'promotion', but it involved loss of salary, and it was instigated by Bacon in the hope that Coke would be less politically mischievous in the King's Bench than in the Common Pleas. Regarding his promotion as 'penal', Coke deeply resented both the obvious motive and the notorious source of it.

Incapable of appreciating the intellectual genius of Bacon, Coke despised him for his conspicuous frailties: for the way in which he fawned upon the great ones of the earth and importuned them for favours for himself. Yet Coke's subsequent conduct was not inspired wholly by personal motives. He was ruggedly and sincerely convinced that it was the proper function of the Judicial Bench, more particularly when Parliament was silenced, to save

the people of England from the encroaching autocracy of
the Crown. In so far as he sought to maintain the supremacy of the Law, Coke was indubitably right; in so far as
he wished to impose quasi-political functions upon the
Judiciary he was, as clearly, wrong.

His error was shared, however, by his rival Bacon and
by the Sovereign himself. Bacon's view of the true relation
between the Executive and the Judiciary was clearly set
forth in one of his most famous Essays. Bacon on Judicature

'It is a happy thing in a State when Kings and States do
often consult with Judges; and again when Judges do often
consult with the King and State: the one when there is matter
of law intervenient in business of State; the other when there
is some consideration of State intervenient in matter of law;
. . . Let judges also remember that Solomon's throne was
supported by lions on both sides; let them be lions, but yet
lions under the throne, being circumspect that they do not
check or oppose any points of Sovereignty.' [1]

Bacon's meaning is not to be mistaken: in technical para-
phrase it amounts to this: the judges should be the hand-
maids of the Executive; the principle which is to-day well
established in many countries that administrative acts are
to be judged by administrative law was to be imported
into English jurisprudence.

The conflicting views of Bacon and Coke were on several
occasions brought to a practical test. In 1615 there was
the case of Peacham. The Reverend Edmond Peacham,
a Somersetshire Rector, had been sentenced by the High
Commission to deprivation of orders for libelling his
diocesan the Bishop of Bath and Wells. A search of his
house revealed certain writings which were said to be of
a treasonable nature. He was committed to the Tower, and
was there put to the torture in the expectation that he
might reveal the existence of a plot among the Somersetshire gentry against the King. No information could be
extorted from him even under torture, but he was subse- Auricular Consultation of Judges

---

[1] *Of Judicature.*

quently put on his trial for treason, sentenced to death, and died in prison at Taunton.

In itself the case was of no particular interest, but incidentally it raised a point of considerable constitutional significance. Before indicting Peacham the King and Council decided to make sure of their ground by consulting the judges, but consulted them not, as was customary, collectively, but individually and separately. The reason for this departure from custom was that Bacon, who as Attorney-General was anxious to secure a judicial opinion favourable to the Crown, well knew that a collective opinion would be dictated by Chief Justice Coke and would not be likely to favour the Crown.

Coke took a strong line against the novel proceeding. That the Crown was entitled to consult the judges he did not deny; but it must be collectively. 'Such particular and auricular taking of opinion', he said, 'is not according to the custom of the realm.' Only under strong protest would he consent to give an opinion, and, when given, it was not favourable to the Crown. The rest of the judges gave a contrary opinion, and on the strength of it Peacham, as already noted, was sent for trial and convicted

The case is important only in that it brought Coke and Bacon once more into sharp conflict and gave the former a further opportunity of reasserting his views on the relation to the Executive.

Writ *De Rege Inconsulto*, 1615   The quarrel between Coke, as the champion of the Common Law, and Bacon, as the champion of Chancery and the defender of the Royal Prerogative, was now coming to a head. It happened that in 1615 a dispute arose between the King's Bench and the Court of Chancery in reference to the case of *Brownlow* v. *Michell*. The Court of Chancery had long claimed and exercised the right to restrict a suitor who had been successful in a Court of Law from obtaining execution, if in the opinion of Chancery the judgement had been obtained by inequitable means. Coke now thought fit to enter a strong protest against this custom. Bacon then unearthed an obsolete writ, well adapted to his immediate purpose: *De Non Procedendo Rege Inconsulto*. By that writ the Common Law Judges were prohibited from dealing with cases in which the interests of the Crown were involved (as they were indirectly in *Brownlow* v. *Michell*) before the matter in dispute had been referred to the Court of Chancery and its permission obtained for the parties to proceed at Common Law.[1]

'The writ', wrote Bacon to the King, 'is a means provided by the ancient law of England to bring any case that may concern your Majesty in profit or power from the ordinary Benches to be tried and judged before the Chancellor of England, by the ordinary and legal part of this power. And your Majesty knoweth that your Chancellor is ever a principal Counsellor and instrument of monarchy, of immediate dependence on the King; and, therefore, like to be a safe and tender guardian of the regal rights.'[2]

The immediate point as between Brownlow and Michell was compromised, though with an inclination towards the King and the Court of Chancery.

But Coke was not to be denied. Certain suitors, described by Mr. Gardiner as 'scoundrels', had obtained judgement in their favour in a Court of Law but had been deprived of the fruits of their victory by the Court of Chancery. Coke, according to the same high authority, thereupon 'instigated'[3] the rascals to prefer indictments of *praemunire* in his own Court of King's Bench, both against the successful appellants to Chancery and against all who had taken part in the Chancery proceedings.

Coke, however, suffered a rude rebuff. When the case came on, the Grand Jury, despite Coke's threats of a committal for contempt, repeatedly refused to find a true Bill. The King, thereupon, referred the whole question

[1] Gardiner, *op. cit.*, iii. 7.

[2] Quoted by Redlich and Hirst, *Local Government*, ii. 363.

[3] Mr. G. P. Macdonell in his biography of Coke ap. *D.N.B.* says that there was 'hardly any direct evidence to prove Coke's intervention'. But Gardiner's view was the one generally believed at the time.

to the Law Officers, who gave a unanimous[1] opinion in
favour of the right claimed by the Court of Chancery.
'The victory of the Chancery was', comments Maitland,
'final and complete—and if we were to have a Court of
equity at all it was a necessary victory.'[2]

Case of Commendams   The quarrel between Coke and Bacon was, however,
carried a stage further by a more famous case, that of
Commendams. Dr. Richard Neile, a leading Arminian, who
held successively the Bishoprics of Rochester, Lichfield,
Lincoln, Durham, and Winchester, and ended his life as
Archbishop of York, was, when Bishop of Lichfield, presented
by the King to a valuable living to be held *in commendam*
with his bishopric. Two gentlemen, named Colt and
Glover, claimed that the presentation belonged to them,
and further that, on legal grounds, it was invalid. As the
case raised a novel and important point it was referred to
the Exchequer Chamber and argued before the whole
bench of twelve judges. The King, whose honour and
interests were directly involved, ordered the judges to stay
proceedings until they had taken counsel with him. The
judges instigated thereto by Coke refused. They were then
summoned before the King in Council and asked 'whether,
if at any time in a case depending before the judges His
Majesty conceived it to concern him either in power or
profit, and therefore required to consult with them, and
that they should stay proceedings in the meantime they
ought not to stay accordingly'.

With the single exception of Coke all the judges made
submission and accepted the contention of the King. The
case was then allowed to proceed, and was decided against
the Bishop, but 'on grounds which left the general prerogative of the Crown untouched'.[3]

The Crown and the Judges   The King, however, thought proper to improve the
occasion, and a few weeks later summoned the judges to

---

[1] In addition to the Attorney and Solicitor, the two King's Serjeants
and the Attorney to the Prince of Wales consented.
[2] *Op. cit.*, p. 270.
[3] Gardiner, iii. 119.

the Star Chamber, where he addressed to them a long and elaborate oration on the relations between the Crown and the Judges.

'. . . . Now having spoken of your office in general, I am next to come to the limits wherein you are to bound yourselves, which likewise are three. First, encroach not upon the prerogative of the crown: if there falls out a question that concerns my prerogative or mystery of state, deal not with it, till you consult with the King, or his council, or both; for they are transcendent matters . . . that which concerns the mystery of the King's power is not lawful to be disputed, for that is to wade into the weakness of princes and to take away the mystical reverence that belongs unto them that sit in the throne of God.

'Secondly, that you keep yourselves within your own benches, not to invade other jurisdictions, which is unfit and an unlawful thing. . . . Keep you therefore all in your own bounds, and for my part, I desire you to give me no more right, in my private prerogative, than you give to any subject, and therein I will be acquiescent: as for the absolute prerogative of the crown, that is no subject for the tongue of a lawyer, nor is lawful to be disputed.

'It is atheism and blasphemy to dispute what God can do: good Christians content themselves with his will revealed in his word, so it is presumption and high contempt in a subject to dispute what a King can do, or say that a King cannot do this or that; but rest in that which is the King's revealed will in his law.'

Such was the Stuart theory of Monarchy stated in all its nakedness. On the narrower point at issue, as between the Chancery and the Common Law, the King's decision in favour of the former was admittedly correct. On the larger question of the Royal Prerogative it is impossible to speak so positively. Had the claims of the Tudors been reduced to theory they might have soared as high as those of the Stuarts: but the Tudors did not invoke theory, they were content as a rule with the substance of power, and were careful to exercise it under legal forms. But the points so unwisely raised by James I were never really settled until the nation had suffered all the horrors of a civil war, until one King had died on the scaffold and a second had been deposed.

Meanwhile, the immediate victory rested with the Crown. Coke tried to avert his doom by partial submission, but the King and Bacon were not content with anything less than unconditional surrender. For that Coke was not prepared, and a fortnight after the delivery of the King's oration he was suspended from office (20 June), and in November was definitely dismissed.

Dismissal of Coke

In another of the elaborate orations so congenial to him, the King announced to the Council his reasons for dismissing the Chief Justice of the King's Bench: Coke's perpetual turbulence towards the Church, the prerogative and the jurisdiction of certain Courts'; his hunting after popular favour; his refractory conduct in the Council rather busying himself in casting fears . . . concerning what they could not do, than joining his advice what they should do'. Chamberlain, who has been described as the Horace Walpole of that day, put the matter more tersely and not less accurately when he wrote to Dudley Carleton (14 November 1616), 'The Common speech is that four p's have overthrown and put him down—that is pride, prohibitions, praemunire and prerogative.'

Though dismissed from the Bench, Coke did not pass entirely out of favour with the King, who restored him to his seat in the Council in 1617, and actually promoted his election, as member for Liskeard, to the Parliament of 1621. The former favour he owed to Buckingham, or rather he purchased it at the price of his young daughter's marriage to Buckingham's elder brother, Sir John Villiers. This odious marriage was strongly opposed by Lady Coke, who appealed to the Privy Council against her husband's abduction of the child—who was but fourteen. Bacon risked the friendship of Buckingham by supporting the wife against the husband, and further embittered his relations with Coke.

Coke had not long to wait for his revenge. Bacon, to

whom the Great Seal had been delivered in 1617, with the
inferior title of Lord Keeper, became Lord Chancellor in
1618, and was raised to the peerage as Baron Verulam.
Three years later he received a further step as Viscount
St. Albans. But that was the zenith of his chequered
career.

His rival Coke, on the contrary, did but exchange his seat Coke in
on the Bench for a seat—ironically provided for him by the Parliament
King in Parliament. Thus at one step he passed from the
leadership of the Judiciary to the leadership of the House
of Commons.

The Parliament of 1621 was perhaps the most important
one of the reign, and Coke, despite nearly twenty years'
absence from the House, at once came forward as the
champion of parliamentary privileges and the keen opponent of every device for securing to the Crown a revenue
independent of Parliament. But it was as a student of
commercial Economics and as a common lawyer that he
was opposed to every practice which could be construed as
a 'restraint upon trade'.

Even under the Tudors Parliament had manifested Mono-
extreme jealousy of monopolists, patentees, and licensees. polies
The practice of granting exclusive rights to privileged
persons had even then assumed alarming proportions. The
Commons protested in 1597, and four years later Elizabeth
made a handsome concession on the subject. But James I,
taking no heed of Elizabeth's concession, revived the
practice and obtained a considerable revenue from the
issue of patents and monopolies. So also it was suspected
did some of his most highly placed courtiers and ministers.

In order to put an end to such abuses the Commons
refurbished in 1621 the rusty weapon of impeachment. Sir
Francis Michell, a magistrate who was accused of having
abused his powers in regard to monopolies, was struck off
the commission of the peace and sent to the Tower. Sir
Giles Mompesson, a member of the House, escaped a worse
fate by flight; but the House flew at higher game.

To the consternation of many and the amazement of

Impeach-
ment of
Bacon

more, a charge of bribery was suddenly preferred against the Lord Chancellor himself. Oblique attacks had been made upon him in connexion with the case of the monopolists; but that any serious charge could be made against him never entered Bacon's mind.

'I know I have clean hands and a clean heart. . . . But Job himself, or whoever was the justest judge, by such hunting for matters against him as hath been used against me may for a time seem foul, especially in a time when greatness is the mark and accusation is the game. And if this be to be a Chancellor, I think if the Great Seal lay upon Hounslow Heath nobody would take it up.'

So Bacon wrote to Buckingham in an impassioned appeal to the favourite for help in the hour of distress.

The King, while promising, if Bacon failed to establish his innocence, 'to show himself a most just King', proposed that a joint Committee of both Houses should be appointed to investigate the charges against the Chancellor. The Commons, however, would have none of the suggestion; fresh evidence against Bacon was coming in almost daily, and they decided therefore to proceed with the impeachment.

Fall of
Bacon

The facts on which the case rested were hardly in dispute. Bacon did not deny them: but he did deny the inferences drawn from them and stoutly maintained the innocence of his motives. It was the system which was to blame, not his own conduct.

'For briberies and gifts wherewith I am charged, when the Book of hearts shall be opened I hope I shall not be found to have the troubled fountain of a corrupt heart in a depraved habit of taking rewards to pervert justice, however I may be frail and partake of the abuses of the time.'

In a word, he had followed the bad custom of taking his remuneration as a judge from the indeterminate fees, not perhaps to be distinguished from the bribes, of suitors; but his judgements had never been influenced thereby. Technically, however, the charges against him could not be resisted, and he made his submission and resigned the

Great Seal. The Lords refused to accept either and proceeded to pass sentence upon him. He was to pay a fine of £40,000, to be imprisoned during the King's pleasure; to be expelled from Parliament and declared incapable of public office or employment and not to come within twelve miles of the Court.

The fallen Chancellor acknowledged 'the sentence just and for reformation fit'; nevertheless, he had been 'the justest Chancellor since his father's death'.

The sentence pronounced upon him, though crushing, was not vindictively executed. The King made over the fine to Trustees to be administered for Bacon's benefit, and his imprisonment lasted only a few days. But though he received a partial pardon he was never readmitted to place; even the Provostship of Eton College was denied to him, and after five years of vain appeals to friends and favourites, varied by unremitting literary labour, he died in 1626.

His rival survived him, as we shall see, by eight years, and played a great part in the earlier Parliaments of Charles I. Two men more sharply contrasted in temper, in outlook, and in fortunes have rarely played leading parts on the same stage. With the literary, scientific, and philosophical achievements of Bacon this book is not concerned. It is, however, a matter of supreme importance to assign to him and to his great rival the place which each is entitled to fill in the history of English Law and English Politics. *Bacon's place in History*

The historian must always be on his guard against giving to past events a retrospective significance which did not in fact inhere in them. Yet it cannot be questioned that the prolonged and embittered conflict between these two great men did correspond to issues of profound and permanent concern to Englishmen and indeed to mankind.

Bacon was no friend to tyranny, though he used the language of servility to kings and favourites; on the contrary, he constantly advised the King to resort to Parliament; he believed in parliamentary government, as then understood, nor did he want to circumscribe the

personal liberty of the subject. But he was better fitted
for the life of speculation than of action. He was indeed
the typical intellectual accidentally plunged into public
affairs. Quite early in life he realized his own limitations
as a politician.

'Knowing myself by inward calling to be fitter to hold a
book than to play a part, I have led my life in civil causes, for
which I was not very fit by nature, and more unfit by the
preoccupation of my mind.'

So he had written to his intimate friend Sir Thomas
Bodley in 1604. Was it then a misfortune that one who,
in the fine critical opinion of Dean Church, afforded 'the
most perfect example that the world had yet seen of the
student of nature, the enthusiast for knowledge', should
have plunged into the turbid stream of politics? Did his
own age commensurately gain from the world's permanent
loss? It is difficult to estimate gain or loss without a
common measure of value, but we may discount at once
the venomous diatribes, the crude antitheses of Macaulay.
It is indeed idle, as Dean Church admits, to 'disguise the
many deplorable shortcomings of Bacon's life', but to
accuse him of being 'a servile advocate that he might
become a corrupt judge', transcends all the bounds of fair
criticism. By his own admission he did not, as a judge, rise
superior to the abuses characteristic of his day: but he was
the victim rather than the author of them. As a politician
he was on the side which eventually lost, and deserved to
lose; he lacked the rugged independence of Coke and the
prescience of Pym. Yet the counsel which he gave to the
King was almost invariably wise, and if James had listened
to it, and had taught his son the lesson he might himself
have learned from Bacon, much of the subsequent mischief might have been avoided.

In regard to the relations between the Judiciary and the
Executive, Coke was less wrong than Bacon, though neither
was entirely right. If Bacon would have made the Judiciary the handmaid of the Crown, Coke would have made
the Bench not merely the interpreter of the law but the

arbiter of the Constitution. Even the judges of the Supreme
Court of the United States of America are not in so exalted
a position as that. If they are in one sense superior to
Congress, in that on the appeal of a suitor they can void
the acts of the Legislature, they can do so only in performing their assigned function of interpreting a Constitution
to which they, like the Legislature, must defer.

A generation ago it was commonly held that Bacon
proved himself inimical to popular liberties by an attempt
to establish an administrative tribunal in England. To-day
there are those who think that such a tribunal would be
less dangerous to liberty than 'the cryptic introduction of
an uncodified and arbitrary departmental *droit administratif*.[1] If Coke is entitled to the gratitude of posterity for
having maintained the authority of the Law against an encroaching Executive, Bacon's 'fundamental strength lay
in recognition of the truth that political wisdom is greater
than legality'.

Could either man have averted the revolution? A recent
biographer of Bacon has suggested that he stood to the
English Revolution 'as Turgot stood to the French revolution'.[2] But the cases are not analogous. France under
Louis XVI was without a Constitution. Turgot, a typical
eighteenth-century reformer, looked to administrative
absolutism as the best hope of reform. Bacon, in the true
Tudor tradition, believed that Parliament, if wisely handled,
could be made the instrument of a beneficent autocrat.
It was the misfortune both of Turgot and of Bacon to serve
masters unworthy of their service and incapable of profit-
ing by their sage counsel.

Coke's work was by no means done when his rival died. Case of
In the Parliament of 1628 he played a part which no the Five
Englishman was so well qualified to play as himself. He Knights
stood forth as the great vindicator of the personal liberty
of the subject.

[1] *The Times*, 6 July 1929.
[2] Gardiner, ap. *D.N.B.*

In the autumn of 1626, Charles I, as we have seen, had recourse to a forced loan. Many of the leading men of the country refused to subscribe: some of them were deported from their homes into distant counties where they could do less harm; others were summoned before the Council and committed to prison. Among the latter were five Knights who were destined to make history—Sir Thomas Darnel, Sir John Corbet, Sir Walter Erle, Sir John Heveningham, and Sir Edmund Hampden. These gentlemen appealed to the Court of King's Bench for a habeas corpus. Relying on the clause of *Magna Carta* which declared that 'no man shall be imprisoned except by the legal judgement of his peers or by the law of the land', they urged that they were at least entitled to know for what cause they were detained in custody. The Crown lawyers contended that it was sufficient return to a writ of habeas corpus to certify that the prisoners were detained *per speciale mandatum regis*—by the special orders of the King. The judges so far accepted the contention of the Crown as to refuse to liberate the five Knights on bail, but, on the other hand, they declined to admit the principle that the Crown might persistently refuse to show cause.

The plea of prerogative was for the moment successful, but the triumph of the Crown—by no means complete—was short lived. Other causes contributed to swell the stream of discontent: the extravagant exaltation of the Royal Prerogative by Arminian preachers in high place; the sufferings of the men pressed for the navy; the outrageous conduct of the youths pressed for the army in the private houses in which they were billeted; above all the failure of the war policy of Charles and his favourite. But deep and wide as was the resentment evoked, it was the denial of the elementary rights of personal liberty and the violation of the principle of no taxation without consent which were immediately responsible for the crisis of 1628.

That public resentment did not issue in active rebellion is not more remarkable than the moderation displayed in Parliament. Even Clarendon admits that it was a marvel that 'all these provocations and many other produced no other resentment than the Petition of Right'.

That Petition is a landmark in the ordered progress of English liberty. After recital of the clause of Magna Carta quoted above and subsequent Statutes the Petition went on to declare that

'against the tenor of the said Statutes ... divers of your subjects have of late been imprisoned without any cause showed, and when for their deliverance they were brought before your Justices by your Majesty's writs of habeas corpus ... and their Keepers to certify the causes of their detainer; no cause was certified, but that they were detained by your Majesty's special command, signified by the Lords of your Privy Council, and yet were returned back to several prisons without being charged with anything to which they might make answer according to the law. . . .'

The Petition, as we have seen, demanded that an end should be put to non-parliamentary taxation, to arbitrary imprisonment, to the billeting of soldiers, and to martial law.

Of the attitude of the King and of the events which followed an account has already been given. It only remains therefore to summarize the subsequent history of the struggle for personal liberty.

The Long Parliament, as we shall see presently, made a clean sweep both of the men and the machinery associated with the attempt of the Stuart Kings to establish personal government in England. Yet after the abolition of the Monarchy and the House of Lords, the House of Commons, relieved for the moment of all the checks which the Crown and the Second Chamber had imposed upon its action, proved itself no less inimical to personal liberty than the Stuart Kings. But the triumph of the Single-Chamber Parliament was short lived. Cromwell, though he dealt roughly with the ridiculous and mischievous pretensions of Parliament, failed in his turn to re-establish a settled form of Government, and the feeble rule of his son

Richard was quickly brought to an end by the intervention of the army and the restoration of the Stuarts.

But the restoration of the Monarchy involved also the restoration of Parliament, and Parliament quickly resumed and completed the work which, begun by the Long Parliament, had been interrupted during the Commonwealth and the Protectorate.

Habeas Corpus

In that work there was no more important item than the guarantee of personal liberty; but the guarantee proved in practice to be inadequate. Consequently after the Restoration, an agitation, more or less persistent, was carried on in the House of Commons to secure more effectual guarantees. The agitation was brought to a head, as generally happens, by a concrete case. In 1676 a London citizen named Jenkes was imprisoned by order of the King in Council. Owing to difficulties interposed by the Lord Chancellor and the Lord Chief Justice it was several weeks before the defendant, who was accused of making a seditious speech at the Guildhall, was released on bail. Public attention was thus called to the inadequacy of the existing procedure for enforcing the right to personal liberty hitherto based only upon Common Law. As a result the *Habeas Corpus Amendment Act* was passed in 1679.

Writs

Ever since Norman times the Common Law right to personal liberty had been secured, though hitherto imperfectly, by a variety of writs. The writ *de odio et atia* was intended to afford protection against malicious accusations of homicide. In consequence of King John's exaction of exorbitant sums for the issue of this writ the Great Charter provided that this 'writ of inquest of life or limb should be granted without payment'; [1] but the use of it gradually became obsolete. A second writ of *mainprize* authorized the sheriff to take sureties (*mainpernors*) for the appearance of a prisoner, and having obtained them to set him at liberty. A third writ *de homine replegiando*, which was of similar import, commanded the sheriff to release a prisoner from custody on repledge or bail.

---

[1]   *Magna Carta*, § 36.

Most important of all was the writ of habeas corpus,[1] which gradually superseded the writs above mentioned. This writ, obtainable from the King's Bench, might be addressed to any person who, under legal pretence or otherwise, detained another person in custody. The detainer was ordered 'to produce the body of the prisoner with the day and cause of his caption and detention to do, submit to, and receive, whatsoever the judge or court awarding such writ shall direct'. Not, however, until 1679 was this procedure, though in use for many centuries, rendered really effective. The Petition of Right had, as we have seen, reaffirmed the principle of personal liberty so manifestly infringed in the case of the *Five Knights*; but it failed to provide an effectual guarantee for its application. The Act of the Long Parliament, which abolished the Star Chamber and all the procedure appertaining thereto, provided that any one committed to custody by the King or by the Council, could claim from the King's Bench or Common Pleas, without delay upon any pretence whatsoever, a writ of habeas corpus; and that within three days the Court should determine upon the legality of the commitment and act accordingly. There still existed, however, various methods of evading the action of the writ, even when it had been issued by the Court.

The Amending Act of 1679 was designed to put a stop to these evasions and delays. It enacted that any person detained in custody (unless committed for treason or felony) should be produced for trial within twenty days at longest, and if the commitment were within twenty miles of the Court whence the writ issued, then within three days. Nor could a person once delivered by habeas corpus be recommitted for the same offence. Further, all prisoners must be tried at the next jail-delivery or else released on bail; and after the second jail-delivery must, if still untried, be discharged. To prevent delays any Court was authorized to issue a writ, or, in vacation, a single judge.

[1] For the Early History of Habeas Corpus, cf. E. Jenks, *Law Quarterly Review*, viii. 164.

Finally, no inhabitant of England, Wales, or Berwick-on-Tweed was, save under certain specified circumstances, to be imprisoned in Scotland, Ireland, Jersey, Guernsey, or Tangiers, or any place beyond the seas.[1]

The Act of 1679 has, from the day of its enactment, remained a corner-stone in the edifice of personal liberty, and its principles have been adopted throughout the English-speaking world. But experience revealed certain weaknesses in the Act. It fixed no limit to the amount of bail that might be demanded. The Bill of Rights (1689) accordingly enacted that excessive bail ought not to be required; while a later Act (1816) extended the action of the writ to non-criminal charges, and authorized the judges to examine into the truth of the facts alleged in the return to the writ, with a view to bailing, remanding, or even discharging the prisoner.[2]

The Revolution of 1688 and the Judiciary
Neither an *Habeas Corpus Act* nor any other Act can, however, secure the liberty of the subject against the Executive, unless those who have to administer the Acts are placed in a position of complete independence. So long as the judges are 'lions under the throne' there can be no effective guarantee for personal liberty. The highest importance must, therefore, be attached to the change in the tenure of the judges effected by the Act of Settlement.

Under the early Stuarts the judges had been repeatedly reminded that they held office at the good pleasure of the King. Sir Edward Coke, as we have seen, was dismissed by James I in 1616 for refusal to assent to the King's wishes in the case of *Commendams*. Chief Justice Crew was dismissed in 1626 by Charles I for his refusal to admit the legality of forced loans. Chief Justice Heath in 1634 incurred a similar penalty for his opposition to ship-money. The later Stuarts dealt not less drastically with the judges. Charles II dismissed, for political reasons, three Lord Chancellors, three Chief Justices, and six judges. James II went even further, and besides a wholesale purge of the

---

[1] Robertson, *Select Statutes, Cases, and Documents*, pp. 46–54.
[2] Hallam, *Constitutional History*, iii. 14–15.

judicial bench, struck off the Commission of the Peace local
justices who showed themselves disinclined to abet his
tyranny. The *Act of Settlement* finally took out of the
King's hands this dangerous weapon. It enacted that
'after the limitations shall take effect as aforesaid, judges'
commissions be made *quamdiu se bene gesserint*, and their
salaries ascertained and established; but upon the address
of both Houses of Parliament it may be lawful to remove
them'. Thus was the independence of the judicial bench
definitely secured. Their salaries are now charged upon
the Consolidated Fund, and they are virtually irremovable.
Incidentally, and to enforce the point by a contrast, it may
be mentioned that the administration of Justice in some
of the State (not in the Federal) Courts of the United States
has become a byword for inefficiency. Nor is the reason
far to seek. Inefficiency (to use no harsher word) is in
direct ratio to the tenure of the judges. In few States is
it sufficiently secure; in some it is purely arbitrary, and
the judges are subject to the mischievous operation of the
Recall. In plain language an unpopular judgement may
result in dismissal.[1]

Yet despite the *Habeas Corpus Act* and *Act of Settlement* General
Warrants
individual citizens were to discover in the course of the
eighteenth century that there still survived 'remnants of
a jurisprudence which had favoured prerogative at the
expense of liberty'.[2] One such survival was illustrated by
the career of that notorious reprobate John Wilkes. In
1763, Lord Halifax, the Secretary of State, issued a general
warrant for the apprehension of the authors, printers, and
publishers of No. 45 of a certain paper, the *North Briton*,
and for the seizure of their papers. No persons were
named in the warrant, but no fewer than forty-nine
persons were arrested under this roving commission—this
'ridiculous warrant against the whole English nation', as
Wilkes himself termed it. Eventually the authorship of

---

[1] Cf. Bryce, *Modern Democracies*, ii. 164; Elihu Root, *Experiments in
Government*, pp. 68 seq.
[2] Erskine May, *Constitutional History*, iii. 2.

the incriminated article was discovered. Wilkes was arrested and brought before the Secretaries of State, and by them committed to close confinement in the Tower, whence he was shortly released, on a writ of habeas corpus, by reason of his privilege as a member of Parliament.

The legality of the whole procedure was promptly questioned in the Courts. Some of the arrested printers recovered £300 damages against the messengers, Lord Chief Justice Pratt having held that the general warrant was illegal, that it was illegally executed, and that the messengers were not indemnified by Statute. The same judge also decided against the competence of a Secretary of State to issue warrants, declaring that such a power 'may affect the person and property of every man in this Kingdom, and is totally subversive of the liberty of the subject'. In this case Wilkes recovered £1,000 damages against Mr. Wood, the Under-Secretary of State, who had personally superintended the execution of the warrant, and eventually got £4,000 damages from Lord Halifax himself for false imprisonment. The Court of Common Pleas also decided against the legality of a search warrant for papers, and Mr. John Entinck obtained £300 damages from a messenger who had executed it. These decisions were subsequently confirmed—so far as the House of Commons can confirm a judicial decision—by resolutions of the House of Commons condemning general warrants, whether for the seizure of persons or papers, as illegal, and declaring them, if executed against a member of the House, to be a breach of privilege.

Recent Tendencies   Thus were the liberties of Englishmen vindicated by our forefathers against the encroachment of the Executive, Regal or Parliamentary. It is, therefore, the more regrettable that this chapter should have to end on the note of interrogation more than once heard in the course of this book. Are those liberties still secure? Have recent tendencies in administration and legislation tended to weaken the force of the guarantees so painfully obtained by

persistent opposition to Stuart autocracy? Words which
have recently fallen from the lips of eminent judges must
needs cause considerable disquietude to those who are still
jealous for the liberty of the subject. Speaking at the
Mansion House on 5 July 1929 the Lord Chancellor (Lord
Sankey) said:

'His Majesty's Judges are charged with the administration
of the law, but there are two matters relating to such administration which have caused some anxiety not only in the public
mind but among trained lawyers. The first is what has been
described as a growing tendency to transfer decisions on points
of law or fact from the Law Courts to the Minister of some
Government Department. The second is the position of the
subject when engaged in a dispute with the Crown or an individual when engaged in a dispute with a Department of
State.' There is, he added, a 'general agreement both within
and without the profession that these matters require further
careful investigation.' [1]

Lord Sankey did not exaggerate the prevalence of public
apprehension on this subject, and it is a disquieting thought
that, should those apprehensions prove to be well grounded,
much of the work of the seventeenth century may have
to be done afresh.

[1] They will, it may be hoped, receive it from the Committee appointed
by Lord Sankey in October 1929.

V. THE EXPERIMENT OF PERSONAL RULE

The System of Thorough. The Gathering Storm

The
Suspen-
sion of
Parlia-
ments THE dissolution of Parliament in 1629 marked the beginning of a new stage in the conflict between the Stuart Kings and their people. The news of the dissolution caused nothing short of dismay; and worse even than the fact of the dissolution was the King's proclamation inhibiting all men to speak of another parliament. Nor was it only upon the opponents of the Crown that the inhibition produced an unfortunate effect. On the contrary, as Clarendon tells us, 'it affected many good men (who otherwise were enough scandalized at those distempers which had incensed the King) to that degree, that it made them capable of receiving some impressions from those who were diligent in whispering and infusing an opinion into men that there was really an intention to alter the form of government, both in Church and State, of which said they, a greater instance cannot be given than this public declaration that we shall have no more parliaments'. [1] The testimony of Thomas May, the Puritan clerk and historian of the Long Parliament, must be received with more caution, but is not less emphatic. 'After the breaking off this parliament', he writes, 'the people of England for many years never looked back to their ancient liberty.' They were 'from that time deprived of the hope of parliaments; and all things so managed by public officers as if never such a day of account were to come.' [2]

Decay of
Parlia-
mentary
Institu-
tions
abroad Contemporaries might well wonder whether they had not witnessed the demise of parliamentary institutions in the only country of western Europe where they had so far survived. The States-General in France had not met since 1614, and was not to meet again until the eve of the Revolution in 1789. Parliamentary institutions in Spain

---

[1] *History of the great Rebellion*, i. 111.
[2] *History of the Long Parliament*, pp. 14, 15.

had suffered earlier eclipse than those of France, though
they were of even greater antiquity than the Parliament
of England. Aragon had its Cortes in 1133; Castille in
1169; yet before the end of the fourteenth century both
assemblies were already in a state of decline; by the end
of the fifteenth they had lost all vitality; early in the
sixteenth they were definitely overthrown, not to be
revived until the nineteenth, when the parliamentary
régime again enjoyed a none too vigorous life.

Many reasons may be suggested for the premature decay
of Parliamentary institutions in the Latin countries.
Among them two stand out pre-eminent. The English
Parliament, as we have seen, assumed gradually a bi-
cameral form. Both in France and Spain, on the contrary,
the form and organization of the representative body corre-
sponded with social distinctions and with the dividing lines
of economic interest. The caste system of society projected
itself into politics: the Cortes and the States-General were
alike assemblies of 'Estates'—Nobles, Clergy, and Towns
—or Communes.[1] Between the different Estates there was
little or no political cohesion. The Kings were consequently
able to drive a wedge into the Representative body, and by
allying themselves now with this Estate and now with
that, to destroy each in turn. A like disaster was averted
in England by the fortunate if fortuitous junction effected
in the fourteenth century by the knights of the shire and
the burgesses of the towns. The knights, drawn mostly
from families which in France and Spain would have been
'noble', thus supplied an invaluable hyphen between the
'Lords' with whom they had social affinities and the
burgesses with whom they acted politically. Political
divisions have never, therefore, in England followed social
lines, to the great advantage of the community as a whole.[2]

There was another reason for the organic weakness and

---

[1] The Cortes of Aragon had in fact four arms or branches, those of
Castille and France three.

[2] The rise of a Labour-Socialist party has weakened to some extent
the strength of this generalization.

ultimate extinction of Parliamentary institutions in France and Spain: neither the States-General nor the Cortes ever obtained a real hold upon the purse-strings.

The
situation
in 1629 These considerations will suffice to show why the situation in 1629 must be regarded as critical. Nothing less than the existence of Parliament was at stake. Contemporary tendencies were all in the direction of Autocracy or Oligarchy. In Spain no limitation upon the power of the absolute monarch survived. In France Richelieu was preparing the way for the autocracy of Louis XIV. In Germany the power of the Emperor was waning, but only because that of the territorial Princes was waxing. Republicanism had indeed achieved a notable triumph in the United Provinces, but their republicanism was of an oligarchical and federal, not a parliamentary type.[1]

This glimpse of continental politics tends to throw into bolder relief the significance of events in England. Here, also, in the one country which seemed to offer some hope for the survival of representative government, Parliament had been dismissed, its leaders imprisoned, and the great mass of the members of both Houses dispersed to their homes, uncertain when, if ever, they would be summoned to Westminster again.

Personal
Govern-
ment of
Charles I So the way was open for the experiment of personal government. In this new act of the great drama the leading parts were played, apart from the King himself, by two men of outstanding personality: Thomas Wentworth, soon to become Earl of Strafford, and William Laud, who in 1633 was promoted to the Archbishopric of Canterbury. Both men have been hardly judged, particularly by the generation which sat at the feet of Hallam and Macaulay.

'He was the first Englishman to whom a peerage was a sacrament of infamy, a baptism into the communion of corruption. As he was the earliest of the hateful list, so he was by far the greatest; eloquent, sagacious, adventurous, intrepid, ready of invention, immutable of purpose, in every talent

[1] See Marriott, *Mechanism of the Modern State*, ii, c. xxxvii.

which exalts or destroys nations pre-eminent, the lost arch-
angel, the satan of the apostasy.'

So Macaulay wrote of Wentworth, not by any means blind Arch-
to his consummate abilities but quite unable to appreciate bishop
his gifts of character. In Laud, Macaulay could perceive Laud
nothing but a 'ridiculous old bigot'. In Laud's case the
pendulum of public opinion has swung almost to the full.
Many indeed still hold that he was mistaken in his ends
and singularly misguided as to the means by which he
hoped to attain them, but no educated person now regards
him as ridiculous, and if he was bigoted it was a quality of
which, in the Stuart period, the Anglican or Arminian party
had no monopoly. 'Laud', in the opinion of a great ecclesiastical historian of the last century, 'saved the English
Church.' [1] Mr. Gladstone in his *Academic Sketch* went out
of his way to pay an almost unique tribute to his work for
the English Church.

'His scheme of Church polity, for his it largely was . . . still
subsists in all its essential features, not as personal or party
opinion, but as embodied in Statute or in usage with no apparent likelihood of disappearance or decay.'

For his memorial we have indeed only to look around:
there is hardly a parish church, throughout the length and
breadth of the land to-day, which does not testify to the
prevalence of Laud's views on the continuity of the
Anglican tradition and the catholicity of its ritual and
doctrine.

As to the wisdom of the policy which he pursued and
recommended to his master, men will continue to differ to
the end of time. In his own day there were few who commended it, but most modern critics, whatever view they may
take of his policy, can now afford to admit Laud's personal
integrity and his single-mindedness of purpose. Even the
Puritan May allowed that 'he had few vulgar and private
vices . . . in a word a man not altogether so bad (in his
personal character) as unfit for the State of England'. For
guiding the destinies of England in those difficult days he

[1] Dr. Mozley, *Historical Essays*.

was certainly unfit. His high capacity for administration no son of Oxford is likely to underrate, for that University was governed by the Statutes which Laud, as Chancellor, drafted for her, until mid-Victorian days. Nevertheless, he was singularly ill-unfitted to be the political adviser of Charles I. He was, as King James had clearly perceived, an idealist. 'He hath a restless spirit', James wrote to George Villiers, 'which cannot see when things are well, but loves to toss and change and to bring matters to a pitch of reformation floating in his own brain.' No one judged Laud more truly than that shrewd old Scot.

Thomas Wentworth, Earl of Strafford   Laud has, however, been more fortunate than his partner Strafford: and for a simple reason. Laud founded a school of churchmanship; his memory is cherished by a cloud of witnesses. Laud was, perhaps, born too soon, and, therefore, had to leave the vindication of his memory to those who have come after. Strafford was, perhaps, born too late. Had England been politically coeval with France, Strafford might have played the part of a Richelieu, and played it with approbation and success, though had he been the Chancellor of a German Emperor in the nineteenth century he might have welded by a policy of blood and iron the States of a loosely compacted confederation into a strong and homogeneous empire. But for the England of the seventeenth century he was born out of due time.

Unlucky in his day he was unlucky in the master who called for his service. It is just conceivable that if from the first Charles had trusted Wentworth instead of Buckingham the breach between Crown and Parliament might have been averted; or failing that, the King might have made a worthier fight for his own policy and principles. For Wentworth had accurately gauged the situation; Charles never really faced the facts. Macaulay has fastened upon Strafford the charge of apostasy: but there is a perfectly simple and perfectly honourable explanation of an apparent change of sides. Strafford's political ideal was an efficient administration. He believed that if government

was to be good it must be strong. So long as Buckingham
was at the King's right hand the administration was
hopelessly inefficient, and Wentworth, therefore, found his
natural place in opposition. When Buckingham was fortunately removed, his place as chief adviser to the King
had to be filled, and Wentworth, conscious of his capacity,
was ready to fill it. An ardent believer in Monarchy he
always was; but not in a Monarchy brought into obloquy
and contempt by the incompetent minister of a second-
rate King.

If this be 'apostasy' every statesman who crosses the
floor of the House to assume the responsibility of carrying
on the King's Government must be in a measure obnoxious
to the charge. 'In a measure', for the analogy is, of course,
far from complete. Yet it is close enough to afford a
reasonable explanation of the conduct of one of the greatest
statesmen of the Stuart period.

Although Wentworth was by far the ablest adviser upon
whom, during the period of personal government, Charles
could rely, it is a mistake to suppose that his influence was
continuously paramount. Apart from the fact that during
the whole period Wentworth was deeply immersed in his
own administrative work—first in Yorkshire as President
of the Council of the North, and from 1633 onwards as
Lord Deputy of Ireland—there is no evidence to show that
the King ever gave him his confidence as completely as he
had given it to Buckingham or as he gave it to Archbishop
Laud. On the contrary, there is the strongest indirect
evidence to prove that he did not. Wentworth was a stern
realist in politics: he knew that there are only two possible
bases of government: consent and force. A government
that does not rest upon consent, must surround itself with
a force adequate to compel obedience. Charles hovered
perpetually between the two alternatives: he never frankly
accepted the principle of consent; he was never prepared
to face the odium and expense in which even the attempt
to raise and maintain a powerful army would have involved
him. Wentworth knew that there was no *sors tertia*, and

when, in 1640, the crisis came it was the enemies of the King who had force behind them; the force with which the prescience of Strafford would have provided the King was still in Ireland.

The Prerogative Courts   Parliament had gone; but the judges remained. The charge of servility brought against the judges of this period has been gravely overstated by those who can see but one side to the constitutional conflict: yet the independence of the Judiciary was necessarily undermined by the fact that the judges held office at the pleasure of the King and by the extended jurisdiction of the 'prerogative' courts. Consequently, the administration of justice became, in this period of personal government, increasingly irregular and oppressive. The extraordinary tribunals strained their jurisdiction to the utmost: the Court of the Marches, set up in the border shires of England and Wales; Strafford's own Council of the North at York; the Stannary Courts in the far south-west; the Court of High Commission which as the *Grand Remonstrance* afterwards complained 'grew to such an excess of sharpness and severity as was not much less than the Roman Inquisition'; above all, the famous Court of the Star Chamber. In the sixteenth century the Star Chamber had been far from unpopular; it had put fear into the hearts of powerful offenders, but for the common sort it had meant cheap and speedy justice. Conditions had, however, altered: a Court which had been tolerated if not esteemed as an appropriate appendage of a popular dictatorship had degenerated into the oppressive instrument of an unpopular despotism. 'The Court of Star Chamber hath abounded in extravagant censure whereby His Majesty's subjects have been oppressed by grievous fines, imprisonments, stigmatizings, mutilations, whippings, pillories, gags, &c.' Thus the *Grand Remonstrance*. Clarendon is not less emphatic in condemnation: 'holding for honourable that which pleased and for just that which profited. . . . Those foundations of right by which men valued their security were to the apprehension and understanding of wise men never more in danger to be destroyed.' How far those apprehensions were consistent with Clarendon's parallel assertion that the country during those years enjoyed 'the greatest calm and fullest measure of felicity' it is not altogether easy for later commentators to understand. Yet the descriptions are not more conflicting than the pictures which Taine and De Tocqueville respectively paint of society in France on the eve of the Revolution.

Meanwhile, in view of the supersession of Parliament, money had to be found by resort to expedients other than that of direct taxation. Indirect taxation in the form of Impositions the King still continued, of course, to collect; but though the duties, 'some so unreasonable that the sum of the charge exceeds the value of the goods', were raised to the highest possible point, the resulting revenue was inadequate to the King's needs. The sale of some articles of daily use such as soap, salt, and wine was, contrary to Statute, handed over to monopolists; obsolete feudal obligations such as 'distraint of Knighthood', whereby country squires were compelled to pay for titles they did not want, or alternatively to pay for not taking them, were revived; the claims of the Crown to royal forests were asserted in the most extravagant manner; in the Forest of Dean alone, seventeen villages had sprung up, and the villagers were now constrained to ransom their property and to come under the jurisdiction of the old forest law; profits were made by the sale of great offices of State, and a petty fraud was practised upon the counties by the exaction of 'coat and conduct money'—provision for the militia regiments which were not in fact called up. In these and other ways, some paltry, all irritating, the necessities of the King were partially supplied.

Of all the devices, however, to which a hard-pressed Treasury found it convenient to resort, none aroused so much popular clamour or evoked such conspicuous and influential resistance as the collection of ship-money.

The suggestion came from Noy, who had acted as counsel for the Five Knights in 1627, who had been foremost in opposition to the King's claim to levy tonnage and

Financial Expedients

Ship-money

poundage, but was now Attorney-General and as zealous
in the King's service as he had formerly been in that of the
opposition. Nor did his suggestion lack ingenuity. Had
not the Plantagenet Kings regularly called upon the coast
towns to furnish ships manned for the defence of the
realm? Had not a fleet been raised in this manner for the
expedition to Algiers so lately as 1626? Two years later an
order for the collection of ship-money had been issued, and
though it was revoked, the right to levy it was not impaired.
Noy's suggestion was approved by Manchester and Coventry, to whom it was referred, and on 20 October 1634 the
writs were issued. They were directed in the first instance
only to London and other seaports, and bade those towns
deliver their quota of ships and men 'to the Port of
Portsmouth, before the first day of March next ensuing'.
The avowed reasons for the levy were set forth in the
writs: 'Because we are given to understand that certain
thieves, pirates, and robbers of the sea, as well Turks,
enemies of the Christian name, as others', have spoiled
'the ships, goods and merchandise of our own subjects and
those of friendly powers'. Moreover, 'we see them daily
preparing all manner of shipping further to molest our
merchants and to grieve the Kingdom'. Reference is also
made to 'the dangers which in these times of war do hang
over our heads, and to the fact that we and our progenitors,
Kings of England, have been always heretofore masters of
the sea, and it would be very irksome unto us if that
princely honour in our times should be lost or in anything
diminished'. The defence of the realm was admittedly a
charge common to the whole Kingdom, but the seaports
were specially concerned, in that their danger was the
more imminent and their interest in foreign trade the most
direct. To them, therefore, the writ was in this first
instance directed.

A year later similar writs were addressed to the inland
counties. The first set merely revised, as we have noted,
an ancient custom which had been enforced without
protest so lately as in 1626. The legality of the second set

of writs was much more disputable, but the judges gave
a strong opinion in favour of it in November 1635, and
again, with even greater emphasis, when it was referred to
the full bench of judges in February 1637:

'We are of opinion that your Majesty may by writ, under the
Great Seal of England, command all your subjects . . . to
provide and furnish such a number of ships with men, victuals,
and munition . . . for the defence and safeguard of this Kingdom . . .: and that by law your Majesty may compel the doing
thereof in case of refusal or refractoriness; and we are also of
opinion, that in such case your Majesty is the sole judge both
of the danger, and when and how the same is to be prevented
and avoided.'

The sting was in the tail. The impost was in itself
bitterly resented: the unlimited discretion which the judges
attributed to the King rendered it doubly unpopular.
London protested, but unavailingly, against the charge;
influential individuals, like Lord Saye and Sele in Oxfordshire, John Hampden in Buckinghamshire, did the same.
Lord Falkland's name also appears in the list of defaulters
in respect of his Hertfordshire property, though he appears
to have paid without protest on his Oxfordshire estates.
That the impost was exceedingly unpopular is certain—
direct taxation is always unpopular; whether it was
illegal is more doubtful. The matter was brought to the
test in the famous trial of John Hampden. St. John,
Hampden's leading Counsel, frankly admitted that the
King as *Pater familiae* was responsible for the maintenance
of peace at home and for the protection of his family from
the attacks of enemies: the law had put 'the means of
defence wholly in his hands'; 'in this business of defence
the *suprema potestas* is inherent in His Majesty as part of
his Crown and Kingly dignity'; but he argued that the
potestas must under ordinary circumstances be exercised
in and through Parliament, and he cited 'a multitude of
records beginning with one in King John's time, and so
downwards' to prove the illegality of taxation without
consent. In a sudden emergency the King, no doubt,

might and must act on behalf of the nation; but in what
sense could emergency be pleaded at the moment? To all
men it was notorious that ship-money was merely one in
a series of devices for enabling the King to avoid the disagreeable necessity of summoning Parliament.

The real   That was the real issue behind the question of the col-
issue   lection of ship-money: but it was naturally ignored in the
speeches for the Crown, by the Attorney-General Bankes
and Lyttelton the Solicitor, and not less in the judgement,
in which seven out of the twelve judges concurred. Two
of the judges dissented on the main issue, and three others
declined, on other grounds, to support the Crown. Among
the majority were Finch, the late Speaker of the House
of Commons, and now Chief Justice of the Common Pleas,
and Sir Robert Berkeley, one of the Justices of the King's
Bench. The latter agreed that Parliament is 'a most
ancient and supreme Court where the King and Peers, as
judges, are in person and the whole body of the Commons
representatively', but utterly denied the main contention
of Hampden's counsel and in particular that of Holborne,
who had argued that final discretion was vested in the
King only when it was impossible to consult Parliament.
'The law', said Berkeley, 'knows no such King-yoking
policy. The law is of itself an old and trusty servant of the
The   King's; it is his instrument or means which he useth to
Judges   govern his people by. I never read nor heard that *lex* was
and the
Crown   *Rex*; but it is common and most true that *Rex* is *lex*, for he
is *lex loquens*, a living, a speaking, an acting law.' 'Though
I have gone very high', he added, 'I shall go to a yet higher
contemplation of the fundamental policy of our laws:
which is this, that the King of mere right ought to have,
and the people of mere duty are bound to yield unto the
King, supply for the defence of the Kingdom, and when
the Parliament itself doth grant supply in that case; it is
not merely a benevolence of the people but therein they do
an act of justice and duty to the King.' If Berkeley went
high, Finch went higher. 'Acts of Parliament', he said,
'to take away [the King's] Royal Power in the defence of

his Kingdom are void. . . . They are void Acts of Parliament to bind the King not to command the subjects, their persons and goods, and I say their money too, for no Acts of Parliament make any difference.'

It has been the fashion to assume that the judgement in favour of the Crown was due to mere servility on the part of the judges. But a layman may well hesitate to say that the judgement was bad in law. What is certain is, that whether good or bad in law, the judgement was in its political effects infinitely mischievous. Clarendon not merely admits but insists upon this. 'I cannot but take the liberty to say that the circumstances and proceedings in those new extraordinary cases, stratagems and impositions were very unpolitic, and even destructive to the services intended.' People are much more roused 'by injustice than by violence'. Men who paid their quota more or less willingly were terrified by the grounds on which the judgement was based. It was 'logic that left no man anything which he might call his own'. 'Undoubtedly', adds Clarendon, 'my Lord Finch's speech . . . made ship-money much more abhorred and formidable than all the commitments by the Council-table and all the distresses taken by the sheriffs in England. . . . Many sober men who have been clearly satisfied with the conveniency, necessity and justice of many sentences, depart notwithstanding extremely offended and scandalized with the grounds, reasons, and expressions of those who inflicted those censures.'

That there was a growing sense of uneasiness in the nation at large is clear not only from the testimony of Clarendon. That the ship-money agitation contributed largely to it is equally certain. But all other causes fade into insignificance as compared with the ecclesiastical policy of Archbishop Laud.

With the ecclesiastical problem this book is not concerned except in so far as it reacted upon constitutional issues. During the years of personal government the reaction was direct and continuous. Ever since the accession of the Stuarts Puritanism had been making headway among the

Laud and the Puritans

masses of the people, but losing it in the high places both
of Church and State. Puritanism, however, is not to be
identified with non-conformity. The term Puritan, as used
in the first half of the seventeenth century, embraced at
least three more or less distinct ecclesiastical parties: the
evangelican churchmen or 'conforming' Puritans; the
Presbyterians; and a party originally known as Brownists
and later as Independents or Congregationalists. In addition there were other less defined sectaries. The position
of the 'Conforming Puritans.' was sufficiently defined in
the Millenary Petition presented to James I on his accession and in the *Apology* of 1604. Briefly it may be said that
they were dissatisfied with the compromise embodied in
the Elizabethan Settlement; were intolerant of all that
savoured of Rome in the doctrine and liturgy of the English
Church, and while rejecting the Presbyterian model of
Church Government, were inclined towards Geneva in
matters of ritual and doctrine. With their claims and
pretensions we shall come to closer quarters in a later
chapter. Here it need only be said that they did not ask
merely for toleration, for inclusion in the English Church,
they asked that their opponents, the Arminians, should be
excluded and that their own views should be accepted as
the orthodox and official views of the State and the State
Church.

The Presby-terians   The position and claims of the Presbyterians were
similarly exclusive. They demanded that the English
Church should follow the example of the reformed Church
of Scotland and take its church government, its ritual, and
doctrine from Geneva. The Presbyterians prevailed upon
the Long Parliament to accept their views, but their
triumph was brief, and was brought to an end by the
accession to power of Cromwell and his army.

The Indepen-dents   The Independents were almost equally opposed to
Roman Catholics, Arminians, Episcopalian Puritans, and
Presbyterians. They disapproved of the connexion between State and Church, refused to accept the government
either of Bishops or Presbyters, and regarded the Church

as coextensive with the 'congregation'. All centralized forms of government were almost equally abhorrent to them, though they were prepared to tolerate all forms of religious belief except those professed by Papists and Jews.[1]

The Stuarts looked with disfavour on all forms of Puritanism, and partly on political, partly on religious grounds, allied themselves closely with the Arminian party. Consequently for a quarter of a century the Arminians had it all their own way in the Church, and during the ten years of personal government their domination extended to politics. When asked what the Arminians held, a contemporary wit replied: 'they hold all the best bishoprics and deaneries in England'. More than that: as soon as Charles I had got rid of Parliament they dictated the policy of the Crown. *The Crown and the Arminians*

If Charles had a Prime Minister during these years it was the man whom in 1633 he advanced to the see of Canterbury, William Laud. Born at Reading in 1573, and educated at the Free Borough School of that town and at St. John's College, Oxford, Laud became Fellow of his College in 1593, and was elected President, despite the protests of the Calvinist party, in 1616. Thenceforward his preferment was rapid. Appointed to the Deanery of Gloucester in 1616, he roused bitter opposition by removing the 'Communion Table' from the middle of the Church to the east end, where it became an 'altar'. Five years later he was consecrated Bishop of St. David's, was translated to Bath and Wells in 1626, and in 1628 from there to London. It was on his advice that Charles, whose close confidence he had now come to enjoy, issued the Declaration on Religion in November 1628.[2] To his other duties he added that of Chancellor of the University of Oxford (1630–41): and to him that office was no sinecure. He did his utmost to restore discipline among the undergraduates, and by his Statutes he left on the University, as we have already noted, a mark which was not erased for two centuries. *Charles and Laud*

[1] Prelatists were also excluded when the Independents came into power.   [2] *Supra*, p. 78.

Appointed to the Archbishopric of Canterbury in 1633, he at once made his hand felt both in Church and State. He took an active part in the work of the Star Chamber, and there in 1637 he confronted the three Puritan pamphleteers, Prynne, Burton, and Bastwick, whose barbarous sentence—a heavy fine, the loss of ears, public shame in the pillory, to be followed by imprisonment for life—evoked a remarkable demonstration of popular sympathy and was reversed, as far as it could be, by the Long Parliament.

Posterity, as already hinted, has come to appreciate the greatness of Laud's intellect, and the purity of his aims. None the less is it necessary to emphasize the mischievous results of his policy. A 'man unfit for the State of England': May's judgement, Puritan though he was, still stands. Even Clarendon admits that Laud was no statesman. 'He did court persons too little, nor cared to make his designs and purposes appear as candid as they were, by showing them in any other dress than their own natural beauty and roughness; and did not consider enough what men said or were like to say.' His objects were partly disciplinary, partly doctrinal. On the one hand a 'restoration of Church ceremonial and external worship'; on the other, 'a doctrinal clearance; the subjugation of the Calvinistic spirit in the reformed Church of England'.[1] The task was difficult enough in England; in Scotland it was hopeless.

Laud and the Scots   To bring the Scotch Church into complete conformity with that of England had always been one of the objects nearest to the heart of Charles I. His ambition was warmly seconded, if not inspired by the Archbishop. On the part of Laud some ignorance as to Scotland might be excused: on the part of the King it was inexcusable. Charles must have known that the Scots were not only devoted on doctrinal grounds to the Presbyterian system, but that they clung passionately to their own Church organization as a symbol of national independence. In 1633 the King, accompanied by the Archbishop, made a magnificent progress into his northern kingdom. Then and there were sown the seeds

[1] Mozley, *Laud*.

destined to produce a terrible harvest later on. What chiefly struck the King in Scotland was 'the want of a Book of Common Prayer and uniform service to be kept in all the Churches, . . . and the want of canons for the uniformity of the same'. He determined, with the aid of the Scotch bishops, to supply these deficiencies, and in 1637 a new book of canons and a revised liturgy were published. The Scotch people desired neither reform of liturgy nor of discipline, least of all did they desire it at the hands of England. They had not thrown off the yoke of Rome to exchange it for the yoke of Canterbury. The new liturgy was appointed to be read for the first time on Sunday, 23 July 1637. The attempt to read it was the signal for the outbreak of a riot at St. Giles's Cathedral—a riot which was in very truth 'the preamble to revolution'. The Scotch bishops with difficulty escaped with their lives, and 'the whole nation, with slight exceptions, bristled into resistance'.[1] The motives of resistance were in part religious, in part political; an attack upon the Presbyterian system from any quarter was hateful, from England it was intolerable. The attempt to force Anglican uniformity upon Scotland practically dissolved the King's authority north of the Tweed. A provisional Government was set up in Edinburgh, and on 27 February, 1638, the Scottish National Covenant 'for the maintenance of the true religion and the King's person' was drawn up and very largely subscribed. The Scotch nation was practically unanimous in defence of the Established Presbyterian Church and national independence. The King now appointed the Marquis of Hamilton as High Commissioner and prepared to announce considerable concessions. The Covenanters regarded the concessions as inadequate: the King must not merely withdraw the new liturgy, but condemn it and acknowledge the justice of the protest against it. Meanwhile, Hamilton summoned a General Assembly to meet at Glasgow. It met on 21 November, and after a week's wrangling was formally dissolved. The act of dissolution

Anglicanism in Scotland

---

[1] The striking phrase is Gardiner's.

was, however, disregarded: the Assembly quietly continued
its business. Every Act concerning the Church passed since
1580 was abrogated; episcopacy was abolished; and a vindication of their proceedings was ordered to be sent 'to all
the sincere and good Christians' in England. War now
became inevitable. 'I have missed my end', wrote Hamilton, 'in not being able to make your Majesty so considerable a party as will be able to curb the insolency of this
rebellious nation without assistance from England.'

Went-
worth and
the Scots

What were the probabilities that such assistance would
be forthcoming? Three months ago Wentworth had
written to advise the King to make no further concessions
to his Scotch subjects, but not to plunge precipitately into
war. Garrison Berwick, Carlisle, and the North of England
strongly and at once; train the garrisons under good
captains; if the Scots show signs of submission, treat them
with all possible leniency and encouragement; if not, make
your preparations for effective coercion. Such was the
advice of Wentworth; but Wentworth had been for years
in Ireland, and was not likely to have learnt from his
correspondence with Laud the strength or volume of the
gathering discontent in England. Is money wanted for a
Scotch war? 'In good faith every man will give it, I hope,
from his children upon such an extremity as this, when no
less verily than all we have comes thus to the stake. In a
word, we are, God be praised, rich and able, and in this
case it may justly be said, *salus populi suprema lex*, and the
King must not want our substance for the preservation of
the whole.' [1] Wentworth, it is clear, was entirely deceived
as to the prevailing temper in England. Events now moved
rapidly. In January 1639 the English nobles were summoned to appear in person, with their due quota of followers, for the defence of the borders. The Earl of Arundel
was appointed Commander in Chief, and Lord Holland
General of the Horse, with Lord Essex as second in command. Clarendon deplores the snub to Essex, 'the most
popular man in the kingdom, and the darling of the sword-

[1] Strafford, *Letters*, ii. 189.

men'; but Holland was a favourite of the Queen, and in war as in politics petticoat influence was becoming supreme. On 14 February the Covenanters published a manifesto appealing from the King to the English people. A fortnight later the King's reply was published, and was appointed to be read in every parish church throughout the land.[1] Charles had taken the first of a series of fatal steps which finally brought him to the scaffold.

The so-called 'Bishops' Wars' were entirely barren in personal distinction to any one concerned, and not less barren, from the King's point of view, in political results. Neither among the English nobles, nor among the English people was there any enthusiasm for the *Bellum Episcopale*. The Bishops' War

'To my understanding we are altogether in as ill a posture to invade others or to defend others as we were a twelvemonth since, which is more than any man can imagine that is not an eye-witness of it. The discontents here at home do rather increase than lessen. . . . I fear the ways we run will not prevent the mischief that threatens us.'

So wrote Northumberland to Wentworth. May probably reflects with accuracy the prevailing temper among the people:

'Never were the people of England so averse from any war, as neither hating the enemy against whom, nor approving the cause for which, they were engaged. Their own great sufferings made them easily believe that the Scots were innocent, and wronged by the same hand by which themselves had been oppressed. And for the cause, it was such wherein they could not desire a victory; as they naturally supposed that the same sword which subdued the Scots must destroy their own liberties, and that the contrivers of this war were equal enemies to both nations.'

The King was entirely deceived alike as to the strength of the Scotch feeling and as to their powers of resistance.

Wentworth was deceived on neither point. News had reached him that guns were being landed from Sweden at Leith. 'Believe it', he wrote to Windebank, 'they fly

[1] Rushworth, ii. 798.

high.' They did; and their preparations for resistance were on a scale with their ambition. They raised an army of more than 20,000 men, well found and well disciplined, many of them seasoned veterans who had seen service in Germany, and placed it under the command of Alexander Leslie.

The King was at the head of an army slightly superior in numbers to the Scots, but in all else inferior. Badly led, ill-armed, ill-fed, undisciplined, and, worst of all, entirely lacking in enthusiasm for the cause in which they were to fight, the English troops would have had small chance against the Scotch. But the issue was never actually joined. Leslie took up his position on Duns Law—a hill which commanded all the roads from Berwick into Scotland: the King faced him on the Tweed. That the Covenanters could have swept the English peasants before them is hardly doubtful, but Leslie was as wise as he was brave. An invasion of England might have brought military glory to the Scots, but it would almost infallibly have converted half-friendly opponents into determined foes. Negotiations were opened between the two camps; a peace was patched up at Berwick (18 June 1639), and the first Bishops' War was at end.

Straf-
ford as
Minister

The pacification of Berwick proved to be a hollow truce. 'Nobody', as Clarendon pithily observes, 'meant what others believed he did.' The English army was disbanded, its leaders were dismissed with scant courtesy, and in August Charles was back in London. The first thing he did was to order the Scotch report of the negotiations at Berwick to be burnt by the common hangman. The second was to summon Wentworth to his aid. Wentworth reached England in September, and for the next fourteen months he was in every sense first minister of the Crown. In January 1640 he received the long deferred mark of royal favour, being created Earl of Strafford.

Strafford, like Bacon, was a thorough believer in Parliament as an instrument of Government. He had bent Parliament to his will in Dublin; might he not succeed in doing the same at Westminster? Scotland had still to be subdued; and subdued it could not be, as Strafford was statesman enough to perceive, unless by some means the King could enlist against it the national sentiment and the material resources of England and Ireland. With Ireland there was not much difficulty. In March 1640 Strafford was over in Dublin and easily secured from the Catholic majority in Parliament four subsidies for the suppression of the Presbyterian heresy in Scotland. A month later he was back in London to take his place in the Parliament which had been called on his advice.

On 13 April 1640 the Short Parliament met; the experiment of 'Personal Rule', protracted for eleven weary years, was a confessed failure; the system of 'Thorough' had broken down. The King was sanguine enough to suppose that Parliament would resent the Scotch 'presumption in their thought of invading England', and 'would express a very sharp sense of their insolence and carriage towards the King and provide remedies proportionable'. Not that the King desired the counsel of Parliament; they were expressly told by the Lord Keeper that he did not; still less were they required 'to interpose in any office of mediation'. What the King wanted was that they should with all convenient speed 'give His Majesty such a supply as he might provide for the vindication of his honour. If they would vote supplies promptly they should have time enough afterwards to represent any grievances to him.' *The Short Parliament*

Many men of distinction entered Parliament for the first time in 1640. Among them was Lucius Cary, Lord Falkland, who as a Scotch peer was eligible (before 1707) for a seat in the House of Commons, and found one at Newport, Isle of Wight. Even the capital of 'the island' could hardly expect in the era of Reform to escape disfranchisement. So Newport lost one of its two members in the redistribution of seats in 1867, and finally ceased to be separately represented in 1885. Let it, therefore, be recorded that there is no constituency in the United Kingdom which showed greater discrimination in the choice of representatives; or, as perhaps it should be put, was more intelligently provided for by its patron. For Newport had the honour of returning no fewer than five first ministers of the Crown—General (afterwards first Earl) Stanhope; Sir Arthur Wellesley (Duke of Wellington); Lord Palmerston; George Canning and William Lamb (Viscount Melbourne); not to mention Lucius Cary (Viscount Falkland), sometime Secretary of State. Most of the members returned in 1640 were new to Parliamentary life, and at their first meeting there was not unnatural embarrassment and hesitation. Then it was, 'whilst men gazed upon each other looking who should begin', that John Pym leapt into the leadership.

John
Pym
By birth a west country squire, educated at Oxford, trained as a lawyer, Pym might now claim leadership not merely in virtue of intellect and character, but by length of Parliamentary experience. He had sat in the last two Parliaments of James I, and had distinguished himself by the vehemence of his views in regard to the enforcement of the laws against the Roman Catholics. He was one of the managers of the impeachment of Buckingham in 1626, and two years later took a leading part in the debates on the Petition of Right. On the dissolution of the third Parliament in 1629 Pym went into retirement and emerged only to appear in that of 1640. The temper of the new House, resolute but moderate, was admirably reflected in the great speech in which Pym unfolded his impeachment of the Government. The speech was of unprecedented length ('a set discourse of about two hours'), and 'very plain', but the House listened and approved. Towards the King personally Pym's tone was one 'of profound reverence', but by the 'long intromission of Parliaments many unwarrantable things had been practised, notwithstanding the great virtues of His Majesty'. That was the point on which Pym throughout laid stress. The list of specific grievances was long, but the root of the matter lay in the 'intromission of Parliaments'. 'The powers of Parliament', he declared, 'are to the body politic as the rational

faculties of the soul to a man.' It was almost an echo of Eliot's language in 1624, and it struck the keynote of much that was to come. But the King wanted not debate but supply. While the Commons talked, Convocation voted. On 22 April, at Laud's bidding, the clergy granted six subsidies. The Commons still dallied, and on the 23rd resolved that the redress of grievances must have precedence. 'Till the liberties of the House and kingdom were known they knew not whether they had anything to give or no.' Strafford urged frank concession; Sir Harry Vane wanted to strike a bargain. If the House would grant twelve subsidies, the claim to ship-money should be unreservedly abandoned. Never did Strafford show greater wisdom. The House would not be bullied; it might still be led. Vane threatened: 'twelve subsidies or nothing'. The need was undoubtedly pressing; dispatches from Scotland announced a renewal of the war. The Commons were unmoved. Vane told the King they would not 'give one penny'; and on 5 May the Short Parliament was dissolved.

Who was responsible for the fiasco? Clarendon, writing in the light of subsequent events, throws the blame on the Secretary of State, the elder Vane, who 'acted that part maliciously and to bring all into confusion . . . being known to have an implacable hatred against the Earl of Strafford . . . whose destruction was then upon the anvil'. Gardiner, while declaring that Clarendon's account of this session is 'nearly worthless', offers no alternative explanation except that dissolution was unavoidable. Whitelocke attributes it—apparently without any authority—to Laud. But wherever the responsibility for the sudden dissolution must lie, the ill effects of it were quickly manifest. All good men deplored the breach: 'there could not a greater damp have seized upon the spirits of the whole nation than this dissolution caused'.[1] The more violent rejoiced. 'All is well', said St. John, 'it must be worse before it is better.' The King was dismayed at his own handiwork. 'He was

[1] Clarendon.

heartily sorry for what he had done and denied having given such authority' to Vane. He even had thoughts, if Clarendon may be trusted, of recalling Parliament by proclamation. Such procedure was impossible; the die was cast. But in May 1640 Charles might still perhaps have saved the situation. Strafford, if given a free hand, might have saved it for him. In November, the Crown, discredited by a second military failure, was compelled to confront a Parliament not unjustly incensed and not unreasonably suspicious.

The events which filled the interval must be briefly told.

After the dissolution of Parliament, Convocation, with questionable legality and still more questionable wisdom, continued to sit, and passed a series of canons binding on clergy and laity alike.[1] Desperate efforts were made to raise money; ship-money, coat and conduct money, forced loans—all the familiar expedients were tried. The Genoese bankers would not lend without the security of the city; the Pope would find funds, but only on the impossible condition that Charles would declare himself a papist. Little money was actually raised except from the clergy and from the Roman Catholic laity at home. Riots broke out in London; the apprentices turned out in crowds; the life of Laud was threatened. Meanwhile, an army must be got together to resist the threatened invasion of the Scots.

Scottish invasion of England   Strafford would have forestalled the invasion, by carrying the war into the enemy's country—in two senses. There must be an end for the moment, to constitutional methods. The position was desperate. The King must not ask for money; but take it. The city must lend; the country find ship-money; above all the war must be waged vigorously, aggressively. And an army? 'You have an army in Ireland you may employ here to reduce this Kingdom. Scotland will not hold out five months. Venture all you have, carry it or lose it.'

[1] The Dean of Winchester (the Very Rev. W. H. Hutton), a high authority, takes the view that the dissolution of Parliament did not necessarily dissolve Convocation (cf. *Hist. English Church*, pp. 80, 87). Laud held otherwise, and cf. Gardiner, ix. 142.

That was, in the circumstances of the hour, the voice of statesmanship, and Laud and Cottington re-echoed it. But Strafford was to pay dearly for the advice then given. The proposal to bring over the Irish army 'to reduce the Kingdom' cost him his life. Meanwhile, the King had little money and few men. But the Scots had somehow to be met. Northumberland and Conway were appointed to the chief commands of the army; Essex was again passed over, though, in Clarendon's opinion, 'he might easily have been caressed'. The troops raised by the press-gang were from the first sullen and averse to the war. Some turned upon their officers and murdered them; many deserted; all became a terror to the country through which they marched. 'The arch-knaves of the country': so they were described by Sir Jacob Astley. 'We are daily assaulted by sometimes 500 of them together', wrote Colonel Lunford, 'and have hurt and killed some in our own defence.' Such an ill-disciplined rabble was not likely to oppose successfully the invasion of the Covenanters. On 20 August the Scots, 25,000 strong, crossed the Tweed at Coldstream. Strafford was summoned from Ireland to take command against them. By 27 August he was at York, but wracked by disease and utterly worn out he could get no farther. Conway was ordered to hold the line of the Tyne; but on 28 August the Scots forded it at Newburn, and the English troops fled in panic before them. Two days later the Scots seized Newcastle; Northumberland and Durham were soon in their hands. In possession of the Northern Counties; convinced, with good reason, of the support of the Parliamentary leaders; surrounded by every evidence of popular goodwill, they could afford to wait.

Meanwhile, the King, putting aside a petition for a new Parliament, decided to have recourse to a constitutional device untried for centuries. A great Council of Peers was summoned to confer with the King, and met at York on 24 September. The King immediately announced that he had resolved to call a new Parliament in November. Clarendon regards this as a blunder. 'It might easily be

Council of Peers at York

foreseen that the calling of so many disaffected, disobliged and discontented men . . . could not but make every man much worse than they came.' Commissioners were appointed to treat with the Scots, who with fervent protestations of loyalty declared 'that their grievances were the cause of their being in arms', and begged the King 'to settle a firm and durable peace by advice of a Parliament'. In October negotiations were opened at Ripon, and there a treaty was concluded. There was to be a truce for two months during which the Scots were to receive £850 a day; the Northern Counties were to be assigned to them as winter quarters, and the terms of a definitive treaty were to be referred to the coming Parliament for adjudication.

While the Scots 'sat still' about Newcastle the elections to the new Parliament were held. 'The Court', wrote Bulstrode Whitelocke, 'laboured to bring in their friends, but those most favoured at Court were little liked in the county, and it was a thing not a little strange to see what an opposition to the Courts proceedings was in the hearts and minds of the people, so that very few of that party had the favour to become members of Parliament.' The meeting of the Parliament thus elected opens a new chapter in English history.

VI. THE LONG PARLIAMENT

The end of Thorough. The Puritans and the Church

THE Parliament which met on 3 November 1640 was not formally dissolved until 16 March 1660. The longest Parliament in English history was also, with one possible exception, the most momentous. If the Reformation Parliament finally 'broke the bonds of Rome' and asserted the national independence of the English Church, the Long Parliament affirmed the principle which has given to the English Constitution its distinctive place in the history of Political Institutions.

The temper of the members was vastly different from that which had animated the House when it assembled in the spring of the same year. Temper of Parliament

'There was observed', says Clarendon, 'a marvellous elated countenance in most of the members of Parliament before they met together in the House; the same men who six months before were observed to be of very moderate tempers and to wish that gentle methods might be applied without opening the wound too wide and exposing it to the air, and rather to cure what was amiss than too strictly to make inquisition into the causes and origin of the malady, talked now in another dialect both of things and of persons.'

Some days before Parliament assembled Pym had met Hyde in Westminster Hall, and conferring together upon the state of affairs had told him that

'they must now be of another temper than they were at the last Parliament, that they must not only sweep the House clean below, but must pull down all the cobwebs which hung in the top and corners that they might not breed dust and so make a foul House hereafter; that they had now an opportunity to make their country happy by removing all grievances and pulling up the causes of them by the roots, if all men would do their duties, and used much other sharp discourse to him to the same purpose, by which it was discerned that the wildest and boldest counsels and overtures would find a much better reception than those of a more moderate alloy, which fell out accordingly.'

The reasons for this change of temper are not difficult to discern. Much, as we have seen, had happened since the dissolution of the Short Parliament on 5 May. During the last six months 'Thorough' made its last desperate venture. As in 1629, so in 1640, members of Parliament were imprisoned; ship-money and coat and conduct money, despite the resolutions of the late Parliament, were collected; forced loans were extorted, and a desperate effort was made to raise an army against the Scots. All to no purpose. The second Bishops' War was a further revelation of military incompetence and divided counsels. Nothing remained but to buy off the hostility of the Scots, and in order to raise the purchase money Parliament must again meet. Clarendon notes two ominous events of the first day of the new Parliament. The King, instead of going in state to open Parliament, sneaked down the river with all possible privacy. The other matter was more serious. Sir Thomas Gardiner, Recorder of London, a zealous adherent of the Crown, whom the King proposed to place in the Speaker's Chair, failed to obtain a seat, and in his place the House chose William Lenthall, an Oxfordshire squire who had attained some eminence at the Bar. Lenthall was a man, according to Clarendon, 'of timorous nature and quite unequal to the difficult task of controlling Parliament in the interest of the King'. But his conduct on the fateful day (4 January 1642), when the King attempted to arrest the five members, belies Clarendon's description and proves that if he could not control Parliament in the interests of the King, he could withstand the King in defence of the liberties of Parliament.

There was, as yet, no clear definition of parties in the new Parliament. The King had personal friends in both Houses, and the Court had its followers, but there was no ministerial party, and the opposition though elaborately organized cannot be described as a 'party'. A small minority showed itself unwilling to proceed to extreme measures against Strafford, but until the development of the attack upon the Church, Parliament was practically unanimous in its desire to amend existing abuses and 'pluck up the causes of them by the roots'.

The House of Lords consisted at this time, in addition to the 26 Spiritual Peers, of 124 Temporal Peers, of whom no less than two-thirds owed their seats to the reigning King and his father.[1] Six bishops and forty lay peers were noted as absent when the roll of the House was called on November 16. At important debates the strength of the House was about one hundred.[2] Among the lay peers Francis Russell, Earl of Bedford, occupied a position of acknowledged pre-eminence. 'A wise man', says Clarendon, 'and of too great and plentiful a fortune to wish a subversion of the Government.' He was the friend of Pym, a Puritan in character as in creed, and a man of agreeable temper and sound judgement. He died unfortunately before the first session was half through. Much afflicted, according to Clarendon, 'with the passion and fury which he perceived his party inclined to: insomuch that he declared to some of near trust with him "that he feared the rage and madness of this Parliament would bring more prejudice and mischief to the kingdom than it had ever sustained by the long intermission of Parliaments".' He was succeeded in the leadership of the popular party in the House of Lords by a much more extreme man, Hampden's friend, William Fiennes, Viscount Saye and Sele. Clarendon speaks of the latter as 'the oracle of those who were called Puritans in the worst sense', and as 'a notorious enemy to the Church'; and, making all allowance for Clarendon's prejudice on such a matter, there can be no doubt that Saye and Sele was a violent opponent not merely of the Laudian system but of the established order in the Church. Among other prominent members of the House of Lords it must suffice to mention the Earl of Essex, a chivalrous opponent and a brave soldier, but ultimately pushed aside by more extreme men; his brother-in-law—by a second marriage—

The House of Lords

[1] Sanford, *Studies*, p. 285.   [2] Firth, *House of Lords*, p. 74.

William Seymour, Earl of Hertford, best known to fame as the husband of Arabella Stuart; Algernon Percy, Earl of Northumberland and Lord High Admiral of England; Robert Rich, Earl of Warwick, who secured for his party the supreme advantage of the command of the sea; his brother Henry, Earl of Holland, a courtier who had no desire for martyrdom; his son-in-law, Edward Montagu, Viscount Mandeville (Baron Montagu of Kimbolton), eldest son of the Earl of Manchester—a man of unbounded popularity among the Puritans whom he courted and (if Clarendon's hint be accepted) sumptuously entertained; and Robert Greville, Lord Brooke, as strong in action as he was eloquent of tongue. The King's party, though commanding a majority in the House, was not too strong in personnel. The Lord Keeper Finch fled from the country in December; Juxon, the Lord Treasurer, and Cottington, Master of the Court of Wards, had no stomach for a fight; Philip Henry, Earl of Pembroke, was dismissed from the office of Lord Chamberlain in July 1641, for hounding on the mob who called for Strafford's head.

The House of Commons: personnel — Among the 493 members of the House of Commons there were not a few members of commanding ability. A glance at the returns will show that most of the constituencies returned men either of high social standing or of distinguished talents. Two Verneys, Sir Ralph and Sir Edmund, father and son, found seats in Buckinghamshire; Sidney Godolphin sat for Helston; Edmund Waller for St. Ives; Edward Hyde for Saltash; two famous lawyers, Oliver St. John and John Maynard, represented Totnes; Denzil Holles, Strafford's brother-in-law and one of the ablest men in the House, sat for Dorchester; Sir John Culpepper and Sir Edward Dering for Kent; Nathaniel Fiennes—as bitter as his father against the Church—represented Banbury; his brother, James Fiennes, with Lord Wenman, represented the county of Oxford, while the University found very distinguished burgesses in Sir Thomas Roe and John Selden; Sir Arthur Hazelrig came in for Leicestershire; Sir Ralph Hopton for Wells; Sir

Benjamin Rudyard and the elder Vane for Wilton, and the younger Vane for Kingston-on-Hull; William Lenthall, the Speaker, represented Woodstock; Cromwell—unnoticed as yet—Cambridge town; John Hampden, returned both for Wendover and Bucks, elected to sit for the county; Pym, with William Lord Russell as his colleague, sat for Tavistock; Falkland, as in the Short Parliament, for Newport, I.W. This catalogue includes only a tithe of the famous men who composed 'that synod of inflexible patriots with some, that conclave of traitorous rebels with others';[1] but the list is long enough to establish the conclusion that rarely, if ever, has there been a Parliament in England which contained so large a proportion of exceptionally brilliant and distinguished men. Falkland and Hyde were destined to a special place as the leaders of the middle party—the constitutional royalists; among the rest two men stand out pre-eminent, John Hampden and John Pym.

Of Hampden we have an imperishable portrait from the pen of Clarendon.

John Hampden

'He was of that rare affability and temper in debate and of that seeming humility and submission of judgement, as if he brought no opinion with him, but a desire of information and instruction. Yet he had so subtle a way of indicating and under the notion of doubts insinuating his objections that he left his opinions with those from whom he pretended to learn and receive them, and even with them who were able to preserve themselves from his infusions and discern those opinions to be fixed in him with which they could not comply, he always left the character of an ingenuous and conscientious person. He was indeed a very wise man and of great parts, and possessed the most absolute spirit of popularity, that is the most absolute faculties to govern the people, of any man I ever knew.'

By the side of John Hampden sat John Pym.

Pym, as we have seen, had leapt into leadership during the Short Parliament; his authority in the new Parliament soon came to be acknowledged on all hands. He was

Pym

[1] Hallam.

essentially a 'House of Commons' man; the first and perhaps the greatest Parliamentary leader whom this country
has produced. A financier of really first-rate ability; a
singularly clear and convincing speaker; a consummate
Parliamentary tactician; a tireless and vigilant leader,
Pym did more than any other single man to impress upon
the House of Commons its modern aspect, and to define
its party system and its methods of procedure. From the
day of meeting until the day of his death he was the soul of
the opposition in Parliament and outside, and was, for all
practical purposes, the leader not merely of a party but of
the nation. Pym sat on the Speaker's left, 'close to the bar
of the House', with Hampden invariably by his side, and
almost immediately opposite to them the equally inseparable companions, Falkland and Hyde. Among others who
sat on the Speaker's right were the elder Vane, 'at the
upper end of the front bench', the Solicitor-General, Sir
Edward Herbert, Sir Benjamin Rudyard, Oliver Cromwell,
and Sir John Culpepper.[1] It is obvious, therefore, that
apart from personal association such as that of Hyde and
Falkland, there was little significance in the choice of seats,
though the extremists sat mostly, as the opposition sit
to-day, on the Speaker's left.

If the personnel of the new House was striking, the
issues before it were momentous. Amidst the mass of questions into the consideration of which the House immediately
plunged three stand out as of pre-eminent importance: the
attack upon Strafford and other agents of 'Thorough'; the
destruction of the machinery of personal government, and
Ecclesiastical Reform.

Impeach-
ment of
Strafford

The new Parliament was scarcely more than a week old
when, on 11 November, Pym suddenly rose and informed
a startled House that 'he had something of importance to
acquaint the House with, and desired that the outward
room be kept from strangers and that the outward doors
upon the stairs be locked'. This being done, Pym put up Sir
John Clotworthy, an Ulster settler, who sat for Malden,

[1] D'Ewes ap. Sanford. Cf. also Verney's *Notes of the Long Parliament*.

to give an account of Strafford's 'tyrannical carriage' in Ireland, of the 'army he had raised there to invade Scotland', and other misdeeds. A proposal for the immediate impeachment of the Lord Lieutenant 'found an universal approbation and consent'. A Committee of seven members, including Pym and Hampden, was appointed to consider all the information against the Earl of Strafford, and within an hour or two reported that 'they did find just cause to accuse the Earl of Strafford of high treason, and further that the House should desire the Lords that he may be sequestered from Parliament and committed, and that within some convenient time this House will resort to their Lordships with particular accusations and articles against him'.

Falkland, though no friend to Strafford or his system, begged the House in a maiden speech to consider 'whether it would not suit better with the gravity of their proceedings first to digest many of those particulars which had been mentioned by a Committee before they sent up to accuse him', though for his own part he was 'abundantly satisfied that there was enough to charge him'.

Pym strongly opposed Falkland's suggestion. Now, as throughout the next three years, he was in possession of exceptional information. Rumours had reached him of an intended *coup d'état*. Strafford might at that moment be on his way to the House of Lords to delate the Puritan leaders for treasonable negotiations with the Scotch rebels. The King was to support the accusation in arms. With Strafford to organize it, the abortive attempt of January 1642 might have been successfully anticipated in November 1640. But even for Strafford Pym was too quick. Forms were impatiently brushed aside. 'To delay is simple ruin', said Pym; 'once let Strafford get to the King and Parliament will be dissolved.' There was no delay. The House followed Pym's advice, and Pym himself carried up the message of the Commons to the Lords. As the Lords debate the question, Strafford himself, having heard of the impeachment, strides in 'with proud gloaming countenance'.

Greeted with shouts of 'withdraw', 'withdraw', he is compelled in confusión to retire. The Lords assent to the Commons' demand. Strafford is called in and stands, 'but is commanded to kneel and on his knees to hear the sentence'. He leaves the House in custody of Black-Rod, 'no man capping to him before whom that morning the greatest in England would have stood discovered, all crying "What is the matter?"' 'A small matter I warrant you', said the Earl. 'Yes, indeed', shouted the crowd, 'high treason is a small matter.' [1] Pym had won the first round; by nightfall the lion was caged.

Months elapsed—months crowded with events of the highest significance—before the great Earl was brought to trial. The elaboratè and complicated charges had to be formulated; a multitude of preliminaries had to be settled; and it was not until 22 March 1641 that the trial was actually opened in Westminster Hall.

Trial of Strafford   Of Strafford's trial we have a singularly vivid and detailed account from the pen of Dr. Robert Baillie, an eminent Presbyterian divine, who had been sent to London by the Scottish Covenanters to draw up the accusation against Archbishop Laud. His first-hand account of the great trial [2] is contained in a report to the Presbytery of Irvine. Baillie brings the whole scene before us: the King's throne set but vacant; the King himself anxiously watching the proceedings from a box with the Queen, the Princess Mary and the Prince Elector, 'little more regarded than if they had been absent'. Crowds of ladies in boxes 'for which they paid much money'; the Lord Steward on the great woolsack; 'two other sacks for the Lord Keeper and the Judges'; the peers fully robed; a little desk set in the midst 'where the prisoner Strafford stands and sits as he pleaseth, together with his keeper, Sir William Balfour, the Lieutenant of the Tower'; other desks for the prisoner's secretaries and 'counsell-at-law'; the eager crowd of the Commons; the general aspect of a great society function; 'the most glorious assemblie the Isle could afford, yet the

---

[1] Baillie, *Letters*, i. 272.   [2] *Ibid.*, i. 313-50.

gravity not such as I expected'; in the intervals 'the Lords always got to their feet, walked and clattered; the Lower House men too loud clattering'; many picnics in the Hall itself; 'much public eating not only of confections but of flesh and bread, bottles of beer and wine going thick from mouth to mouth without cups'. But though the scene was gay the matter was grave, and in the main, with some unfortunate exceptions, the conduct of it was not unworthy.

Disentangled from technicalities, the charge against Strafford was in reality twofold: that he had ruled tyrannically in Ireland, and that he meant to make Ireland the 'jumping off ground' for an attack on the liberties of England. The case rested mainly on the notes taken by the elder Vane of Strafford's advice to the King in Council. Of these entirely confidential notes the younger Vane had by an accident got view; most dishonourably he copied them, and even more dishonourably showed them to Pym. The incriminating words were: 'Your Majesty having tried all ways (against the Scots) and being refused, in this case of extreme necessity and for the safety of your kingdom, you are loose and absolved from all rules of Government. You are acquitted before God and man. You have an army in Ireland; you may employ it to reduce this kingdom.' Strafford defended himself with splendid courage, with touching eloquence and consummate ability. And he was obviously producing an effect. 'Three whole kingdoms', says May, 'were his accusers, and eagerly sought in one death a recompense of all their sufferings.' But Strafford met them face to face. Against the doctrine of cumulative treason Strafford had throughout protested. Misdemeanours he frankly admitted, but he contended, with unanswerable logic, that no amount of misdemeanours could make a felony. 'He made', says Baillie, 'one general answer, and almost in every article repeated it, though the point alleged against him were proved, yet it would be but a misdemeanour; an 100 misdemeanours would not make one felonie, and an 100 felonies not one treason, being a crime of a different kind and nature.' That Strafford was at least technically right no one can doubt, but in the Debate on 15 April Falkland brushed the subtleties impatiently aside. 'How many haires' breadths makes a tall man, and how many makes a little man, noe man can well say, yet wee know a tall man when wee see him from a low man. Soe 'tis in this, how many illegal acts makes a treason is not certainly well known, but wee well know it when wee see.' Strafford, he concluded, 'in equity deserves to die'. Yet Falkland, out of regard for the King, would have spared Strafford's life. Even his enemies could not fail to be impressed by Strafford's undaunted courage and the ability of his defence. 'Never man acted such a part on such a stage', writes Bulstrode Whitelocke, 'with more wisdom, constancy and eloquence, with greater wisdom, temper and with better grace in all his words.' The grim Covenanter Baillie allows that 'the matter and expression was exceeding brave; doubtless if he had grace and civil goodness he is a most eloquent man'. Strafford was visibly gaining ground; the impeachment was foredoomed to failure; even prejudiced judges could not convict on such evidence. But the 'inflexibles' were determined that Strafford should die. The trial had already dragged on for more than a fortnight when suddenly the impeachment was abandoned. A Bill of Attainder was brought in on 10 April, and 21 April it passed the Commons by 209 votes to 59 —a large majority, but in a thin House. Among those who voted in the minority, John Selden, the great lawyer who sat for Oxford University, and Lord George Digby were the most distinguished. They not only voted but spoke against the Bill, not out of pity for Strafford, nor yet out of regard for the King, but solely out of respect for the law.

'I do not say', said Digby, 'but the charges may represent him as a man worthy to die, and perhaps worthier than many a traitor. I do not say but they may justly direct us to enact that they shall be treason for the future. But God keep me from giving judgement of death on any man upon a law made *a posteriori*. Let the mark be set on the door where the plague is, and then let him that will enter, die. I believe his practices in themselves as high, as tyrannical, as any subject ever ventured on; and the malignity of them largely aggravated by those rare abilities of his, whereof God has given him the use, but the devil the application. In one word, I believe him to be still that grand apostate to the Commonwealth, who must not expect to be pardoned in this world till he be despatched to the other. And yet let me tell you, Mr. Speaker, my hand must not lie to that despatch.'

The assent of the Lords and the King was still necessary. On the 23rd the King wrote to his faithful servant to assure him 'upon the word of a King' that he should not suffer 'in life, honour, or fortune'. The King then entered into negotiations with the Puritan leaders. Bedford, Saye and Sele, and Pym himself were to have high office. Not even this could stay the hand of the 'opposition'. 'Stone dead hath no fellow' was the grim verdict of Essex. By the 8th of May the Bill of Attainder was through the Lords; Strafford's fate now rested with the King. Fears for the safety of the Queen at last overcame his hesitation; the Royal assent was given on 10 May, and two days later, Strafford was brought to the block. At last the fiery and fretted spirit was at rest.

Until the day of his death Strafford filled the stage. But the *Journals* of the House prove its manifold activities in other directions. Before Strafford was sent to the block much of the machinery of 'Thorough' had been destroyed and many of its agents brought to account. Of all the questions dealt with by the Long Parliament, in its first session, none was so insistent as that of the Church; but this will be reserved for separate and continuous treatment. Meanwhile, Parliament listened to the long tale of grievances detailed in county petitions; it impeached Laud, Finch, and Windebank; it vindicated the 'distressed ministers and other persecuted people' such as Prynne, Bastwick, and Burton; it questioned and committed 'many doctors and divines that had been most busy in promoting the late Church innovations'; it swept away the Prerogative Courts,

End of Thorough Reforms of the Long Parliament

the Star Chamber, the High Commission Court, the Stannary Courts, the Council of the North, and the Court of the Marches; it reversed, so far as Parliament can by resolution or legislation reverse, many unpopular judgements; it declared the illegality of Impositions and Tonnage and Poundage without the consent of Parliament; it restricted Purveyance; determined forest boundaries and abolished compulsory knighthood; above all it provided, by the Triennial Act, against the intermission of Parliamentary Sessions for the future, and, by a flagrant, though under the peculiar circumstances of the moment not perhaps an unjustifiable invasion of the Prerogative, made it impossible for the Crown to dissolve the existing Parliament without its own consent. None of these questions really evoked any serious difference of opinion. In both Houses there was practical unanimity as to the expediency of sweeping away the abuses of the old régime, and rendering their recurrence impossible.

Resolutions against Ship-money

Of all these abuses there was none, perhaps, against which feeling was more bitter than the collection of ship-money, and the action of the judges, in particular of Lord Keeper Finch, in relation thereto.

On 5 December 1640 there was presented to the House 'a humble petition of divers inhabitants in and about the Town of Watford complaining of the Sheriff for rigorous levying of ship-money'. The petition was referred to a Committee; two days later the House resumed consideration of the subject, and after an elaborate speech from Falkland, passed without a dissentient voice the following resolutions:

(1) 'That the charge imposed upon the Subjects for the providing and furnishing of ships, and the assessments for raising of money for that purpose, commonly called ship-money, are against the laws of the realm, the subjects right of property and contrary to former resolutions in Parliament and to the Petition of Right.

(2) 'That the extra-judicial opinions of the Judges published in the Star Chamber and enrolled in the Courts of Westminster

in haec verba, &c., in the whole and in every part of them are against the Laws of the Realm, the Right of Property, and the Liberty of the Subjects, and contrary to former resolutions in Parliament, and to the Petition of Right.

(3) 'That the writ following *in haec verba*, &c., and the other writs commonly called the ship writs, are against the laws of the Realm (&c., *ut supra*), and

(4) 'That judgement in the Exchequer in Hampden's case in the matter and substance thereof, and in that it was conceived that Mr. Hampden was any way chargeable, is against the Laws of the Realm, &c., *ut supra*.' [1]

Further, on the motion of Hyde, a Committee of sixteen members was appointed 'to go forthwith to the several judges to know how they were solicited or threatened, and in what manner, and by whom, to give any opinion or judgement concerning ship-money, and they are to go two to a Judge'. Leave was likewise given to this Committee 'to acquaint the Judges what hath been voted this day in the House touching ship-money, and to use their own discretions to ask such questions as shall be material to the matter contained in the order'. Falkland, Hyde, and Sir John Culpepper were among the members appointed to serve. In view of the 'ministry' afterwards formed by these three men the conjunction of their names at this point is significant. As a result of their investigations the House resolved, on the motion of Falkland, to proceed to the impeachment of Lord Keeper Finch. Finch prayed that before matters went further he might be heard at the bar in his own defence. To this request the House, though not without 'great controversy', acceded, and on 21 December the 'great officer of the Law' appeared at the bar. A chair was set for him, and 'when the Speaker told him that his lordship might sit, he made a low obeisance, and laying down the Seal and his hat on the chair made a speech standing and bare-headed'.

The speech, 'elegant and ingenious',[2] and delivered with 'an excellent grace and gesture', was an effective plea

---

[1] Rushworth, iv. 88, and Nalson.　　　　[2] Whitelocke.

for clemency, and it made an obvious impression upon a curiously sympathetic House. 'Many', says Rushworth, 'were exceedingly taken with his eloquence and carriage; and it was a sad sight to see a person of his greatness, parts, and favour to appear in such a posture before such an assembly to plead for his life and fortunes.' But his eloquence did not suffice to save him; the House resolved on his impeachment, and Falkland was appointed to carry up the accusation to the Lords. Finch, however, had no mind for martyrdom. 'The next day he was accused before the Lords, but he got up earlier and escaped into Holland.'[1] The impeachment, of course, went on. Hyde was 'at the request of the Lord Falkland' appointed 'to be assistant unto him for the reading of the articles against the late Lord Keeper'. The articles of impeachment were read and in due course the Lords sent back a message to the Commons that they had taken into consideration the charges against the late Keeper of the Great Seal; but having received intimation that he was not to be found, they had ordered him into safe custody as soon as he could be discovered. Finch remained in exile for eight years, after which, having made abject submission, he was permitted to return to England. On the day after the formal impeachment of Finch before the Lords, the King announced his pleasure that the judges should henceforth hold office *quamdiu se bene gesserint*, and no longer *durante bene placito*. The House of Commons recognized its debt to its Committee, and on 14 January it was ordered by the House that 'thanks be rendered from the House to Mr. St. John and Mr. Whitlock, the Lord Falkland and Mr. Hide for the great service they have performed to the Honour of this House, and good of the Commonwealth, in the transferring the business of the ship-money and the other matters concerning the Liberty and Property of the Subjects and the articles against the late Lord Keeper'.

Once more it may be observed that the main objection of Parliament and people to such fiscal devices as ship-

Change in Judges Tenure

Parliament and the Judges

---

[1] Rushworth.

money was less to the impositions themselves than to the misuse of the judicial bench in connexion with them. They apprehended, dimly it may be, that the question went to the very roots of political society and affected principles which were at once elementary and fundamental. To the leaders of the Long Parliament, as to Bacon, the position of the judges in the State, and their appropriate functions in the general scheme of polity, were matters of first-rate importance. Bacon frankly desired that the Judiciary should be regarded as the handmaid of the Executive. To Hyde, Falkland, and their colleagues such a doctrine was abhorrent. The primary function of the judges was to protect the liberty of the individual, not to enlarge the prerogative of the Crown. 'If they neither deny nor delay us justice . . . the greatest person in this kingdom cannot continue the least violence upon the meanest.' It was the misuse of their function that was condemned; that the judges had 'delivered an opinion and judgement in an extra-judicial manner, that is such as came not within their cognisance, they being judges, and neither philosophers nor politicians'. The judgement may in itself have been perfectly sound in law, and yet at the same time the grounds on which it was based may have been politically mischievous beyond all computation. Clarendon's criticism is eminently to the point. 'The damage and mischief cannot be expressed that the Crown and State sustained by the deserved reproach and infamy that attended the judges by being made use of in this and the like acts of power.' People might well condone some stretching of the Prerogative 'upon an emergent occasion'; what they would not stand was 'apothegms of State urged as elements of law, judges as sharp-sighted as Secretaries of State and in the mysteries of State; judgement of law grounded upon matter of fact of which there was neither inquiry nor proof'.[1]

It was essentially the old question at issue between Bacon and Coke reappearing in a new form. Was there

[1] *Op. cit,.* i. 116.

to be in England 'one law for all', or was the Executive to be strengthened by the admission of the principle of the *droit administratif*? Regarded from this point of view, the 'ship-money question' assumes a fresh importance; it is seen to be not merely a temporary expedient to raise money by extra-parliamentary means but an essential part of a coherent and cunningly compacted scheme. 'Thorough' was impracticable without *tribunaux administratifs*; English judges must be taught to dance to the pipe of the Executive. It would be fantastic to suppose that these considerations in their full significance were present to the minds of the squires and lawyers of the Long Parliament;' but it is indubitable that in their denunciation of ship-money and in their attack upon Lord Keeper Finch they were dimly feeling after a constitutional principle of the first importance.

The Long Parliament and religion   If there was any question on which the members of the Long Parliament felt more strongly than on fiscal abuses, and the attitude of the Judiciary thereto, it was that of religion. And in no matter did they act more promptly. Within three days of its first meeting the House of Commons appointed 'a Committee of the whole House for Religion to meet every Monday at two of the clock'. 'Let religion,' said Rudyard speaking on 7 November, 'be our *primum quaerite*; for all things else are but *et ceteras* to it: . . . Believe it, sir, religion hath been for a long time and still is the great design upon this kingdom.' Speaking on the same occasion Pym laid stress upon the 'Encouragement of Popery', the introduction of innovations in religion, and 'last and greatest grievance', 'the ambitious and corrupt clergy preaching down the laws of God and liberties of the kingdom'. Meanwhile, petitions were pouring in upon the House from every side. Nearly all made the same complaints and the same demands: they denounced the removal of the communion table to the east end, and the railing it in; they complained of the oath and articles imposed upon churchwardens; the false doctrines and irregularities of the clergy. But from the country

came no hint of a demand for revolution in Church government. It was otherwise in Presbyterian London. There
the tide was running strong against Episcopacy. On 11
December the monster petition signed by 15,000 laymen
and 1,640 ministers in London was, amid considerable
tumult, presented to the House. This was the famous
'Root and Branch Petition', praying that 'the government The 'Root
of archbishops and lord bishops, deans and archdeacons, Branch
etc., . . . with all its dependencies, roots and branches, may Petition'
be abolished, and all laws in their behalf made void, and
the government according to God's Word may be rightly
placed among us'.[1] The presentation of this petition
marked the beginning, faint as at first it was, of the definition of parties in Parliament. 'It was well received,' says
Baillie; 'there were many against, and many for the same,'
wrote his colleagues. Clarendon denounced the 'strange
uningenuity and mountebankry that was practised in the
procuring these petitions', but it seems idle to deny that
they represented a considerable body of opinion.

How far did they represent the ecclesiastical opinion
of the nation as a whole? It is not easy to answer that
question. As to the growing unpopularity of the Laudian
régime there can be no doubt; but it is exceedingly difficult,
in view of much conflicting evidence, to gauge public feeling
as to any particular method of reform. Were the people
sick of Episcopacy and panting for Presbyterianism?
Baillie evidently thought so, and wrote to his friends on
18 November 1640 in the highest spirits.

'Episcopacie itself beginning to be cryed down, and a
covenant cried up, and the Liturgie scorned. The toun of
London, and a world of men, minds to present a petition for the
abolition of Bishops, Deanes and all their aperteanances. It is
thought good to delay it till the Parliament have pulled down
Canterburie and some prime Bishops, which they minde to doe
so soon as the King has a little digested the bitterness of his
Lieutenant's censure. Hudge things are here in working: The

---

[1] Text in Rushworth, iv. 93, and accessible to all in Gardiner's
Constitutional Documents, pp. 67–73.

mighty hand of God be about this great work! We hope this
shall be the joyfull harvest of the teares that this manie yeares
has been sawin in this kingdomes. All here are wearie of
Bishops.'

Baillie judged of England—not unnaturally—from London. And Baillie himself becomes less confident as the
months pass on. In December he still believed that the
popular voice favoured the 'root and branch' policy. 'All
are for bringing them (the Bishops) verie low; but who will
not root them clean away are not respected.' Later on
comes the fear lest the action of the Brownists may save
Episcopacy. 'The Separatists are like to be some help to
hold up the Bishops through their impertinencie.' Towards
the end of December the dread increases. 'There was some
fear for those of the new way who are for the Independent
congregations.' By the middle of March the tone of his
reports is becoming distinctly more cautious. 'To propone
the rooting out of the Bishops had been by pluralitie of
voices to have established them.' Clearly Presbyterianism
was not to be rushed through, and it is painful to observe
in this typical Presbyterian an increasing reliance upon the
secular arm. No permanent harm was likely to come to the
cause of God, either from Brownists or Prelatists, 'so long
as the lads about Newcastle sitts still'.

Clarendon and Baillie are of course at opposite poles,
but Clarendon, while not denying the unpopularity of the
Bishops in London—'the sink of all the ill humour of the
kingdom'—bitterly condemns the apathy and weakness
of the Executive at this crisis. 'It had been no hard matter
to have destroyed those seeds and pulled up those plants
which (being) neglected grew up and prospered to a full
harvest of rebellion and treason.' But Clarendon probably
underrates the depth of the feeling against Laud as much
as Baillie exaggerates it.

Attack on the Bishops   In Parliament the tide was running strong, if not against
Episcopacy, at least against the Bishops. The first blow
was aimed at Laud. On 18 December he was committed
to the custody of Black Rod until the charges against him

could be formulated. Two months later (26 February 1640) he was impeached at the bar of the Lords and committed to the Tower, only to issue therefrom three years later to be tried before the Peers for his life. As in Strafford's case, it soon became clear that the impeachment would fail: recourse, therefore, was had to an Ordinance of Attainder, which was eventually passed by the Lords on 4 January 1645. The King's pardon, signed nearly two years earlier, was pleaded in vain, and on the 10th the Archbishop died on the scaffold.

If a martyr be one who voluntarily undergoes the penalty of death for the sake of his opinions, Laud cannot claim the title. Unlike his master, he had no opportunity of saving his life by abandoning his faith. But he was certainly the victim of a cruel murder, judicial only in the sense that it was committed under such pretence of legal forms as were at the moment available. An Act of Attainder required the assent of the King; in the King's absence the Rump of Parliament could legislate only by Ordinance, which had less legal sanction than the Proclamations of the Stuarts. In fact, the Ordinance had, at the moment, little more validity than a resolution of the House of Commons, for the judicial proceedings before the House of Lords were a farce, and in the end the remnant of that House yielded only to the intimidation of the mob.

Execution of Laud

The London mob, always strongly Presbyterian in its sympathies, clamoured loudly for the blood of the man who to them was anti-Christ. The Solemn League and Covenant had made the same party for the moment dominant in Parliament. 'Little Canterbury' could look for no mercy from them; and he received none. Posterity has vindicated the purity of his aims if not the wisdom of his policy, but he was indeed 'unfit for the times'.

The rancour with which Laud was pursued by his enemies in Parliament was extended to his disciples. 'Many doctors and divines', writes May, 'that had been most busy in promoting the late Church innovations were then questioned and committed.' A great popular demonstration, on the other hand, marked the return from exile of Prynne, Bastwick, and Burton. The judgements given against them by the Court of High Commission were declared by the Commons to be illegal, unjust, and opposed to the liberty of the subject; and large damages, £5,000 to £6,000 apiece, were voted to them, to be levied upon Laud and the other High Commissioners who had voted against them. Clarendon broadly hints that the 'vindication of the distressed ministers' was a piece of skilful stage management. 'This insurrection and frenzy of the people,' he writes, 'was an effect of great industry and policy to try and publish the temper of the people.' Be that as it may, the results were indisputable—the pulpits were delivered over to 'the schismatical and silenced preachers'; the presses began to pour forth 'the most invective seditions and scandalous pamphlets'; the King's judges and the Council ceased to exercise any jurisdiction.

Signs of reaction

Yet the more discerning could perceive signs of a reaction against the extremists. The 'Root and Branch Petition' had alarmed the moderate Episcopalians.

'Doubtless', said the Puritan D'Ewes,[1] 'the Government of the Church of God by godly, zealous, and preaching bishops hath been most ancient, and I should reverence such a bishop in the next degree to a King. But I protest in the presence of God that if matters in religion had gone on twenty years longer as they have done of late years, then would not in the issue so much as the face of religion have continued amongst us but all should have been overwhelmed with idolatry, superstition, ignorance, profaneness and heresy. As I allowed ancient and godly bishops, so I disliked their baronies and temporal honours and employments.'

Further evidence of the growth of this moderate party is afforded by the presentation on 23 January 1641 of the 'Ministers' Petition and Remonstrance'.[2] This demanded not revolution, but reform, and on it was founded the sub-

[1] Quoted by Shaw, *History of the English Church during the Civil War*, i. 17.
[2] See Shaw, *op. cit.*, i. 24, for Summary of its 'near four score heads.'

sequent proposal for the removal of the bishops from secular employment in general and the House of Lords in particular.

On 8 February 1641 the two great petitions—the 'Root and Branch Petition' and the 'Ministers' Remonstrance'— were taken into consideration by the House, and one of the most important debates of the session ensued. Of many noteworthy speeches, perhaps, the most noteworthy was Falkland. Its keynote was a statesmanlike avoidance of extremes. He did not spare the Arminian bishops—those who have been 'the destruction of unity under pretence of uniformity', nor did he deny their responsibility for the outbreak of rebellion; but he candidly distinguished between the men and their order, and his essential conservatism comes out indisputably. It was not the part of statesmanship 'to abolish upon a few days' debate an order which hath lasted in most Churches these sixteen hundred years, and in all from Christ to Calvin'.

Falkland was preceded in the debate by Rudyard and Digby, and followed by Fiennes, Bagshaw, Harbottle, Grimston, and others. Rushworth describes the debate as 'great and tedious', but the speeches may be read at length in his collection. In the main the debate would seem to have been maintained on a high plane of seriousness and excellence. Rudyard favoured the scheme of limited Episcopacy which afterwards took shape in the Lords' Bill on Church Reform. Digby argued for the reform but against the abolition of episcopacy. Fiennes was frankly Presbyterian in tone. 'Until the ecclesiastical government be something of another twist and be more assimilated to that of the Commonwealth, I fear the ecclesiastical government will be no good neighbour unto the civil.' With the exception of Pleydell's there is no reported speech which could possibly have satisfied the Arminian party. But the ultimate issue of the debate was by no means disconcerting to the moderate Episcopalians. The general sense of the House was clearly in favour of a reform of the 'excrescences' of Episcopacy, but against the

Debate on Religion

destruction of the institution itself. In the event, the
House resolved

'that the Committee of twenty-four with the addition of these
six—Sir Thos. Roe, Mr. Holles, Mr. Palmer, Mr. Holborne, Mr.
Fiennes, Sir H. Vane—do take into consideration that part of
the Ministers' Remonstrance that has been read, and the
petition of the inhabitants in and about the city of London,
and other petitions of the like nature that have been read, to
prepare heads out of them for the consideration of the House,
the House reserving to itself the main point of Episcopacy for
to take it into their consideration in due time.'

The result may be described as a compromise, but there
can be no doubt that the balance of victory inclined towards
those who, following the lead of Falkland, declined to play
into the hands of the enemies of the established order in the
Church. Episcopacy was not, for the moment at least, to be
flung into the crucible. Baillie's comment reflects, accurately enough, the existing position. 'All are for the
erecting of a kind of Presbyteries, and for bringing down
the Bishops in all things, spiritual and temporal, so low
as can be with any subsistence: but their utter abolition,
which is the only aim of the most Godlie, is the knott of
the whole question: we must have it cutted by the axe of
prayer; God, we trust will doe it.' Baillie plainly is still
hopeful, but no longer confident.

In March things moved on faster. Bills were introduced
for the ejection of the bishops from the House of Lords and
the Privy Council, and for disabling any clergyman from
being in the Commission of the Peace or performing any
secular functions. The first of these—popularly known as
the First Bishops [Exclusion] Bill—was read a first time
on 30 March 1641, and finally passed the House of Commons on 1 May.

The House of Lords and the Bishops   The Lords, however, drastically amended the Bill. They
agreed to the exclusion of the clergy generally from civil
functions, but they declined to approve so revolutionary a
change in the composition of their own House as the
exclusion of the Bishops, the most ancient element in the

Second Chamber, would involve. Nevertheless their attitude was not unconciliatory, and on 27 May they appointed a Committee to confer with the Commons on the Bill. The Commons, on their part, determined to prepare a statement of 'reasons' on behalf of it.

In view of the intrinsic importance of a question still unsolved those 'reasons' may be quoted in full:

'Reasons of the House of Commons why bishops ought not to have votes in the House of Peers:

'(1) Because it is a very great hindrance to the discharge of their ministerial function.

'(2) Because they do vow and undertake at their ordination when they enter into holy orders that they will give themselves wholly to that vocation.

'(3) Because councils and canons in several ages do forbid them to meddle with secular affairs.

'(4) Because the twenty-four bishops have a dependence on the two archbishops, and because of their canonical obedience to them.

'(5) Because they are but for life, and therefore are not fit to have legal power over the honours, inheritances, lives, and liberties of others.

'(6) Because of bishops' dependency and expectancy of translation to places of greater profit.

'(7) That several bishops have of late much encroached upon the consciences and liberties of the subject, and they and their successors will be much encouraged still to encroach, and the subject will be much discouraged from complaining against such encroachment, if twenty-six of that order be to be judges upon those complaints. The same reason extends to their legislative power in any bill to pass for the regulation of their power upon any emergent inconveniences by it.

'(8) Because the whole number of them is interested to maintain the jurisdiction of bishops, which hath been found so dangerous to the three kingdoms that Scotland hath utterly abolished it, and multitudes in England and Ireland have petitioned against it.

'(9) Because the bishops, being Lords of Parliament, it setteth too great a distance between them and the rest of their brethren in the ministry, which occasioneth pride in them, discontent in others, and disquiet in the Church.

'To their having votes a long time. *Answer:* If inconvenient, time and usage are not to be considered law makers. Some abbots voted as anciently as bishops, yet they were taken away. That for the bishops' certificate for plenary of benefice and loyalty of marriage the bill extends not to them. For the secular jurisdictions of the Dean of Westminster, the Bishops of Durham and Ely and the Archbishop of York, which they are to execute in their own persons the former reasons show the inconveniences therein. For their temporal courts and jurisdiction, which are executed by their temporal officers, the Bill doth not concern them.'

In spite of these formulated 'reasons' the Lords remained unconvinced, and on 8 June the Bill was rejected on the third reading.

'Root and Branch' Bill

Meanwhile the bolt had fallen. On the very day on which the Lords held their conference with the Commons (27 May), a Bill was introduced into the Lower House 'for the utter abolishing and taking away of all archbishops, bishops, their chancellors, commissaires, deans, deans and chapters, archdeacons, prebendaries, chanters and canons, and all other their under officers'. The nominal sponsor for the Bill was Sir Edward Dering, the weakly consequential member for Kent, but he himself tells us that the Bill was 'pressed into his hands' by Sir A. Hazelrig, who similarly received it from Sir H. Vane and Oliver Cromwell. The leadership of the extremists was already falling into the hands of Cromwell and the younger Vane.

Nobody seems to have expected the 'Root and Branch Bill' to pass into law; but there are various theories as to the object with which it was brought in. Some hold that it was merely intended to frighten the Lords into acceptance of the less radical proposal; but the dates negative this view. Others suppose that the purpose was to test the feeling of the House of Commons. Be this as it may, the reception of the Bill was unexpectedly favourable. Mr. Hyde indeed 'moved with great warmth that the Bill might not be read', and he adds that 'the rejecting it was earnestly urged by very many'. Yet the measure excited, it would seem, little general interest in the House; the extreme Puritans mustered in force, but the attendance in Committee was so thin, especially after dinner, that Falkland used mockingly to say that 'they who hated bishops hated them worse than the devil: and that they who loved them did not love them so well as their dinner'. Notwithstanding Hyde's ingenious obstruction, facilitated by his having been put into the Chair in the Committee on the Bill, it made considerable progress in Committee, but after the King's departure for Scotland it was virtually dropped; and when Parliament reassembled after the recess (20 October 1641) it was abandoned.

On the following day (21 October) the Second Bishops Bill was introduced; in two days it had passed through all its stages in the Commons, and was read a first time in the Lords on 23 October. There the matter rested for two months, and the Lords showed no disposition to resume consideration of it. But at the end of December the bishops—or a party of them—played into the hands of their enemies. Feeling was running high against them in London, and more than once bishops had been mobbed on their way to the House of Lords. On 30 December twelve bishops, swayed, as Clarendon puts it, 'by the pride and insolence of that anti-prelatical Archbishop' (Williams of York), entered a formal protest against 'all laws, orders, votes, resolutions and determinations, as in themselves null and of none effect', passed in their absence since 27 December, or hereafter to be passed 'during the time of this their forced and violent absence'. The protest may, considering the circumstances, have been indiscreet, but it afforded no ground whatever for prosecution. The temper of both Houses was, however, curiously aroused; the twelve bishops were impeached for high treason and were committed to the Tower. Next day the Commons reminded the Lords of the neglected Bill. The Lords gave it a second reading on 4 February 1642, and a third, under protest from the Bishops of Winchester, Worcester, and Rochester, on the 5th. On 14 February, to the dismay of Clarendon, it

The Second Bishops [Exclusion] Bill

received the Royal assent. It was the last Act of real
importance to which the King gave his assent before the
outbreak of the Civil War.

To this step he was persuaded, according to Clarendon,
by Sir John Culpepper; but Culpepper's arguments were
warmly seconded by the Queen, who seems to have been
afraid that, if the concession were not made, her journey to
the Continent might be stopped.

The Bishops Exclusion Act, seriously as it affected
the fabric of the State, did not in itself essentially touch the
fabric of the Church. The 'Root and Branch Bill' did. That
Bill, however, was for the moment dropped. The reason
for the abandonment is somewhat obscure. Had the Bill
served its purpose? Did Pym think that enough had been
done? Was he afraid of consolidating the Royalist party?
Were the extremists satisfied for the time being with
exclusion? Were they too fully occupied with other things?
All these reasons may well have been present to the minds
of the leaders. But the essential reason was that they were
not prepared with an alternative.

It requires some little effort to enable the critic of to-day
to grasp the situation. The 'root and branch' reformer of
to-day is, as regards the ecclesiastical establishment,
merely destructive. He is content to sever the connexion
of Church and State, and to leave it to 'the Churches' to
rebuild the spiritual edifices as they will. Not so the 'root
and branch' reformer of 1641. He still deemed it incumbent
upon him to rebuild. The fibres of Church and State were
too closely interwoven to permit the passing of an Act
simply destructive in its operation. It was easy enough,
for example, to abolish, by a stroke of the pen, the Ecclesiastical Courts: but what was to be put in their place?
Parliament might get rid of bishops and deans, but some
provision would still have to be made by the State for the
government of the Church. This is the essential point of
difference between the 'root and branch' man of 1641 and
the 'liberationist' of to-day. The former had to deal with
the Church; the latter is concerned with the churches.

Much as men might then differ among themselves as to the particular form of ecclesiastical organization which should represent the State in its spiritual aspect, most, if not all, were agreed in the passionate conviction that such a representation was essential to the body politic. After the first Civil War the Independent ideal forged, indeed, more rapidly to the front, but as late as 1645 the main point at issue between the 'out and out Presbyterians', like Baillie, and the 'lame Erastian lawyers', such as Selden, was whether the State should be subordinate to the church, or the Church to the State. Vane's proposal, when the Commons were in Committee on the 'Root and Branch Bill', not less than the Bill on Church Reform [1] read twice in the Lords, made it clear that had bishops been 'extirpated' Parliament would still have felt it necessary to provide for the performance of many of their functions.

The fact is that the dominant sentiment of the Long Parliament as regards the Church was neither Episcopalian, Presbyterian, nor Independent; it was Erastian. Amid infinite variety of opinions, two conclusions more and more clearly emerged: first, that there must be some form of ecclesiastical organization; and, secondly, that whatever the form might be, its government must be strictly controlled by Parliament. It was this Erastian temper which in the autumn of 1641 secured for the King the adherence of the High Episcopalians, in 1642 that of the Broad Churchmen, and in 1646 that of the Presbyterians. Arminians like Clarendon, liberal Churchmen like Falkland, and Presbyterians like Baillie, were equally opposed, though on different grounds, to the dictation of a Parliamentary majority in the spiritual sphere. Yet no party was prepared to accept, perhaps none perceived, the only ogical alternative.

[1] See Gardiner, *Documents*, p. 94, for text of this interesting proposal.

VII. PYM AND THE GRAND REMONSTRANCE

The Problem of the Executive

ON the 8th of November 1641 Pym presented to the
House of Commons the *Grand Remonstrance*. Though
primarily intended as a manifesto against the Crown and
an apology for the conduct of Parliament, that memorable
document possesses another and more permanent significance. Admirably conceived to promote its immediate
purpose, it owes its unique place in the literature of Political
Science to the fact that it enshrines the embryonic idea of
that species of Democracy which is now known throughout
the world as 'Responsible Government'.

How to retain the institution of Monarchy and simultaneously to transfer Sovereignty to a King-in-Parliament,
how, while permitting the Legislature to control the Executive, to make the Executive strong enough for the efficient
conduct of the daily business of State—how, in a word, to
reconcile strength with freedom in the machinery of
Government, this was the central problem of constructive
statesmanship in the seventeenth century. The solution
was ultimately discovered in the slow and gradual evolution of a Cabinet under the presidency of a Prime Minister.
That evolution had only, in fact, reached the middle stage
when the century closed. But the germ is discoverable in
the *Grand Remonstrance*. The genesis of that document is,
therefore, a matter of supreme interest to the student of
Political Institutions.

When Parliament, on 9 September, adjourned for a brief
recess it could look back on a ten months' session of solid
achievements. It had scrapped the whole machinery of
'Thorough' and had brought to justice the two chief
engineers. Strafford was in his grave; Canterbury was
caged. Once for all it had been decided that whatever
form the Government of England might in future assume
it would not be personal monarchy. By putting on the

Statute book the Triennial Bill and the Bill against the dissolution of Parliament without its own consent, the Legislature had taken every possible precaution against even a temporary intermission of parliamentary control. England was not, in respect of representative institutions, going the way of France and Spain. But though the destructive work had been done thoroughly the much more difficult task of reconstruction had not been begun. The slate was now clean: what were the statesmen of the Long Parliament going to write on it?

A strong Executive is the primary need of every civilized society. No political architects ever perceived this truth more clearly than the group of singularly wise and prescient statesmen who drafted the Constitution of the United States of America. They perceived also that a strong Executive is not inconsistent with, nay, is peculiarly indispensable to, a democratic Constitution. *The problem of the Executive*

'There is an idea,' writes Alexander Hamilton in the *Federalist*, 'which is not without its advocates that a vigorous Executive is inconsistent with the genius of Republican Government. The well-wishers of this species of Government must at least hope that the supposition is destitute of foundation since they can never admit its truth without at the same time admitting the condemnation of their own principles. Energy in the Executive is a leading character in the definition of good government. It is essential to the protection of the community against foreign attacks; it is not less essential to the steady administration of the laws; to the protection of property against those irregular and high-handed combinations which sometimes interrupt the ordinary course of justice; to the security of liberty against the enterprises and assaults of ambition, of faction, and of anarchy. . . . The ingredients which constitute energy are, first, unity; secondly, duration; thirdly, an adequate provision for its support; fourthly, competent powers.'[1]

How was the England of the seventeenth century to obtain such an Executive?

[1] *The Federalist*, No. lxx.

Throughout the greater part of world history the problem was solved by the institution of hereditary monarchy. The King was the actual ruler of the State. In his own person he combined, in primitive days, the functions of lawmaker, judge, administrator, leader of the host in war, supreme lord of the soil, and master of his people in peace. England afforded no exception to this rule. The gradual evolution of an administrative system, the setting up of Courts of Justice, and not least the calling of a Parliament, relieved the King by degrees of some of his functions. But he remained solely responsible.

Personal Monarchy   Down to the death of Queen Elizabeth the strength of the Executive had depended wholly on the personality of the reigning Sovereign. A strong King meant a strong government; a weak King exposed the country to all the evils inseparable, as Hamilton perceived, from a weak Executive. The *Apology* of 1604 makes it clear, however, that in the opinion of Parliament the era of Personal Monarchy was, for England, at an end. It may well be that not one of the men who assented to that momentous declaration had formed any clear idea of possible alternatives; but the document itself could never have been presented to a King who was intended in future to exercise personal supremacy over the government. If, however, the King was henceforward to reign but not any longer to rule, who was to rule in his stead? If the King was no longer to be Sovereign, in whom was Sovereignty to rest? In Parliament? Or in the people? In either case, who was in practice to exercise it? If the Judges were no longer to hold merely at the good pleasure of the Crown, what was to be the relation between the Judicature and the Executive, the Judicature and the Legislature? Similarly in the ecclesiastical sphere. It was easy to imprison Arminian Bishops and clergy, to abolish the Court of High Commission and to compensate those who had suffered under its arbitrary verdicts; but how was the Church to be governed, and in what relation was it to stand to the State? If Convocation was to be abolished, was Parliament to assume

the sole responsibility for ordering the Services of the
Church? Or was the historic system of the English Church
to give place to an alien hierarchical system imported
from Geneva? If so, was the Genevan system to have
coercive jurisdiction over Anglicans and Independents as
well as over Presbyterians? Our immediate concern is not,
however, with the Government of the State, nor with the
position of the Judges in the Polity, but with the constitution of the Executive and its relation to the other organs
of Government, legislative and judicial. The problem
which confronted the Long Parliament has never been
better stated than in a work, now undeservedly neglected,
by Dr. William Smyth.

'Control,' he writes, 'executive power must be lodged somewhere; and the question is not as the friends of liberty sometimes suppose, how the executive power can be made sufficiently
weak but how it can be made sufficiently strong, and yet
brought within the influence of the criticism of the community,
i.e. in other words, how it can secure the people from themselves,
and yet be rendered properly alive to feelings of sympathy and
respect for them. . . . This indeed is a problem in the management of mankind not easy to be solved; but it is the real
problem, the proper problem to exercise the patriotism of wise
and virtuous men.' [1]

That was the problem presented to English statesmen in
the seventeenth century, and immediately in the winter
of 1641-2. The Long Parliament in the preceding twelve
months had accomplished much, but their work had been
mainly destructive. The more difficult task of reconstruction lay immediately ahead of them. 'Pigmies,' said
Mirabeau, 'can destroy; it takes giants to build.' The
Pyms and Hampdens were no pigmies: but they had yet
to prove themselves giants.

Pym has been described as the 'English counterpart of   Pym's
Mirabeau'.[2] But he was much more than that. He, more   leadership
than any other single man, save Sir Robert Walpole,

[1] *Lectures on Modern History*, Cambridge, 1839, ii.495 (Bohn's edition).
[2] Goldwin Smith, *Three English Statesmen*, p. 16.

impressed on the English Constitution its permanent form. In a long line of great parliamentarians he was the first and perhaps the greatest: a greater than Walpole, since the times of Charles I were far more critical than those of George I; a greater than Sir Robert Peel, as Stuart days were more difficult than those of Victoria. Not so accomplished an orator as Eliot, Pym far excelled him as a parliamentary debater, as a tactician, as a leader of men. Not endowed with the mellow philosophical insight of a Falkland, he could pierce remorselessly into the heart of a political situation as Falkland never did. The situation called for such a man in the autumn of 1641.

The King's journey to Scotland

A month before Parliament adjourned, the King, despite the urgent entreaty of Parliament, had set out for his northern kingdom. In this journey Parliament found fresh ground for the suspicions which for the last six months at least had never been long absent from their minds. Throughout that period their debates had been conducted under the constant dread that the King would throw himself upon the army and effect a *coup d'état*. The precise truth as to successive 'Army Plots', with reports of which Pym periodically alarmed the House, is still a matter for conjecture. Fortunately it is not essential to the immediate purpose to attempt a disentanglement of the confusion. All that need be said is that, as the archives are being gradually compelled to reveal the secrets of all hearts, it becomes increasingly clear that Pym's information, though rarely precise, was in the main substantially accurate. We may indeed take it for granted that had the King and Queen seen a favourable opportunity for the employment of force against Parliament they would not have scrupled to use it. What is more difficult to appreciate is the moral guilt which such action would have involved. That it would have been politically suicidal is indisputable, but why it should be more morally reprehensible for the King to employ the English army to coerce Parliament, than for Parliament to employ the Scotch army to coerce the King, is one of the many cases in which the orthodox historians have confused simple issues. It is, however, none the less important to remember that most of the work of the Long Parliament was done under the shadow of this fear.

When Parliament reassembled on 20 October it became immediately apparent that Pym and his friends of the extreme left had made up their minds to provoke an open rupture with the King.

Nor is it difficult to appreciate their reasons. The recess had witnessed a distinct and increasing reaction in the King's favour. Such reactions are common phenomena in the history of popular movements, and we need be at no special pains to account for the reaction with which Pym was confronted on the reassembling of Parliament. None the less it is important to understand the reasons for the movement of opinion in the King's favour. Among these the most potent was probably the violence of the Parliamentary attack upon the Church. Even the Puritan May admits that 'if Parliament had not so far drawn religion into their cause it might have sped better'. The people had no love for the Arminian bishops, and had a wholesome dread of the jurisdiction of their courts; but there is no evidence that they desired a radical change of system. Still less is it clear that they were ready to embrace Presbyterianism. The bitter Presbyterianism of London gave it an entirely disproportionate influence upon the proceedings in Parliament; outside London there was no enthusiasm for the Genevan system, except perhaps in Lancashire. On the other hand, there was a growing disgust at the outrages which were perpetrated in the churches. Clarendon declares that these outrages were actually instigated by the Parliamentary majority, and even May admits that Parliament did nothing to restrain them, being 'either too much busied in variety of affairs, or perchance too much fearing the loss of a considerable party, whom they might have need of against a real and potent enemy'.

Another reason for reaction was the pressure of Parlia-

Royalist reaction

Heavy taxation

mentary taxation—imposed largely for the support of their Scotch allies. For eleven years the mass of the people had been virtually ignorant of taxation; individuals suffered, but the country at large escaped. The revival of Parliamentary sessions of course brought a renewal of regular taxation, a species of 'constitutionalism' which could not be expected to enhance the value of popular institutions in the eyes of the taxpayers. Finally, things looked hopeful for peace. The King, contrary to expectation, had passed through the armies encamped in the North without an attempt to tamper with their loyalty. Those armies were now happily disbanded; the Scots had recrossed the Tweed before the end of September, and the English troops had dispersed.

Was there not, then, a reasonable chance that the quarrel might still be composed, and that the King might be induced loyally to accept the position of a constitutional sovereign? So far as the country knew, his conduct, since Parliament met, had been irreproachable. He had refused nothing that Parliament asked. He had assented to the revolutionary proposal that the existing Parliament should not be dissolved without its own consent; he had not withheld the sacrifice of his ablest and most devoted counsellor. More than that, he had been anxious to call to his counsels the leaders of the party which was predominant in Parliament. Something in the nature of a modern 'ministry' might have been formed, including Lord Saye, Lord Essex, Denzil Holles, and Lord Bedford, with Pym himself as Chancellor of the Exchequer. No stronger proof of good faith could have been given by the King, and but for the death—ever to be lamented—of Lord Bedford, such a ministry would probably have been formed in the spring of 1641. Is it wonderful, in view of such considerations, that the country should, in the early autumn, have begun to settle down, or that men should have turned hopeful eyes towards the dawn of a brighter day?

The 'Incident'   It was this growing confidence in the King's good faith which Pym set himself steadfastly to combat. In this endeavour he was powerfully assisted by the current of events in Scotland and Ireland. Parliament had no sooner reassembled than Pym laid before it information as to the existence of a widespread conspiracy in the royalist interest. In the midst of the debate letters arrived from Hampden, who was still in attendance on the King in Edinburgh, containing news of the 'Incident'. This was a plot, disclosed on 11 October, for the assassination of Argyle and Hamilton. No evidence has ever been produced to connect the King with this murderous design, but the news was sufficiently alarming to enable Pym to carry his point. Falkland and Hyde ridiculed the idea that danger could arise to England from an attack upon the Covenanter leaders in Scotland, and proposed that the business of Scotland should be left in the hands of the Scottish Parliament. But the fears of the Commons were aroused; resolutions were adopted for immediate conference with the Lords on the safety of the kingdom, and it was ordered that an express messenger be sent to the Committee of both Houses in Scotland to let them know 'that the Parliament takes well their advertisement and that they conceive the peace of that kingdom concerns the good of this'. The Lords immediately agreed that a hundred men from the trained bands of Westminster should be called up to guard the two Houses by day and night.

Ten days later news reached London of the outbreak of the Irish Rebellion. The wildest reports were quickly in circulation. Rumour had it that almost the whole Protestant population of Ulster had been put to the sword: Clarendon declares that 40,000 or 50,000 were murdered, and May puts it at 200,000. The lowest estimates were largely in excess of the truth. The news, however, was nothing less than a godsend to Pym. That the King had long been in negotiation with the Irish Lords was notorious: what more natural than to suppose that the explosion was due to his intrigues? Historical research has acquitted the King of all direct complicity in the rebellion, but as to the

The Irish
Rebellion

precise truth of the details we are not for the moment concerned.[1] It is sufficient to note the effect of the news upon the political situation in England. Pym had long been anxious that Parliament should formulate and publish a manifesto against the King. His opportunity had come.

On 4 November Parliament, despite the warnings of Culpepper and Falkland, decided to accept the offer made by the Scottish Parliament to provide 1,000 men for the suppression of the Irish Rebellion. Anything more calculated to pour oil upon the flames in Ireland can hardly be conceived; but Pym was playing his game with consummate skill, and under repeated shocks administered by him Parliament was giving way to panic. On 5 November Pym again startled the House by a declaration which alike from the point of view of immediate results and of ultimate significance can only be described as epoch-making. No man was readier than himself, he declared, 'to engage his estate, his person, his life for the suppression of the Irish Rebellion, but all that they did would be in vain as long as the King gave ear to the counsellors about him. His Majesty must be told that Parliament finds evil counsellors to have been the cause of all these troubles in Ireland; and that unless the Sovereign will be pleased to free himself from such, and take only counsellors whom the kingdom can confide in, Parliament will hold itself absolved from giving assistance in the matter'. In these words Pym announced the central point of the scheme of reform to be subsequently embodied in the Grand Remonstrance.

The Grand Remonstrance The House seems instantly to have apprehended the significance of the declaration. A scene of great excitement ensued. Amid shouts of 'Well moved, well moved', Hyde rose to oppose Pym's motion on the ground that by such an instruction 'we should, as it were, menace the King'. Pym was obliged for the moment to give way, but three days later (8 November) he again proposed his resolution and carried it by a majority of 151 to 110. In its later and amended form the resolution declared that the King should

[1] But cf. *infra*, c. xiii.

be asked 'to employ only such counsellors and ministers as should be approved by his Parliament; failing which Parliament would be compelled to take measures on their own part for the defence of Ireland and their own liberties, and to commend those aids and contributions which this great necessity shall require to the custody and disposing of such persons of honour and fidelity as we have cause to confide in'.

On the same day the Grand Remonstrance was presented to the House.

Prefixed to the Remonstrance proper was a Petition which, after tendering a welcome to the King on his safe return from Scotland, referred to the false scandals and imputations cunningly insinuated and dispersed among the people to blemish and disgrace the proceedings in this Parliament, and attributed them largely to 'the subtile practice of the Jesuits and other engineers and factors for Rome'. To the same dangerous influence Parliament attributed the Scottish war, 'the increase of jealousies' between the King and his 'most obedient subjects', the 'violent distraction and interruption of this Parliament', and 'the insurrection of the Papists' and massacre of the Protestants in Ireland. These things compelled Parliament, 'without the least intention to lay any blemish upon your Royal person', to issue a declaration on the state of the Kingdom, and to petition the King:

Preliminary Petition

(1) to deprive the Bishops of their votes in Parliament and of their coercive powers, and by removing 'some oppressions and unnecessary ceremonies by which divers weak consciences have been scrupled', to unite all loyal Protestants against the Papists;

(2) to remove evil counsellors from the Council and replace them by such 'as Parliament may have cause to confide in'; and

(3) not to alienate any of the forfeited and escheated lands in Ireland, but to retain them for the support of the Crown and the payment of the expenses of the (Irish) war.

Of the 204 clauses of the Remonstrance itself, the first 190
consisted mainly of an historical recital of the 'pressing
miseries and calamities, the various distempers and dis-
orders' which had marked the reign of the present King.
Among other topics the recital touched on the evil designs
of Papists and Arminians; their baneful influence on
foreign policy and on the relation between the Crown and
Parliament; on the breaches of parliamentary privileges;
the persecution of Protestants; on unparliamentary taxation; on monopolies; on the denial of justice and the
iniquities of the Prerogative Courts; on the attack on
Scottish religion and liberties; on the oppressions of the
Arminian clergy, and so forth. The Remonstrance then
(clauses 105–58) summarized the work so far accomplished
by the Long Parliament, and after referring to Army Plots
and the intrigues of 'venomous counsellors', proceeded
with its substantive proposals. These included the calling
of an Ecclesiastical Synod to draft proposals for a reformation of religion and report thereon to Parliament; a
measure for reforming and purging Oxford and Cambridge;
a standing Parliament Commission to watch the activities
of the Papists; above all, the appointment of ministers in
whom Parliament can confide.

Germ of the Cabinet

Here we have the kernel of the document; here most
distinctly can we trace the influence of the constructive
genius of Pym. The method of procedure by impeachment
was hopelessly ineffective and palpably obsolete; and the
reason is clearly stated in § 198: 'It may often fall out
that the Commons may have just cause to take exceptions
at some men for being councillors, and yet not charge
those men with crimes, for there be grounds of diffidence
which lie not in proof. There are others which, though they
may be proved, yet are not legally criminal.' Known
favourers of Papists; apologists for 'great offenders' questioned in Parliament; contemners and libellers of Parliament; agents of Popish foreign Kings; corrupt purchasers
of public offices—'for all these and divers others we may
have great reason to be earnest with His Majesty, not to

put his great affairs into such hands, though we may be unwilling to proceed against them in any legal way of charge or impeachment.'

The only solution then of the difficulties of the situation is for the King to 'have cause to be in love with good counsel and good men'.

Several clauses of the Remonstrance were debated *seriatim*, often with great heat, between 8 and 20 November. On the latter date the Remonstrance was laid upon the table in its complete form. Thereupon Pym, yielding to the pressure of Falkland and his friends, fixed the final debate for Monday, 22 November. The extremists were disgusted at the delay. Cromwell, 'who at that time was little taken notice of',[1] asked Falkland as they left the House 'why he would have it put off, for that day would quickly have determined it'? He answered: 'There would not have been time enough, for sure it would take some debate.' 'A very sorry one,' retorted Cromwell. 'They supposing,' adds Clarendon, 'by the computation they had made, that very few would oppose it.'

Monday, the 22nd of November, was one of the most fateful days in the history of the Long Parliament, and indeed in the history of England. The debate, contrary to Cromwell's expectation, was long and fierce. Starting 'about nine of the clock in the morning, it continued all that day; and candles being called for when it grew dark . . . the debate continued, till after it was twelve of the clock with much passion'. Hyde himself led off and was immediately followed by Falkland. 'Lord Falkland (says Forster) rose immediately after Hyde, and, as his wont was, spoke with great passion in his warmth and earnestness, his thin high-pitched voice breaking into a scream, and his little, spare, slight frame trembling with eagerness. He ridiculed the pretension set up in the Declaration to claim any right of approval over the councillors whom the King should name; as if priest and clerk should divide nomination and approval between them. He denounced it as

Debate on the Remonstrance

Falkland's speech

---

[1] Clarendon, iv. 42.

unjust that the concealing of delinquents should be cast upon the King. He said (forgetting a former speech of his own going directly to this point) that it was not true to allege that Laud's party in the Church were in league with Rome, for that Arminians agreed no more with Papists than with Protestants. And, with the power to make laws, why should they resort to declarations? Only where no law was available were they called to substitute orders and ordinances to command or forbid. Reminding them of the existing state of Ireland, and of the many disturbances in England, he warned them that it was of a very dangerous consequence at that time to set out any remonstrance: at least such a remonstrance as this, containing many harsh expressions. Above all, it was dangerous to declare what they intended to do hereafter, as that they would petition his Majesty to take advice of his parliament in the choice of his privy council; and it was of the very worst example to make such allusion as that wherein they declared that already they had committed a bill to take away bishops' votes. He pointed out the injustice of imputing to the bishops generally the description of the Scotch War as *bellum episcopale*, which he asserted had been so used by only one of them. He very hotly condemned the expression of "bringing in idolatry", which he characterized as a charge of a high crime against all the bishops in the land, and he denounced it as a manifest contradiction and absurdity that after reciting, as they had indeed sufficient cause to do, the many good laws passed by a parliament of which bishops and Popish lords were component members, they should end by declaring that while bishops and Popish lords continued to sit in parliament no good laws could be made.'[1]

Pym's reply   Dering followed Falkland in his opposition; Rudyard warmly approved the narrative portion of the Remonstrance, but objected 'to what he would call the pro-

---

[1] Forster, *Grand Remonstrance*, p. 287. Forster's account is obviously coloured by his own sympathies; but it is skilfully compiled from the notes of Verney and D'Ewes.

phetical part'. Pym's powerful reply was addressed, with
true debating instinct, to Falkland; but neither now nor
at any time during the last weeks did he lose hold of the
vital clause of the Remonstrance. 'We have suffered so
much by counsellors of the King's choosing that we desire
him to advise with us about it.' Many speakers followed
Pym, and not until after midnight was the question at last
put. On the final division the Remonstrance was carried The
by 159 votes to 148. Both Clarendon and Whitelock division
declared that the Puritans wore down their opponents by
sheer physical endurance, and Rudyard compared the
result to the 'verdict of a starved jury'. But in view of
the fact that large numbers of members refused to return
to Westminster for the autumn session, the division was a
large one, and there is no reason to suppose that the
Royalists were inferior in endurance to their opponents.

Even now the fight was not ended. The numbers were Scene in
no sooner announced than Peard jumped up and moved the House
that the manifesto should be printed. A scene of un-
paralleled confusion followed, which, but for Hampden's
tact, might well have ended in a hand-to-hand fight.
Palmer moved that the clerk should take down the names
of the opponents of the Declaration with a view to ultimate
protest. 'All, all,' shouted Hyde and his friends. 'All,
all,' re-echoed from all sides of the House. 'Some,' says
D'Ewes,[1] 'waved their hats over their heads, and others
took their swords in their scabbards out of their belts, and
held them by the pummels in their hands, setting the lower
part on the ground; so, as if God had not prevented it,
there was very great danger that mischief might have been
done.' Sir Philip Warwick recalls with even more picturesque imagery his recollection of the famous scene: 'I
thought we had all sat in the valley of the shadow of
death, for we, like Joab's and Abner's young men, had
catcht at each others locks, and sheathed our swords in
each others bowels, had not the sagacity and great calm-
ness of Mr. Hambden by a short speech prevented it'.[2]

[1] *Ap.* Forster, p. 324.   [2] *Memoirs*, p. 202.

The House rose 'just when the clock struck two the ensuing morning', after deciding by 124 to 101 that the Declaration should 'not be printed without the particular order of the House'. As the members hurried out of the House Falkland paused to inquire sarcastically of Cromwell 'whether there had been a debate'? To which Cromwell answered 'that he would take his word another time': and whispered him in the ear with some asseveration 'that if the Remonstrance had been rejected he would have sold all he had the next morning, and never have seen England more; and he knew there were many other honest men of the same resolution'. 'So near,' adds Clarendon in relating the story, 'was the poor kingdom at that time to its deliverance.'

Case for and against the Remonstrance No apology is needed for having described in considerable detail the circumstances attendant upon the passing of the Grand Remonstrance. In the history of the rebellion it marks the parting of the ways. At this point every student of the period is compelled to pause and ask: 'Should I have voted Aye or No; should I have stood with Falkland or with Pym?' No attempt can be made to answer the question here; but whatever the answer of individuals may be, no one will deny that the Remonstrance is a document of the first importance. Consisting, as we have shown, in part of an historical retrospect recounting all the grievances which had accumulated since the accession of the King; in part of an outlined scheme of constructive reform, the Remonstrance was primarily intended to excite popular feeling against the reigning sovereign, to reanimate, as Hallam puts it, 'discontents almost appeased', and to guard the people 'against the confidence they were beginning to place in the King's sincerity'.

Two questions, therefore, may fairly be asked: (i) Was the appeal to the people against the Crown a political necessity? And (ii) Was the scheme of reform statesmanlike and sound? That nothing but necessity can justify a step which led inevitably to civil war needs no arguing.

Lord Lytton, writing in 1860, regarded the Remonstrance as either a great blunder or a great crime—a blunder if Pym was sincere in his desire to retain the monarchy, a crime if he was not. Hallam, a generation earlier, held much the same view. Gardiner's guarded but decided approbation rests mainly upon the documents which in recent years have come to light, and which in the main tend to confirm Pym's deep-rooted conviction of the King's duplicity. If Charles I was really sincere in the concessions which in the last twelve months he had made; if he was minded to play with straightforward honesty the part of a constitutional sovereign, the work of Hampden and Pym was both a blunder and a crime. The difficulty of the popular leaders was this. They were, as we now know, in possession of information sufficient to satisfy their own minds as to the intrigues of the Court, but not circumstantial or precise enough to convince others. Could they, in view of their own knowledge, take the responsibility of allowing the country at large to bestow upon the King a renewal of confidence? But for the Scotch 'Incident' and the Irish Rebellion they would probably have been compelled to run the risk. Puritans as they were, they could hardly fail to discern in those opportune events the hand of the Lord pointing in the direction in which they were already anxious to go.

To Falkland, on the other hand, the balance of argument seemed decidedly against a step which was admittedly revolutionary, and could hardly fail to embroil the country in a fierce fratricidal war. The danger of a *coup d'état* was not present to his mind, as it was to Pym's. Events in Scotland and Ireland would naturally wear a very different aspect to one who was not yet convinced of the duplicity of the King, and was entirely ignorant of the intrigues of the Queen. Moreover, he was not prepared to face the risks involved in the overthrow of the Monarchy and the Church. The Church of England, with all its defects, stood in his eyes for intellectual freedom and for moral order against the narrow intolerance, not to say the social anarchy, threatened by a Puritan ascendancy. The Crown stood for ordered political progress against the encroachments of a usurping assembly. And who shall say that Falkland was wrong? True it is that the cardinal clause (197) of the Grand Remonstrance is the protoplasm of constitutional evolution as we in this country have conceived it. But that clause had no immediate results. The written Constitutions of the Commonwealth and Protectorate make no attempt to develop the idea of a Parliamentary executive, and the Cabinet system might, in its entirety, have been long deferred but for the accident that George I had no English and Walpole no German. For all that, the secret of the future was with Pym; and Pym, as a constitution-maker, is entitled to all the credit which properly belongs to one who is ahead of his time. But it must be remembered that England had to wade through a sea of blood to the realization of Pym's ideal. His opponents may have seen less clearly the ultimate solution, or may have been less unwilling to postpone it, but they were more keenly alive to the immediate risks.

VIII. THE PRELUDE TO WAR

The final Issues

THREE days after the passing of the Grand Remonstrance The King's return the King made a semi-triumphal entry into his capital (25 November). The Remonstrance was formally presented to him on 1 December. On the 10th he issued a Proclamation expressing his concern in regard to the 'present division, separation, and disorder about the worship and service of God', enjoining obedience to the 'laws and statutes ordained for the establishing of the true religion in this country', and commanding that Divine Service be performed 'as is appointed by law'. On the 23rd he replied His reply to the Remonstrance to the Petition accompanying the Grand Remonstrance —a 'declaration of a very unusual nature', which ought not to have been published until the answer thereto had been received. Nevertheless, while 'very sensible of the disrespect' involved in this procedure, and though quite at a loss to understand some of the allusions, the King deigned to reply to the Remonstrance.

As to religion, the King was prepared to concur with all the just desires of his people for preserving the peace and safety of the Kingdom from the design of the Popish party 'in a parliamentary way'; for the restraint of illegal innovations; and for the defence of the Church in its 'purity and glory', as well against all invasions of Popery, and against 'the irreverence of schismatics and separatists'; but as for depriving the Bishops of their votes in Parliament, the King (while deferring his final answer until the Bill was formally presented for his assent) would have the Remonstrants consider that the right of the Bishops 'is grounded upon the fundamental law of the Kingdom and constitution of Parliament'.

As to the removal and choice of councillors, the King was at a loss to know at whom the proposals were aimed; he had proved that there was 'no man so near to him in

place or affection' whom he would protect from punishment if found guilty by due process of law, but he resented
general aspersions upon unnamed councillors.

On the cardinal question of the appointment of ministers,
the King firmly declined to give way. He would use the
utmost care to appoint fit persons, but to ask him to give
up the right of appointment was 'to debar [him] that
natural liberty all freemen have'; and to deny 'the undoubted right of the Crown of England'.

What other answer could have been expected from the
King? It is true that Pym had, with rare political prescience, hit upon a device which, after a civil war, after the
trial and failure of a military dictatorship, after a second
trial of the Stuart Monarchy, and after a bloodless revolution consummated in 1714 by the accession of a German
princeling to the English throne, was gradually incorporated in the fabric of the English Constitution to our own
satisfaction and to the imitative admiration of other
nations. But while this is true, and should be emphasized,
it is also true that Charles I accurately interpreted the
Grand Remonstrance as being less a petition to the Sovereign
than a manifesto issued to the people in justification of
that appeal to arms which now appeared inevitable.

The Militia Bill   Foiled by the Peers in an attempt to limit the King's
right to compel men to military service beyond the borders
of their own counties, the Commons now brought in a Bill
to transfer the control of the armed forces of the realm to
the nominees of Parliament. Intended, perhaps, for the
moment only as a warning, the Bill roused a deep resentment among the Royalists, and was not immediately
pressed. It was, however, on this issue that the final
breach was presently to take place.

A new Ministry   Meanwhile the King took an important step. On
1 January 1642 he appointed to the vacant Secretaryship
of State Lucius Cary, Viscount Falkland, and offered
the Chancellorship of the Exchequer to Pym. Whether Pym
refused or the King withdrew the offer 'cannot', says
Gardiner, 'now be known'. The office was in fact conferred

upon Sir John Culpepper, and at the same time the Solicitor-Generalship was offered to Hyde. The latter declined it on the ground, as he assured the King, 'that he should be able to do much more service in the condition he was in'; and he added that 'he had the honour to have much friendship with the two persons who were very seasonably advanced by His Majesty, when His Majesty's service in the House of Commons did in truth want some countenance and support; and by his conversation with them . . . he should be more useful to his Majesty than if he were under a nearer relation of dependence. Hyde became, in fact, if we may anticipate future terminology, a minister without portfolio.

Falkland undertook a tremendous responsibility, but Falkland most reluctantly. Yet a man with his fine sense of honour could hardly have evaded the obligations imposed upon him by his vote against the *Grand Remonstrance*. Down to that moment he had acted, on the whole, with Pym and Hampden: down to that moment, indeed, there had been no coherent Royalist party. Falkland, though no Round-head, never became a Cavalier. His ecclesiastical views were not indeed those of Baillie, still less of Milton, but neither were they identical with Laud's. With men of the type of Hales and Chillingworth he was a 'bigot for tolera-tion'. He favoured episcopacy as the most convenient and orderly form of Church government, but he attributed no Divine Right to the Bishops, and laid no stress upon the formal continuity of apostolic succession. The violence of the Puritan leaders drove him into opposition to their ecclesiastical policy, and prepared the way for his adherence to the Royalist party. On the Divine Right of Kings he laid no more stress than upon the Divine Right of Bishops. To the experiment of Personal Monarchy and to the whole machinery of 'Thorough' he was no less strongly opposed than Pym, and to Strafford's death he was a consenting party. He saw, more clearly perhaps than any one, except his friend Hyde, how fatally the course of monarchy was injured by the resort to such expedients as ship-money and by the substitution of Administrative Law and Administrative Courts for the ordinary law administered in the ordinary courts. He perceived, also, the harm inflicted if not upon religion, at least upon ecclesiastical order by the coercive policy of Laud and his Arminian associates.

Effect of the Grand Remonstrance upon Parties With the *Grand Remonstrance* there came the final parting of the ways. The debates, and still more the divisions, on that measure made it manifest that the House of Commons would no longer present a united front of opposition to the Crown. Parties were becoming rapidly and clearly defined. Just as the 'Root and Branch Bill' had given strength and coherence to an Episcopalian (as distinct from a Laudian) party, so the *Grand Remonstrance* provided common ground for the scattered adherents of the Monarchy.

The Royalist party rapidly increased in numbers and even in coherence. For this Pym was primarily responsible. During the few weeks which had elapsed since the passing of the Remonstrance Pym had made it clear that he would stick at nothing to attain his ends. He was determined to get control of the armed forces of the Crown. If the Peers thwarted him, he would follow up his attack upon the monarchy by an attack upon the House of Lords. Nay, he would bring pressure to bear upon the House of Commons itself by an appeal to the London mob.

It is difficult to believe that under these circumstances the movement in the King's favour, already noted, could have failed to gain ground rapidly. But to the success of such a movement one thing was essential. The King must give no fresh grounds for offence. He had called moderate men to his counsels. He had given them a promise that 'he would do nothing that in any degree concerned or related to his service in the House of Commons without their joint advice and exact communication to them of all his own conceptions'. Yet the King 'in a very few days', as Clarendon tells us, 'very fatally swerved', and by an act of almost incredible folly played straight into the hands of Pym.

On 3 January 1642 Sir Edward Herbert, the Attorney-General, suddenly appeared in the House of Lords to impeach for high treason Lord Kimbolton,[1] and five members of the House of Commons, Pym, Hampden, Holles, Haselrig, and Strode, the charge being that 'they had traitorously conspired to levy and actually had levied war upon the King'. Immediately afterwards the Serjeant-at-Arms appeared in the Commons to demand in the King's name the arrest of the incriminated members. The Commons thereupon appointed a Committee to attend his Majesty and to acquaint him 'That this message from his Majesty was a matter of great consequence, that it concerneth the privilege of Parliament . . . that this House will take it into serious consideration . . . and in the meantime the said members shall be ready to answer any legal charge laid against them'. It is worthy of note that Culpepper and Falkland—the recently appointed ministers—were two of the four members thus appointed to wait upon the King.

Attempted arrest of the five members

On the following day (Tuesday, 4 January)

'the Lord Falkland reported the King's answer to the message of this House delivered the last night to his Majesty, that his Majesty asked them, whether the House did expect an Answer? They replied, they had no more in Commission to say, but only to deliver the message: the King asked them as private Persons, what they thought of it? They said, they conceived the House did expect an answer; but his Majesty was informed the House was up, so he said he would send an Answer this morning, as soon as this House was set; but in the meantime he commanded them to acquaint the House, that the Serjeant at Arms did nothing but what he had directions from himself to do.[2]

The five members were all present; but later in the day news reached the House, through the perfidy of Lady Carlisle, that the King was coming in person to arrest them. The members were bidden to withdraw. The King arrived with an armed force, passed through the lobby and entered the House. The scene that followed is thus quaintly described by an eye-witness, Verney:

---

[1] Afterwards Earl of Manchester. [2] Nalson, ii. 816.

'Then the kinge steped upp to his place and stood uppon the stepp, but sate not doun in the chaire. And, after hee had looked a greate while, hee told us, hee would not breake our priviledges, but treason had noe priviledge; hee came for those five gentlemen, for hee expected obedience yeasterday, and not an answere. Then hee calld Mr. Pim, and Mr. Hollis, by name, but noe answere was made. Then hee asked the Speaker if they were heere, or where they were. Uppon that the Speaker fell on his knees, and desired his excuse, for hee was a servant to the House, and had neither eyes, nor tongue, to see or say anything but what they commanded him. Then the king told him, hee thought his owne eyes were as good as his, and then said his birds were flowen, but hee did expect the House should send them to him, and if they did not hee would seeke them himselfe, for there treason was foule, and such an one as they would all thanke him to discover. Then hee assured us they should have a fair triall, and soe went out, putting off his hat till hee came to the dore.' [1]

Baffled at Westminster the King sought the fugitives in the City; but the Common Council was as firm as Parliament. Meanwhile a Committee of twenty-four members was appointed by the Commons to sit at the Guildhall. It is significant of their relations to the House that of this Committee also Falkland and Culpepper were members. London was strongly moved by the attack on Parliament. The City trained-bands were called out: Skippon was appointed to the command: the seamen in the Thames volunteered for the defence of Parliament. Even Charles felt that in London the game was up; on 10 January he and the Queen left Whitehall; on the 11th the impeached members returned in triumph to Westminster.

The incident has been endlessly discussed, and in particular many words have been wasted in demonstrating the unconstitutional character of the King's proceedings. Such demonstration would seem to be beside the point. The King's action was of course, from first to last, hopelessly irregular; but who among the supporters of the Grand Remonstrance could afford to cast the first stone? The

[1] Verney, 139.

King's real crime was not the attempt but the failure. Nothing could justify such outrageous conduct except complete success. A wise man, or even a clever man, would have left nothing to chance in an enterprise on the success of which everything depended. Charles, hesitating to the last, uncertain whether to proceed by quasi-legal methods or to employ force, left everything to chance. Why, if an arrest was intended, it was not quietly effected without the gratuitous violation of Parliamentary privileges must for ever remain a mystery. Perhaps the King's precipitate haste was simply due to the fatuous instigation of the Queen. Perhaps it was due to the folly of Digby 'thinking difficult things too easy'. It is impossible definitely to say. But out of a maze of uncertainties one or two certainties emerge. First: it is certain that no atom of responsibility can attach to the recently appointed Secretary of State. The action of the House in naming Falkland to be a member of the Committee at the Guildhall is conclusive proof that not even his opponents imputed complicity to him. Clarendon speaks of the 'discouragement they had so lately received in the King's going to the House to demand the five members, without ever communicating his intention to them, and which had made a deep impression upon them'.[1] A modern Secretary of State would, of course, under similar circumstances have tendered his resignation at once. Danby, under circumstances exactly parallel, was impeached. But between 1642 and 1679 the doctrine of ministerial responsibility had obtained larger acceptance. Falkland may well have despaired of the cause which he had espoused, and of the master whom he had undertaken to serve, but he did not feel justified in deserting him because he had been guilty of criminal folly.

A second point emerges with equal clearness. The King's action 'much advanced the spirits of the disaffected' and correspondingly depressed those of his wellwishers. It was indeed fatal to the cause of peace. Lord Macaulay speaks of the attempt as 'undoubtedly the real

Effect of King's failure

[1] *Life*, i. 102.

cause of the war'. But to ascribe the Civil War to any single cause, most of all to ascribe it to a single incident, is curiously unphilosophical. Forster [1] is substantially in accord with Macaulay. With more accuracy Clarendon speaks of it as 'the most visible introduction to all the misery that afterwards befell the King and kingdom'. The 'visible introduction' it was; but not the cause.

The embryo Cabinet

Before leaving Whitehall the King renewed his commands to Falkland, Culpepper, and Hyde 'to meet constantly together and consult upon his affairs, and conduct them the best way they could in the Parliament, and to give him constant advice what he was to do, without which, he declared again very solemnly, he would make no step in the Parliament. Two of them were obliged by their offices and relations, and the other by his duty and inclination, to give him all satisfaction'.[2] The following passage in Clarendon's autobiography throws additional and interesting light alike upon the political organization of the day, and upon the mutual relations of the three principal advisers of the unhappy King: 'They met every night late together, and communicated their observations and intelligence of the day; and so agreed what was to be done or attempted the next; there being very many persons of condition and interest in the House who would follow their advice, and assist in anything they desired.'

The problem of an army

Meanwhile Parliament, flinging aside all constitutional restraint, set itself to raise an armed force. Apart from ultimate possibilities two immediate necessities might be held to justify such action. Parliamentary privileges had to be protected from armed invasion, and the Irish Protestants to be rescued from Catholic violence. But it is characteristic of the situation that debate on constitutional aspects of the 'Militia' question proceeded simultaneously with decisive action on the part of both combatants. On 17 December a Militia Bill had been introduced into the House of Commons, and before the end of the month had passed its second reading. It is justly described by Gardiner as a

[1] *Five Members*, 184–200.   [2] Clarendon, *Life*, i. 102.

'root and branch Bill to regulate the army'. Had it become law the King's command over the armed forces of the realm would have been transferred to Parliament. And it was on this issue that the rupture finally took place. It was one on which neither side could give way. Anxious as the English Puritans were to send relief to their co-religionists in Ireland, they were not prepared to place in the King's hands a powerful engine to be used against themselves. The King, professing equal solicitude for his Irish subjects, was not disposed to part with a power which alike by law and constitutional convention was indisputably his own.

On the other outstanding question—the exclusion of the bishops from the House of Lords—the King, as we have seen, gave way. On the militia question no compromise was possible. Meanwhile, pending a legislative decision, Parliament hastened to usurp a power which they could not legally obtain. The London trained-bands had been already called out and placed under the command of Major-General Skippon, a stout soldier well affected to Parliament. Towards the end of January the Commons demanded that the fortresses and militia should be placed in the hands of persons in whom Parliament could confide. The Lords refused to join in the demand, and the King returned an evasive answer which was formally voted to be a denial. On this the Commons produced the 'Militia Ordinance', conferring power upon persons to be subsequently named to train the inhabitants in each county for war. To this 'Ordinance' the King's final answer was a proclamation that no one should presume 'upon any pretence of order or ordinance to which his Majesty was no party concerning the militia or any other thing to do or execute what was not warrantable' by the laws. On the receipt of this answer Parliament in 'choler and rage' took the matter into their own hands. Hull—the most important arsenal, and perhaps the most important seaport in the kingdom—had been already secured by the Hothams despite the King's efforts to anticipate them. On 23 April Charles in vain demanded admission 'to view his maga-

The Militia Ordinance

Acts of war

zines'. Newcastle was occupied by its Earl in the King's interest (17 June), but only just in time. Portsmouth was held for him by the double-traitor Goring. But Newcastle and Portsmouth were of little value without a fleet, and on 2 July the fleet accepted the command of Warwick, and Warwick secured its allegiance to the Parliament.

The Navy   'This loss of the whole Navy' was, as Clarendon justly observes, 'of unspeakable ill consequence to the King's affairs.' The influence of sea-power upon the progress and ultimate issue of the English Civil War has been curiously neglected by most historians. Clarendon's strong hint might have been expected to stimulate curiosity in this direction, but it has signally failed to do so. Yet it is not too much to assert that the strategy of the struggle was largely determined by the fact that Parliament had command of the sea, and were thus able to sustain the resistance of Gloucester, Plymouth, and Hull—three ports in the heart of Royalist country, and vitally important to the prosecution of the King's plan. The whole subject is well worthy of detailed investigation, but it cannot be pursued here.

Notwithstanding overt acts of war, negotiations between King and Parliament were continued until the middle of July. From the time, however, when the King left London there was little hope of an amicable issue. February was spent mostly at Theobalds; on the 25th the King got the Queen safely away to Holland with the Crown jewels, and on 3 March, against the wish of both Houses, he himself set out for the North. On the 19th he rode into York, which became for the next few months the head-quarters of the Royalist party. The Lord Keeper Littleton, to the consternation and confusion of Parliament, carried off the Great Seal to York, and to York the Courts of Law and the two Houses of Parliament were ordered by the King to adjourn.

Parliament intervened to prevent obedience to the former order, but day by day, despite efforts to restrain them, its own members slipped away. Ultimately, not more

than thirty peers and three hundred commoners were left
at Westminster, a large majority of the Upper House and
a considerable minority of the Lower having thrown in
their lot with the King.[1] Falkland and Culpepper joined
the Court early in June, having stayed in London until the
last moment in order to draft the answer to the Nineteen
Propositions. The latter document was approved in Parliament on 1 June.

During the last months before the actual outbreak of
the war the air was positively laden with Remonstrances,
Petitions, Counter-petitions, Proposals and Counter-pro-
posals. Many of these may be read at length in Clarendon,
who was largely responsible for the papers which emanated
from York. In all these it was his supreme object to
exhibit the King as the champion of law against the assaults
of lawless innovators. 'The King's resolution was', writes
Clarendon, 'to shelter himself wholly under the law; to
grant anything that by the law he was obliged to grant;
and to deny what by law was in his own power, and which
he found inconvenient to consent to.' 'I speak knowingly',
he adds with truth. But though the documents are
voluminous, the points really at issue were comparatively
few. The approval of ministers, councillors, and the
two Chief Justices and the Chief Baron by Parliament
which was to have a veto upon their appointment and
upon the admission of new peers to sit and vote in the
House of Lords; similar approval of the governors and
tutors of the Royal children, and of their marriages; the
execution of the laws against Jesuits and Popish recusants;
the reformation of Church government and liturgy as
Parliament shall advise after consultation with divines;
and the settlement of the militia on the lines of the ordinance; the punishment of 'delinquents'; alliance with
Protestant States on the Continent: these were the more
prominent requirements of the Nineteen Propositions.
They mostly reappear in the subsequent negotiations.

The time for argument had, however, gone by. The

The Nineteen Propositions (margin note)

[1] Firth, *Cromwell*, p. 69.

O 2

two parties had reached a position from which neither could
recede. The one struggled to obtain, the other to retain
the essence of sovereignty. Negotiations were drawn out
mainly for the purpose of informing the minds and enlisting
the sympathies of the nation to which both sides were now
compelled to appeal.

The Com-
missions
of Array
On 11 June the King issued his Commissions of Array;
on the 13th he announced that he would not engage his
supporters in any war against Parliament 'except it were
for his necessary defence and safety against such as did
insolently invade or attempt against His Majesty'. To
this appeal Falkland and the peers at York responded
with a promise to stand by the King's prerogative, and on
15 June the peers joined the King in a solemn declaration
that they desired only 'the law, peace, and prosperity of this
kingdom'. Falkland, Culpepper, Lord Keeper Littleton,
Chief Justice Bankes and thirty-four peers were among the
signatories. If the King and Court desired peace, so did
the country at large. Petitions praying for an accommodation poured into York from all parts of the country. Falkland's answers to the petitions are models of dignity and
sober eloquence, and testify, as far as words can testify, to
the King's earnest desire 'that all hostility may cease, cease
for ever, and a blessed and happy accommodation and
peace be made; that God's honour and the Protestant
religion may be maintained; that the privileges of Parliament and the laws of the land may be upheld and put in
execution that so his good people may be freed from their
fears, and secured in their estates'.

But the sands were running out. On 4 July the Houses
named a Committee of Safety; on the 6th they ordered
a special army of 10,000 men to be raised, and on the 12th
they appointed Essex to command it.

The King's friends were, meanwhile, chafing at the
delay in raising his standard. But it was not easy to decide
where it should be set up. The Derby family desired to
secure the honour for Lancashire and promised strong
support: York was considered, but was less eager for the

distinction; on 12 August the King summoned his loyal subjects to rally round the standard at Nottingham, and there on the 22nd it was set up.

On the eve of the war it is desirable to pause awhile and attempt to gauge the state of public feeling, and estimate the forces which were at work to dispose the plain citizen to this side or that.

One thing is abundantly and honourably clear, that the aversion to the idea of war was deep and general, and that out-and-out partisans on either side were few. Round the King was a small and devoted band of people who had adopted in its integrity the Stuart theory of monarchy. They held with Charles himself—

The choice of Sides

> Not all the water in the rough rude sea
> Can wash the balm from an anointed King;
> The breath of worldly men cannot depose
> The deputy elected by the Lord.

On the other side there were some who could re-echo the splendid confidence of that stout-hearted but rather stupid republican, Edmund Ludlow:

'The question in dispute between the King's Party and us being, as I apprehended, whether the King should govern as a God by his Will, and the Nation be governed by force like Beasts; or whether the People should be governed by Laws made by themselves, and live under a Government derived from their own consent. Being fully persuaded that an accommodation with the King was unsafe to the people of England, and unjust and wicked in the nature of it. The former, besides that it was obvious to all men, the King himself had proved by the duplicity of his dealing with the Parliaments, which manifestly appeared in his own papers, taken at the battle of Naseby and elsewhere, of the latter I was convinced by the express words of God's law: "that blood defileth the land, and the land cannot be cleansed of the blood that is shed therein, but by the blood of him that shed it" (Num. xxxv. 33). And therefore I could not consent to leave the guilt of so much blood on the nation, and thereby to draw down the just vengeance of God upon us all, when it was most evident that the war had been occasioned by the invasion of our rights and open breach of our laws and constitution on the King's part.' [1]

But unhesitating, convinced and thorough going partisans like Ludlow were few; the vast majority of citizens were distracted as to the choice of sides, and detested the idea of civil war. A conversation reported by Clarendon gives us an insight into the feelings of one such citizen, Sir Edmund Verney, the King's standard bearer, 'a man of great courage and generally beloved'. He came to Hyde one day and said

'he was very glad to see him in so universal a damp, under which the spirits of most men were oppressed, retain still his natural vivacity and cheerfulness. My condition', he continued, 'is much worse than yours . . . and will very well justify the melancholie that I confess possesses me. You have satisfaction in your conscience that you are in the right, that the King ought not to grant what is required of him; and so you do your duty and business together. But, for my part, I do not like the quarrel, and do heartily wish that the King would yield, and consent to what they desire, so that my conscience is only concerned in honour and gratitude to follow my master. I have eaten his bread and served him near thirty years, and will not do so base a thing as to forsake him, and choose rather to loose my life (which I am sure I shall do) to preserve and defend those things which are against my conscience to preserve and defend; for I will deal freely with you—I have no reverence for bishops, for whom this quarrel subsists.'

Sir Edmund Verney, it cannot be doubted, spoke the thoughts of thousands of those who took service under the banner of the King. There was just the same temper on the other side. Sir William Waller writes thus to his friend Ralph Horton:—

'The great God who is the searcher of my heart, knows with what reluctance I go upon this service and with what perfect hatred I look upon a war without an enemy. The God of Peace in His good time send us peace, and in the meantime fit us to receive it. We are both on the stage, and we must act the parts

[1] *Memoirs*, i. 267.

that are assigned to us in this tragedy. Let us do it in the way of honour and without personal animosities.'

Such was the honourable temper of both sides as they embarked on this great contest. And who will deny that there was ground for hesitation?

'There was', as the judicial Hallam says, 'so much in the conduct and circumstances of both parties to excite disapprobation and distrust that a wise and good man could hardly unite cordially with either. On the one hand he would entertain little doubt of the King's desire to overthrow by force or stratagem whatever had been effected in Parliament, and to establish a plenary despotism; his arbitrary temper, his known principles of government, the natural sense of wounded pride and honour, the instigations of a haughty woman, the solicitations of favourites, the promises of ambitious men, were all at work to render his position as a constitutional sovereign, even if unaccompanied by fresh indignities and reproaches, too grievous and mortifying to be endured. . . . But on the other hand the House of Commons presented still less favourable prospects. . . . After every allowance has been made he must bring very heated passions to the records of those times, who does not perceive in the conduct of that body a series of glaring violations not only of positive and constitutional, but of those higher principles which are paramount to all immediate policy.'[1]

A further question demands an answer.

Is it possible to draw any broad lines of division between the two parties? 'Saints and Sinners' is the natural suggestion of the keen partisan: but there is a good deal of contemporary opinion to contradict it. 'Think not', said Thomas Fuller preaching in London, 'that the King's army is like Sodom, not ten righteous men in it, and the other army like Zion, consisting all of saints.' An echo comes from Chillingworth, preaching before the Court at Oxford:—

'Publicans and Sinners on the one side, against Scribes and Pharisees on the other; on the one side hypocrisy, on the other profaneness. No honesty or justice on the one side, and very little piety on the other. On the one side horrible oaths, curses

[1] *C. H.* ii. 139, 140.

and blasphemies, on the other pestilent lies, calumnies and perjuries. . . . I profess that I cannot without trembling consider what is likely to be the event of these distractions.'

Fuller and Chillingworth were surely right. Neither side had a monopoly of morals—good or bad. But though morally the line of division is happily blurred, ecclesiastically it is clearly defined. On the side of King Charles all the Romans and Anglicans; on that of 'King Pym' all the many varieties of Puritanism. But even on the ecclesiastical stage there was a large middle party of which Falkland was typical—anti-Laudian but not anti-Episcopal, a party which had 'contracted some prejudice to the archbishop', but which liked still less the prospect of Genevan domination.

Geographically, parties were roughly divided by the line that has been an immemorial dividing-line in English history—the line from the Humber to the Severn—or perhaps more accurately from the Humber to Southampton. The strength of the King lay in the comparatively wild districts to the north and west of the line, where great lords like Newcastle, Derby, and Worcester still ruled in semi-feudal state. To the Parliament adhered the rich and comparatively civilized districts of the east and south. The great agricultural plain contained at that day almost the whole wealth of England. London was at least as pre-eminent among the towns as it is to-day. Exceptionally bitter in its Puritanism, and containing not less than a tenth of the whole population, its support was a tower of strength to the Parliamentary party. Bristol and Norwich, the only considerable towns outside London, were both Parliamentarian, though Bristol fell before the intrepid attack of Rupert. Hull, Plymouth, and Gloucester were secured to Parliament, by the adhesion of the fleet, and no words can exaggerate the advantage they thus obtained. The industrial towns in the west and south-west not less than in the south-east were at the opening of the struggle on the same side; but they were unable to resist the pressure of the surrounding country. Wales, with the exception of Pembroke, was solidly Royalist from the first, as were the four Northern Counties.

Socially, the line is, fortunately, less easy to draw. The Civil War was a war of creeds and parties; it was not a war of classes. The townsmen were generally on the side of Parliament; the great lords and their retainers fought mostly for the King; but the Puritan trained-bands were officered by squires, and many a stout yeoman rode with Rupert. Pym could count on thirty peers, and Charles on nearly two hundred members of the Lower House. There was, therefore, no question of property at issue. Later on, the Levellers developed socialistic opinions, but they got no countenance from the responsible leaders.

Politically, the line must be drawn at the divisions on the Grand Remonstrance. How close they were we have already seen, and that they reflected with substantial accuracy the balance of parties in the country we cannot doubt.

But though we may thus discriminate between Cavaliers and Roundheads, it still remains true that the mass of the nation was neither one nor the other. Many of the counties would gladly have followed Yorkshire in an attempt to contract themselves out of the war, and the peasants of Dorset and Wilts.—subsequently organized as *The Clubmen*—represented, in their anxiety to keep both parties at arm's length, the feelings of most of their class. 'The number of those who desired to sit still was greater', as Clarendon pithily observes, 'than of those who desired to engage in either party.'

ENGLAND
in the
Civil War
Autumn 1643

Districts held by Parl.
" " " King
Parl. strongholds in the
Kings Country = Plymouth

Kilsyth
Falkirk
Edinburgh
Dunbar
Dunse Law
Philiphaugh
Newburn on Tyne
Newcastle

York
Marston Moor
Hull
Preston
Lathom House
Manchester
Gainsborough
Chester
Rowton Heath
Nantwich
Winceby
Newark
Belvoir
Shrewsbury
Ashby de la Zouch
Norwich
Birmingham
Naseby
Hotmby House
Worcester
Cropredy
Cambridge
Edge Hill
Gloucester
Oxford
Bristol
Chalgrove
LONDON
Lansdown
Roundway Downs
Reading
Brentford
Bath
Newbury
Basing House
Langport
Wardour Cas.
Winchester
Taunton
Southampton
Exeter
Lyme Regis
Portsmouth
Plymouth
Corfe

IX. POLITICS AND WAR

DURING war constitutional history is a blank. Although *Inter arma silent leges* true in one sense this oft-quoted aphorism obscures an even more important truth. War is indeed apt to arrest constitutional development. Or if progress is made it cannot easily be registered while attention is concentrated on the achievement of victory in the field. Nevertheless, war acts as a solvent of established institutions and equally as a forcing house of political ideas. The fruit cannot be immediately gathered, yet the ripening process tends to be exceptionally rapid.

The English civil war affords no exception to this rule. The forcing house of war Not until the sword was drawn, nor indeed till long afterwards, did a republican party emerge; still less a communist party seeking to attain its ends by means of a political revolution. Nor is it even possible to discern until the eve of war any movement against the co-ordinate legislative authority of the House of Lords. Yet in 1649 the House of Lords followed the Monarchy into the abyss, and by that time there had emerged the nucleus of a party which, though never dominant, anticipated, in certain leading ideas, the Jacobinism of the French Revolution, and the Bolshevism of modern Russia.

But in 1642 all this was in the distant future. Before Proclamations, and Counter-proclamations battle was actually joined, both sides, with a view to impress waverers, put out proclamations and counter-proclamations. On 9 August 1642 the King issued a proclamation declaring Lord Essex and his officers traitors, but offering a free pardon to him and to all who should lay down their arms. On the 18th the Houses issued in their turn a counter-proclamation denouncing as traitors all those who in arms supported the King; yet, despite this, the King was persuaded, much against his will, to renew his offer of peace, and on 25 August the Earls of Southampton and Dorset set off with Culpepper and Sir William Udall from Nottingham to Westminster, as the bearers of the King's message to Parliament. It was received as the King had anticipated, 'with unheard of insolence and contempt'; Parliament refused to negotiate unless the King would unconditionally haul down his flag, abandon his friends, put his person at the disposal of Parliament, and agree to abide by their advice.

The terms were impossible and further negotiation was palpably vain; nothing but the sword could cut the gordian knot. But before the King left Nottingham to recruit an army on the Welsh marches he published, 'as a farewell to his hopes of a treaty and to make the deeper sense and impression in the hearts of the people', an admirably conceived manifesto to the nation. To the pathos of its concluding words no one could be insensible:

'The God of Heaven direct you, and in mercy divert those judgements which hang over this nation; and so deal with us and our posterity as we desire the preservation and advancement of the true Protestant religion; the law and liberty of the subject; the just rights of Parliament, and the peace of the Kingdom.'

The two sides   In which of the two armies should a man have enlisted who sincerely desired the 'law and liberty of the land and just rights of Parliament'? Before the sword was finally sheathed the 'rights of Parliament' had been swept aside no less ruthlessly than the rights of the Monarchy; nor can it be contended that the liberty of the subject was more respected by Cromwell than by Charles I. It is true that all comparisons were as vitiated by the fact that war had intervened and that the situation, after a civil war, must necessarily be, for a time at any rate, abnormal. Yet the fact remains that the restoration of the Monarchy was an essential preliminary to the re-establishment of the 'just rights of Parliament', and that only under a restored Monarchy was the liberty of the subject placed under guarantees which proved finally sufficient and satisfactory.

A detailed narrative of military events does not fall within the scope of this book, but it is essential to its

purpose to scrutinize the terms offered from time to time
by negotiators on either side so far as they throw light
upon the evolution of political institutions or the development of political ideas.

The first series of negotiations lasted almost continuously The First Campaign
from December 1642 to April 1643. Many men had hoped,
perhaps had believed, that a month's campaign would
settle the whole business in favour of Parliament. They
were painfully undeceived. Neither side was ready for war;
but the King was more favourably placed for improvisa-
tion than Parliament. Consequently, the first campaign
was decidedly favourable to the Royalist cause. The first
important skirmish of the war took place at Powick
Bridge, just outside Worcester, on 23 September. The
King, while marching from Nottingham to Chester, learnt
that Worcester was threatened by Essex. Accordingly,
Prince Rupert was sent to its relief, and at Powick Bridge
he encountered Essex's advance-guard. Sandys was at the
head of a thousand men, the flower of the Roundhead
cavalry, but Rupert's charge was irresistible. The Roundheads broke and fled, leaving 400 of their thousand dead
upon the field. The Prince had drawn first blood, but he was
not strong enough to hold Worcester, and on the 24th the
city was occupied by Essex without resistance. The skirmish
at Powick Bridge had, however, 'rendered the name of
Prince Rupert very terrible' to the enemy. But in the field,
as in the closet, Rupert had the defects of his qualities.
Unequalled in courage and dash he was overbearing in
temper, impatient of control, and reckless of consequences.

The same qualities were displayed at Edgehill, the first
serious battle of the war. The King, advancing from Chester
to London, found his way barred by Essex, who lay about
Banbury. On 23 October the armies met at Kineton or
Edgehill. The issue is commonly described as doubtful:
but the fact remains that the King had pushed Essex
aside, safely reached Oxford, 'the only city of England that
he could say was entirely at his devotion', and from Oxford
was able to advance on Reading.

So marked and unexpected was the King's initial success that the peace party in Parliament was encouraged to open negotiations. But the King's march on London was not meanwhile stayed. He got as far as Brentford on 12 November, but on the following day he suffered a decisive check at Turnham Green and was compelled to fall back on Reading, whence he made his way to Oxford.

Having failed to push through to London, the King was now anxious to reopen negotiations. Accordingly, Falkland was commanded to forward to Lord Grey of Warke, as 'Speaker of the Peers *pro tem.*', the King's reply to the answer of Parliament to his message of 12 November.[1] This document was, in effect, an elaborate vindication of the King's good faith in regard to the action at Brentford. Rupert's conduct was bitterly and not unnaturally resented by Parliament, and they were now willing to treat only on condition that the King would return to the capital and abandon the 'delinquents' to their mercy. The condition was impossible. Rupert's impetuosity—not without justification from the purely military standpoint—had shattered for the moment the hopes of the peace party.

The winter brought no formal cessation of arms, but despite desultory fighting in the North and West, the real business of the winter was not war but diplomacy. During the months between December 1642 and April 1643 negotiations between Oxford and London were carried on practically without intermission.

The country had as yet seen little of war, but it had seen enough to make it long for peace. In particular, the City of London, without whose loyal support Parliament would have been powerless in its contest with the King, was already beginning to feel the pinch of commercial depression, combined with the burden of war taxation. On 12 December the Common Council resolved to present petitions to the King and the Parliament respectively in favour of peace. The remnant of the House of Lords at West-

[1] It may be read in *S. P. Dom., Car. I*, ccccxcii. 59; or Rushworth, v.

minster was at one with the City. The lawyers in the
House of Commons were not less eager than the merchants.
It is plain that nothing but the indomitable resolution of
Pym kept Parliament firm to its purpose. Pym was not
averse to negotiation, so long as there was no sacrifice
of the essential ends for the attainment of which he had
embarked on war; and he took care that there should be
none. On 26 December the Commons agreed to open
negotiations with the King, on the basis of the terms proposed to them by the Lords. About a month later they
were formally laid before the King at Oxford.

Meanwhile, a deputation from the City arrived at Oxford.
Their reception was not encouraging: they were hooted in
the streets, and received with scant ceremony by the King.
Their proposals were not indeed such as to conciliate the
Court. They amounted to a suggestion that the King
should forthwith disband his army, and put himself at the
absolute disposal of Parliament. The King's answer was in
effect a haughty offer of pardon to such as would make
unconditional submission. It is difficult to understand how
such terms could have been proposed, for it is undeniable
that the merchants were sincerely desirous of peace. Nor
was their attitude due merely to the selfish interests of the
wealthier citizens. On 3 January a vast crowd of London
apprentices, three thousand strong, besieged Parliament
with similar petitions. The home counties, Hertfordshire,
Essex, and Bedford, did the same. The desire for peace
was well-nigh universal, but no man could suggest how it
was to be attained.

On 1 February the Parliamentary Commissioners arrived
in Oxford, and the peace proposals were immediately laid
before the King. The full text may be read in Rushworth's
Collection or in Gardiner's *Documents*. The propositions
afforded no possible basis for negotiation, still less for
compromise. It is true that some of the more objectionable
demands made in the *Nineteen Propositions* disappear from
the Oxford proposals. There is no mention in the latter of
an oath to be taken by all Privy Councillors and Judges to

Negotia-
tions at
Oxford

maintain the Petition of Right and other Statutes to be specified by Parliament; of the demand for the dismissal of all Privy Councillors and Ministers of State not approved by Parliament, or that the Privy Councillor or Ministers should not hereafter be appointed without the same approval; or the insulting demand that no order emanating from the King-in-Council should be recognized unless signed by a majority of the Council; for parliamentary control over the education and marriages of the King's children, and for a veto of both Houses on the right of peers, hereafter created, to sit or vote in the House of Lords.[1] On the other hand, very objectionable demands were inserted or retained. The King was to disband his armies; to return to Parliament; to leave 'delinquents' to the judgement of Parliament and a legal trial; to disarm the Papists; to compel them to abjure their creed; to assent to legislation for the education of the children of Papists by Protestants in the Protestant religion; to leave the Militia Settlement to Parliament, and to accept Parliamentary nominations to the high judicial offices. In regard to the vital question of the Church, Parliament demanded the King's assent to the Root and Branch Bill, and a promise that he would pass such other bills for Church reform as Parliament after consultation 'with godly, religious and learned divines should present to him'. Had the military situation of the King been desperate, such propositions might conceivably have obtained a hearing. But so far the balance of military advantage lay decidedly with the King. Under these circumstances to propose terms which involved the surrender of principles and persons dearest to the King was mere futility. The King's answer,[2] though not unconciliatory in tone, was naturally firm. He expressed his willingness to assent to 'any good act for the suppressing of Popery and for the firm settling of the Protestant religion now established by law', and suggested that a Bill should be framed

[1] Gardiner, *Documents*, p. xli.
[2] Rushworth, v. 168. The answer is not printed in Gardiner's *Documents*.

for 'the better preserving of the Book of Common Prayer from the scorn and violence of Brownists, Anabaptists, and other Sectaries, with such clauses for the ease of tender consciences as His Majesty hath formerly offered'. Finally, the King proposed a cessation of arms and 'free trade for all His Majesty's subjects'.

This last point was hotly debated in both Houses. The Lords favoured a cessation; the Commons desired to insist on disarmament. Eventually a compromise was reached, and Parliament resolved to ask for a cessation of arms limited in duration to twenty days. These 'articles of cessation' were presented to the King on 1 March, and on the 6th the King's reply was communicated to Parliament. Neither proposal was satisfactory, but Parliament 'being still carried on with a vehement desire of peace', sent further instructions to the Commissioners at Oxford on 18 March. For a whole month negotiations continued at Oxford.

But it was all to no purpose. The King insisted that his revenue, magazines, ships, and forts should be immediately restored to him, and on 14 April the Parliamentary Commissioners were recalled from Oxford. With so excellent a disposition on both sides, how came the negotiations at Oxford to fail? The answer to this question has more than an immediate significance. Pym was doubtless as obstinate as the King; but Pym disappeared from the stage before the end of the year, and still Charles proved unyielding.

Clarendon's account makes it abundantly clear that the King did not give his entire confidence to his official advisers, to the devoted men without whose 'joint advice' he had promised to take no important step. Behind the 'cabinet' there were the Princes and Digby, and behind both there was the Queen. The picture which Clarendon draws of the relations between Charles and Henrietta Maria is idyllic. 'The King's affection to the Queen was of a very extraordinary alloy; a composition of conscience and love and generosity and gratitude and all those noble affec-

The King and his advisers

tions which raise the passions to the greatest height; insomuch as he saw with her eyes and determined by her
judgement.' [1] But a domestic idyll may mean a political
tragedy. When the Queen left England to labour for his
cause abroad, the King had promised that 'he would never
make any peace but by her interposition and mediation
that the kingdom might receive that blessing only from
her. This promise (of which His Majesty was too religious
an observer) was the cause of his rejecting or not entertain-
ing their last overture.' 'Where the fault lay I judge not',
says May; [2] but Whitelocke—himself one of the Parliamentary Commissioners at Oxford—concurs with Clarendon.[3] At the same time he gives a favourable impression
of the King's conduct during the negotiations. At all times
it seems the Commissioners had access to him and were
allowed 'very free debate with him'. He was generally
attended in these conferences by Rupert, Lord Southampton, the Lord Keeper,[4] and the Lord Chief Justice,[5] besides
the lords of his council. But these played a subordinate
part. They never, says Whitelocke, 'debated any matters
with us, but gave their opinions to the King in those things
which he demanded of them, and sometimes would put the
King in mind of some particular things, but otherwise they
did not speak at all.' The King 'manifested his great parts
and abilities, strength of reason and quickness of apprehension, with much patience in hearing what was objected
against him. . . . His unhappiness was that he had a better
opinion of others' judgements than of his own.' Among the
'others', Rupert and the Queen, who had landed in Yorkshire in the middle of the negotiations, were unquestionably the most influential.

The
Scotch
Commis-
sioners at
Oxford

It was not only with Parliament that the King was in
treaty during the winter of 1642-3. Scotch Commissioners
reached Oxford on 17 February—among them Lord
Loudoun and Mr. Alexander Henderson—Lord Lanark [6]

[1] *Life*, i. 185.   [2] *Long Parliament*, 278.
[3] *Memorials*, 68.   [4] Littleton.
[5] Bankes.   [6] Baillie's 'Lanerick', afterwards Duke of Hamilton.

arrived later. From a letter of Baillie's [1] it would appear
that 'their life was verie uncomfortable all the tyme at
Oxford. . . . None durst shew them any sensible favour.
In the streets, and from windows they were continually
reviled by all sorts of people.' The King's treatment of the
Scots seems to have been the height of impolicy, and
strangely lacking even in common courtesy. 'Before any
answer was given twenty dayes would passe; for His
Majesty had no leasure. When they did in 24 houres give
in their replyes, other 20 dayes would passe before the
Secretaries, Nicolas, Falkland, Hyde, Ashburnham, Lanerick could have leasure to answer: so the year should have
passed in vaine, had they not been recalled.' There is some
ground perhaps for Baillie's comment uttered more in
sorrow than in anger: 'This policie was, lyke the rest of
our unhappy malcontent's wisdom, extreamlie foolish; for
it was verie much for the King's ends to have given to our
Commissioners farr better words, and a more pleasant
countenance'. On the other hand there was at least an
element of truth in the common rumour reported by Wood:
'it is thought that there is some double dealinge on the
Scott's side in this businesse'. At Oxford, in 1643, as elsewhere and always, the one supreme object of the Scots was
to force upon the King and the people of England an
ecclesiastical system which they detested. On this point
no compromise or accommodation was possible until the
King's will was broken, and his plight was desperate.

That was far from being the case in the summer of 1643.
On the contrary, everything seemed to point to the speedy
triumph of the Royalist cause. The King, whose ability
as a soldier was rated highly by the Duke of Wellington,
had conceived the idea of a triple advance on London:
Newcastle, having cleared Yorkshire of rebels, was to pierce
through Cromwell's force in Lincolnshire and march on the
capital by the great north road. Grenville and Hopton,
having made all safe for the King in Cornwall and Devon,
were to come up from the West, and keeping south of the

The King's plan of campaign

---

[1] *Letters and Journals*, ii. 66.

Thames to march on Southwark. The northerners were to
join hands with the men of Cornwall and Devon to the
east of London; the King was to clinch matters by advancing from Oxford and Reading, while the Welshmen were to
cross the Severn and hold the country between Severn and
Thames.

The summer of 1643 saw the partial achievement of this
scheme. Hopton cleared Cornwall; all Devonshire except
Dartmouth and Plymouth gradually came in for the King,
and Hopton pushed on through Somerset and Wilts.
Bristol, the second city of the Kingdom, surrendered to
Prince Rupert towards the end of July; Dorset was
cleared of rebels in August; and though the seaports of the
west, Plymouth and Dartmouth, Poole and Lyme Regis,
held out for the Parliament, the continuity of the King's
country, between Mount's Bay and the Mersey, was broken
only by the obstinate resistance of Gloucester. The news
of the surrender of Bristol had come to London, as Thomas
May tells us, 'as a sentence of death'. 'The Parliament',
he adds, 'was at that time so sunk both in strength and
reputation and so much forsaken by those who followed
fortune that nothing but an extraordinary providence
could make it again emergent.'

Meanwhile, Newcastle was, on the whole, successful in
the North. By the end of February most of the north-
midland towns were in the King's hands except the cloth-
ing towns of the West Riding, and a great victory won by
Newcastle's 'Papists' over the Fairfaxes near Bradford
on 30 June, brought their resistance to an end. The Queen,
who had landed at Bridlington in February, bringing with
her much needed supplies of money and arms, reached
Oxford safely in May. But one obstacle obtruded itself
between Newcastle and complete success in the north.
Hull, succoured from the sea, still held out, and while Hull
was untaken, the squires and yeomen and peasants of the
north refused to come further south.

Sir Philip Warwick hints indeed that the stubborn
resistance of Hull was not the sole reason for Newcastle's

refusal to come south. Having been sent by the King to persuade him to do so, Warwick found the nothern Earl 'very averse to this, and perceived that he apprehended nothing more than to be joined to the King's army or to serve under Prince Rupert; for he designed himself to be the man that should turn the scale and to be a self subsisting and distinct army wherever he was'. Warwick may have been over suspicious of Newcastle; but that there was serious friction between the several Royalist commanders is certain.

Yet on the surface things looked black for the Parliamentary Party. Essex's failure to reach Oxford (June) only accentuated the gloom caused by the Royalists victories in the west and the north. But there were weak links in the chain of Royalist successes. Parliament never lost the command of the sea, and so long as they held it, they could succour important seaports like Plymouth and Hull. So long as Plymouth held out, the men of the west moved eastwards with hesitation: Hull, as we have seen, stayed the southward march of the northerners. But even more significant at the moment was the resistance of Gloucester. It was thought that the surrender of Bristol would be the prelude to that of Gloucester. Not so; Gloucester held out, and until it was taken the Welshmen would not cross the Severn. Taken it never was: on the contrary, the brilliant march of Essex and his London train-bands through Bucks and Oxon., along the Cotswold ridge from Chipping Norton to Cheltenham, saved Gloucester. Rupert raised the siege on 8 September, and with the failure to take Gloucester the tide of Royalist success turned.

Thus, if it is too much to say that the King's plan was broken by the three cities of Hull, Gloucester, and Plymouth, their resistance at least affords striking testimony to the importance of sea-power—even in our own insular civil war.

Gloom had, however, settled down on the Parliament, and Baillie might, therefore, with some justice take credit for the Scots in going to the assistance of a ruined cause.

Gloom in Parliament

'Surely', he writes, 'it was a great act of faith in God and huge courage and unheard of compassion that moved our own nation to hazard their own peace and venture their lives and all for the sake of a people irrecoverably ruined both in their own and all the world's eyes.' [1] Almost any candid contemporary observer would have taken Baillie's view of the situation. Yet it is not difficult in retrospect to perceive that the more permanent forces were operating in favour of the Roundheads. The ultimate victory of Parliament was in truth implicit in their command of the sea, in the unshaken tenacity of Hull, Plymouth, and Gloucester; in the proven unwillingness of the King's local levies to go far from home; in the new military organization adopted as yet only by a single regiment in the eastern counties, but soon to be extended to the whole 'new model' army; above all, in the germinating genius of the man by whom that organization was devised. But the full effect of all this had yet to be revealed.

For the moment the King's cause was clearly in the ascendant, and in their desperation the English Parliament turned for help to the Scots. The price demanded for that help was the acceptance of the *Solemn League and Covenant*. The more foresighted perceived that though it might secure the indispensable assistance of the Scots, it would render infinitely more difficult any accommodation with the King; but Gloucester was still unrelieved; needs must when the devil drives; and with certain amendments the *Solemn League and Covenant* was taken by the House of Commons.[2]

Under the terms of this famous engagement the English Parliament pledged itself to preserve 'the reformed religion in the Church of Scotland, in doctrine, worship, discipline, and government, to reform religion in England and Ireland 'according to the word of God and the example of the best

Marginal notes: Factors making for success of Parliament

The Solemn League and Covenant

---

[1] *Letters*, ii. 99.

[2] The formal date of acceptance was 25 Sept.: Essex had entered Gloucester on 8 Sept.: but the Commons had discussed the Covenant on 1 Sept.

reformed Churches, and to 'endeavour to bring the Churches of God in the three Kingdoms to the nearest conjunction and uniformity in religion, confession of faith, form of Church Government, directory for worship and catechizing, and 'without respect of persons' to 'endeavour the extirpation of Popery, prelacy', &c. In plain words, Presbyterianism, on the Scottish model, was to be imposed by authority of Parliament, and at the point of the sword not only upon an England, which, though Protestant, was Episcopalian, but upon Roman Catholic Ireland. From this Established Presbyterian Church no deviation, to right or left, was to be permitted, nor was any other form of religion to be tolerated.

As regards temporal affairs, the King's 'person and authority' were to be preserved and defended, 'together with the rights and privileges of the Parliaments and the liberties of the Kingdoms', and 'malignants' were to be hunted down and to receive 'condign punishment . . . as the supreme judicatories of both Kingdoms respectively, or others having power from them for that effect shall judge convenient'.

A few months later (16 February 1644) a Committee of Lords and Commons was appointed, 'to join with the Committees and Commissioners of Scotland', to manage the affairs of both nations, and to carry into effect the terms of the Covenant. Among those thus appointed to represent the English Parliament were the Lords Northumberland, Essex (Lord General), Warwick (Lord Admiral), Manchester, Saye and Sele, the two Sir Henry Vanes, and Oliver Cromwell. The Joint Committee

The Covenant was the high-water mark attained by the Presbyterian party in the English revolution. From the list of the Committee named to give effect to it two names will be missed: John Hampden had been mortally wounded on Chalgrove Field in June, and on 8 December John Pym had passed away. That either of them would have exercised a moderating influence upon affairs is not to be supposed; but their deaths at this juncture undoubtedly facilitated the transfer of supreme authority from the Parliament at Westminster to the Generals in the field; from the General of the parliamentary army to the organizer and commander of the 'new model', from the Presbyterians to the Independents.

Hampden   Hampden was one of those men who make more impression by character than by achievements. Apart from his almost accidental association with the ship-money case, it is difficult to connect his name with any of the outstanding events of those stirring times. Yet the impression which he made on contemporaries is indelible. On that point Clarendon's testimony is conclusive, though the portrait he draws of Hampden is not entirely flattering: 'a man of much greater cunning [than Pym], who spoke rarely but listened carefully, and having observed how the house was like to be inclined, took up the argument, and shortly, and clearly and craftily, so stated it that he commonly conducted "it to the conclusion he desired", or failing that, had "the dexterity to direct the debate to another time"; a man who led when he appeared to follow'. Clarendon, it would seem, never forgave Hampden for his influence, in the earlier days of the Long Parliament, over Falkland, but he acknowledges his 'flowing courtesy to all men', and confesses that 'his carriage throughout this agitation was with that rare temper and modesty that they who watched him narrowly to find some advantage against his person ... were compelled to give him a just testimony'. Of his death Clarendon writes that it caused 'as great a consternation of that party as if their whole army had been defeated or cast off'. Posterity has accepted the verdict of contemporaries.

Pym   Of Pym it is not too much to say that great as was his repute among contemporaries, the passage of time has enhanced it. 'The most popular man and the most able to do hurt that hath lived in any time.' Such is Clarendon's verdict. 'One of the greatest revolutionary leaders known to history', said Leopold von Ranke. But Pym was more than a great revolutionary leader. Danton was that: but what permanent mark has Danton left upon the face of France? Pym was a great constructive statesman, and in our Parliamentary constitution his memory is enshrined.

Yet Pym can claim no exclusive proprietorship in the political device which he did so much to develop. Lord Lytton, no mean critic, argues that even in this respect the claims of Falkland are superior to those of Pym. In their deaths the two men, who had parted company on the *Grand Remonstrance*, were not far divided. Three months before Pym died Falkland had been killed in the first fight at Newbury. Clarendon's portrait of his closest friend is familiar to every lover of English prose: [†]Falkland

'At the battle of Newbury was slain the Lord Viscount Falkland; a person of such prodigious parts of learning and knowledge, of that inimitable sweetness and delight in conversation, of so glowing and obliging a humanity and goodness to mankind, and of that primitive simplicity and integrity of life, that if there were no other brand upon this odious and accursed civil war than that single loss it must be most infamous and execrable to all posterity.'

Clarendon wrote under the poignant sense of personal bereavement. Lord Lytton did not; but his eulogy of Falkland is hardly less warm than Clarendon's. Moreover, he raises a point of special significance in connexion with the problems which this book attempts to analyse. Did Pym or Falkland see further into the future of our constitutional evolution? Pym, as we have seen, fixed on the principle of a responsible Executive as the ultimate solution of the constitutional problem of his day. The King must take 'Councillors whom the parliament had cause to confide in'. Herein he proved his prescience. In the crucial division on the *Grand Remonstrance* Falkland voted against Pym. Was Pym right and Falkland wrong?

Had the issue been simply a constitutional one Falkland might have been in the majority with Pym; but the problem was complicated by the presence of an ecclesiastical factor not less difficult and insistent than the constitu- *Was Pym right or Falkland?*

tional factor. The historical continuity of the English Church was at stake, if not the historical continuity of the English Monarchy. By the autumn of 1641 much had been achieved. The Monarchy had been stripped of the accretions with which it had been overlaid by the Stuarts. The machinery of 'Thorough' had been broken beyond repair. Falkland, Clarendon, and the moderate Royalists were prepared to give the Monarchy another chance. Pym and Hampden were not. The *Grand Remonstrance* was not an academic resolution; it was a trumpet call to civil war. Falkland feared that war would endanger all that had been gained during the first months of the Long Parliament; and who shall say that his fears were not justified? Pym was prepared to take the risk. It is customary to claim that Pym's principles, though submerged under the military autocracy of Cromwell and temporarily rejected at the Restoration, were triumphantly and permanently vindicated by the Revolution of 1688. As regards the constitutional issue the claim can be justified. But the Revolution was a triumph for the Established Church not less than for the principle of Constitutional Monarchy. The triumph of Pym's policy would have involved the establishment of Presbyterianism, the extirpation of 'prelacy' and the effacement of the Monarchy. Had Pym propounded a scheme for the supersession of the Monarch, instead of for the destruction of the Monarchy; for the enlargement of the borders of the Anglican establishment, instead of the substitution of Presbyter for Priest, Falkland might have remained at his side. But Falkland, though he cared little for the Monarch, believed in Monarchy; though he loved not the Laudian bishops, he dreaded the intellectual intolerance of the Puritan. With Falkland, therefore, rather than with Pym lay the secret of the future. Shall we then accept Lord Lytton's claim on his behalf?

'Could Falkland look from his repose on England as England is now, would not Falkland say, "This is what I sought to make my country. This is the throne which I would have reconciled with Parliamentary freedom; this is the Church that

I would have purified from ecclesiastical domination over secular affairs and intolerant persecution of rival sects. To make an England such as I now see, I opposed the framers of the Grand Remonstrance and the Nineteen Propositions; and England as seen to-day is the vindication of my policy and the refutation of Pym's''.'

The argument is specious, but is it conclusive? Undeniably the England of to-day corresponds more closely with Falkland's ideal than with Pym's, but who shall say that if Pym had not done the rough work in his day, the delicately poised machinery of a Parliamentary monarchy would ever have been evolved?

For this digression on persons no apology is offered: the persons represented the principles which in that phase of the revolution were essentially in conflict. Moreover, the exit of these actors from the stage coincided with the opening of a new act of the drama.

The acceptance of the Covenant marked, in truth, the last effective effort of Parliament to retain control of the situation. Pym had controlled it until his death; but he left no successor at Westminster; control was soon to pass to the army and its generals.

One great military success was, however, reserved for the Covenanters. In January 1644 the Scots crossed the Tweed; Newcastle was like to be crushed between them and the Fairfaxes in Yorkshire, and ultimately found himself besieged in York; Rupert, however, fought his way through to him, and on 2 July the battle was joined on Marston Moor. The defeat of the parliamentary forces under the Fairfaxes was more than retrieved by Cromwell and David Leslie; the day ended in the rout of the Cavaliers. A fortnight later York surrendered, and the King's cause in the North was ruined.

Cromwell's brilliant victory in Yorkshire was thrown into bolder relief by the defeat of Essex in Cornwall, and by the failure of Manchester and Waller to wrest victory from the King in the second battle of Newbury (27 October).

After the failure at Newbury Cromwell lost patience with his colleagues. He bluntly ascribed the failure to 'some principle of unwillingness to have the war prosecuted to a full victory; and a desire to have it ended by an accommodation on some such terms to which it might be disadvantageous to bring the King too low'. He had some ground for his suspicions; but the Presbyterian party was still powerful enough to insist on the reopening of negotiations with the King. Peace propositions were accordingly agreed upon in Parliament on 9 November, and were presented to the King 'a fortnight later at Oxford. The King agreed to send Commissioners to discuss them on his behalf to Uxbridge, where they met a deputation from Parliament and the Scotch Commissioners.

The Uxbridge Proposi- tions, January 1645 Gardiner has described the terms offered to the King at Uxbridge as 'insulting'. They were nothing less. Several of the more objectionable demands put forward in the Nineteen Propositions, but omitted, as we have seen, from the Propositions presented to the King at Oxford (1 February 1643), now reappeared,[1] and in addition the King was asked to agree to share with Parliament his right of declaring war and peace, and to set up a permanent body of Commissioners, English and Scotch, with the most extensive power to control all the military forces of England and Scotland. A long list of delinquents was included, together with several categories of unnamed persons, and upon them all the expenses of the war were to be charged. Finally, not only were the two Kingdoms to be brought into complete religious uniformity, but the King himself was to subscribe the Covenant.

The King's reply demanded in effect that the *status quo ante*, the *Grand Remonstrance*, should be restored, and suggested that a National Synod should be 'legally called' to deal with the suppression of Popery, the 'firmer settling of the Protestant religion established by law', the 'better preserving of the Book of Common Prayer from scorn and violence, and the easing of tender consciences'. It has

[1] For details, cf. *supra*, p. 207, and Gardiner, *Documents*, p. xliv.

been observed that the offer now made by the King did
not fall far short of the Settlement ultimately effected by
the Revolution of 1688. That is true, but it ought to be
added that the Revolution Settlement was guaranteed by
the execution of one Stuart King and the expulsion of a
second. In 1645 Parliament was as little likely to accept
the King's terms as Charles was to accept theirs. Had
Parliament but known it, Uxbridge was their last real
chance either of offering or accepting terms.

The breakdown of the Uxbridge negotiations was immediately followed by a great victory—his first—won by
Cromwell at Westminster. In the House of Commons he
pressed for a reorganization of the army and a change in
its commanders.

The Self-Denying Ordi-nance, April 1645

'Without a more speedy, vigorous, and effectual prosecution
of the war we shall make the kingdom weary of us, and make it
hate the name of a Parliament. . . . If the army be not put into
another method and the war more vigorously prosecuted, the
people can bear the war no longer, and will enforce you to a
dishonourable peace.'

Cromwell spoke the blunt truth, and on 23 November the
Commons ordered the Committee of both Kingdoms to
consider forthwith the reorganization of the whole army.
This was followed on 19 December by a drastic Ordinance
to deprive members of both Houses of all offices or commands, civil or military. The Lords after some delay
rejected the Ordinance, but ultimately (3 April 1645)
accepted it in a modified and much less stringent form.
The new Self-Denying Ordinance merely required all
members of the two Houses to resign their offices or
commands within forty days, but no obstacle to their
reappointment was raised, if Parliament thought fit.
Meanwhile the supreme command of an army, completely
remodelled, was entrusted to Sir Thomas Fairfax. Skippon,
an experienced soldier, was appointed a Major-General, but
the intermediate place was not filled. Cromwell had, however, been specially ordered by Parliament to continue his
work in the army, and on 10 June—just before the fight

at Naseby—Fairfax and his Council of Officers petitioned that he might be appointed Lieutenant-General, with the command of the cavalry. To this petition the Commons assented; the Lords returned no answer. After the great victories of 1645 no answer was needed.

The New Model Army The effect of the New Model was soon demonstrated. The great victory at Naseby (19 June 1645) was followed by a successful campaign in the west: Bath was taken on 29 July; on 10 September Rupert was forced to surrender Bristol, and by the end of October all the west, except Devon and Cornwall, was cleared of Royalists. In Scotland, Montrose, after a year of brilliant and unbroken successes, was surprised and defeated by David Leslie at Philiphaugh (13 September); in the early part of 1646 the south-west was won for the Roundheads, and on 24 June the devoted city of Oxford was forced to surrender. The fall of Oxford marked the end of the first Civil War.

The Newcastle Propositions The King escaped from Oxford just before it was invested by Fairfax and took refuge with the Scots, who presently carried him off a prisoner to Newcastle. To that city Parliament sent further propositions for peace (July 1646). The terms offered to the King varied little from those he had rejected at Uxbridge. The militia was to be controlled by Parliament for twenty years, but the demands for Parliamentary control over the education of the Royal children and the determination of peace and war were dropped. Presbyterianism, however, was to remain established, and the King was to take the Covenant and to agree to the proscription of a large number of his best and bravest supporters. 'Little wonder is it,' as Mr. John Morley said, 'that these proposals, some of them even now so odious, some so intolerable, seemed to Charles to strike the Crown from his head as effectually as if it were the stroke of the axe.'[1] Even less wonder, I would add, if his replies were regarded as unsatisfactory and evasive. In the event, Parliament claimed the custody of his person, and in February 1647 he was escorted to Holmby House.

[1] *Cromwell*, p. 207.

The breakdown of the negotiations at Newcastle marked a decisive moment in the history of the English Revolution. The King, had he accepted the terms then offered to him by Parliament, would have impaled Cromwell and the Independents on the horns of a dilemma. The latter would have found themselves compelled either to accept the yoke of an Erastian Presbyterianism or again to take up arms against a combination of the King, both Houses of Parliament, and the Scots. From making that difficult choice they were relieved only through the obstinacy or the high principle of the King. If Charles had been a greater statesman or a wiser man he might have accepted the terms offered at Newcastle and have won at least a respite from the divisions of his enemies.

Even as it was his enemies were sorely divided. Perhaps the knowledge of those divisions explained the King's refusal and induced the high spirits in which he arrived at Holmby. They rose still higher when he found himself courted by the army. Nor were they wholly unjustified. Despite his defeat in the field the King's position was inherently a strong one. The English people as a whole were essentially monarchical. The Stuarts had tried them sorely, and in the middle and upper classes there were many who had suffered in person, in goods and in consciences, from the tyranny of King and Bishops. But the more thoughtful must have known, as Cromwell knew, that a King was an indispensable element of the English Polity, while among the masses the hereditary instinct for an hereditary monarchy was part of the very fibre of their being. *Army and Parliament*

On the other hand it is true that the new military organization, the long discussions around camp-fires, and the growing revolt against authority in State and even more perhaps in Church, were factors making for a new temper among both officers and men of Cromwell's army. That temper was democratic if not republican. It recked little of the craft of Kings, of priests or presbyters. Cromwell and the Independents were not anarchists; far

from it; but they held that authority was lent to law by
the will not of governors but of the governed. When after
Naseby fight Baxter visited Cromwell's army in camp, he
found a state of things he had never dreamt of. 'I heard,'
he says, 'the plotting heads very hot on that which
intimated the intention to subvert Church and State . . .
I found many honest men of ignorance and weak judgement seduced into a disputing vein to talking for Church
democracy or State democracy.' [1] Baillie, writing of the
same period, notes: 'In all the sects, notably the Anabaptists, there is a declared averseness from all obedience
to the present magistrates and laws and frequent motions to
have the very fundamentals of government new módelled;
they do no more dissemble their detestation of monarchy.' [2]
In short, the Levellers were at work in the army. To their
influence Baxter ascribed the new temper which he discerned among the soldiers: 'A great part of the mischief
was caused by distribution of the pamphlets of Overton
and Lilburne and others against the King and the Ministry
and for Liberty of Conscience, and the soldiers in their
quarters had such books to read when they had none to
contradict them.' [3]

To what such reading tended the sequel will show.

[1] *Life*, 50–3, quoted *ap*. G. P. Gooch, *British Democratic Ideas in the
Seventeenth Century*, p. 136—an admirable essay.
[2] *Letters*, ii. 117.   [3] *Ap*. Gooch, p. 141.

X. THE FALL OF THE MONARCHY

Army and Parliament

THE rise of the Levellers marks the opening of yet another act in the drama of the Puritan Revolution. The new movement was in part the product of war waged by a democratic army, in part the product of the ecclesiastical ideas which were wafted back to England from the Puritan exiles in Holland and New England. The Levellers represented, in short, the political application of Brownist or Independent principles of Church Government. They rejected the sovereignty of Parliament as decisively as they rejected the sovereignty of the King or the supremacy of the Pope. Sovereignty belonged only to the people. Baxter found the soldiers in camp 'vehement against the King, and against all government but popular' Their immediate quarrel, however, was with the King.

'I perceived,' writes Baxter, 'that they took the King for a tyrant and an enemy, and really intended absolutely to master him or to ruin him, and that they thought that if they might fight against him they might kill or conquer him; and if they might conquer they were never more to trust him further than he was in their power.'

In their crusade against monarchy they looked to Crom- well as their natural leader. But Cromwell was not merely a popular leader, nor merely a great soldier, but a statesman of profound sagacity. He was indeed impatient of what seemed to him the pedantry of Parliament and its Presbyterian masters. Comradeship in arms with men of widely differing opinions had taught him lessons hidden from the eyes of those who lived and worked under the shadow of the Westminster Assembly. In the Presbyterian creed there was no room for toleration. 'To let men serve God according to the persuasion of their own consciences was to cast out one devil that seven worse might enter.' That was the prevailing temper at Westminster.

Q

Around the camp-fires of the New Model army men saw things differently; most of all did the General. 'Honest men served you faithfully in this action; they are trusty; I beseech you in the name of God not to discourage them. He that ventures his life for the liberty of his country, I wish he trust God for the liberty of his conscience, and you for the liberty he fights for.' Thus Cromwell wrote to Parliament from the field of Naseby. But his plea for toleration was deeply resented at Westminster. Nevertheless, he repeated the plea a few months later, when the great campaign in the west had been crowned by the capitulation of Bristol.

'Presbyterians and Independents all here have the same spirit of faith and prayer . . . they agree here, have no names of difference; pity it should be otherwise anywhere. All that believe have the real unity which is most glorious because inward and spiritual. . . . From brethren in things of the mind we look for no compulsion, but that of light and reason.'

If the King had accepted the terms offered to him at Newcastle a compulsion, not of light and reason, had indeed been legally established. From that peril the nation was saved, as we have seen, by the obstinacy or optimism of the King.

The King's hopes   The rejection of the terms offered to the King at Newcastle gave Cromwell his chance, and he determined to seize it by seeking an accommodation with Charles. For he understood, as his fanatical followers did not, that without *a* King, if not without *the* King, no permanent settlement was possible. The King, needless to say, shared Cromwell's conviction. 'Men will begin to perceive', he wrote, 'that without my establishing there can be no peace.' His immediate anxiety, however, was to get into personal touch with the leaders of the two parties in Parliament. 'Now for my own particular resolution. It is this, I am endeavouring to get to London, so that the conditions may be such as a gentleman may own, and that the rebels may acknowledge me King, being not without hope that I shall be able so to draw either the Presbyterians or Independents to side with me for extirpating the other that I shall be really King again.' So he wrote to Digby. But his hopes were destined to disappointment. Both parties wished indeed to retain him on the throne; neither was willing (as the terms offered to him proved) that he should be, in his sense, 'really King again '.

Meanwhile, in January 1647, the Presbyterian leaders sent secretly to the King a draft letter which, if approved by him, was to be sent to Parliament as a further reply to the Newcastle proposals. The King accepted it with unimportant modifications, and returned it to Parliament in May. He offered to come to London and 'heartily join in all that shall concern the honour of his two Kingdoms', and to confirm the establishment of Presbyterianism for three years (provided that he and his household should be free to use the Anglican liturgy in private), and then to settle religion in consultation with the Westminster Assembly. He agreed to strong measures against Popish recusants, and to leave the militia for a period of ten years in the hands of the nominees of Parliament. The Presbyterians and the King

Great stress is laid by Dr. Gardiner on these documents as marking the first step in that alliance between the King and the Presbyterians which led to the second Civil War in 1648 and to the Restoration in 1660. In return for the temporary establishment of Presbyterianism and a temporary control of the militia, the King was to be restored to the position he had occupied before the war. But the agreement was not a satisfactory one, for as Sir Charles Firth has observed, 'it left unsettled the questions which had caused the war and threw away all the fruits of the victory'.[1]

What would the army say to the agreement? The Presbyterian leaders showed no anxiety to find out. The war was over—except in Ireland—and in February and March 1647 Parliament passed a series of resolutions for the disbandment of the army. The army was to be reduced at once from 40,000 to about 16,000, of whom only 4,000 Parliament and Army

[1] *Cromwell*, p. 156.

horse were to be retained for service in England, the rest were to be employed for the reconquest of Ireland. Fairfax was to be retained as General, but all the other Generals and all Independent officers were to be dismissed; only Presbyterians were to be employed. No member of Parliament was to hold a commission, and the soldiers were to receive on disbandment only one-sixth of the arrears of pay.

The Parliament which had raised the army was plainly within its constitutional rights in disbanding it; but the terms offered to the soldiers were insulting in their inadequacy. A great meeting of officers was held at Saffron Walden to protest against them and to formulate the counter-demands of the army: these included a legal indemnity for their actions as soldiers; payment of arrears in full; pensions for widows and orphans of soldiers killed in service; exemption from imprisonment in any future war, and pay till disbandment.

The agitators' To those not unreasonable demands Parliament replied by a resolution declaring those who joined in the army petition to be enemies of the State and disturbers of the public peace (30 March). The army, in reply, vindicated their right as soldiers and citizens to petition Parliament, and proceeded to elect agents or agitators from each regiment to represent them. They thus came near to the establishment of a rival Parliament.

Cromwell looked with mistrust upon this quasi-political development and did his utmost to induce in both parties a more conciliatory temper. But Parliament was determined to disband the army; the army refused to be disbanded or deported to Ireland until it had received satisfaction for its grievances. Meanwhile, both Parliament and army realized with increasing vividness that the King held the key of the situation.

King abducted by Army The custody of the King's person became, therefore, a matter of vital importance. But while Parliament was considering his removal from Holmby House to London, Cornet Joyce, with a troop of Horse, suddenly appeared at Holmby and carried the King off to his own house at

Newmarket. Newmarket, though hard by the army head-quarters, was selected by the King himself in preference to Oxford or Cambridge. He was received there by the villagers with demonstrations of loyalty and was treated by the army with respect.

A week after the King's arrival at Newmarket, a rendez-vous of the army was held on Triploe Heath. Commissioners appointed by Parliament laid before the army further proposals from both Houses: complete indemnity for acts done in the war; the repeal of the offensive Declaration of 30 March, and an addition to the sum voted for the speedy payment of arrears after disbandment. The reply of the army was a demand that the terms should be submitted to the Council of Officers and agitators; that the Presbyterian leaders should be excluded from Parliament; and that the army should have a voice in the final settlement of the nation. Army Convention at Triploe Heath 10 June

At the same time the army advanced a stage nearer London—to Royston, and addressed an appeal not to Parliament but to the City. Army appeal to the City

'We desire', it declared, 'a settlement of the Kingdom and of the liberties of the subject . . . but no alteration of the civil government. As little do we desire to interrupt, or in the least to intermeddle with, the settling of the Presbyterian Government. Nor do we seek to open a way for licentious liberty under pretence of obtaining ease for tender consciences. We profess as ever in these things, when once the State has made a settlement; we have nothing to say but to submit or suffer. Only we could wish that every good citizen, and every man who walks peaceably in a blameless conversation, and is beneficial to the Commonwealth, might have liberty and encouragement; this being according to the true policy of all States, and even to justice itself.'

To this appeal the Common Council returned a temporizing answer, repudiating any intention of resisting the just demands of the soldiers, but requesting the army not to advance within thirty miles of London, lest they should enhance the price of provisions for the citizens.

Declara-
tion of
the Army
To this the Council of the Army replied with a Declaration (15 June), in which the army claimed the right to speak in the name of the English people, asked the House of Commons to fix a date for its own dissolution; demanded that in future Parliament should sit for a fixed period, and should not be adjourned or dissolved without its own consent; that the right of petitioning should be acknowledged; that offences should be punished by law and not by Parliament; and that, after a few examples had been made of delinquents, there should be a general act of oblivion.

Parliament refused even to discuss these demands, or to suspend the eleven members impeached by the army; but as the army, despite the request of the City, continued their advance on the capital, the eleven members voluntarily withdrew from the House. Parliament then made some concessions to the demands of the army, which retired to Reading, and established the King at Caversham, where Cromwell began the series of conversations with his sovereign intended to prepare the way for a final settlement.

Hampton
Court
Proposi-
tions
August
1647
These overtures unfortunately led the King to overrate the strength of his own position. Important he was: but he regarded himself as indispensable.

'The King,' writes that stout old republican, Colonel Ludlow, 'finding himself courted on all hands became so confident of his own interest as to think himself able to turn the scale to what side soever he pleased, which Commissary General Ireton, discerning said these words to him: Sir, you have an intention to be arbitrator between the Parliament and us, and we mean to be so between you and the Parliament.'

Ireton, Cromwell's son-in-law, a constitutional jurist of high intelligence and the skilled draughtsman of the Army Council, had accurately diagnosed the situation, and to him was committed the task of drafting the Proposals which, after they had been informally submitted to the King, were amended by the Council of the Army and on 1 August were published.

Formally presented to the King at Hampton Court these

Heads of Proposals were, in more senses than one, a notable advance on any plan of settlement hitherto drafted. They were at once more democratic and less anti-monarchical. 'They did not,' as Gardiner observed, 'like the various propositions laid before Charles on former occasions, seek to establish a Parliamentary despotism upon the ruins of the despotism of the King. They proposed indeed to make the King's power subservient to that of the Parliament,' but at the same time to make Parliament itself more amenable to the constituencies, and to restrict the powers of the State over the liberty of the individual citizen. Clarendon does not take this view, but Clarendon could not, like Gardiner, view such proposals from the standpoint of a late Victorian critic. To him they appeared 'as ruinous to the Church and destructive to the regal power as had yet been made by the Parliament, and in some respects much worse and more dishonourable '.

How far can this opinion be sustained? The existing Parliament was to be dissolved within a year at most. In future, Parliament was to be brought into closer touch with the electorate by biennial elections which were to be 'free', and by a drastic redistribution of seats based on some intelligible 'rule of equality or proportion', such as rateable value. The militia was to be controlled by Parliament for ten years, and after that to be commanded by the King, but with the advice and control of Parliament. The great offices of State were to be at the disposal of Parliament for ten years, after which the King was to appoint to each vacancy from a list of three names submitted by Parliament. Parliament was to appoint committees to function in its name during the recesses, and for seven years there was to be a Council of State to 'superintend' the militia and to conduct foreign affairs, though the final decision of peace and war was to be reserved to Parliament. Peers created after 21 May 1642 were not to sit without the consent of both Houses; Acts under the Great Seal, from the date when it was carried off from Westminster, were to be invalid, while the Acts under the Parliament Seal were validated. There was to be an act of oblivion for all except five royalist 'delinquents'. As regards religion there was to be complete freedom: Episcopacy might survive, but the Bishops were to have no coercive power; there were to be no civil penalties for spiritual offences; and no one was to be compelled to take the Covenant and to be punished for attending or not attending any particular form of public worship.

It is easier for us than it could have been for Charles or Clarendon to appreciate the good points in these proposals. We have the history of the Interregnum to demonstrate that the conduct of an unreformed Parliament can be at least as arbitrary as that of a Stuart King. We know that the solution of the problem of the Executive was ultimately found in a Cabinet, nominally appointed by the King, but actually responsible to Parliament. Even Charles, however, might have been expected to see that though restraints were imposed, and inevitably, upon him, the dignity and utility of the monarchy were not permanently impaired; that he himself was spared the humiliation of subscribing a Covenant which outraged his most sacred convictions; and that in common with the meanest and the proudest of his subjects he would still be free to worship God in the manner approved by himself, and to remain in communion with a Church governed by the successors of the Apostles.

Parliament and the City But Charles had persuaded himself that he could get much more than this; that if he played off the Parliament against the army, the Presbyterians against the Independents, he could be 'really King again'. That conviction proved his undoing.

At this point a fresh complication arose. Parliament having given way to the demands of the army was confronted by the demands of the City, more Parliamentarian, or at least more Presbyterian, than the Presbyterian Parliament itself. The London mob, its political appetite whetted by the food which for years Parliament had served out to it, demanded the control of the London militia, the restoration of the eleven secluded members, and insisted that the King should be invited to return to London 'with safety, honour, and freedom'.

Parliament now appeared to be between the devil and the deep sea. Yet real power rested not with the City, its train-bands and militia, but with the disciplined and experienced troops under the command of Fairfax and Cromwell. Early in August the army made a triumphal march through London; the Presbyterian leaders again withdrew from Parliament, and the fugitive Independents were restored.

Yet despite this fresh proof of the supremacy of the army, the King still refused to accept the terms suggested in the Heads of the Proposals.

Cromwell's patience was wellnigh exhausted, but he still held grimly on to his determination to retain the monarchy, if the monarch's obstinacy would permit. Meanwhile, he was confronted by a critical situation in his own party.

New ideas, almost as repugnant to Cromwell as to Charles, were beginning to permeate the army. Men like Hugh Peters who, after exile in Holland and a sojourn in New England, had returned to serve as a chaplain in the New Model army, and John Lilburne, one of the many Puritan victims of the Star Chamber, were disseminating by tongue and pen new and strange doctrines among their comrades. From those doctrines, democratic and communistic, a new party known as the *Levellers* drew their inspiration. Sovereignty belonged neither to the Prince nor to Parliament; it was vested in the people, from whom Prince and Parliament alike derived any authority they exercised. Why should political power be based on the possession of property? Had not the poor a birthright as inalienable as that of the rich? Such was the language which began to be heard round the camp-fires. More sinister things began to be whispered. What did the meetings between Cromwell and Royalists portend? Was it true that Cromwell and Ireton had knelt to the King and kissed his hand? Nay, had they not succumbed to the promise of earldoms?

The Levellers

'The King's flatteries', said Wildman, 'were like poisoned arrows, infecting the blood in the veins of Cromwell and Ireton.'

'The Case of the Army' Loose talk of this kind began, in the autumn of 1647, to take form in concrete propositions. Specific demands were embodied in *The Case of the Army*. No more privileges, sinecures or monopolies, the restoration of the common lands to the poor from whom they had been stolen by enclosers—these were among the demands of the *Case*.

The Agreement of the People Of much greater and more permanent significance was *The Agreement of the People*. This document was originally drawn up in October 1647, and copies of it were flaunted by the Levellers when mutiny broke out at Ware in November; but it was not presented to the House of Commons until 20 January 1649—ten days before the execution of the King. As it was the first of several attempts made between 1649 and 1659 to reorganize the government of England on the basis of a written Constitution it may be more convenient to consider its terms presently in connexion with the other experiments of the Commonwealth and Protectorate.

Its immediate significance lay in the fact that, together with *The Case of the Army*, it supplied a rallying point for the critics of Cromwell who, on 15 November 1647, led the mutiny at the rendezvous at Ware.

Cromwell and the Levellers Cromwell was gravely perturbed by the growing influence of Lilburne and the spread of the Levellers' doctrines among his soldiers. Not only did he deprecate the attack on the monarchy, which he was still anxious to conserve in the interests less of the monarch than of the people, but he staunchly championed the principle of authority, wheresoever it might reside. 'No men', he declared, 'could enjoy their lives and estates quietly without the King has his rights.' The monarchy, in short, was essential to personal liberty and the rights of property. Throughout the whole of this tangled time between the two Civil Wars, while the triangular duel was in progress between the King, the Army, and the Parliament, Cromwell held steadfast to his main purposes: in State, a settled and orderly government; in Church, freedom of conscience for all within the pale of Christianity. Favourable to monarchy and tolerant of episcopacy, he held that both must be deprived of the power to tyrannize over the bodies or minds of men. Yet he was no Leveller. Worse even than tyranny was anarchy, and anarchy there must needs be if the private soldiers took it upon themselves to issue orders, or if the officers refused to acknowledge the civil authority of Parliament. He would himself lay hold of anything 'if it had but the face of authority' rather than have none.[1]

A critical moment was reached when the army held a convention or *rendezvous* in Corkbush Field, between Hertford and Ware. Prompt action was needed if the spreading spirit of mutiny was not to triumph; nay, if the Commonwealth was not to be plunged into anarchy from which it could only issue under the heel of a tyrant, crowned or uncrowned. Cromwell did not hesitate. Eleven of the chief mutineers were called out from the ranks; condemned by drum-head court-martial to die; lots were cast among the condemned men; the lot fell upon Trooper Arnold: he was shot there and then. A dangerous mutiny was thus for the moment quelled. But the spirit which inspired it was unbroken, and manifested itself afresh, as we shall see, after the execution of the King. *Rendezvous at Ware 15 Nov. 1647*

Towards that crisis of the drama the action now moves fast. In the autumn of 1647 Cromwell began to be alarmed for the King's safety. Would not the Levellers take it on themselves to execute justice upon the 'chief delinquent'? Charles was at the moment under the care of Colonel Whalley at Hampton Court, and Cromwell thought it well to warn his cousin: 'There are rumours abroad of some intended attempt on his Majesty's person. Therefore I pray have a care of your guards. If any such thing should be done it were accounted a horrid act.' Perhaps the same *Charles at Carisbrooke*

---

[1] Cf. Carlyle, *Letters and Speeches*, vol. i, part iii. Firth, *op. cit.*, c. ix *passim*; F. Harrison, *Cromwell*, c. vi.

rumours had reached the King. Anyway, on the same night (11 November 1647) he fled from Hampton Court and took refuge in the Isle of Wight, at Carisbrooke. The motive of the King's flight remains uncertain. The theory that it was due to a sinister suggestion of Cromwell, though supported by the well-known lines of Marvell, may be dismissed at once.[1] That it was planned with the connivance of Colonel Robert Hammond, Governor of the Isle of Wight, who had visited the King at Hampton Court, is more likely. But Hammond was a connexion by marriage of Cromwell's, and though 'tempted' by the King continued to be his vigilant though respectful gaoler. Escape from custody of the army had in fact been urged upon the King by the Scots, who suggested Berwick as his refuge; but the King preferred the Isle of Wight as being handier, should necessity compel, for flight to France.

The King and the Scots

Not that the King regarded his plight as by any means desperate. From Carisbrooke—'a place where he conceives himself to be at much more freedom and security than formerly'—he wrote to the Speaker of the House of Lords refusing to abandon Episcopacy but offering to continue the Presbyterian establishment for three years, with freedom of conscience for others, and then to promote a settlement of religion with the consent of King and Parliament, to abandon the control of the militia for his own lifetime, and, as regards Parliaments, to give favourable consideration to the army proposals for reform. Parliament's reply was to embody an ultimatum in Four Bills and a series of propositions which virtually reaffirmed the Newcastle Propositions.

The 'Engagement'

The King thereupon turned to the Scottish Commissioners who had arrived at Carisbrooke and concluded with them an *Engagement* (26 December 1647) by which

[1] 'Twining subtle fears with hope
He wove a net of such a scope
As Charles himself might chase
To Carisbrooke's narrow case,
That thence the royal actor borne
The tragic scaffold might adorn.'

the Scots undertook to restore the monarchy in full regality in return for the three years' establishment of Presbyterianism, the suppression of sectaries, and certain privileges for the Scots. The Scottish Parliament was to require from the English Parliament the disbandment of all armies, and if this were refused to demand the restoration of the King to his full regality. If this were refused the Scots would invade England to insist on these concessions and to summon a 'free and full Parliament in England'.

Neither party was in truth in a position to fulfil the terms of this *Engagement*. Nevertheless, on the strength of it, the King refused his assent to the Four Bills, and prepared for flight to France. But the door of escape was now closed to him. He was for the first time a close prisoner at Carisbrooke. Parliament countered by the vote of No Addresses, which recorded their resolution to break off negotiations with the King (17 January 1648). *No Addresses*

The army leaders presently arrived at a similar resolution. Towards the end of April they held a convention at Windsor, where a momentous resolution was adopted: *The Army resolution*

'That it was our duty, if ever the Lord brought us back again in Peace, to call Charles Stuart, that man of blood, to account for that blood he had shed, and mischief he had done to his utmost, against the Lord's Cause and People in these poor Nations.' [1]

Cromwell could no longer resist this resolution. Charles was impossible; yet might not the monarchy survive the deposition of the King? According to Sir Charles Firth, there is evidence that during the Spring of 1648 the Independent leaders discussed a scheme for deposing Charles I and placing the Prince of Wales or the Duke of York upon the throne—a plan frustrated by the unwillingness of the Prince and the flight of the Duke to France. [2]

[1] *Somers Tracts*, vi. 501, quoted *ap.* Carlyle, i. 290, where there is a vivid account of the Windsor 'Prayer Meeting'. Gardiner (*Civil War*, iv. 117) fixes the date of this momentous meeting as 29 April to 1 May, and the wording of the resolution seems to point to a date subsequent to the outbreak of the second Civil War.

[2] *Cromwell*, p. 190.

For the moment, however, the King himself had sealed the fate of the monarchy.

The second Civil War

The second Civil War was, in even greater degree than the first, fought over the heads of the common folk. Only in Kent and Essex, perhaps the most truly English parts of England,[1] was there any popular rising in favour of the King, and Fairfax suppressed it by his victory at Maidstone in June and a second at Colchester in August. Meanwhile, in West Wales the stubborn defence of Pembroke Castle kept Cromwell employed for six weeks, but Pembroke surrendered on 11 July, and Cromwell was free to meet the more serious danger which threatened in the north. Three days before Pembroke surrendered a large Scottish army, under the Duke of Hamilton, crossed the border and moved south, not, as Cromwell had expected, by the east coast route but by the west. Cromwell joined Lambert near Knaresborough on August 12, and learning that Hamilton was advancing through Lancashire he crossed the Pennines and fell upon the Royalist army at Preston. A running fight lasting three days (17–19 August), and extending from Preston to Wigan and Warrington, annihilated Hamilton's army, and practically ended the war. Cromwell then marched with his victorious army into Scotland, and, having come to an arrangement with Argyle that the Hamiltonian royalists should be permanently excluded from office in the Northern Kingdom, he returned to deal with the situation in London.

Parliament and the King

While the army had been busy in the field Parliament had plucked up courage to reopen negotiations with the King who, in September, accepted the terms offered to him at Newport (Isle of Wight). The appointment of officers, the command of the military forces of the Crown, and the appointment of the chief officers of State were to be in the hands of Parliament for twenty years; the Bishops were to be suspended and the Presbyterian Establishment continued for three years; there was to be an amnesty for all members of Parliament and punishment for a few Royalist

[1] Cf. H. G. Wells, *Mr. Britling Sees it Through.*

'delinquents'. Charles was avowedly playing for time: 'The great concession I made this day—the Church, militia and Ireland—was made merely in order to my escape.' So he wrote to a friend. But escape was no longer open to him.

The 'Treaty of Newport' served only to embitter the feelings with which the army returned to London. Petitions poured in from regiment after regiment. All protested against the Treaty concluded between Parliament and the King and demanded that the authors of the war should be brought to justice. Cromwell shared to the full the exasperation of his troops. The Army and the King

In forwarding their petitions to the General, Cromwell wrote:

'I find a very great sense in the officers . . . for the sufferings and ruin of this poor Kingdom, and in them all a very great zeal to have impartial justice done upon all offenders; and I do in all from my heart concur with them, and I verily think they are things which God puts into our hearts.' [1]

But if coercion was to be applied to Parliament it must needs be justified by an appeal to principle. That principle he discovered in the 'Divine Right' of the army and disclosed it in one of the most interesting of all his letters— that addressed to the 'Dear Robin' who was still the King's gaoler. Colonel Hammond's conscience was distracted by a dual if not a triple allegiance. The anointed of the Lord was in his custody. True, Charles had been in treaty with Parliament, but was not Parliament still the constitutional authority? The General had recalled him to head-quarters on 21 November, and he prepared to obey the summons. Hammond, therefore, handed over his charge to three officers on the 27th, but with instructions to prevent the removal of the King from the island 'unless by direct order of Parliament'. The army head-quarters had been moved to Windsor. On his way Hammond was met at Farnham by orders from Parliament to return to the island and The Divine Right of the Army

[1] Carlyle, ii. 79.

resume his charge. Thereupon he was arrested by an army escort and conveyed to Windsor.

Cromwell's letter of reassurance and remonstrance, written on 25 November from Knottingley, near Pontefract, could not yet have reached him. But as a revelation of Cromwell's mind it is none the less of supreme importance. To Hammond's scruples as to Divinely ordered authority of Parliament he replies with a series of characteristic questions: Are there no limits to the obligations of passive or active obedience? Is not *salus populi* a sound doctrine? Has not Parliament broken its covenants with the army? Has not God's will been manifested in the great victories vouchsafed to the army? 'Let us look into providences; surely they mean somewhat.' Did not the God-given victories point to the transfer of lawful authority from a Parliament which had betrayed His cause to the army which had vindicated His purposes to man? [1]

Of Cromwell's own passionate conviction that he was himself guided by the hand of God there cannot, to any candid mind, be question. In that conviction he pursued his grim task.

Pride's Purge December 6–7

Events now moved rapidly. On 30 November Parliament refused to take into consideration the Army Remonstrance. On 1 December the King was removed, a close prisoner, from the island to Hurst Castle on the opposite shore. On the 2nd the army moved up to London and quartered itself in Westminster. Nevertheless, Parliament resolved to continue negotiations with the King. On the 6th the army discharged the City train-bands, who had acted as the guard of Parliament, and occupied Palace Yard and Westminster Hall with horse and foot under the command of Colonel Rich and Colonel Pride. Only members well affected to the army, some fifty or sixty, were allowed to enter the House. Forty-five were arrested and ninety-six others excluded from the House.

The Fate of the King

What should be the next step? What was to be done with the King? Differences of opinion manifested them-

[1] Carlyle, ii. 84.

selves among the officers. Cromwell still pleaded, on
grounds of policy, that the King's life should be spared,
provided he would accept the terms now offered to him.
The King refused even to consider terms. Cromwel
therefore, in despair, gave way to the extremists. On
1 January 1649 the Independent Rump in the House of
Commons passed an Ordinance to set up a special Court
to try the King. A handful of Peers refused to concur.
The Commons then resolved that 'the people are under
God the original of all just power', and that the 'Commons
of England in Parliament assembled, being chosen by and
representing the people, have the supreme power in the
nation', and may lawfully legislate without the concurrence of King or Peers. Two days later an Act was
passed setting up a Commission of one hundred and thirty-
five persons to hear, try, and adjudge Charles Stuart.
This step was justified in an elaborate preamble on the
ground that the King had 'a wicked design totally to
subvert the laws and liberties of this nation, and in
their place to introduce an arbitrary and tyrannical
government', that he had maintained a civil war against
the Parliament and Kingdom, and had only taken
advantage of the forbearance of Parliament to raise
'new commotions, rebellions, and invasions'. To prevent
any future attempt 'traitorously and maliciously to
imagine or contrive the enslaving or destroying of the
English nation', Charles Stuart must be brought to
justice.

The King had been brought up to Windsor on 23 Trial and
December, and on 19 January was transferred to St. James's execu-
Palace. Brought before the Commissioners on the 20th the King
the King naturally refused to acknowledge the jurisdiction
of the Court, but despite grave differences of opinion among
the Commissioners sixty-seven of them were found to
sentence the King to death as 'tyrant, traitor, murderer,
and a public enemy to the Commonwealth of England'.
Fifty-nine signatures were, by one means or another,
collected to the warrant for his execution, and on the

30th King Charles, with perfect dignity and pious resignation, met his fate.

The well-known lines of Andrew Marvell testify to the
impression made by the King's Execution upon those who
witnessed it:

> He nothing common did or mean
> Upon that memorable scene,
> But with his keener eye
> The axe's edge did try;
> Nor call'd the gods with vulgar spite
> To vindicate his helpless right,
> But bow'd his comely head
> Down, as upon a bed.

Thus the curtain falls upon the last act of a great
tragedy. Modern usage has vulgarized the word: yet a
'tragedy' in the strict sense Charles's death unquestionably was. From that day to this the act of the regicides
has continued to excite bitter controversy. Justified by
Cromwell as a cruel necessity; denounced by others as a
foul murder, the execution of the King has been very
differently judged even by the most impartial of historians.
Legal justification, in the narrower sense, there could be
none. The remnant of a Legislature, acting under military
coercion, set up an irregular tribunal whose jurisdiction
the King properly denied. Justification must be sought on
other grounds. Can it be found?

Did the King's execution make for liberty?

'For the people I desire their liberty and freedom as much
as anybody whatsoever; but I must tell you that their liberty
and freedom consists in having government, those laws by
which their lives and their goods may be most their own. It is
not their having a share in the Government; that is nothing
appertaining unto them. A subject and a sovereign are clean
different things; and therefore until you do that—I mean that
you put the people in that liberty—they will never enjoy
themselves.'

Such were the King's own words upon the scaffold.
Harsh as his denial of the root principle of democracy may

sound in some modern ears, can it be denied that they contain more than a germ of truth? Has 'democracy' secured 'liberty'? But that is a large question, too remote from the circumstances of the hour to justify discussion in this place. Certain it is that the King's death brought no access of liberty to that generation of men.

Historians, have, for the most part, tended to condemn the deed.

'I cannot perceive', writes the judicial Hallam, 'what there was in the imagined solemnity of this proceeding, in that insolent mockery of the forms of justice, accompanied by all unfairness and inhumanity in its circumstances, which can alleviate the guilt of the transaction; and if it be alleged that many of the regicides were firmly persuaded in their consciences of the right and duty of condemning the King, we may surely remember that private murderers have often had the same apology.'

Ranke concedes to Charles at least a fragment of the martyr's crown:

'In misfortune he appears not without moral greatness. It would have been easy for him to save his life, had he conceded to the Scots the exclusive domination of Presbyterianism in England, or to the Independents the practical freedom of the army, as they themselves descried. That he did not do so is his merit towards England. Had he given his word to dissolve the episcopial governments of the Church, and to alienate its property for ever, it is impossible to see how it could ever have been restored. Had he granted such a position to the army as was asked in the four articles, the self-government of the corporations and of the Commons, and the later parliamentary governments itself would have become impossible. So far the resistance which he offered cannot be estimated highly enough. The overthrow of the constitution, which the Independents openly intended, made him fully conscious, perhaps not of their ultimate intention, the establishment of a republic, but certainly of his own position. So far there was certainly something of a martyr in him, if the man can be so called who values his own life less than the cause for which he is fighting, and in perishing himself saves it for the future.'

Gardiner refrains from a final judgement:

'All can perceive that with Charles's death the main obstacle to the establishment of a constitutional system was removed. . . . The monarchy, as Charles understood it, had disappeared for ever. . . . The scaffold had accomplished that which neither the eloquence of Eliot and Pym, nor the Statutes and Ordinances of the Long Parliament had been capable of doing.'

But even Gardiner admits that thus far the work of Cromwell and his comrades had been 'purely negative'; they had 'cleared the ground'; it was left to others to build the 'edifice of constitutional compromise'.

Was the building of that compromise impossible without the commission of a deed which led first to the despotism of Parliament, then to a military autocracy, and finally to a royalist reaction, followed in turn by a second revolution? Who shall say? For the time being Charles had in truth made all compromise impossible; for 'he could not be bound'. His word was given only to be broken. An opportunist, living only from hour to hour, he was 'a double-minded man', and therefore in all his ways unstable. On such instability no sure foundations could be laid.

XI. THE RUMP AND THE REPUBLIC

Constitutional Experiments. Democracy and Communism

THE downfall of the monarchy inaugurated a period of constitutional experiments, which, evanescent as they were, are of supreme and permanent interest to the student of political institutions.

Of those experiments the first was a Republic dominated by a uni-cameral Parliament, with a Council of State strictly subordinated to the Legislature. Resolutions for the abolition of the House of Lords and the monarchy were passed by the emasculated Commons on 6 and 7 February respectively. Not, however, until 17 March was the Kingship formally abolished; the House of Lords was abolished two days later. Meanwhile, the Rump had passed an Act for constituting a Council of State for the 'Commonwealth of England'. This Council, consisting of forty-one members, with nine as a quorum, was charged to 'oppose and suppress' any who might assert the claim of the Prince of Wales, or any other member of the Stuart family, or 'any other single person whatsoever' to the throne; to take measures for the reconquest of Ireland, the Channel Islands, and the Isle of Man, for the encouragement of trade in England, Ireland, and 'the dominions to them belonging', and all oversea plantations, to maintain friendly relations with foreign powers, and to appoint and receive ambassadors, &c. The Council was to have command of the militia, and to maintain such forces by land and sea as were necessary for the defence of the country. It was to continue in office for one year, 'unless otherwise ordered by the Parliament'. It formed, in brief, a Parliamentary Executive in all things responsible to Parliament, and its members were to take an oath of secrecy and of loyalty to the Republic 'without King or House of Lords'. Whether they were to be members of the Legislature was not specifically stated, though in fact thirty-one out of its forty-one members were also members of Parliament, which remained in continuous session.

Abolition of the Monarchy and the House of Lords

On 17 March the 'Rump' passed an Act declaring that the office of King was 'unnecessary, burdensome, and dangerous to the liberty, safety, and public interest of the people', and that it should be forthwith abolished. This Act was immediately followed (19 March) by another which declared that 'the Commons of England . . . finding by long experience that the House of Lords is useless and dangerous to the people of England to be continued have thought fit to ordain and enact . . . that from henceforth the House of Lords in Parliament shall be and hereby is wholly abolished and taken away; and that the Lords shall not from henceforth meet or sit in the said House, called the Lords' House, or in any other house or place whatsoever, as a House of Lords; nor shall sit, vote, advise, adjudge, or determine on any matter or thing whatsoever, as a House of Lords in Parliament'. Further: provision was in the same Act made that 'such Lords as have demeaned themselves with honour, courage, and fidelity to the Commonwealth' should be capable of election to the uni-cameral Legislature. The Acts of 17 and 19 March 1649, having neither the sanction of the Crown nor the House of Lords, had obviously no more legal force than any other resolution of the House of Commons. As the work of a House of Commons from which a majority of the elected representatives had been excluded by force of arms, they had less than the usual moral significance. Such considerations were, however, lost upon the Rump which from the first was plainly bent upon entrenching itself in a position of permanent authority. On 19 May 1649 it passed an Act declaring England and 'all the dominions and territories thereunto belonging' to be a Commonwealth and Free State; on 2 January 1650 it ordered an engagement of fidelity to the Commonwealth 'as now established without a King or House of Lords to be taken by all men of the age of eighteen; but there was no hint of any restrictions upon its own omnipotence, nor of any bill for the reform of the electoral franchise or the redistribution of seats; least of all of any date for its own dissolution.

In all these latter respects the policy of the Rump was in direct conflict with the principles laid down and the programme formulated in the *Agreement of the People*. To the history of that remarkable document we must now return. The Agree-ment of the People

The *Agreement of the People* was originally drawn up in October 1647, nominally by the agents elected by the soldiers of the New Model army, in fact by John Lilburne. A declaration which was at the same time laid before the General (Fairfax) asserted freedom of conscience, liberty of person, freedom from impressment, and equality before the law to be the native and fundamental rights of every Englishman—rights which no Parliament or Government had power to diminish or take away. This was, in short, a counter-manifesto to the *Heads of the Proposals of the Army* which had been drawn up by Ireton and published by the Council of Officers on 1 August 1647. The Heads of Proposals represented, as we have seen, the minimum demands of Cromwell and the Officers for a settlement of the Kingdom. They assumed the continuance of the monarchy and the House of Lords. The *Agreement of the People* was couched in a very different tone. It demanded 'a democratic republic based on a written constitution drawn up in accordance with abstract principles new to English politics'.[1] It anticipated the *Charter* of 1837 in asking for manhood suffrage, equal electoral districts, and biennial parliaments.[2] Supreme power was declared to reside in the representatives of the nation in Parliament, 'without the consent or concurrence of any other persons'. The authority of the King and the House of Lords was thus implicitly abrogated. Nor were the soldiers much more

[1] Firth, *Cromwell*, p. 177.
[2] Annual in the Charter and indeed in the final version (Feb. 1649) of the Agreement.

tender to the House of Commons. They had evidently in mind a direct as opposed to a representative democracy, for they demanded that their scheme should be submitted not to the obsolescent Parliament, which was to be dissolved within a year, but directly.to the people by plebiscite.

The Council of the Army strongly opposed these proposals. Not only would they have blasted all hopes of an accommodation with the King and of a settlement of the affairs of the Kingdom, on which Cromwell and the Officers were at the moment set, but would have imported into the Government of England principles as dangerous as they were new.

Cromwell's opposition
'This paper', said Cromwell, 'doth contain in it very great alterations of the government of the Kingdom— alterations of that government it hath been under ever since it was a nation.' Against this all the conservative in Cromwell (and it was a large element) strongly revolted. That the soldiers' scheme had good points he did not deny; but was the nation ready for so drastic a revolution? He gravely doubted 'whether the spirits and temper of the people of this nation are prepared to receive it'. In any case it was bound to provoke endless debate, and the promulgation of other schemes, emanating from this quarter and that, all, it might be, equally plausible. 'And not only another and another, but many of this kind, and if so, what do you think the consequences of that would be? Would it not be confusion? Would it not be utter confusion? Would it not make England like Switzerland— one canton of the Swiss against another, and one county against another? And what would that produce but an absolute desolation to the nation?' It is all very well, he added, to say that we ought to have faith, that faith will remove mountains, but 'give me leave to say there will be very great mountains in the way of this'.

Colonel Rainsborough
Such language, albeit obviously the language of sober sense, was deeply resented by the fanatical democrats. This party, though much stronger among the private

soldiers and their 'agents', was not unrepresented even
among the Officers, of whom Colonel Rainsborough was
the spokesman. Thomas Rainsborough, or Rainborrow, had
done good service to the parliamentary cause both on land
and at sea. He was rewarded in 1645 with the command of
a regiment, and in 1646 entered parliament as member for
Droitwich. But when Parliament proposed to disband the
army Rainsborough was among the stoutest champions
of the army. A man of hot temper and rough manners he
came to be regarded as the leader of the extreme republican
party on the Council of Officers. Cromwell's plea for
moderation roused in him bitter opposition. He would
hear nothing of the 'difficulties' urged by men of little
faith: in matters of conscience difficulties obtruded themselves only to be overcome.

'I hear it said', he continued, 'it's a huge alteration, it's a
bringing in of new laws', and 'this Kingdom hath been under
this Government ever since it was a Kingdom.' If writings be
true, there hath been many scufflings between the honest men
of England and those that have tyrannized over them, and
there is none of those just and equitable laws that the people of
England are born to but were intrenchments on the rights of
these tyrants. But if they were those laws that the people have
been always under, if the people find they are not suitable to
freemen, I know no reason should deter me, either before God
or the world, from endeavouring by all means to gain anything
that might be of more advantage to them than the Government
under which they live.' [1]

Nor was Rainsborough alone in his protest. Why
maintain the 'negative voice' of King or peers? asked
Wildman. 'Both the power of King and Lords,' urged
another, 'was ever a branch of tyranny, and if ever a
people shall free themselves from tyranny certainly it is
after seven years' war and fighting for their liberty.'
Despite the vehement eloquence of these fanatical doc-
trinaires Cromwell and Ireton maintained their position,

[1] For these illuminating debates, cf. the *Clarke Papers* (i. 236 seq.)
bequeathed to the library of Worcester College and edited by Sir Charles
Firth for the Camden Society.

and, as we have seen, the Army Proposals were in due course laid before the King; only, however, to be contemptuously rejected by him. Yet the grim struggle sustained by Cromwell was amply justified by the event. Neither then, nor at any other time, has the sober judgement of the English people paid much heed to abstract reasoning in politics. Their trusted leaders have almost invariably been, in the best sense, opportunists—men not of theory but of expedients, men who like Pym and Cromwell, Walpole and Peel, saw the next thing to do, and did it.

The King, like the Levellers, was an idealist, or if we will, a staunch adherent to principle. The plans of Cromwell and Ireton, in essence conservative, were frustrated by his 'diplomacy'; and violence, consequently, claimed its victim. Nevertheless, the event vindicated the wisdom and clearsightedness of Cromwell. No sooner had the grave closed on the King than the infant Republic was confronted with the impossible demands of the men who had urged, against the better judgement of the army chiefs, the abolition of the monarchy and the House of Lords.

The Sovereignty of the People Meanwhile, the *Agreement of the People*, considerably amended during the protracted debates in the Council of Officers, was presented to the Rump on 20 January 1649. In presenting it the Officers declared that they were far from desiring to impose their private apprehensions on the judgement of any man, much less on members of the Parliament. If not accepted, the document would at least testify to their anxiety for a settlement. Accepted it was not likely to be by a Parliament which hoped to perpetuate its own existence. For the first article demanded that 'the present Parliament end and dissolve upon, or before, the last day of April 1649'. The second set forth in detail a scheme for a reformed House of 400 members and a redistribution of seats. The franchise was extended to all resident householders and ratepayers of twenty-one years and upwards, except wage-earners and 'persons receiving alms'. Members of Parliament were to be similarly quali-

fied. Sixty was to be the minimum quorum for debates and
150 for legislation. Parliaments were to be elected bienni-
ally and to sit in each year for six months. No member was
to sit in two successive Parliaments, nor to hold executive
office except as a member of the Council of State, which was
to be appointed for two years, but to act strictly on the
instructions of Parliament.

As to religion, the Christian religion was to be established,
but there was to be toleration and protection for all who
'profess faith in God by Jesus Christ', except Papists and
Prelatists.

A novel feature of the document was the distinction Funda-
drawn between 'fundamentals' and things 'useful and mentals
good for the people'. This distinction, hitherto unknown
to the English Constitution, was strongly emphasized,
later on, by Cromwell: and it may indeed be regarded as
an essential characteristic of a written constitution. Even
more alien to English tradition was the attempt to impose
limitations upon the legal omnipotence of Parliament, by
excepting and reserving from the competence of the
representatives certain enumerated points. The eighth
clause, which was intended to define the position of the
Legislature, runs as follows:

'That the representatives have, and shall be understood to
have, the supreme trust in order to the preservation and
government of the whole; and that their power extend, without
the consent or concurrence of any other person or persons, to
the erecting and abolishing of Courts of Justice and public
offices, and to the enacting, altering, repealing and declaring
of laws, and the highest and final judgement, concerning all
natural or civil things but not concerning things spiritual or
evangelical. Provided that, even in things natural and civil,
these six particulars next following are, and shall be, understood
to be excepted and reserved from our representatives, viz. . . .'

There then follow five points of detail which do not
immediately concern us. The sixth is, however, of first-
rate importance; it declares

'that no representative may in any way render up, or give or
take away any of the foundations of common right, liberty, and

safety contained in this agreement, nor level men's estates, destroy property, or make all things common; and that, in all matters of such fundamental concernment, there shall be a liberty to particular members of the said representatives to enter their dissents from the major vote.'

What the legal effect of such dissent would be is not indicated, but the clause would alone suffice to render the *Agreement* of supreme interest to the student of political institutions. Here we have for the first time in the annals of the English race an attempt not only to embody the Constitution in a written document, but to give to that document the authority of an unalterable instrument, and so render rigid the Constitution itself. Parliament is to exercise only a defined and limited power. Sovereignty is implicitly vested in the people. The *Agreement* never attained legal validity, but the attempt to establish a written and rigid Constitution was, as we shall see, renewed a few years later, and with equal lack of success. Meanwhile it is pertinent to observe that the *Agreement*, like the *Instrument of Government*, prescribed no method for constitutional amendment. Before 1653, however, Parliament itself had noted the lacuna, and in its alternative sketch of a Constitution proposed to supply it.

The authors of the *Agreement* in its amended form expressed the hope that it would satisfy all ingenuous people that they were not such wild, irrational, and dangerous creatures as they were 'aspersed'. Assuming the transformation of the monarchy into a republic and the supersession of the Second Chamber, the hope was not unjustified. The *Agreement*, at any rate, took all the precautions which a written and rigid Constitution could afford against the abolition of private property, or other equalitarian and communistic schemes.

Mutiny in the Army — The precautions themselves suggest that such schemes were in the air, and the pamphlet literature which was poured out in such profusion at this moment confirms the suggestion. There were indeed considerable groups both of soldiers and civilians whose ideas went far beyond the relatively moderate limits of the *Agreement*. 'We were ruled before by King, Lords and Commons, now by a General Court Martial and Commons; and we pray you what is the difference?' The question was put in one of these many tracts, *The Hunting of the Foxes from Triploe Heath to Westminster by Five Small Beagles*, and it was not an easy one to answer. Criticism of Cromwell himself was not lacking. It was couched in the usual tone adopted by the rank and file of all revolutionary movements towards the leaders who have already mounted into power on their shoulders. 'You shall scarce speak to Cromwell about anything,' wrote Lilburne, 'but he will lay his head on his breast, elevate his eyes, and call God to record. He will weep, howl and repent, even while he doth smite you under the fifth rib.'

At the end of February 1649 Lilburne and his friends supplemented the too-moderate *Agreement* by fresh proposals presented to Parliament in a pamphlet with the suggestive title of *England's New Chains*. The primary object of attack was the new Council of State. It was denounced in now-familiar phrase as anti-democratic, and the demand was made that it should be superseded by 'committees of short continuance frequently and exactly accountable for the discharge of their trusts'. Parliament itself was to be re-elected annually and to remain in continuous session in order to control its executive committees. There were to be no special courts of justice set up, no imprisonment for debt, and no collection of tithes; above all, work and a comfortable maintenance was to be provided for the poor and impotent.

England's New Chains

But the opposition to the new government was not confined to words written or spoken. An attempt was made to re-establish the Council of the Army and to give the soldiers an equal voice with the Officers in directing its political action. Failing concessions, the soldiers were incited to mutiny. This was trying Cromwell's patience too far. Lilburne and three other ringleaders were arrested and brought before the Council. Through the door he

heard Cromwell thumping the table and in loud and angry
tones exclaiming, 'I tell you, you have no other way to
deal with these men but to break them, or they will break
you; yea, and bring all the guilt of the blood and treasure
shed and spent in this Kingdom upon your heads, and
frustrate and make void all that work that with so many
years' industry, toil and pains you have done; and, therefore, I tell you again, you are necessitated to break them'.

New
Treason
Law
In the prevailing temper of the London mob, even
Cromwell could not break them. Lilburne and his comrades were sent to the Tower, but from the Tower they
poured forth a stream of pamphlets. One of these, *Impeachment of High Treason against Cromwell and Ireton*, was
so violent that the Government determined to put Lilburne
on his trial (October). Before this, however, the Rump had
passed two precautionary measures. The first was a new
Treason Law (17 July 1649), which made it high treason
to declare that the Government now established 'is tyrannical, usurped, or unlawful; or that the Commons in
Parliament assembled are not the supreme authority of
the nation', or to 'plot, contrive, or endeavour to stir up or
raise force against the present Government'. A second
Act (September) forbade the publication of any 'book or
pamphlet, treatise, &c.' without a licence, and imposed
penalties not only on the author, printer, and seller but on
the purchaser, if he did not inform within twenty-four
hours.

Trial of
Lilburne
In October Lilburne was put on his trial. A large force
of soldiers was brought into the court. But all to no purpose. Lilburne maintained that it was for the jury alone
to decide whether he had, by his writings, broken the law,
and despite the new treason law and all the extraordinary
precautions of the Government the jury acquitted him.
Mr. Gardiner compares the enthusiasm evoked by the
verdict to that which nearly forty years afterwards greeted
the acquittal of the Seven Bishops. The verdict, says a
contemporary account, called forth 'such a loud and
unanimous shout as is believed was never heard in Guild

Hall, which made the Judges for fear turn pale and hang down their heads.' Nor had the Government heard or seen the last of 'Freeborn John'.

For the moment, however, the mutineers had been crushed. In March an example had been made by the execution of a soldier named Lockyer in front of St. Paul's Cathedral, but in his speech from the scaffold Lockyer boldly declared his confidence that God would make his blood speed liberty to all England, and thousands of demonstrators followed his corpse to the grave.

A few weeks later (May) three of the regiments selected for service in Ireland broke out into mutiny at Salisbury, declaring for 'England's freedom, soldiers' rights', and refusing to embark until the liberties of England had been secured. Fairfax and Cromwell, however, took prompt measures, chased the mutineers, caught them at Burford in Oxfordshire, shot three non-commissioned officers, and took four hundred prisoners. The mutiny was at an end. Further
mutinies

The ferment of revolutionary ideas was not, however, confined to the soldiers, nor to those who were concerned solely with constitutional readjustments. It is customary to affirm that the English revolution of the seventeenth century was directed exclusively to the achievement of certain political and religious objects. In the main that is true. The men who brought Charles I to judgement, who transformed England into a Parliamentary Republic, were 'hard-bitten' lawyers, substantial merchants, and country squires. They had a firm grip upon the root principles of Parliamentary Democracy, but they were not political idealists, still less were they social visionaries. The London apprentices played a conspicuous part in the Civil War, so long as it was dominated by the Presbyterians, and John Lilburne, as we have seen, was the hero of the London mob. But the peasantry played little part in the struggle, and would like to have played even less. There are indeed, as Mr. Trevelyan has sagely remarked,

'few things in the history of Europe so unaccountable as the ebb and flow of political agitation among the peasantry. Wat the Tyler had stirred the English peasants to revolt in 1381 when the manorial lords attempted to reimpose upon them the fetters of serfdom. The enclosures of the sixteenth century and the dislocation of social life due to the suppression of the monasteries drove them into revolt again under Edward VI, but from these last stirrings of medieval revolt down to the time of Cobbett the social agitator was almost unknown on the village green. Even under the Commonwealth, when 30,000 political pamphlets were issued and all men were united by the spirit of the age to question the very basis of social convention, there was no important movement among the peasantry on their own behalf'. [1]

Gerard Winstanley   That is as true as it is remarkable. But it would have been even more remarkable had such an upheaval as the Puritan Revolution given birth to no equalitarian ideas, to no utopian schemes of social readjustment. Among a group of social visionaries who, after the establishment of the political Commonwealth, hoped to achieve a reorganization of society on a communistic basis the most conspicuous was Gerard Winstanley. Winstanley was a consistent communist. Private property, especially in land, was to him anathema. The land belonged to the 'people' and ought to be restored to them. The buying and selling of this prime necessity of life ought to be prohibited. 'This is the beginning of particular interest, buying and selling the earth from one particular hand to another, saying "This is mine" . . . as if the earth were made for a few and not for all men. All the men and women in England are all children of this land; and the earth is the Lord's, not particular men's, who claim a proper interest in it above others.' [2] Such language anticipates almost verbally that of Rousseau; [3] it is in fact found in Winstanley's *New Law of Righteousness* (1649). A year or two earlier the *Light Shining in Buckinghamshire* had attributed the origin of political and social slavery to the institution of private property in land: 'Man following his sensuality became an encloser, so that all the land was enclosed in a few

---

[1] *Op. cit.*, pp. 39–40.   [2] Quoted by Trevelyan, *op. cit.*, pp. 282–3 n.
[3] Cf. *Discourse on the Origin of Inequality*.

mercenary hands and all the rest made their slaves. This usurpation was abetted by priests, who provided Divine sanction for the crimes of men. The base priests preach all our powers and constitutions to be *jure divino*. Shake off these locusts and be no more deluded by them; cast off these abominable deceivers.' [1]

In April 1649 a score or so of these visionaries, led by Winstanley and one Everard, squatted down upon some waste land at St. George's Hill, near Walton-on-Thames in Surrey, 'began to dig and sowed the ground with parsnips, carrots, and beans'. A few days later they took up a more menacing attitude: 'They do threaten to pull down and level all park pales and lay open and intend to plant them. They give out that they will be four or five thousand within ten days, and threaten the neighbouring people they will make them all come up to the hills and work.' [2]

If such a threat was in fact uttered it was empty. Important though Winstanley may be in the history of ideas, the movement which he led had no political or social significance. The 'diggers' were almost immediately dispersed. Winstanley himself was summoned before the local magistrates and sentenced to pay a fine, with costs, of £9 11s. 1d. But he was not silenced. He promptly addressed an 'Appeal to Parliament desiring their Answer whether the Common People shall have the quiet enjoyment of the Commons and Waste Lands or whether they should be under the will of Lords of the Manor still'. The House of Commons, like the army leaders, treated the whole matter with the contempt it deserved; yet the notes sounded by Winstanley have not ceased to resound.

Apart from the Extremists on the left, the Government of the Rump was confronted by other difficulties. Royalism was not buried in the grave of King Charles I. Charles II was alive, and within a fortnight of his father's death was proclaimed in Scotland King of England, Scotland, and Ireland (12 February). In Ireland, Ormonde, the Lord-

The 'Diggers'

Difficulties of the Commonwealth

---

[1] Quoted by Gooch, *op. cit.*, pp. 213–14.
[2] *Clarke Papers*, ii. 209–12.

Lieutenant, performed the miracle of uniting all parties in his favour, and asserted his authority throughout the whole country except in Dublin and Londonderry. A substantial portion of the Fleet had gone over to the Royalists, and so Prince Rupert, with the support of the Royalist islands of Jersey and Scilly, was able to hold the channel. The Isle of Man, too, was Royalist, and privateers issuing from its ports, as from those of the Channel Islands, were able to prey upon the commerce destined for the sustenance of the rebels in England. Continental powers, notably France and Spain, refused to acknowledge the English Republic, and succoured and gave refuge to its enemies. Dr. Dorislaus, the envoy of the Republic to the United Provinces, was murdered at the Hague by some of Montrose's men on the night of his arrival. Ascham, who had been sent to represent the Republic in Spain, met a like fate at Madrid.

With all these external enemies Cromwell dealt firmly in due course, but the most serious difficulty of the Commonwealth arose from the narrowness of the base on which it rested at home. Representing only a small minority of the nation it increased its unpopularity by imposing crushing taxation upon the majority. Whereas the revenue of Charles I was estimated (1633) at £618,000 that of the Republic in 1649 amounted to about two millions.[1] In many parts of the country there was serious scarcity of food, except for the soldiers, and half-starved people bitterly complained that 'the bread was eaten out of their mouths by the taxes'.[2]

Eikon Basilike   The revival of Royalist sentiment was not, however, due solely to the unpopularity of the Republic. It found positive sustenance in the publication, within a fortnight of the King's execution, of a little book which provided for the adoration of his disciples a Kingly Image (*Eikon Basilike*). Purporting to be written by the King's own hand during his captivity at Carisbrooke it appeared to reveal the innermost mind of the Royal Martyr: his unshaken belief

---

[1] Firth, *Cromwell*, p. 246.   [2] Whitelocke, *Memorials*.

in his Divine mission, his solicitude for the well-being of
his people, his patience under persecution, his submission
to the chastening hand of the Almighty, and not least his
constant prayers for the forgiveness of his misguided
enemies. That the book was in fact a skilful forgery, the
work of Dr. Gauden, who was rewarded after the Restoration with the bishopric of Exeter, detracted nothing from
its effectiveness as propaganda, and a sale of nearly 50,000
copies in the first year of publication testified not only to
the skill of the author but to the pervasiveness of the
sentiment to which the booklet ministered. Milton, who
had lately been appointed Secretary for Foreign Tongues
to the Council of State, was instructed to prepare a
counterblast. The *Eikonoklastes* was completed before
October; but couched in a tone of 'rude railing and
insolent swagger'[1] it proved wholly ineffective for the
purpose.

Of all the dangers, however, which confronted the Situation
Republic the most pressing, if not the most inherently in Ireland
formidable, was that threatened by the temporary conjunction of anti-republican parties in Ireland. The Council of
State realized the gravity of the situation, and on 15 March
nominated Cromwell to the command of the army which
was to be dispatched forthwith to Ireland. Cromwell was
no less quick than his colleagues to perceive the danger.
'Your old enemies,' he told his officers, 'are uniting against
you'—in England, in Scotland, not least in Ireland, where
all parties were joined together 'to root out the English
interest there and set up the Prince of Wales'. Now, as
always, Ireland was likely to become the jumping-off
ground for an attack on England. 'If we do not endeavour
to make good our interest there, and that timely, we shall
not only have our interest rooted out there, but they will
in a very short time be able to land forces in England and
put us to trouble here.' Moreover, just as the Levellers
had aroused all the conservative in Cromwell, so the

---

[1] The description, which I should hardly have ventured myself to
employ, I borrow from Mark Pattison, *Milton*, p. 102.

threatened attack from 'papist' Ireland roused all the Puritan and the Englishman in him.

'I confess I have often had these thoughts with myself, which perhaps may be carnal and foolish: I had rather be overrun by a Cavalierish interest than a Scotch interest, I had rather be overrun by a Scotch interest than an Irish interest, and I think that of all this is the most dangerous. . . . The quarrel is brought to this state: that we can hardly return to that tyranny which formerly we were under the yoke of, but we must at the same time be subject to the Kingdom of Scotland or the Kingdom of Ireland for the bringing in of the King. It should awaken all Englishmen.'

Yet Cromwell, gravely as he viewed the situation, was not prepared to start off without such preparations as he deemed adequate to the discharge of a difficult job. He insisted upon a large force, ample money, complete equipment, and full authority for himself. The Council assented: appointed him Lord-Lieutenant and Commander-in-Chief for a period of three years, voted him a salary of £13,000 a year, and gave him a well-equipped army of 12,000 men. By August his preparations were complete, and on the 13th of that month he landed at Dublin. Cromwell's campaign in Ireland, his victories, and his plan for the settlement of the country open a new chapter in the tangled story of the relations between England and Ireland in the seventeenth century. Of the interaction and reaction of the politics of the two countries, the one upon the other, nothing has yet been said. A somewhat prolonged parenthesis becomes, therefore, at this point inevitable.

XII. ENGLAND AND IRELAND

Plantations and Parliaments. Chichester and Wentworth·

FOR eight hundred years Ireland has been to England as the heel of Achilles. Not least in the seventeenth century. Yet England had, in that period, an opportunity of effecting a settlement of the Irish question such as she had never had before; such as she was never, perhaps, to have again. When James I ascended the English throne Ireland presented a *tabula rasa* for a great political experiment. On that clean slate the Stuarts might have written what they would. For four hundred years their predecessors in title had been lords of Ireland, but not until the last year of Elizabeth's reign had their lordship been effectively asserted.

The reasons for this paradoxical state of affairs were admirably set forth by Sir John Davies. Davies was Attorney-General for Ireland (1606–19), served on the Commission for the plantation of Ulster, and for a short time acted as Speaker of the Irish House of Commons. His Book, published in 1612, bears the lengthy but significant title: *Discoverie of the True Causes Why Ireland was Never Entirely Subdued nor Brought under Obedience of the Crown of England until the Beginning of His Majesties happie Raigne James 1st.* The root cause of this disaster—a disaster for both countries—is to be found in the half-completed conquest of Henry II. Unlike the England which William the Bastard subdued with such comparative ease and so completely, Ireland had not, even a century later, emerged from the tribal stage of development. A country in that condition is too weak and distracted to offer effective resistance to external attack, but its very weakness and lack of cohesion render it difficult of conquest.

'For a barbarous country', as Davies wrote, 'is not so easily conquered as a civil, whereof Caesar had experience in the wars

The Heel of Achilles

The Anglo-Norman Conquest

Lough Swilly

Lough Foyle

Culmore
Coleraine
Londonderry
Lifford

U L S T E R

Carrickfergus
Newtown
Ards
Belfast
Lisnegarvy
Charlemont
Benburb
Enniskillen
Portadown
Armagh
Downpatrick

Foyle R.

Newry

Sligo

Boyle
Jamestown
Cavan
Carlingford
Dundalk

Elphin
Tulsk
C O N N A U G H T
Ardmoor
Castlecoote
Roscommon

Kells
Slane
Drogheda
Athboy
Navan
Trim

Galway

Boyne

Rathmines
Naas
Dublin

Loughrea
Portumna

Maryborough
Wicklow

C L A R E

Shannon

L E I N S T E R

Ennis
Carlow

Limerick
Kilkenny
Kilrusk

Shannon R.

M U N S T E R
Clomnel

Tralee
Wexford

Waterford
Dungarvan
Tallow
Cork
Youghall

Bantry B.

IRELAND

Miles

0   20   40   60   80

☐ Royalist Ireland in 1643
Athboy Royalist towns
▨ Cromwellian Settlement

against the Gauls. A country possessed with many petty lords and states is not so soon brought under as an entire kingdom governed by one prince or monarch.'

Failing to subdue the Irish chieftains, the Plantagenet Kings planted, and did their best to maintain, a district, chiefly along the east coast, known as the Anglo-Norman Pale. The expedient thus adopted was fated to the natural and national development of Ireland. The Barons of the Pale were not strong enough to impose English rule upon the whole of Ireland, but their presence served to perpetuate Irish divisions and to prevent any one of the native princes from conquering the rest, and the growth of a healthy national life. Moreover, many of the Anglo-Norman barons found it to their advantage to adopt Irish customs, to use the Irish language and dress, to assume Irish names, and practically to exchange the status of Anglo-Norman barons for that of Irish chieftains. Thus they became, according to the proverbial saying, *Hibernicis ipsis Hiberniores*—more Irish than the Irish themselves. Attempts were periodically made to arrest the 'degeneration', but mostly in vain; and when the Tudors came to the throne English authority in Ireland was verging on extinction.

The Tudors reasserted it. 'Poyning's Law' (1494) made English law applicable to Ireland and brought the Irish Parliament into dependence on the English Privy Council. So it remained until 1782. Henry VII was too busy and too insecure on the throne to do more. Henry VIII not only assumed the title of 'King' instead of 'Lord' of Ireland but asserted English authority throughout the land. A real effort was at the same time made to assimilate both the laws and the social customs of Ireland to those of England. The new policy was moderately successful until it was ruined by the attempt to impose upon Ireland the essentially 'English' Reformation. In law, the Church in Ireland was brought into conformity with the established Church of England; in fact, the great mass of the Irish people not only maintained their old Catholic faith

Tudor rule

but became, for the first time, devoted adherents of
Rome.

Rebel-
lions
under
Elizabeth

Throughout the latter half of the sixteenth century,
Ireland—one part of it after another and finally the whole
of it—was in perpetual revolt against the English Crown.
From the days of Elizabeth the Irish 'problem' begins,
indeed, to assume its modern aspect. Three factors have
during the last three hundred years entered into that
problem: the religious, the agrarian, and the political.
Ardent in their Roman Catholicism, the great mass of the
Irish people have clung tenaciously to the land which they
have always contended was the property of the native
tribes, not of the intruding conqueror or planter, and have
neglected no opportunity to assert their national independence. Yet the domestic problem, in itself sufficiently difficult, has been complicated by another. The continental
enemies of England have from the sixteenth century onwards
regarded Irish soil as peculiarly favourable for the cultivation of conspiracies directed against the monarchy and the
people of England. In each of the four great conflicts in
which during the last four centuries the might of England
has been engaged the foreign foe attempted to use Ireland
as a pawn in the game against England: Philip II of Spain;
Louis XIV of France; the French Republic at the end of
the eighteenth century; the German Emperor early in the
twentieth—all attempted to play the same game; and in
each case with similar lack of success.

The
Eliza-
bethan
Conquest

Elizabeth's foothold in England was too insecure to
allow her to ignore the Irish danger. Mr. Lecky has
declared that the wars of Elizabeth in Ireland were not
wars of nationality, nor, to any great extent, wars of
religion, but that their motive was primarily agrarian—
the fear of the Irish people lest they should be driven from
the soil to which they were so deeply attached. In fact,
however, the Irish chieftains who led successive revolts
against Elizabeth, the O'Neills in Ulster, the Geraldines
in Munster, and, most formidable of all, Tyrone, hoped to
achieve three objects at one blow: the restoration of their

religion, the security of their property, and the independence of their country. Intrigues with the foreign enemies
of England rendered these revolts additionally dangerous.
Elizabeth was compelled to put forth her strength. Ireland
was for the first time really conquered; but the land thus
conquered was a desert. Very horrible is the description
of Munster given by the poet Edmund Spenser, himself one
of the 'colonists' or 'planters' in that province: 'In short
space there were none almost left, and a most populous
and plentiful country suddenly left void of man and beast,
yet, sure, in all that war there perished not many by the
sword, but by all the extremity of famine, which they
themselves had wrought.' [1]

This *tabula rasa*, though horrible to contemplate, Ireland under the Stuarts
afforded a unique opportunity for constructive statesman-
ship. Nor were the Stuart Kings ill qualified to give Ireland
what Ireland most needed. The Tudor policy, based on
uniformity and simultaneity of treatment for two countries
at very different stages of political development, may have
been inspired by praiseworthy motives, but it was bound
to lead to disaster. England and Ireland were unequal
yoke fellows. England by the end of the sixteenth century
had, as we have seen, outlived the need for paternal
government; Ireland had not. Ireland urgently needed the
discipline of a strong and centralized administration such
as that which centuries earlier Henry II and Edward I
had given to England, but of which Ireland, to her permanent loss, had been deprived by the half-completed
conquest of Henry II and the fatal policy of the Pale. It
is indeed one of the many tragedies of Irish history that
a free hand given at this critical juncture to the two great
English statesmen who were entrusted for a time with the
Government of Ireland might have conferred upon that
country the incomparable benefit of a strong, just, and
equal administration, and have given her the training
without which the grant of representative institutions is
a cruel mockery. But neither Chichester nor Strafford

[1] *View of the State of Ireland*, p. 144.

was permitted to work out to completion his beneficent designs for Ireland.

Sir Arthur Chichester as a sailor had served against the Armada, and in the expeditions of Drake and Essex, and as a soldier in the Low Countries and in Ireland under Mountjoy. He became Lord Deputy of Ireland in 1604, and for ten years brought to the service of that country all his gifts of firmness and sympathy. His first efforts were directed to the disarmament and pacification of the country and to eradicating from Irish land tenure the last remnants of the tribal system. His aims are well expressed in the Proclamation which he issued:

'To the end of the said poor tenants and inhabitants and everyone of them may from henceforth know and understand that free estate and condition wherein they were born, and wherein from henceforth they shall all be continued and maintained, we do by this present proclamation in His Majesty's name declare and publish that they and everyone of them, their wives and children, are the free natural and immediate subjects of His Majesty, and are not to be called or reputed the natives or natural followers of any lord or chieftain whatsoever, and that they and everyone of them ought to depend wholly and immediately upon His Majesty, who is both able and willing to protect them, and not upon any other inferior lord or lords, and that they may and shall from henceforth rest assured that no person or persons whatsoever, by reason of any chiefry or seignory or by colour of any custom, use, or prescription hath or ought to have, any interest in the bodies or goods of them; and that all power and authority which the said lords of counties may lawfully claim or challenge is not belonging to their lordships chiefries or seignories, but is altogether derived from His Majesty's grace and bounty whereby divers of the said lords have received and do enjoy their lands, lives, and honours; and that His Majesty, both can and will, whensoever it seem good to his princely wisdom make the meanest of his said subjects, if he shall deserve it by his loyalty and virtue, as great and mighty a person as the best and chiefest among the said lords.'

The effect of this policy is further emphasized by Davies:

'First, the common people were taught by the justices of

assize that they were free subjects to the kings of England, and not slaves and vassals to their pretended lords. That the Cuttings, Cosheries, Sessings, and other extortions of their lords were unlawful, and that they should not anymore submit themselves thereunto since they were now under the protection of so just and mighty a Prince as both could and would protect them from all wrongs and oppressions. They gave a willing ear unto these lessons; and thereupon the greatness and power of those Irish lords over their people suddenly fell and vanished.'

Compelled by James I, albeit unwillingly, to enforce the recusancy laws against Roman Catholics, Chichester did all in his power to improve the condition of the Protestant establishment in Ireland. He urged that the English Liturgy should be translated into Irish, and that in other ways efforts should be made to render Protestantism more acceptable to the King's Irish subjects. Nor was legal and administrative reform neglected. The English common law was made applicable to the whole of Ireland, a more efficient police system was introduced, the whole country was gradually divided into shires, and regular judicial circuits were instituted. Thus, as Davies complacently remarks, the 'streams of the public justice were derived into every part of the Kingdom, and the benefit and protection of the law of England communicated to all as well Irish and English without distinction or respect of persons.' How far that 'communication' was appreciated by the recipients was one of those questions which English administrators, set to govern for their good backward or inferior peoples, do not stay to ask. As to the beneficent effect of these reforms Davies at least had no misgivings.

In 1607, however, progress in reform was suddenly interrupted by the flight of the northern earls, Tyrone and Tyrconnell. Information reached the Government that, backed by Spain, the Earls intended to raise the country, to seize Dublin Castle and murder the Lord Deputy. How far the information was correct has never been known. Chichester himself disbelieved it, but the Earls took alarm and fled from Ireland, never to return. Their flight was interpreted as an admission of guilt, and it was followed by a succession of risings in the north of Ireland. As a result the greater part of Ulster was declared confiscate to the Crown.

It was the age of colonization and settlement. Here was an opportunity for plantation on a vast scale, and the English Government determined to utilize it. Chichester was enthusiastically in favour of the policy of plantation, and his plan was to treat the Irish as the actual possessors of the soil, to satisfy their claims on a generous scale, and then to offer the residue of the land to English and Scottish settlers. He recognized that, rightly or wrongly, the peasants regarded the land as belonging to them as tribesmen, subject only to the claims of their chiefs.

'You must note that many of the natives in each county do claim freeholds in the lands they possess, and albeit their demands are not justifiable in law, yet it is hard and almost impossible to displant them; wherefore I wish that a consideration may be had of the best and chief of them, albeit they were all in Tyrone's last rebellion. . . .'

These are the words of wise and humane statesmanship, but they did not commend themselves to the Commissioners appointed by the English Government. Consequently the scheme for the plantation of Ulster, as ultimately adopted, reversed the order of precedence. The greater part of the land of Ulster was assigned to retired military and civil servants of the Crown and to English and Scottish colonists. Such inferior lands as remained over might be left to the natives. Chichester had to perform the hateful task of displacing the tribesmen, but it wellnigh broke his heart. 'I have both studied and laboured the reformation of that people and could have prevailed with them in any reasonable matter, though it were new unto them; but now I am discredited among them.' So he wrote to Salisbury. As a fact the task of displacement was very imperfectly accomplished: the new settlers could not dispense with the labour of the native inhabitants. They remained as hewers of wood and drawers of water to masters alien from themselves in blood, in tradition, and in creed.

The final result has made history. A substantial part of northern Ireland was planted with a British garrison. It has had its differences from time to time with the British Government, but divided from the rest of Ireland by blood and creed, its sentiment of attachment to the British Crown and the Protestant faith has deepened as the years have passed, and the six counties are now among the most intensely loyal portions of the Empire. But for this indubitable gain a heavy price has been paid, in the increasing alienation of the other parts of Ireland, perhaps also in the misunderstandings between the two main branches of the English-speaking race on the opposite shores of the Atlantic.

The plantation of Ulster is the most lasting memorial of Chichester's rule in Ireland, but brief mention must also be made of his attempt to revive parliamentary institutions in that country. *Chichester and the Irish Parliament*

The last Parliament had met under Sir John Perrot in 1587. Chichester, however, was anxious to obtain Parliamentary recognition of the King's title to the escheated lands of Ulster and a confirmation of the recent settlement of that province. But no Parliament elected on the existing basis would be likely to give it. The native and Roman Catholic party was bound to be in a large majority. To avert this difficulty forty new constituencies on which the King could count were created, and thus a substantial government majority was secured. In the House of Lords the Roman Catholic Peers were in a large majority, but were entirely outvoted by the Bishops. Against the packing of Parliament the Roman Catholic party naturally protested, and in retrospect it is clear that from such an ill-judged pedantic experiment nothing but confusion could ensue. Nevertheless, it seemed to Chichester and Davies important to attempt it.

Parliament was opened in person by the Lord Deputy,

now raised to the peerage as Lord Chichester of Belfast. The first business before the House of Commons was the election of a Speaker. Religious passion broke out at once. Sir Thomas Ridgeway proposed the election as Speaker of Sir John Davies, intimating that the choice would be acceptable to the King. Upon this Sir James Gough, a well-known Roman Catholic, vehemently protested against the packing of the House, and proposed the name of Sir John Everard, a staunch Roman Catholic. A division was called. The Protestant majority filed out into the Lobby; the Catholic minority remained behind, and took advantage of their opponent's absence to seat their champion Everard in the chair. When the majority returned, Everard refused to budge, whereupon Sir Oliver St. John and Ridgeway took Sir J. Davies by the arms, lifted him from the ground, and placed him in the chair in Everard's lap.

The situation was not without its humour, but it did not advance the business of the session. The Roman Catholics appealed to the King, who pronounced judgement on all matters substantially in favour of the Protestants.

In June 1614 Chichester, who had been brought over to London in connexion with this business, returned for the last time to Ireland. He took with him instructions from the King to republish the proclamation for the banishment of Jesuits; to exact the 1s. fine for recusancy; to send over the sons of Catholic lords to England for education; and if the towns persisted in electing magistrates who refused the oath of supremacy to confiscate their charters.

Thus the old dreary game was to be played anew. But not by Chichester. On 29 November 1615 he was recalled. The precise reasons for his recall remain a mystery; but it is conjectured that it was due to Chichester's obvious unwillingness to embark upon a fresh series of persecutions. If this be really the case, 'all that can be said is', as Dr. Gardiner justly observes, 'that it was a worthy end to the government of such a man'.

Save by Dr. Gardiner, the episode of Chichester's rule in Ireland has been, as a rule, grotesquely misrepresented or, more often, totally ignored by English historians of this period.[1] Yet of the many turning-points in Irish history this was one of the most critical. A strong ruler, just, fearless, and untrammelled, might at this point have given to the whole subsequent history of Anglo-Irish relations a bias at once beneficent and decisive. Honourable, courageous, disinterested in his motives, and just in his intentions Chichester indisputably was, but not untrammelled. He saw the way the path of safety and honour lay; he was not free to follow it. He had a great opportunity; through no fault of his own he lost it.

Chichester left Ireland in November 1615. Wentworth landed in Dublin on 23 July 1633. The interval of eighteen years was relatively uneventful and unimportant. Under Sir Oliver St. John (1615–22), who succeeded Chichester, further plantations were carried out in the counties of Leitrim, Longford, Westmeath and, most important of all, in Wexford. Only one-fourth of the land was assigned to English settlers, but the tribal rights of large numbers of Irishmen were ignored, much suffering was inflicted on them, and the plantations accentuated the sentiment—destined to become a tradition—of English injustice. St. John's successor was Sir Henry Cary, first Viscount Falkland, father of a famous son, but himself as weak as he was well-meaning. His reign in Ireland was noteworthy only for the invention of a device for dealing with the two obstinate problems by which all English administrators in Ireland have been confronted. 'Graces' were issued to landowners and Roman Catholics. A grace gave an indefeasible title to landowners who could prove sixty years' possession, while the religious graces eased the consciences of Roman Catholics by substituting for the oath of supremacy, involving repudiation of Papal authority, a

---

[1] Professor Trevelyan, *England under the Stuarts*, makes no reference to the man or his work; nor does Dr. Franck Bright, *Personal Monarchy*. J. R. Green (*Short History*) devotes a page to them.

new oath of allegiance to the Crown. It was hoped that in return for these concessions the Irish gentry would be willing to make to Crown such grants as would enable the distracted Deputy to satisfy at least some portion of the arrears due to the army. In default of pay the soldiers preyed upon the inhabitants, and thus to the other grievances of Ireland was added the presence of an ill-paid and undisciplined force.

Went-
worth in
Ireland This was only one of many difficulties with which the new Lord Deputy had to deal. But he was not the man to quail before them. His three years' Presidency of the Council of the North had proved his capacity for rule. Of Wentworth's career in English politics mention has already been made; but it is with Ireland that his name will be imperishably associated. There he found exactly the same sort of field for the display of his peculiar gifts that India has afforded to a long series of great administrators, and that some have found in Egypt. When Wentworth landed in Ireland in 1633 he found the country ecclesiastically and socially distraught, and in respect of political and economic development some centuries behind the sister island.

'If', wrote one of the most discerning of Wentworth's biographers,[1] 'the advantage of a minister's post is to be measured by the scope it gives for his talents, no more fortunate department could have fallen to Strafford than Ireland. The country presented at that time, in most awkward combination, the difficulties of a civilized and an uncivilized state. . . . The power of the chieftains had been succeeded by the licence of a disorderly nobility, who, if they could not control their inferiors as they had before, had no notion of being controlled themselves; corruption had crept into every department of the public service; justice was feebly and partially administered; an ill-disciplined and ill-provided army preyed upon the substance of the common people; monopolists swallowed up one source of revenue, the nobility who had possessed themselves of the Crown lands the other. Church property was in as bad case, devoured wholesale by the nobility, and the wretched remnants seized, in the shape of commendams and fraudu-

[1] Canon J. B. Mozley, *Historical Essays.*

lent wasting fines, by a covetous puritanical episcopate and higher clergy.'

Wentworth's own account of the situation does not differ greatly from Dr. Mozley's analysis.

'I find them', he wrote to Portland, 'in this place a company of men the most intent upon their own ends that I ever met with, and so as those speed, they consider others at a very great distance.' The army was one 'rather in name than in deed, whether it was considered in numbers, in weapons, or in discipline'. He was almost frightened to see the work before him. 'Yet', he encouraged himself by saying at the end, 'you shall see I will not meanly desert the duties I owe to my master and myself. Howbeit, without the arm of his Majesty's counsel and support, it is impossible for me to go through with this work.'[1]

The first necessity was an adequate army well disciplined and regularly paid. Wentworth set himself to create it without delay, and so great was his success that he could presently inform the Privy Council that he had transformed a half-clothed, half-armed, undrilled, unpaid, ill-conducted rabble into an effective and orderly force. This he had done by indefatigable personal supervision: 'I had visited the whole army, seen every single man myself as well in person as in exercising.' He expended £6,000 out of his own pocket on his own troop, and the troop became in equipment and in discipline a model for the whole army. He even made the English garrison popular in Ireland. 'Formerly they took the victuals and paid nothing, as if it had been an enemy's country.' All that was changed. 'In the removes and marches the army paid justly for what they took, and passed along with civility and modesty as other subjects without burdens to the country through which they went.' Consequently 'the soldier was now welcome in every place, where before they were an abomination to the inhabitants'.[2]

The Army

[1] 3 Aug. 1633. S. P. Ireland, i. 96, quoted *ap.* Gardiner, viii. 35.
[2] Quoted *ap.* Traill, *Strafford*, p. 138.

Dealings with the Irish Parliament

As Wentworth disciplined the army so he hoped to discipline Parliament and make it subserve his high purposes in Ireland. Of parliamentary life and parliamentary leadership he had himself had experience, and like Bacon he was a believer in Parliament, if properly used, as an instrument of government. Not that Parliament must be permitted to encroach on the prerogative of the Crown His view was, as Sir George Radcliffe, his devoted secretary, explains:

'that regal power and popular privileges might well stand together; yet it being hard and difficult to keep the interests of the King and people from encroaching on one another, the longer he lived his experience taught him that it was far safer that the King should increase in power than that the people should gain advantage on the King. That may turn to the prejudice of some particular sufferers; this draws with it the ruin of the whole.'

Yet recent experience of Irish Parliaments should hardly have tended to encourage over-sanguine hopes. It is true, indeed, that Parliamentary institutions in Ireland were almost coeval with those of England, but they had never taken deep root in that country. Nor was there any real basis on which to build them in the Ireland of the seventeenth century. Rulers like Chichester might strive to break down the tribal system, but they could not suddenly erect a nation on its ruins; and unless there be a nation to represent, representative institutions can be none other than a mockery.

'An honest, able, and humane Lord Deputy with full powers would probably have done more at that moment than the largest measure of Parliamentary liberty for the pacification and civilization of the country.'

Such is the shrewd judgement of an ardent lover of liberty, the late Mr. Goldwin Smith. Dr. Gardiner is of a similar opinion:

'What Ireland needed was a government like that of India in the present day, supporting itself on an irresistible army and guided by statesmanlike intelligence. It was unfortunate that, in their honourable anxiety to raise Ireland to the level of England, English statesmen had thrust upon the country institutions for which it was manifestly unfit.'[1]

Nor was the King so sanguine as his Deputy. 'As for that hydra,' he wrote, meaning thereby his faithful Commons in Parliament assembled, 'take good heed, for you know that here I have found it cunning as well as malicious.'

Nevertheless on 15 July 1634 the Lord Deputy met Parliament. He begged them to take warning from the unhappy fate of the Parliament in England—to lay aside suspicion and not to permit an opposition of interests to emerge between King and people:

'Suffer no poor suspicion or jealousies to vitiate your judgement, much rather become you wise by others' harms. You cannot be ignorant of the misfortunes these meetings have run of late years in England; strike not, therefore, upon the same rock of distrust which hath so often shivered them. . . . Above all, divide not between the interests of the King and his people, as if there were one being of the King and another of his people. This is the most mischievous principle that can be laid in reason of State, and that which, if you watch not very well, may the easiliest mislead you. For you might as well tell me a head might live without a body, or a body without a head, as that it is possible for a King to be rich and happy without his people be so also. Most certain it is that their wellbeing is individually one and the same, their interests woven up together with so tender and close threads as cannot be pulled asunder without a rent in the commonwealth.'

These were wise words and evidently reflected the profound conviction of the speaker. Nor was Parliament wholly unresponsive to the Deputy's mood. Two sessions were held in 1634; six subsidies were voted without opposition, and despite some obstruction from the Roman Catholics, when they found themselves in an accidental and temporary majority, much useful work was accomplished. But the King's suspicions were not allayed, and

[1] *op. cit.* viii. 30.

though Parliament met for two more sessions in 1635 Charles insisted on its dissolution. 'Parliaments', he wrote, 'are of the nature of cats, they ever grow curst with age; so that if ye will have good of them put them off handsomely when they come to any age, for young ones are ever most tractable.'

Yet despite discouragement from his master the Lord Deputy repeated his experiment, and almost the last incident of his Irish administration was a unanimous vote of four subsidies (£180,000) obtained from the Parliament of 1640 as a contribution to the expenses of the Bishops' War against the Scottish Covenanters. In view of subsequent events that vote, and the expressions of exuberant loyalty to the Crown with which it was accompanied, were not without significance. In March, Strafford (as he had by then become) wrote confidently to Secretary Windbank that the Irish would be as ready to serve with their persons as with their purses, and that by the middle of May he would be ready, provided the money could be advanced from England in anticipation of the subsidies, to take the field with 9,000 men.[1]

Notwithstanding Wentworth's success in handling his Irish Parliaments, in playing off Protestant against Catholic and Catholic against Protestant, the doubt still persists whether his parliamentary policy was either wise or ingenuous. But as to his attitude towards Parliament there was no obscurity. A strong administration was his political ideal; if Parliament could be made to subserve it why not utilize it? That inexperienced Irish squireens (or for that matter English squires and merchants) should ever be permitted to become a co-ordinate organ of Government, still more to control the Executive, was an idea which did not come within his political horizon. He had, as we have seen, supported the English Commons in their attack on Buckingham and in their demand for the Petition of Right, not because he shared the political or religious views of Eliot and Hampden, but because he wanted to see the

[1] *Strafford Letters*, ii. 398, and ix. 96.

English monarchy strong and respected. The influence of an incompetent favourite weakened and degraded it. Attacks on the personal liberty of well-affected subjects served only to make it an object of general and well-grounded suspicion.

To respect for a Government nothing contributes more than strong and even-handed justice. In England we have long been accustomed to associate the administration of justice and he liberty of the citizen with the device of trial by jury. But if there was one English institution less adapted to the needs of Ireland than a parliament it was the jury system. Of this Wentworth was well aware. Consequently, while he had a genuine desire to attain the essential ends of justice he exhibited (to English and indeed to Anglo-Irish eyes) a gross and flagrant carelessness in methods and means. In his great apology for his Irish administration he claimed, not without reason, that while keeping the Judiciary (like every other organ of Government) 'in that due subordination to the Crown as is fit' he had ever kept in view the interests of the great mass of the King's Irish subjects. Justice was dispensed, he averred, 'without acceptation of persons'. It was: as powerful and high-placed malefactors could sorrowfully testify. 'The poor knew where to seek and to have relief without being afraid to appeal to his Majesty's Catholic justice against the greatest subject,' and that, as he justly claimed, was 'a blessing to the poorer sort' and 'a restraint the richer had not formerly been acquainted with in that kingdom.' Towards the great, who were 'as sharp set upon their own wills as any people in the world', and sought only 'to fill their greedy appetites', he showed little mercy. That his methods with men like Lord Clanricarde, Lord Cork, Lord Wilmot, Lord Chancellor Loftus, and above all perhaps Lord Mountmorris, were somewhat high-handed cannot be denied. He was himself conscious that he had the defects of his qualities, but he pleaded that his policy was from first to last inspired by a passionate desire to inaugurate a purer and better administration in a country too long neglected by

Administration of justice

its nominal rulers. And who could gainsay his own pathetic plea?:

> . . . so as if I stood clear in all these respects, it was to be confessed by any equal mind that it was not anything within, but the necessity of his Majesty's service which enforced me into a seeming strictness outwardly. And that was the reason indeed. For where I found a Crown, a Church, and a people spoiled, I could not imagine to redeem them from under the pressure with gracious smiles and gentle looks; it would cost warmer water to do so. True it was that when a dominion was once gotten and settled, it might be stayed and kept where it was by soft moderate counsels, but where a sovereignty (be it spoken with reverence) was going down the hill, the nature of man did so easily slide into the paths of an uncontrolled liberty, as it would not be brought back without strength, nor be forced up the hill again but by vigour and force.'

But he had to pay the penalty. The vengeance of power-ful victims pursued him to his death. Laud had long since warned him of the risks he was running:

> 'I know', wrote the Archbishop to his friend, 'you have a great deal more resolution in you than to decline any service due to the King, State, or Church, for barking or discontented persons, and God forbid but you should; and yet, my Lord, if you could find a way to do all these great services and decline these storms, I think it would be excellent well thought on.'

Ecclesias-
tical
policy

The advice was shrewd, and in his own interests Went-worth would have been wise to heed it. But his imperious temper led him to hack his way through scandals and abuses which a more patient man might have circum-vented. No scandal that he found existing in Ireland was more glaring than that of the Church. The Tudors had destroyed the Church (though not the religion) beloved of the great mass of the Irish people; they had put nothing in its place. The established Protestant Church presented indeed a sorry spectacle. The fabrics were in ruins or put to base uses; Church property had been filched to 'fill the greedy appetites' of the great lords; an unlearned Pro-testant clergy, though adding benefice to benefice, rarely

visited their parishes, and were too unlearned to perform
their duties had they done so.

Wentworth did what he could to mend matters. He
refused to fine recusants for not going to Church until
Churches were provided for them to attend. He issued
Commissions for the repair of fabrics and to find a remedy
for the worst abuses. Powerful despoilers of Church
property were compelled to disgorge £30,000 a year; the
clergy were forced to reside in their parishes and give up
pluralities; schools were built, and education was encouraged. If this was the work of a 'corrupt and capricious
tyrant' Ireland might well have stood larger doses of the
prescription.

Of the several aspects of Wentworth's work for Ireland
not the least important and perhaps the most enduring was
the economic. His first task was to clear the Irish Sea of
the pirates of whose predatory attacks he had himself been
a victim when he first crossed the channel. He then
reformed the Customs administration with such success
that, without adding to the burden of the Irish consumer,
he increased the yield from £12,000 to £40,000 a year, and
so reorganized the whole fiscal and financial system as to
convert an annual deficit of £24,000 into a substantial
surplus of £8,500. In three years he had, by careful
husbandry, increased the annual revenue by £180,000; the
servants of the Crown, civil and military, were punctually
paid, Crown rents were regularly collected—in a word,
order was evolved out of chaos and imminent bankruptcy
was averted. But Wentworth was less intent upon an
immediate increase of revenue than upon the development
of the permanent resources of the country. Then, as
always, Ireland relied mainly upon the cultivation of its
soil and the utilization of its extensive grass-lands. Wool
was its only important article of export, and woollen manu-
facture its only industry. Wentworth is accused of having
discouraged it. The accusation is true; but it is proof of
his prescience rather than of his malignant indifference to
Irish interests. High protection was the fiscal fashion of

Fiscal and com- mercial reforms

the hour. For Irish wool and cloth England was the main
if not the sole market. But the more Ireland prospered, the
greater the jealousy of English competitors, the higher the
walls of their protective tariffs. The event exactly accorded
with Wentworth's anticipation. With rare foresight, therefore, he furnished the Irish with a substitute. Largely at
his own expense, he laid the foundations of that linen
industry in Ulster which from that day to this has been
the mainstay of Irish industry.

As Mr. Goldwin Smith, no friend to autocracy, has justly
said:

'The resources of the country rose buoyantly beneath his
master hand: the value of land was increased, shipping multiplied, and if his government had not been tainted by a sinister
object he would have proved decisively that the temporary
rule of a beneficent despot was the remedy required by the
maladies of the country.'

Dr. Mozley is admittedly a less impartial witness, but he
is entitled to be heard in Strafford's defence:

'Strafford's great experiment had now been tried, and succeeded; and in one part of the dominions, at any rate, a lazy,
timorous government had become an effective and bold one.
His great theory and *beau-ideal* of a *popular monarchy*, a
monarchy that did its work and looked after the people, was in
a measure fulfilled, and his government was grateful to the
mass. He liked the Irish, notwithstanding some sharp dicta;
and the Irish took to the Lord Deputy's bold, frank carriage,
which set off the *bona fide* attention to their interests. The
people cheered him as he went his progress on the plantation
scheme, because, said Strafford, they were better off than they
had been for ages, and felt the leniency of the royal arm, compared with the "oppression of their petty imperious lords".'

Is Mr. Goldwin Smith accurate in attributing to Strafford
a 'sinister object'? That he had grave defects of character, and that these were reflected in his administrative
methods, cannot be disputed. Conscious of unselfish aims
he was too little regardful of the means employed to achieve
them; anxious to improve the lot of the defenceless poor,

he was careless in offending the powerful and the rich. His violation of the 'graces' was indefensible and his treatment of individuals was high-handed and arbitrary. Yet the apology he offered for his conduct cannot be lightly set aside; his surgery, like Cromwell's, was rough; it was no time nor place for 'gracious smiles and gentle looks'; but the main accusation is unanswered: was his whole policy tainted by a sinister motive?

That Strafford went to Ireland with the deliberate object of providing his master with an army for the subjugation of England would seem to be the fantastic suggestion of bitter enemies determined at all costs to secure his conviction and compass his death. 'Stone dead hath no fellow.' Essex was right. Strafford, if permitted to live, might well have frustrated the efforts of Pym. That does not prove, however, that he deserved to die. If, as he consistently maintained, the force he raised in Ireland was intended for the defence of his King and his country against the Scots, wherein was his conduct treasonable or even blameworthy? That the weapon if used with effect against the Scots might later have been turned against their allies in the English Parliament is possible: but by 1641 the scheme, if ever entertained, had been frustrated. Strafford was already disarmed. Nevertheless, he was condemned to die. Already Ireland had lost the greatest ruler she had ever known. Strafford's death

Within six months of Strafford's death England was confronted with massacre and rebellion in Ireland. A new chapter in Irish history had opened.

XIII. THE IRISH REBELLION AND AFTER

The Cromwellian Conquest and Settlement

IRISH politics, always difficult of comprehension by Englishmen, were during the years that followed Strafford's departure exceptionally difficult and confused. Royalists and Parliamentarians, Scottish Presbyterians and Irish Catholics, Anglo-Irish noblemen and Celtic clansmen, cross-purposes, shifting alliances—the picture is an almost inextricable medley.

Parties in Ireland

Out of the welter and confusion four more or less clearly defined parties did, however, gradually emerge, and it may conduce to the lucidity of the narrative which follows to enumerate them at the outset. The first, and perhaps the least important of the four, consisted of the adherents of the English Parliament, led by Lord Justices Borlase and Parsons, who, on Strafford's departure, had been left in charge of the government in Dublin. Their strength lay in the fact that they represented constituted authority in Ireland, but their position gradually weakened after the King had appointed Lord Ormonde as Lord-Lieutenant, and after the widening of the breach (reflected even in their own faction in Ireland) between the Presbyterians and the Sectaries. Secondly, there were the Royalists, headed by James Butler, Earl of Ormonde, one of the few great nobles who had cordially supported the policy of Strafford, and almost the only man of note who, throughout this troubled period, played a perfectly consistent, straightforward, and honourable part. Himself a Protestant, he strove to combine all those who were, like himself, loyal to the English Crown and the English connexion. Thirdly, there were the Anglo-Irish nobles and gentry who, although they were Roman Catholics first, were prepared to remain loyal to the King provided they received satisfactory guarantees for the security of their religion and their property. Finally, there was the great mass of Celtic Irishmen, largely dispossessed by recent plantations of the tribal lands which they had regarded as their own, devoted to the Roman Catholic Church, and anxious to rid their land of the foreign conquerors. They found an intrepid leader in Owen Roe O'Neill.

On 1 November 1641 news reached Westminster that a rebellion had broken out in Ireland, and that large numbers of Protestants had been massacred in the northern counties. Rumour exaggerated the horrors of a situation, in itself sufficiently horrible, and Pym, as we have seen, took advantage of the fears excited in Parliament to press on the *Grand Remonstrance*, and, later on, to claim for Parliament the control of the armed forces of the Crown. *The Ulster rebellion*

Many circumstances combined to complicate the situation. The King was in Scotland; opinion in England was veering in his favour; yet information, more or less circumstantial, was reaching the Parliamentary leaders almost daily of some fresh negotiation between the Queen and her co-religionists on the continent or in Ireland, of an army 'plot', or a meditated *coup d'état*. On the top of all came the news of an Irish rebellion and a 'St. Bartholomew in Ulster'. That the rebellion if not the massacre had been instigated by the King was commonly believed in London.

What are the facts? That the King was in any way privy to the rebellion of October 1641 is not true, but it is true that the Queen had been in constant communication (as was natural enough) with the Irish Roman Catholics, and that in August the King had been negotiating with Lord Ormonde and Lord Antrim. A promise of concessions was to be held out to the Catholics, and Ormonde and Antrim were to get together the remnants of Strafford's Irish army, now in process of disbandment, obtain the authority of the Irish Parliament for the seizure of Dublin Castle and use it as a base of operations against the English Parliament. This plan was betrayed to the Lord Justices just in time to enable them to prevent an outbreak in Dublin and secure the capital.

Simultaneously, the dispossessed natives in Ulster rose *Ulster massacre* under Sir Phelim O'Neill and put to the sword all the Protestants within their reach. As to the extent of the massacre controversy still rages. Clarendon says the victims numbered 40,000 to 50,000. Other contemporary accounts put the numbers even higher. Froude speaks of 'scenes which rivalled in carnage the horrors of St. Bartholomew'.[1]

Lecky, after analysing with characteristic impartiality and detachment the causes of the rebellion, is disposed to restrict the 'pretended massacre' to very narrow limits.

'The rebellion,' he writes, 'represented the accumulated wrongs and animosities of two generations. The influence of the ejected proprietors . . . the rage of the Septs . . . the animosity which very naturally had grown up between the native population and the alien colonists planted in their old dominions; the new fanaticism which was rising under the preaching of priests and friars; all the long train of agrarian wrongs . . . all the long succession of religious wrongs contributed to the result. . . . These considerations restrict the pretended massacre to very narrow limits and are sufficient to show that it has been exaggerated in popular histories almost beyond any other tragedy on record. There can, however, be no question that the rebellion in Ulster was extremely horrible and was accompanied by great numbers of atrocious murders.'[2]

Side by side with this we may put an extract from Sir John Temple's letter to the King (12 December 1641) which, if less detached, bears the impress of the emotions of the hour:

'Thus enraged and armed they march on furiously, destroying all the English, sparing neither sex nor age throughout the kingdom, most barbarously murdering them, and that with greater cruelty than ever was used among Turks and infidels. . . . Many thousands of our nation are already perished under their cruel hands, and the poor remainder of them go up and down, desolate, naked, and most miserably afflicted with cold and hunger.'

Sir John Temple, who was Master of the Rolls in Ireland, had, no doubt, personal motives for exaggeration; yet his evidence cannot on that account be totally ignored.

[1] *The English in Ireland*, i. 91.   [2] *History of England*, ii. 123.

Gardiner, like Lecky, questions the evidence for any
'general massacre' but admits that there were cases of
'unimaginable brutality' and a wholesale eviction of
Anglo-Scottish settlers. The most careful estimate suggests
that out of a total of 120,000 settlers some 20,000 to 25,000
perished either by the sword or by starvation in the first
weeks of the insurrection.

But whatever the precise number of victims (and it can
only be roughly estimated) there can be no question that
the fact of the massacre made an ineradicable impression
upon the Puritans of England and Scotland, and has
coloured for all time the history of the relations between
Great Britain and Ireland. The British electorate has
never been willing to put 'Protestant' Ulster against its
will under the jurisdiction of a 'Catholic' Parliament in
Dublin, and it is safe to predict that, however blurred the
memories of 1641 may have become, it will never under
any circumstances consent to do so. But swifter vengeance
awaited the transgressors. English Puritans looked for
their ensamples to the Old Testament rather than the New.
'An eye for an eye and a tooth for a tooth' was an injunction which they were quick to obey. The 'terrible surgery'
applied by Cromwell in 1649 was not an operation dictated
merely by the necessities of the hour; the surgeon had not
forgotten the St. Bartholomew of Ulster.

The question as to the King's complicity, so hotly
debated at the time, may now be dismissed in a few
sentences. 'The fools,' said the Earl of Antrim, 'well liking
the business, would not expect our time and manner for
ordering the work, but fell upon it without us, and sooner
and otherwise than we would have done, taking to themselves and in their own way the management of the work
and so spoiled it.' Lord Antrim and Lord Ormonde were
the two leaders of the Irish nobility with whom the King
had been in negotiation during the summer. What the
King wanted was to keep together or get together Strafford's army, in order that it might be available, if required,
for use in England. The last thing he wanted was an Irish

Question of the King's complicity

rebellion. Nevertheless, he may well have unwittingly precipitated a movement with which he was totally un-connected and which was even more disastrous to him than to his enemies.

That his enemies should none the less have suspected his complicity was not merely natural but almost inevitable. Sir Phelim O'Neill, Owen Roe's cousin, who with Roger Moore led the attack on the Ulster Protestants, exhibited a commission signed by the King over the Great Seal of Scotland and dated 1 October 1641. It is at least a curious coincidence that the seal was on that very day changing hands, and Gardiner, while admitting that O'Neill's com-mission was certainly forged, is led to suggest that the forgery might have been based upon another commission issued by the King on the same date authorizing the Irish lords to occupy fortresses, &c., on his behalf.

The English Parlia-ment and Ireland   The points which are at once certain and relevant to our present purpose are that the Irish rebellion gave Pym his majority on the *Grand Remonstrance,* and that it rendered immediate the question of the control of the militia and so precipitated, if it did not cause, the Civil War in England. Nor, finally, is it open to doubt that the measures taken by the English Parliament poured oil on the flames in Ireland. Not only did they pass (8 December) a resolution against any toleration for 'Papists', but they adopted a suggestion made by the City that 2,500,000 acres of good Irish land should be allotted to the subscribers to a special fund of £1,000,000 for the suppression of the rebellion. A force was rapidly mobilized. Sir Simon Harcourt arrived in Dublin in December at the head of an advanced guard of 1,500 men, and was followed in February by a large force of foot under George Monk and some horse under Sir Richard Grenville.

Early in April the King announced his intention of taking the field in person in Ireland, but Parliament formally requested him to desist, and Hotham was in-structed to deny him the equipment which he proposed to obtain from the magazine at Hull.

Meanwhile despite, or perhaps in consequence of, some A national revolt in Ireland success achieved by the Parliamentary army in Ireland, the movement in that country gradually assumed more of a national character. The Roman Catholic nobles of the south threw in their lot with the Ulster rebels. In May 1642, a Provisional Government was set up at Kilkenny; in June, the Roman Catholic members were expelled from the Dublin Parliament, and in October a General Assembly representative of every county in Ireland and of every borough not actually in enemy occupation met at Kilkenny. This Assembly resolved to set up a Provincial Council invested with administrative and judicial authority in each Province, to form a Supreme Executive Council of twenty-five members, and to re-establish and re-endow the Roman Catholic Church in Ireland. The English Parliament might still function in such towns of Ireland as were held by its armed forces; the rest of Ireland was ruled by the Supreme Council and the General Assembly at Kilkenny.

Things had gone far towards the erection of a national Ireland and the King Government in Ireland: but the national movement was not essentially republican; it was indeed ready to lay itself—on conditions—at the feet of the King. In March 1643 the King was petitioned to redress the grievances of his Irish Roman Catholic subjects and to assent to the repeal of Poyning's Law and the creation of an independent Irish Parliament. In return, Ireland would provide him with 10,000 troops for use against the English Parliament.

The King's position in Ireland at this moment depended The Marquis of Ormonde almost entirely on the fidelity of a single person. Throughout these troubled times James Butler, twelfth Earl and first Duke of Ormonde, played a great and consistently honourable part. A real patriot, a staunch Protestant and an ardent Royalist, he was created a Marquis by the King in August 1642, in January 1643 was commissioned to act on his behalf in Ireland, and in October was nominated as Lord-Lieutenant. Despite his adhesion to Protestantism no man was better fitted to act as intermediary between

the King and the Roman Catholic confederates, and on
15 September 1643 he concluded, on the King's behalf, a
twelvemonth's truce with the Confederacy.

The 'Cessation', as it was called, provided in effect for
a resuscitation of the 'Pale'. A strictly defined district on
the east coast, another and smaller district round Cork, and
such strong places in the north and west as were in the
actual occupation of English troops, were to remain in the
hands of the English commanders. Over the rest of Ireland
the Confederate Government was to be recognized as
effective. The Royalist troops in Ireland would then be
liberated for service in England. The conclusion of this
truce made a profound impression on the minds of English
and Scottish Puritans, and, according to Baillie, induced
large numbers to subscribe the Solemn League and Covenant. 'Most of all,' writes the Scottish Divine, 'the Irish
Cessation made the minds of our people embrace that
means of safety.'

All that the King got out of the Cessation were two
English regiments from Munster. But the men proved, as
Byron wrote to Ormonde, 'very cold in this service; they
broke and fled when engaged with the Roundheads at
Nantwich, and of the 1,500 who were taken prisoners 800
were easily persuaded to subscribe the Covenant'. Byron's
advice to Ormonde was to send over only Irish troops,
officered by Englishmen who could be trusted. Though
the regiments from Munster were in fact English, their
employment gave offence to the King's English supporters,
and if *The True Informer* (3 February 1644) may be trusted
'His Majesty lost more of the English Cavaliers than there
have been Irish come over'.[1]

The Larger schemes for securing Roman Catholic support
for the King's cause were, however, afoot. In November
1644 Queen Henrietta Maria arrived in Paris to confer
with a Joint Committee of English and Irish Catholics that
had been formed to promote a restoration of Roman
Catholicism in both countries. Every possible source of

The Cessation (margin note)

The Glamorgan Treaty (margin note)

[1] Quoted by Gardiner, *Civil War*, i. 296.

assistance was explored, and in January 1645 an arrangement was concluded by which Charles Duke of Lorraine
agreed to bring over 10,000 of his troops to the aid of the
Stuart King, and the Prince of Orange undertook to
provide transport for them. Meanwhile the King himself
had been negotiating at Oxford with agents of the Supreme
Council of Irish Confederates, and in particular with Lord
Herbert of Raglan, the son of the Marquis of Worcester, and
himself a zealous Roman Catholic. Lord Herbert was
created Earl of Glamorgan and was commissioned to
organize an extensive combination of Irish, Welsh, and
continental Catholics to revive, if it might be, the drooping
fortunes of the King. The King, on his part, engaged to
suspend all the Penal Laws in favour of the Catholics; but
it is noticeable that even in this dark hour Charles, consistent in his devotion to the Established Church, would not
hear of repealing the great Statutes, such as the Statute
against Appeals to Rome, on which the Reformation
Settlement rested.

Nevertheless, the King's negotiations with the Catholics
caused great disquietude among his Protestant friends.
The capture of the King's papers at Naseby enabled the
Puritan leaders to make the whole story public, and the
sensation thus caused was profound and painful, and withal
exceedingly damaging to the Royalist cause.

Two months after Naseby fight, after many accidents Negotia-
and long delays, Glamorgan managed to reach Ireland and tions with
concluded with the Confederates at Kilkenny the famous Roman
Treaty which bears his name. It had, however, little Catholics
practical significance. Large promises were made to the
Catholics, but the Parliamentarian forces under Sir George
Monro were making considerable headway in Ireland, and
the arrival of a Papal nuncio, Rinuccini, served only to complicate the situation. At the end of December 1645
Glamorgan was arrested in Dublin, and in January the
terms of his Treaty were published in London together
with those of a Treaty which Sir Kenelm Digby had concluded directly with Pope Innocent X. Ormonde concluded

with the Confederates a Treaty of more limited scope (March 1646), but before the promised Catholic army was ready to embark the military situation in England rendered all such assistance impracticable. The expedition was accordingly countermanded, and Ormonde was instructed to abandon further negotiation with the Confederates. But events in Ireland made literal fulfilment of his instructions impossible. A crushing defeat inflicted by the Confederate army on Monro (June 5) impelled the Lord-Lieutenant to come to terms with the Supreme Council. But the terms were distasteful to the nuncio, who, naturally enough, thought relatively little about Ireland, but thought a great deal about the European situation in general, and, in particular, about the position of the Pope. In short, Ireland was once more becoming involved in continental politics; Rinuccini was claiming, as Papal nuncio, to control the situation, and Ormonde, Irish patriot and loyal Protestant as he was, had no option but to apply to the *de facto* Government at Westminster. He offered either to carry on as Lord-Lieutenant, on behalf of the English Government, or, with the permission of the Sovereign, from whom he held his Commission, to resign. The Westminster Parliament, without reference to the King, forthwith accepted his resignation and appointed Lord Lisle, eldest son of the Earl of Leicester, in his place. But Lord Lisle had hardly begun his reign before he was recalled.

Parlia-
ment,
Army,
and
Ireland

Not that Parliament was disposed to neglect Irish affairs. For once, indeed, Ireland seemed likely to be a convenience instead of an embarrassment to the politicians at Westminster. The quarrel between Parliament and the army was now (March 1647) approaching a crisis.[1] The Civil War was over. Parliament was therefore supremely anxious to disband the army which had won it and to regain control of the situation. But the soldiers refused to be disbanded. So they should be sent to Ireland. But the bulk of the army would not go except under their own

[1] Cf. *supra* c. x.

Generals, Fairfax and Cromwell, nor until Parliament had met their demands as to arrears and pensions.

Meanwhile Parliament had made other arrangements as to the Irish commands. Among them was the appointment of Colonel Michael Jones, a rough but highly efficient soldier, to command in Dublin. Jones, accompanied by Parliamentary Commissioners, reached Dublin on 7 June 1647, and Ormonde, though anxiously striving to the end to consolidate parties in Ireland in the King's interests, had no option but to hand over the reins of Government to them. On 8 August Jones inflicted a severe defeat on the Confederate army at Dungan Hill, and by his brutal treatment of the enemy taught the Irish Catholics what they might expect from victorious Puritans. Shortly afterwards he effected a junction with General Monk, who had been appointed to command for the Parliament in Ulster. Lord Inchiquin, commanding in Munster, gradually made himself master of the south. *Colonel Michael Jones*

Never had the prospects of the Puritans in Ireland looked so bright; but the situation was again complicated by the outbreak of the second Civil War in England. In March 1648 Lord Inchiquin declared for the King, and Monro, who had for years been making a valiant and, in the main, successful fight for Parliament in Ulster, also adhered to the new Coalition between Royalists and Presbyterians. But in September Monk took Belfast, Carrickfergus, and Coleraine, captured Monro, and sent him over as a prisoner to England. These victories averted a threatened invasion of Ulster by the Scots, and so far as Ireland was concerned virtually decided the second Civil War (September). *The second Civil War*

Lord Ormonde, however, having received a renewed Commission from the King as Lord-Lieutenant, landed in Cork (4 October) with instructions to take his orders from the Queen, so long as the King remained in custody, and meanwhile to use his best endeavours to consolidate the Royalist position in Ireland. *Ormonde*

The execution of the King facilitated his task. The Papal nuncio had alarmed the Catholic nobles whose sympathies were Anglo-Irish rather than Papist, and his departure in February untied one of the many knots in the tangled skein of Irish politics. The savagery of Michael Jones had evoked no love for New Model Puritans. The Ulster Presbyterians naturally looked for a lead to their brethren in Scotland. Consequently, Ormonde had relatively little difficulty in bringing the Anglo-Irish Catholics, the Episcopalians, and the Presbyterians into temporary union, and in proclaiming Charles II as King. Munster, Connaught, and Ulster were practically solid in his favour; only by the continued occupation of Dublin did the English Parliament maintain a precarious hold on the island.

Cromwell in Ireland

The menace to the infant Commonwealth was a real one; not only was Ireland on the verge of independence, but it was like to become a base for an attack on England. 'If', as Cromwell said to his officers, 'we do not endeavour to make good our interest there, and that timely, we shall not only have our interest rooted out there but they will in a very short time be able to land forces in England and put us to trouble here.' It was truly spoken. Cromwell was appointed Lord-Lieutenant and Commander-in-Chief. After some months of careful preparation he landed at Dublin, with a large and well-equipped force, on 13 August.

The spirit in which Cromwell's expedition to Ireland was undertaken is clearly set forth in a Declaration [1] which in January 1650 he issued from Youghal:

'We are come to ask an account of the innocent blood that hath been shed; and to endeavour to bring to an account, by the presence and blessing of the Almighty, in whom alone is our hope and strength, all who, by appearing in arms, seek to justify the same. We come to break the power of lawless Rebels, who, having cast off the authority of England, live as enemies to Human Society; whose principles, the world hath experience, are, to destroy and subjugate all men not complying with them. We come, by the assistance of God, to hold forth and maintain the lustre and glory of English Liberty in a nation where we have an undoubted right to do it;—wherein the people of Ireland (if they listen not to such seducers as you

[1] For the whole Declaration cf. Carlyle, *Speeches*, ii. 207–25.

are) may equally participate in all benefits; to use liberty and fortune equally with Englishmen, if they keep out of arms.'

A statement more characteristic of the temper in which the Englishman, Unionist and Protestant, has throughout the ages attacked the problem of Irish Government has never been conceived or set forth. 'Rebellion is as the sin of witchcraft.' Is it not England's manifest right, as well as her simple duty, to extend the blessings of English liberty to all the peoples on earth? What better fortune can come to any people than to be delivered by England from the seductions of Rome and permitted to share her own goodly (Protestant) heritage? Some years earlier (1641) Sir John Clotworthy had advised that Englishmen should go to Ireland with the sword in one hand and the Bible in the other. Cromwell was literally obeying his injunction.

For the moment the sword was even more prominent than the Bible. A fortnight before Cromwell's arrival in Dublin Michael Jones had inflicted a crushing defeat on Ormonde's army at Rathmines, and the latter sought refuge, with the pick of his troops, in Drogheda. On Drogheda, accordingly, Cromwell marched, summoned it to surrender, and on its refusal stormed it and, according to his word, put to the sword every man of the garrison, about 3,000 strong. 'I do not think', he wrote to Bradshaw, 'thirty of the whole number escaped. Those that did are in safe custody for the Barbados.' 'Truly I believe', he added, 'this bitterness will save much effusion of blood.' Trim and Dundalk surrendered, and then, having dispatched a force for the relief of Londonderry, Cromwell marched southwards and on 11 October the scenes enacted at Drogheda were repeated at Wexford. Cromwell estimated the enemy's loss at 'not many less than two thousand'; not one priest was believed to have escaped. Cromwell's own loss numbered a bare score.

(margin: Drogheda and Wexford)

Town after town, warned by the fate of Drogheda and Wexford, opened its gates to Cromwell. Waterford alone checked his triumphal march; but by the end of 1649 the whole coast of Ireland from Londonderry to Cape Clear was, save for Waterford, in his hands. Before Waterford's stout resistance even Cromwell recoiled, though it was eventually taken by Ireton in August 1650.

Cromwell had long since been recalled to meet a more pressing danger. Before he left Ireland, however, in May 1650 he had reduced the whole of Leinster and Munster to obedience, and, by allowing the garrisons of towns which surrendered to take service abroad, had rid the country of some 45,000 soldiers. The back of resistance was broken and Ireton was left to complete Cromwell's work. Before the end of 1650 almost all the garrisons in Ulster and Munster had surrendered and the remnants of the armies were driven across the Shannon into Connaught where desultory fighting continued among the bogs and mountain fastnesses for another twelvemonth or more. Galway, the last stronghold held by the Irish, capitulated in May 1652. The reconquest of Ireland was at last accomplished.

Execution of the Ulster rebels A High Court of Justice was set up under General Fleetwood in Kilkenny, and there the survivors of the Ulster rebellion of 1641 were at length brought to justice. Sir Phelim O'Neill and two hundred others were convicted and executed. The Irish slate was once more cleaned ; what would England write on it ?

Before proceeding to answer that question and to examine the details of the Cromwellian settlement a word must be said about Cromwell's destructive work.

His methods of warfare in Ireland have excited, needless to say, the bitterest controversy.

The Cromwell controversy Carlyle had as little doubt as Cromwell himself that he was but the human instrument chosen to execute the will of the Almighty:

'To those who think that a land overrun with Sanguinary Quacks can be healed by sprinkling it with rose-water these letters [from Ireland in 1649] must be very horrible. Terrible Surgery this : but is it Surgery and Judgment or atrocious murder merely? That is a question which should be asked ; and answered. Oliver Cromwell did believe in God's judgments ;

and did not believe in the rose-water plan of Surgery. Which, in fact, is this editor's case too.'

Carlyle's sentiments, like Cromwell's, are in complete harmony with the views which prevailed in Puritan England. The massacres at Drogheda and Wexford were just reprisals for the massacres perpetrated by the Papists in Ulster in 1641. That this view can be justified only by profound ignorance of Irish social history prior to 1641 is, as Gardiner has pointed out, little to the point. Such ignorance did, in fact, prevail in England; Cromwell shared it, and his conduct was its natural product. That Cromwell intended to exterminate the Irish, Mr. Goldwin Smith held to be 'an exploded fable'. But the fable has been accepted as Gospel truth in Ireland from that day to this; and if extermination was not in Cromwell's mind he did not stop far short of expatriation. The real excuse for Cromwell can be found only in the application of the Positivist method of criticism; and of such a method we have an admirable example in Frederic Harrison:

'Cromwell, not worse than the Puritans and English of his age, but nobler and more just, must yet for generations to come bear the weight of the legendary "curse". He was the incarnation of Puritan passion, the instrument of English ambition; the official authority by whom the whole work was carried out, the one man ultimately responsible for the rest: and it is thus that on him lies chiefly the weight of this secular national quarrel.' [1]

A 'secular national quarrel' was Cromwell's legacy to England and Ireland. Yet, at the moment, his duty must have seemed as clear as it was unquestionably stern. The English Republic could not afford to ignore an Ireland which had declared for Charles II any more than William III could afford to ignore an Ireland which welcomed James II as King. But if Ireland was not to be ignored it had to be reconquered. Cromwell and Dutch William were in successive generations entrusted with the task. Colonization was, in the seventeenth century, the natural

[1] *Oliver Cromwell*, p. 147.

The Cromwellian Settlement

sequel of conquest, and, in his scheme of land settlement Cromwell (or those who acted in his name) did but carry to their logical conclusion the schemes of 'plantation' attempted by his predecessors.

According to this scheme Ireland was divided into two unequal parts by the Shannon. Ireland west of the Shannon—the land of bogs and mountains—was to become an Irish 'Wales'. Its population was to consist entirely of Catholic Celts. Into it were to be driven all the 'Innocent Papists'—Celtic chiefs, 'open' Papists and other opponents of the English Parliament who had not actually drawn the sword, and such 'Inferior Swordsmen' or private soldiers, as had escaped Cromwell's sword and preferred Connaught to foreign service. The towns of Connaught and Clare were to be reserved for English and Scottish settlers, and a military cordon, one mile in breadth was to be drawn round the sea coast and the river bank, in order to cut the Celts off from all possible contact with the outside world or the rest of Ireland. The Celts were in fact to be herded behind a human barbed-wire fence. Ulster, Munster, and Leinster were to be peopled exclusively by settlers from England and Scotland, save for a certain number of 'poor labourers', 'husbandmen, ploughmen, labourers, artificers, and others of the meaner sort' to whom pardon and oblivion were graciously extended on condition that they consented to act as hewers of wood and drawers of water for the new settlers. The priests were to be shipped off wholesale to Spain, or the West Indies. The Dublin Parliament was to be abolished; Ireland was to have representatives at Westminster and to enjoy complete equality of trade with England.

Criticism   To examine critically and in cold blood the details of such a scheme is almost impossible for those who cannot scrutinize it through seventeenth-century spectacles. Nor is it really necessary to do so since the scheme was never carried out in its entirety, and was abandoned when Charles II came into his own again. The physical difficulties in the way of wholesale deportation of the Celtic population were in fact less formidable than appear since their numbers did not exceed some 700,000. That, however, in no way diminishes the brutality of the intention. On the other hand, it is hardly disputable that had the scheme taken full effect, free trade and a legislative Union would have given to Ireland a half-century's lead of Scotland and have avoided the worst features of the 'ascendancy' government of the eighteenth century. That Ireland did, during the years which followed the Cromwellian settlement, enjoy an exceptional measure of economic prosperity is a fact well established by contemporary evidence.

But prosperity was bought at a terrible price. On this point Mr. Lecky's judgement is inexorable. 'The Cromwellian settlement', he writes, 'is the foundation of that deep and lasting division between the proprietary and the tenants which is the chief cause of the political and social evils of Ireland.' Of the social evils unquestionably; but Mr. Lecky belonged to a generation which held that economic and ecclesiastical reforms would solve the 'Irish Question'. The event disappointed their expectations. The disestablishment and disendowment of the Anglican Church in Ireland, the concessions contained in successive Land Acts, even the final expropriation of the Anglo-Irish proprietary failed to provide a solution. Where was their diagnosis at fault? Perhaps the communication from 'The Provisional Government of the Irish Republic' to President Wilson in 1919 supplies a key to the paradox. 'Our Nationalism', it ran, 'is not founded upon grievances. We are opposed not to English misgovernment but to English Government in Ireland.' No one more truly representative than Oliver Cromwell of all that has been best and worst in the English Government of Ireland ever set foot on Irish soil.

'The Irish Question'

XIV. THE COMMONWEALTH AND THE PROTECTORATE

Constitutional Experiments

AFTER Ireland, Scotland. Long before his task in Ireland was completed Cromwell, as we have seen, was recalled by Parliament to take the command, persistently declined by Fairfax, of the English army against the Scots.

Situation in Scotland

The situation in Scotland, though less confused than in Ireland, was not wholly free from complications. Three parties stand out: the old Royalists under the Marquis of Montrose, who was taken in battle by the Covenanters in the spring of 1649 and died gallantly on the scaffold (21 May); the strict Covenanters, headed by the Duke of Argyll, whom Cromwell had installed in power after his victories in the second Civil War, and the 'Law' Covenanters, 'Engagers' or Hamiltonians who headed by Hamilton, Lauderdale, Huntley and Middleton had been responsible for the invasion of England in 1648.

Battle of Dunbar

In the summer of 1649 a second Scottish invasion, in the interests of Charles II and the Covenant, was plainly imminent, but Fairfax declined to march against the Scots unless and until they crossed the border. Cromwell was willing to anticipate the attack and crossed the Tweed at the head of 16,000 on 22 July. But the eastern lowlands had been swept bare of men and provisions, and Cromwell could feed his troops only by supplies provided by the navy who protected his right flank. For several weeks David Leslie, at the head of 24,000 troops refused to be drawn from his entrenchments in front of Edinburgh; nor was Cromwell strong enough to attack. Towards the end of August however, Leslie saw a chance of cutting off the retreat of the enfeebled invaders, marched from Edinburgh and blocked the Berwick road to the south of Dunbar. There on 3 September Cromwell won the great victory which takes its name from the fishing village of Dunbar.

Of the Covenanters 3,000 were slain, and 10,000 taken prisoners, and Cromwell having captured all the baggage and guns of the enemy marched on Edinburgh. The Scottish Parliament, however, met at Perth, the Covenanting army was reformed and admitted the Royalists and Engagers to its ranks; Charles II was crowned at Scone (1 January 1651), and being cut off from the Highlands by the advance of Cromwell, decided to march south and raised his standard at Worcester (22 August). Cromwell, leaving 5,000 men under Monk to complete the conquest of Scotland, started in hot pursuit and on 3 September the 'crowning mercy' of Worcester was achieved. Leslie was taken prisoner as were many English and Scottish notables, but Charles, after forty-four days of hiding and wandering, escaped to Normandy (16 October).

Cromwell's victories in Ireland, Scotland, and England produced a marked effect upon the attitude of continental governments towards the Commonwealth. Monarchies and Republics vied with each other in their haste to resume polite relations with England. Diplomatic representations were exchanged with Sweden, Denmark, Portugal, the Swiss Cantons, and the Cities of the Hanseatic League, Tuscany, Venice, Geneva, Spain, and finally even with France. Meanwhile, the Commonwealth Navy had chased Prince Rupert not merely from the Channel but out of the ports of the Mediterranean and the West Indies. By the end of the year 1652 the authority of the Commonwealth was acknowledged in all the British Plantations oversea and indeed throughout the world. *Foreign Countries and the Commonwealth*

One quarrel, however, remained to be adjusted. Between England and the United Provinces there had long been friction, particularly between the merchants of the two countries in the East. A massacre of English merchants at Amboyna (1623) had driven our countrymen out of the spice islands and compelled them, fortunately for the Empire, to take refuge on the eastern coast of the Indian Peninsula. Neither James I nor Charles I had ever been able to extract apology or reparation for this brutal *The Dutch War*

act. Nor were there wanting causes of friction nearer
home.

The Navigation Act and the Dutch War
War broke out between the two countries in 1652.
Fought out between Blake and Van Tromp with varying
fortunes, it ended with a series of English victories, the
death of the Dutch admiral and the conclusion, in 1654,
of a Peace by which the United Provinces acknowledged
the supremacy of the English flag in the narrow seas.
They also agreed to exclude English Royalists, to make
reparations for the Amboyna massacre, and to accept the
terms of the Navigation Act which had been passed by
Parliament in 1651. Frankly protectionist in scope the
Navigation Act was nevertheless lauded by Adam Smith as
a triumph of statesmanship. No goods were henceforward
to be imported into England save in English ships, or in
ships belonging to the country of origin. Whether or no
the Act served only to register an economic change already
in progress, the fact remains that from that day onwards
the carrying trade of Holland waned and that of England
waxed. Holland continued to be a great financial and commercial entrepôt, but supremacy at sea passed to this island.

The Settlement of the Kingdom
Meanwhile, in England itself, things had been moving,
though slowly, towards a settlement. Parties there were
in England as in Ireland, but they were much more clearly
defined. Such remnant of 'constituted' authority as survived the execution of the King and the abolition of the
House of Lords was vested in the House of Commons.
That House, or the pitiful remnant of it, was supremely
anxious to perpetuate its power and in effect to render
itself independent of the electorate. It had the support of
such 'honest republicans' as Colonel Ludlow (whose description of his own party is here borrowed), Vane and
Martin who dreaded, not without reason, the domination
of the army. The Royalists, after the failure of their King
at Worcester, lay low and waited on events, but kept their
ears open to any sympathetic whispers from the Scotch and
English Presbyterians. Of the position of the 'Levellers'
enough has been said already.

Parliament was seemingly bent on alienating every party and interest in the State. It wantonly confiscated the property of 'malignants' to enrich its own members and adherents; it contravened all sound principles of government by acting simultaneously in a legislative and judicial capacity, and in March 1650 it set up what was in effect a new Star Chamber. The Court was to sit without a jury and to have power of life and death. Its duration was, it is true, limited to six months, but its appointment was one of many indications both of the arbitrary temper of the Rump and of the fears which inspired its action.

Most of all were the fears and suspicions of Parliament revealed in the measures proposed with the object of rendering it independent of the electorate and perpetuating its own power. Under the Act of 11 May 1641— an Act which had of course received the assent of the King and the House of Lords—the Long Parliament could not be dissolved, prorogued, or adjourned except by Act of Parliament 'passed for that purpose'. The Act contained a further provision that 'the House of Peers shall not at any time . . . during this present Parliament be adjourned unless it be by themselves or by their own order'. But, this notwithstanding, the Act was deemed to be still in force, and it did provide a certain measure of sanction for the impudent claim now put forward by the remnant of the House of Commons. On 4 January 1649 that House had resolved that 'the Commons of England in Parliament assembled, being chosen by and representing the people, have the supreme power in this nation'. Never, as Sir Charles Firth says, was the House

'less representative than at the moment when it passed this vote. By the expulsion of royalists members during the war, and of Presbyterians in 1648, it had been, as Cromwell said, "winnowed and sifted and brought to a handfull". When the Long Parliament met in November 1640 it consisted of about 490 members; in January 1649 those sitting or at liberty to sit were not more than ninety. Whole districts were unrepresented.

. . . At no time between 1649 and 1653 was the Long Parliament entitled to say that it represented the people'.[1]

Nevertheless the position it assumed possessed this element of strength: in the absence of a King, a House of Lords, and a written Constitution, there was absolutely no legal check upon its unlimited and irresponsible authority.

'This', said Cromwell, addressing his second Parliament, 'was the case of the people of England at that time, the Parliament assuming to itself the authority of the three Estates that were before. It had so assumed that authority that if any man had come and said, "What rules do you judge by?" it would have answered, "Why, we have none. We are supreme in legislature and judicature".'

Supreme the Rump claimed to be; but it ignored the dominant factor in the situation—the new model army and its general, and it chose to forget that its usurped authority rested in fact upon the power of the sword. It was soon to be uncomfortably reminded of this fact. By 1651 there was a clamorous demand for a settlement of the kingdom. The external enemies of the Commonwealth were now scattered, and so the victorious party had leisure and opportunity to quarrel among themselves. Petitions poured in from the army praying for reforms—long delayed—in law and justice; for the establishment of a 'gospel ministry'; above all, for a speedy dissolution of the existing Parliament. The officers were ready to employ force to effect the last object: but Cromwell was opposed to it and restrained his colleagues. Meanwhile the Rump pushed on their 'Bill for a New Representation'. This Bill suggested that the New House should consist of 400 members, but further proposed that the existing members should retain their seats without re-election, and should have a veto upon all new members elected not merely to the next but to all future parliaments. This provision has commonly been regarded as a gross usurpation of the rights of the electorate, but it is noteworthy that so strict a constitutionalist, so unimpeachable a democrat as the late

---

[1] *Cromwell*, p. 235.

Mr. John (Viscount) Morley held this was 'perhaps the least unpromising way out of difficulties when nothing was very promising'.[1] At least it did avoid the most fatal of all the errors committed by the Constituent Assembly in the French Revolution. Be that as it may, the officers strongly protested against this proposal; even Cromwell's patience was exhausted: 'You must go, the nation loathes your sitting.' Later on, he gave his opinion of this 'Perpetuation Bill': 'we should have had fine work then ... a Parliament of four hundred men executing arbitrary government without intermission except some change of a part of them; one Parliament stepping into the seat of another, just left warm for them; the same day that the one left, the other was to leap in. ... I thought and I think still, that this was a pitiful remedy.'

In his estimate of the position and policy of the uni-cameral Rump Cromwell was undeniably right. It was in plain truth the 'horridest arbitrariness that ever existed on earth'. It was judicially held that the Rump had become a sort of residuary legatee of all the powers previously possessed by either House. 'Whatsoever authority was in the Houses of Lords and Commons the same is united in this Parliament.' Such was the theory held by Lord Chief Justice Glyn. In particular the judicial power of the House of Lords was held to be vested in the Rump, while Major-General Gough went so far as to assure his fellow members 'that the ecclesiastical jurisdiction by which the Bishops once punished blasphemy had since the abolition of the bishops devolved also upon the House'.[2] The union of executive, legislative, and judicial authority more than justified Cromwell's famous description. No man's person or property was safe. It was a repetition of all the arbitrary tribunals of the régime of *Thorough* rolled into one. Hence

'the liberties and interests and lives of people not judged by any certain known Laws and Power, but by an arbitrary Power ... by an arbitrary Power I say: to make men's estates

Cromwell and the Rump

[1] *Cromwell*, p. 347.   [2] Firth, *Last Years of the Protectorate*, i. 9.

liable to confiscation, and their persons to imprisonment—
sometimes by laws made after the fact committed; often by
the Parliament's assuming to itself to give judgment both in
capital and criminal things, which in former times was not
known to exercise such a judicature'.[1]

Cromwell and Whitelocke   That Cromwell did not overstate the case against the
arbitrary behaviour of a House of Commons, acting with-
out a sense of immediate responsibility to the nation, and
unchecked by any external authority, is unquestionable.
But what were the alternatives? In order to discover them
many conferences, formal and informal, were held during
the eighteen months which elapsed between the 'crowning
mercy of Worcester' (3 September 1651) and the *coup
d'état* of 20 April 1653. Of these conferences the best
contemporary account is furnished by Whitelocke in his
Memorials of English Affairs (1625–1660). The *Memorials*
were not, it is true, published until 1682, and Carlyle's
hints as to the possible bias of a post-Restoration writer
must not be ignored; but Whitelocke was a trained
lawyer, the learned son of a learned father; he played an
honourable part in difficult days and little deserved the
derisive epithets which Carlyle was pleased to heap upon
him. 'The dancing hippopotamus', the 'dull fat Bulstrode',
with his 'fat terrene mind' had the misfortune to differ in
some degree from Cromwell as to the most hopeful lines
on which a permanent settlement of the Kingdom could
be effected. For Carlyle that is enough, but it was John
Morley's opinion that Whitelocke 'better than any of those
about him represented the solid prose of the national mind',[2]
and Cromwell himself thought well to seek Whitelocke's
counsel even if he did not abide by it.

Constitutional Conferences   When the Conference met at the house of Speaker
Lenthall, Cromwell propounded the question, 'Whether
a Republic or a mixed Monarchical Government will be best
to be settled, and if anything Monarchical, then, in whom
that power shall be placed?' Between the soldiers and
the lawyers a sharp difference of opinion at once manifested

[1] *Speeches*, iv. 50.   [2] *Cromwell*, p. 343.

itself. The soldiers were strongly in favour of a Republic. Whitelocke, on the contrary, gave his opinion in favour of a Monarchy.

'The Laws of England', he said, 'are so interwoven with the power and practice of Monarchy that to settle a government without something of Monarchy in it, would make so great an alteration in the Proceedings of our Law that you will scarce have time to rectify it, nor can we well foresee the inconveniences which will arise thereby.'

Sir Thomas Widdrington suggested that the Crown might be vested in the late King's third son the Duke of Gloucester as he was 'too young to have been in arms against us or infected with the principles of our enemies'. Whitelocke thought that terms might be made with the Prince of Wales or the Duke of Gloucester. Cromwell himself avoided the question of persons, but concluded 'that a settlement with somewhat of Monarchical power in it would be very effectual, if it may be done with safety and preservation of our Rights both as Englishmen and as Christians'. [1] The question was indeed one, as all parties agreed, 'of no ordinary difficulty'. The whole fabric of the Body Politic presupposed the existence of a King, and to effect a settlement without one meant a fundamental remodelling of Law and of Institutions.

For a settlement of some sort there was, indeed, urgent need and Cromwell recurred to the matter again and again. Meeting Whitelocke one day in St. James's Park he reopened it with him. 'There is very great cause for us to improve the mercies and successes which God hath given us and not to be fooled out of them and broken in pieces by our particular jarrings and animosities against each other.' The army had come to loathe the Parliament. 'And I wish there were not too much cause for it. For really their pride and ambition and self seeking, their daily breaking forth into new factions, their delays of business, and design to perpetuate themselves, these things, my lord,[2] do give

[1] Whitelocke, *Memorials*, iii. 372–4.
[2] Whitelocke was one of the Commissioners of the Great Seal.

too much ground for people to open their mouths towards them. So that unless there be some authority so full and so high as to restrain and keep things in better order, it will be impossible to prevent our ruin.' But who, objected the lawyer, can restrain a body acknowledged to be 'Sovereign'? 'What if a man should take upon him to be king', retorted Cromwell. 'Surely', he urged in answer to Whitelocke's cautious remonstrance, 'the power of a King is so great and high and so universally understood and reverenced by the people of this nation that it would be of great advantage in such times as these.' [1]

Nor was it Cromwell or the soldiers only who desired a separation of the Executive from the Legislative power. As far back as February 1650 Isaac Pennington, the younger, a son of one of the Councillors of State, put forward in *A Word for the Commonwealth* a plea for a stronger and more independent Executive. Complaint was made, he declared, of three evils: 'multitude of affairs, prolixity in your motions, and want of an orderly Government of your own body.' The remedy he proposed was the separation of the Executive from the Legislature. 'It seemeth to me', he wrote, 'improper for Parliaments to meddle with matters of Government further than to settle it in fit hands and within just bounds.' . . .

Parliament, however, would part with no tittle of sovereignty; the members of the Rump would not even submit themselves to the ordeal of a 'free' election. Would the army have been more ready to do so? Parliament and army both knew well that a 'free' election would have meant the recall of the Stuarts. Yet army and people were alike becoming increasingly impatient of Parliament.

Accordingly, on 19 April 1653, Cromwell summoned a Conference between the Generals and some Parliament men at his own house. Twenty-three members attended. Vane, on behalf of Parliament, promised that the Perpetuation Bill to which the soldiers objected should not be proceeded with until further conference had been held.

[1] Quoted by Gardiner, *Commonwealth and Protectorate*, i. 245.

Cromwell and the soldiers, so Ludlow reports, would give no securities for future government, saying: 'It was necessary to pull down *this* Government, and it would be time enough then to consider what should be placed in the room of it.' 'So both parties', adds Ludlow, 'understanding one another prepared to secure themselves.'

On the following day, news reached Cromwell that Parliament, despite Vane's undertaking, were pressing on their Perpetuation Bill. Summoning a company of musketeers to attend him, and accompanied by Lambert and other officers, he strode down to the House and took his place. As the Speaker was putting the question he said to Harrison 'This is the time, I must do it'. Then he rose and spoke with rising passion: 'You are no Parliament; I say you are no Parliament,' he shouted. 'Come, come, we have had enough of this; I will put an end to your prating. Call them in.' The musketeers filed in. 'What shall we do with this bauble?' he cried, and snatching up the mace from the table he gave it to a musketeer: 'Here, take it away.' Then pointing to the Speaker: 'Fetch him down,' he shouted to Harrison. Lenthall sat still. 'Sir, I will lend you a hand,' said Harrison, and the Speaker, yielding to a show of force, vacated the chair. The House was then cleared and the door locked. 'It is you that have forced me to do this,' cried Cromwell to Vane and other members as they passed out; 'I have sought the Lord night and day that He would rather stay me than put me on the doing of this work.' The expulsion of the Rump

What shall be said of this, one of the most famous and dramatic incidents in the history of the English Parliament? The 'honest republicans', even if soldiers like Ludlow, definitely parted company with Cromwell at this point. Clarendon, on the contrary, declares that Parliament had 'become odious throughout the Kingdom' and that the dissolution was 'generally very grateful and acceptable to the people'. 'Not a dog barked' was Cromwell's own comment. Among modern commentators the orthodox constitutionalists, typified by Hallam and John Morley, regret Cromwell's break with the remnant of legalism. Cromwell's biographers and apologists, led by Carlyle, while generally deploring the passion and coarseness displayed by the Lord-General, in the main approve the act itself.

Cromwell's act must in truth be judged by the results. Had it opened out the way to a settlement, not even the most pedantic would withhold approval. It did, in fact, initiate a series of constitutional experiments immensely interesting to students of politics but not conducive to that settlement and repose so ardently desired by the mass of the people, not least by the merchants and other men of business who were suffering severely from the prolongation of unrest and uncertainty.

The Puritan Convention Cromwell held himself to be, by virtue of the commission as Commander-in-Chief he had received from Parliament, the sole residuary of constituted authority. But he had no wish to prolong his dictatorship. A temporary Council of State of thirteen persons, mostly officers, was set up to carry on the daily business of the State. Even in this small body disputations as to the future form of Government ensued, but it was quickly decided to summon a Convention of Puritan notables, selected by Cromwell and the Council from a list submitted by the congregational churches, the godly clergy, and the chief Puritan lights in each county. Of the 140 men thus selected six represented Ireland, six Wales, five Scotland, and the rest England. They were all men 'fearing God, of approved Fidelity and Honesty , and were mostly persons of position and substance. But their discretion proved unequal to their zeal. 'I am more troubled now,' said Cromwell, 'with the fool than with the knave.'

In his opening speech Cromwell traced the hand of God in the winnowing of the nation's forces; in the marvellous successes won by men 'neither versed in military affairs nor having much natural propensity to them'; and in each successive event from the King's leaving Westminster to the battle of Worcester. After Worcester the one desire of the nation was to be allowed to reap the fruit of all the blood and treasure it had spent, but its hopes were persistently frustrated by the remnant of the Long Parliament. The army had besought Parliament to act spontaneously and without even the semblance of outside coercion. When they realized that this was hopeless 'the thinking of an act of violence was to us worse than any battle that ever we were in'. When the Perpetuation Bill had necessitated a forced dissolution no time was lost in summoning the Convention in order to 'divest the sword of all power in civil administration'. Finally, he adjured them to seek power from above to execute the judgement of mercy and truth.

The Puritan zealots then set about the task of accomplishing in a few months a work which called for years of thought and labour. They proposed to get rid of the Court of Chancery in teeth of bitter opposition from the lawyers; to abolish tithes, to the consternation alike of patrons and ministers; to abolish imprisonment for debt; to make civil marriage and the registration of marriages and births compulsory. Bills were also drafted for fixing lawyers' fees, for establishing County Courts accessible to the poor, and for registration of titles to land.

The 'Barebones Parliament', as it was afterwards nicknamed, allowed itself to be dominated by Puritan socialists in a hurry; the Moderates, as Gardiner says, 'lost power by neglect of business'. Not for the last time. But they plucked up energy to attend the House betimes one day, and finding themselves in a majority carried a resolution resigning their power into the hands of the Lord-General. The minority found themselves too few to make a quorum, and on the appearance of a military guard quietly departed (12 December 1653).

Ludlow, growing daily more rabid in his detestation of Cromwell, does not hesitate to accuse him of having called the Puritan Convention into being with the deep design of 'rendering them odious and to secure the lawyers and clergy into a compliance with his ambitions'. He appealed to 'the corrupt part of the lawyers and clergy and so he became their protector, and they the humble supporters of his tyranny'.[1]

The *Instrument of Government*   If this were indeed Cromwell's object he showed himself curiously eager to share the responsibilities of a tyrant with an elected Parliament. The Assembly of Saints was, as Cromwell afterwards confessed, a complete failure; it was heading straight for 'confusion of all things'. Lambert and a Committee of Officers had for some time been at work on the draft of a new Constitution. On the dissolution of the Little Parliament it was quickly completed, submitted to a conference of officers and civilians, and accepted by the Lord-General, who was solemnly installed as Protector on 16 December 1653.

The new Constitution embodied in the *Instrument of Government* has been described as 'a cross between the Elizabethan system and *The Agreement of the People*'.[2] But the description is picturesque rather than exact. To the scientific student of Political Institutions the *Instrument* is profoundly interesting. For the first time in its history England was placed under the government of a Constitution which was certainly written and was perhaps intended to be 'rigid'. On the latter point there has indeed been some controversy. The twenty-fourth clause conferred upon the Protector a suspensive veto on legislation. Did it do more? The clause runs as follows:

'That all Bills agreed unto by the Parliament shall be presented to the Lord Protector for his consent; and in case he shall not give his consent thereto within twenty days after they shall be presented to him, or give satisfaction to the Parliament within the time limited, that then, upon declaration of the Parliament that the Lord Protector hath not consented nor given satisfaction, such Bills shall pass into and become law although he shall not give his consent thereunto; *provided such Bills contain nothing in them contrary to the matters contained in these presents.*'

What is the precise meaning of this clause and, in par-

[1] *Memoirs*, ii. 272.   [2] By Gardiner, *Oliver Cromwell*, p. 86.

ticular, of the words here italicized? Dr. Gardiner contends that the intention was to devise a rigid Constitution and to limit the authority of Protector and Parliament by the terms of the Constitution as defined by the *Instrument*. The Protector was, according to this view, invested with a short suspensive veto on ordinary legislation, but ·neither he nor Parliament, nor both combined, could alter or amend the Constitution itself. It is noticeable that this is not the interpretation placed upon the clause by a contemporary—Colonel Ludlow. His summary of the clause runs as follows:

'that whatsoever they (Parliament) would have enacted should be presented to the Protector for his consent; and that if he did not confirm it within twenty days after it was first tendered to him it should have the force and obligation of a Law; provided that it extended not to lessen the number or pay of the army, to punish any man on account of his conscience, or to make any alteration in the *Instrument of Government*; in all which a negative was reserved to the single Person' (i.e. the Protector).[1]

Ludlow obviously regards the Protector and Parliament as being conjointly competent to alter even the terms of the Constitution itself, and that was the opinion of Dr. Dicey.[2] It would seem, moreover, to be confirmed by the draft of *The Constitutional Bill of the first Parliament of the Protectorate*, clause 2 of which runs as follows:

'that if any Bill be tendered at any time henceforth to alter the foundation and government of this Commonwealth from a single Person and a Parliament as aforesaid that to such Bills the single Person is hereby declared shall have a negative.'

Clearly, if the single Person did not veto the constitutional amendment, it was to become law. This 'Constitutional Bill' never passed into law, and can be cited, therefore, only in illustration. But so far as it goes it would seem to support the contention of the lawyers that in a legal sense

[1] Ludlow, *Memoirs*, p. 478.
[2] As expressed in conversation with the present writer and recorded at the time by Dr. Dicey's permission. Cf. Marriott, *English Political Institutions*, p. 132.

the *Instrument of Government* was not a 'rigid' but a 'flexible' Constitution. On the other hand the *Instrument* does not provide any machinery for constitutional amendment, and we know from external sources that Cromwell's own intention was that the Parliament should exercise merely legislative, and not constituent functions. In consequence of its determination to debate these constitutional questions it was, as we shall see, summarily dissolved by the Protector.

A contemporary pamphlet—written, it would seem, under official sanction—throws some light upon the point under discussion.

'If it be objected, that in the twenty-fourth article a negative voice is placed in the Protector, as to whatever is contained in the said establishment; and that in the twelfth article, the members elected are, by their indentures, to be debarred from altering the government, as it is declared to be a single person and a Parliament; and that thereby the supreme power is limited and restrained in things most natural to their trust and employment; it is answered, that though it be not of necessity, yet it were a thing to be wished, that popular consent might always, and at all times, have the sole influence in the institution of governments; but when an establishment is once procured, after the many shakings and rents of civil divisions and contestings for liberty, as here now in England, doubtless we have the greater reason to value it, being purchased at the price of our blood, out of the claws of tyranny; and we conceive it highly concerns us, to put in some sure proviso to prevent a raging of those foundations of freedom that have been but newly laid; especially in such an age as this, wherein men are very apt to be rooting and striking at fundamentals, and to be running out of one form into another. . . . Which being considered, it was high time some power should pass a decree upon the wavering humours of the people, and say to this nation, as the Almighty himself said once to the unruly sea, "Here shall be thy bounds, hitherto shalt thou come, and no further".[1]'

That this pamphlet represents the wish if not the inten-

---

[1] *A True State of the Case of the Commonwealth* 1654, p. 33 (quoted by Firth, *House of Lords*, p. 242).

tion of those who framed the *Instrument* can hardly be questioned. Nor can there be any doubt as to Cromwell's own conception of the functions of Parliament. They were to be purely legislative not 'constituent'; their business was to make laws, but only under the limitation that such laws did not infringe the 'fundamentals' of the Constitution as embodied in the *Instrument*. To this important point, however, we must return.

One of the 'fundamentals' on which Cromwell insisted was that the Executive power should reside in a 'Single Person'. On this point no debate could be permitted. The *Instrument* vested the 'chief magistracy and the administration of the Government . . . in the Lord Protector, assisted with a council' of not less than thirteen or more than twenty-one members. Oliver Cromwell was nominated Lord Protector of 'the Commonwealth of England, Scotland and Ireland, and the dominions thereto belonging, for his life'; but the office was to be 'elective not hereditary', and after Cromwell's death the Council was to elect his successor, excluding only any member of the Stuart family. *Position of the Executive*

The original members of the Council, fifteen in number, were likewise nominated in the *Instrument* for life. By a temporary provision the Protector and Council might, before Parliament met, co-opt not more than six additional Members of Council. A similiar power was also conferred upon them to make *Ordinances* which should have the force of law until revoked by Parliament. Full use was, as we shall see, made of this provision. *The Council*

The Protector was to control the military forces of the country, to conduct foreign affairs, and to declare war or make peace, by consent of Parliament, if Parliament was in session; by consent of the Council if it was not. On a declaration of war Parliament was to be forthwith summoned, and the Protector and Council had power to summon it for an extraordinary session at any time when deemed necessary.

Yearly revenue for the ordinary expenses of civil government was fixed at £200,000 a year, and in addition a sum sufficient to maintain 10,000 horse, 20,000 foot, and 'a convenient number of ships for guarding of the seas' was to be raised by Customs and in such other ways as were agreed by the Protector and Council. But the revenue was not to be diminished, nor the mode of raising it altered, save by consent of the Protector and Parliament.

The Council was evidently intended to be something very different from the Privy Council of the old monarchy. Its powers were specific and large, and it was evidently intended to act as a check upon the autocracy of the 'Single Person'. The Protector could do nothing without the consent of his councillors.

'No doubt,' as Dr. Gardiner says, 'his power of influence over its members was considerable, but in his dealing with them he had to rely on influence, not on authority. Though unfortunately we have little knowledge of anything that took place in the council beyond mere official routine, we know enough to convince us that the ordinary belief that Oliver was an autocrat and his councillors mere puppets is a very incorrect view of the situation.'[1]

The high officials of State, including the Chancellor and the Chief Justices, were to be 'chosen by the approbation of Parliament', presumably by the Protector. If Parliament was not sitting the Council was to approve such appointments, but subject to subsequent confirmation by Parliament.

The Legislature   Legislative power was vested in a single chamber to consist of 400 members for England and Wales, 30 for Scotland, and 30 for Ireland. The scheme for the redistribution of seats was substantially on the lines of *The Agreement of the People*; borough representation was greatly reduced and that of the counties increased, and there was to be a high property qualification—£200 of real or personal property—for all electors. Roman Catholics and Irish rebels were to be permanently excluded from the franchise or a seat in Parliament, and enemies of Parliament were to be similarly disqualified for twelve years.

[1] *Cromwell*, p. 86.

Parliament was to be re-elected triennially and to sit for not less than five months, and elaborate precautions were inserted in the *Instrument* to prevent any possible intermission of Parliament. Parliament was not to 'have power to alter the Government, as it is hereby settled in one single person and a Parliament', and it was, as we have seen, to share while in session various executive functions with the Protector.

As regards ecclesiastical affairs, the *Instrument* reflected the all but universal idea of the age that the maintenance of the 'Christian Religion' was the business of the State. This in effect meant an established and endowed Church on the congregational model, but there was to be toleration for all Christians except Papists, Prelatists, and 'such as under the profession of Christ hold forth and practise licentiousness'. The Church

Such were the main provisions of the *Instrument of Government*, but the first Parliament was not to meet until 3 September 1654. For nine months, therefore, the Protector and his Council had a clear field for the display of their activity, legislative and administrative. Nor did they neglect to cultivate it. No fewer than eighty-two Ordinances dealing with a great variety of subjects were issued between January and September 1654; many of them were confirmed by the Second Parliament of the Protectorate, and if they failed to leave a permanent impress upon the English Statute-book it was only because the legislation of the interregnum was repealed at the Restoration. Cromwell's domestic reforms

Cromwell, as Protector, proved himself to be not only an ardent reformer but a keen Imperialist and Unionist. Ireland was, as we have seen, to be represented at Westminster, and thirty members from Ireland sat in the Parliaments of 1654, 1656, and 1659: it was also to enjoy equal rights with regard to foreign and colonial trade and to pay identical Customs and Excise duties. Scotland also was 'united with the people of England into one Commonwealth' with equal privileges of trade and representation. The Irish and Scottish Unions

But there the similarity between the treatment of the two incorporated countries ended. The Irish Papists were regarded as barbarians to be hunted to death or into banishment: the Scots were weaker brethren but still brethren. Only twenty-four of the Scottish leaders lost their property altogether; minor offenders were fined. There was no general confiscation, still less any scheme of colonization by aliens.

Nor was the Faith of the people proscribed. The General Assembly was dissolved and the Church was deprived of its civil power and coercive jurisdiction. Feudal tenures were abolished and the administration of justice was, even on the admission of Scotsmen, greatly improved. Burnet indeed declared that 'those eight years of usurpation [were] a time of great peace and prosperity'; but Baillie's account is nearer the truth: 'A great army in a multitude of garrisons bides above our heads and deep poverty keeps all estates exceedingly under; the taxes of all sorts are so great, the trade so little, that it is a marvel if extreme scarcity of money end not so in some mischief.' Scotland, after all, had had fifteen years of intermittent fighting, and Cromwell himself admitted that at the end of it they were 'a very ruined nation'. But whether English rule brought ruin or riches it was deeply resented, and Scotland hailed the Stuart Restoration as the re-birth of national independence. Yet Cromwell's work in Scotland was not wholly effaced, and his policy had but to wait another half century for complete vindication.

Foreign affairs   Wars with Portugal and (as we have seen) with Holland were ended on terms favourable to English trade, and commercial treaties were concluded with Sweden and Denmark. 'There is not a nation in Europe', as Cromwell boasted to his Parliament, 'but is willing to ask a good understanding with you.' The two great continental rivals eagerly competed for the friendship of the great captain of the Ironsides. Cromwell's inclination was towards France rather than Spain. Spain not only persecuted heretics at home but jealously excluded English traders from all share in her colonial trade. Only on the basis of free trade for English merchants and toleration for English sailors would Cromwell consent to offer the hand of friendship to Spain. 'To ask liberty from the Inquisition and free sailing in the West Indies is,' said the Spanish ambassador, 'to ask my master's two eyes.' Blake was accordingly dispatched to the Mediterranean in October 1659, and Penn sailed for the West Indies in December of the same year. Blake made the English flag respected in the Mediterranean, released English traders held captive by the Dey of Algiers, and inflicted drastic punishment on the pirates who interfered with English shipping. In 1655 war broke out with Spain, and in the three years that followed Blake, Penn, and Venables rivalled the exploits of the Elizabethan sea-dogs. The treasure-laden galleons of Spain were captured; England's mastery in the South Atlantic was asserted, and her possessions in the West Indies were consolidated by the conquest of Jamaica. The anxiety of the French for an alliance with Cromwell gave the Protector an opportunity of succouring the Protestants in the Canton Vaud. He did not miss it, and Protestant Europe resounded with his fame. France reaped her reward in 1657, when an English force was dispatched to co-operate with Turenne in the campaign against the Spaniards in Flanders. Turenne's great victory at Dunkirk (4 June 1658) brought the long-drawn war between France and Spain to an end. The fortress of Dunkirk was the stipulated reward for the timely help of the English Ironsides. Dunkirk would serve, as Thurloe said, 'as a bridle to the Dutch and a door into the continent'. Cromwell had at one time contemplated getting another door into the continent and a bridle to the Spaniards by an attack on Gibraltar, but prudential reasons restrained him. Even so, his brief tenure of power had made the English flag respected abroad as it had never been respected since the spacious times of Queen Elizabeth, and England's position under the Protector was a far greater one than it had been even under the Queen. By the exercise of infinite patience and by ceaseless circumspection Elizabeth had been able, with small resources in men and money, to do little more than hold the balance between the two great continental Powers. At the zenith of Cromwell's power they were both suppliants for his aid. His alliance with France may, as Bolingbroke afterwards complained, have upset the European balance and given France a pre-eminence which proved dangerous in after years to his own country. But that pre-eminence would never have been gained had Cromwell found a worthy successor to his sceptre. If Louis XIV was able to threaten the independence of Europe the blame must rest largely on Charles II and the disgraceful Treaty of Dover, not on that alliance between equals which gave us Dunkirk. To round off the story we have anticipated events: we must return to the first months of the Protectorate.

Church reform

Cromwell was not only one of the founders of our Imperial polity but a great domestic reformer. His first care, indeed, was for the religious nutriment and the moral well-being of the people committed to his charge. That the State could cut itself adrift from the Church never entered his head, nor that of any other responsible statesman of that age. The State must provide a godly and learned ministry, even though Episcopacy was abolished and Presbyterianism little liked. Accordingly, an Ordinance was issued (20 March 1654) to set up a Board of thirty-eight Commissioners to examine into the qualifications of all candidates for livings. No one was to be admitted to a benefice without a certificate from these Commissioners or 'Triers', testifying to his 'holy and unblameable conversation and also for his knowledge and utterance and fitness to preach the gospel'. Local commissioners were also appointed (August) in every county charged with the duty of ejecting unfit ministers and schoolmasters. Large parishes were subdivided and small ones were united. Baxter, Presbyterian though he was, and suspicious of the partiality of the 'Triers' for 'Independents, Separatists, Fifth Monarchy-men, and Anabaptists', was forced to admit that 'they did abundance of good to the Church', and that 'many thousands of souls blessed God for the faithful ministers whom they let in'. The appointment of a University Commission and a Board of Visitors for the Public Schools afforded further proof of the Protector's anxiety for the intellectual and spiritual welfare of the people and for the training of their pastors and teachers.

Second only in importance to the purity of religion was the purity of law. The administration of justice was, there- fore, carefully overhauled. By a reform of the criminal code Cromwell might, if permitted, have anticipated much of the work accomplished by Romilly and Peel. A scheme was devised by which procedure in Chancery was simpli- fied and fees were cut down; and bills were prepared for the establishment of local courts where justice might be obtained promptly and cheaply, and for county registers.

Despite the driving power of the Protector nine months were little enough for the accomplishment of such exten- sive reforms; much of the work remained only in draft; for on 3 September the Protector had to face Parliament.

It was a critical moment in the history of parliamentary government. That Cromwell was anxious to share his responsibility with Parliament can be questioned only by those who regard him as a conscious hypocrite. But Parliament, though composed for the most part of moderate men, was bent on asserting its claim to sovereignty; and sovereignty Cromwell was no more disposed than the Stuart Kings to concede to it. We are here for 'healing and settling'; for a long while there has been nothing in the hearts and minds of men but 'overturn, overturn, overturn'. At home disunion and trouble, of which foes, external and internal, have taken advantage, and which would have resulted in great misery but for the remedy provided in the *Instrument of Government*. . . . 'I have not spoken as one who assumes to himself dominion over you, but as one who doth resolve to be a fellow-servant with you in the interests of these great affairs.'

Thus Cromwell addressed Parliament in his opening speech. But Parliament was not disposed to accept the

Law reform

The first Protec- torate Parlia- ment

Instrument as a constitutional *terminus a quo*. They claimed, in technical terms, to be not merely a legislative but a *constituent* body. It was for them—the elect of the people—not for any self-appointed body of soldiers or civilians, to draft a Constitution and to determine the relations of Legislature and Executive. For a full week members continued to debate the 'form of Government', whether it shall be by a single person and parliament.

Cromwell was chafed by their delay in getting to work, and with rising temper came down and addressed a second speech to them on 12 September:

Funda-
mentals
and cir-
cumstan-
tials

'I said you were a free Parliament: you are; but you must acknowledge the *Instrument of Government* under which you were summoned. I called not myself to this place; God and the People did so, and if so I will not lay it down unless God and the People take it from me. After Worcester I hoped and expected to live privately in peace and liberty; God be my witness that I longed to be dismissed from my charge. I urged the Long Parliament to dissolve themselves; my marches with the army had taught me the temper of the Nation which loathed their sitting.'

After the dissolution of the Rump the

'Little Parliament was called to settle the nation and for myself to lay down the power which was in my hands. . . . I accepted the *Instrument of Government* because by it I was not put into a higher capacity but rather *limited*. My position was confirmed by the People, the proofs are presentable: express approbations from counties, grand juries, &c.; the judges acted under commissions from me; the sheriffs also; you are here in answer to my writs of summons; you are my witnesses: for you to sit and not own the authority by which you sit is absurd, it is true as there are some things in the Establishment which are *fundamental*. So there are others which are not but are *circumstantial*. Of these no question but I shall easily agree to vary, to leave out, according as I shall be convinced by reason. But some things are Fundamentals! About which I shall deal plainly with you; these may not be parted with; but will I trust be delivered over to Posterity as the fruits of our blood and travail. The Government by a Single Person and a Parliament is a Fundamental. It is the *esse*; it is constitutive. . . . Liberty of Conscience is a Fundamental: So is the Militia in the hands of one person along with Parliament.

'As to Fundamentals we must have agreement. Regretfully, therefore, I inform you that only those will be, after to-day, admitted to Parliament who sign an engagement to be true and faithful to the Lord Protector and the Commonwealth of England, Scotland and Ireland . . . and not to alter the Government as it is settled in a single Person and a Parliament.' [1]

About three hundred members signed the engagement, but among the excluded members were stout republicans like Bradshaw and Haslerig, and Levellers like Wildman. The 'purge', however, had little effect. Parliament continued to debate constitutional points; friction ensued between the Protector and Parliament as to the size of the army and the control of the armed forces. Consequently, on the first possible date Cromwell dissolved Parliament (22 January 1655). 'Dissettlement and division, discontent and dissatisfaction, together with real dangers to the whole, have been more multiplied within these five months of your sitting than in some years before.' With these stern words Cromwell bade good-bye to his first Parliament. *Dissolution of Parliament*

The words were true: Royalists and Levellers, Fifthmonarchy men, and fanatics religious and political, plotted the overthrow of the Protectorate. An actual rising of Royalists took place in Wilts., but was sternly repressed.

Another experiment was then tried. For eighteen months the country was handed over to military administration. England was divided into twelve districts, and each was placed under the charge of a Major-General. Order was thus maintained, but the administration was a bad compound of the rule of the sword and the rule of the saints. Many ale-houses were suppressed; race meetings, cockfights, and bear-baiting were prohibited; the performance of stage-plays was forbidden; Royalist gentry were imprisoned by the score, and a special supertax of 2s. *The Major-Generals 1655-6*

---

[1] The argument is compressed but, I hope, substantially reproduced. Cf. *Speeches*, iii, pp. 20–109.

in the £1 was imposed on their estates. Many of the worst features of the Personal Government of Charles I were reproduced with sinister exactitude and with results not dissimilar. The administration of justice recalled the days of the Star Chamber: the Major-Generals ejected ministers quite in the mode of the High Commission Court; Lord Grey of Grooby, denied his writ of Habeas Corpus, presented a parallel case to that of the Five Knights; Sir Peter Wentworth continued the family tradition by resisting the imposition of a duty on merchandize much as Hampden had resisted ship-money or Bates had refused to pay the duty on currants. Chief Justice Rolle resigned his place rather than give judgement in Wentworth's case; other judges declined to act on Commissions to which they were appointed; Whitelocke and Widdrington, two of the Commissioners of the Great Seal, resigned. But embarrassing as were such resignations the Protector's most pressing need, like that of the Stuart Kings, was money. The Spanish war [1] could not be carried on without it and the Protector summoned a second Parliament. Great efforts had been made to secure the election of the well-affected, but even so it was found necessary to exclude as many as one hundred irreconcilables.

The second Protectorate Parliament 1656–8   This renewed 'sifting and winnowing' did not solve the difficulty. There were in truth only two genuine alternatives: 'government by consent' or government by the sword. The 'honest republicans', like Ludlow, wanted the former. 'What would you have?' asked Cromwell of Ludlow. 'That which we fought for,' replied the colonel, 'that the nation might be governed by its own consent.' 'I am as much for government by consent as any man,' said the Protector, 'but where shall we find that consent?'

The question denotes the practical statesman as against the doctrinaire. 'Government by consent' could mean only a freely elected Parliament with constituent powers. Such a Parliament meant a Stuart restoration. And Cromwell knew it. Nevertheless he was almost pathetically anxious

[1] *Supra*, p. 316 seq.

to keep the sword out of sight, and arrive, if by any means possible, at a constitutional settlement. 'It is time to come to a settlement and to lay aside arbitrary proceedings so unacceptable to the nation.' The lawyers, the merchants, and the middle party generally, were of one mind with the Protector, and early in the year 1657 a demand arose from many quarters for a revision of the Constitution. Alderman Sir Christopher Pack, one of the members for the City of London, was put up to propose revision—a Second Chamber and increased power for the Protector, who was to be 'something like a king'.

By the end of March the demand took practical shape in the *Humble Petition and Advice*. The Protector was to be transformed into a king, with the right to nominate a successor; Parliament was once more to be bi-cameral; the 'other House' was to consist of not more than seventy and not less than forty members, nominated for life by 'his Highness', and approved by 'this' House; the Commons were again to secure control over their own elections, and none duly elected was to be excluded; the Council of State was to be known henceforth as the Privy Council; a permanent revenue was to be secured to the king, and there was to be toleration for all: 'so that this liberty be not extended to Popery or Prelacy or to the countenancing such who publish horrible blasphemies or practise or hold for licentiousness or profaneness under the profession of Christ.' In a word, the old Constitution, so far as the circumstances of the moment would allow, was to be restored. *The Humble Petition and Advice*

Cromwell was well pleased with the scheme, and, had his officers permitted, would have accepted it in its entirety. 'The things provided in the Petition', he declared, 'do secure the liberties of the people of God so as they never before had them.' But on one point the leading officers and the 'honest republicans' were alike immovable: they would have no king. They were backed in their opposition by the extremer Puritan sects. *Cromwell and the Crown*

'We cannot but spread before your Highness our deep resentment of, and heart bleedings for, the fearful apostasy which is endeavoured by some to be fastened upon you . . . by persuading you to assume that office which was one declared and engaged against by the Parliament . . . as unnecessary, burdensome and destructive to the safety and liberty of the people.' [1] So ran an address from nineteen Anabaptist ministers in London. Cromwell himself was in two minds. His reason assented to the *Humble Petition*, but policy required that he should not break with the masters of the sword. The extremists prevailed, and after five weeks of discussion and hesitation Cromwell refused the offer of the crown.

A new Second Chamber

The prosposal for a revived Second Chamber was, on the contrary, carried with an unexpected degree of unanimity. The Protector pressed it strongly upon the officers.

'I tell you,' he said, 'that unless you have some such thing as a balance we cannot be safe. Either you will encroach upon our civil liberties by excluding such as are elected to serve in Parliament—next time for aught I know you may exclude four hundred—or they will encroach upon our religious liberty. By the proceedings of this Parliament you see they stand in need of a check or balancing power, for the case of James Naylor might happen to be your case. By the same law and reason they punished Naylor they might punish an Independent or Anabaptist. By their judicial power they fall upon life and member, and doth the *Instrument* enable me to control it? This *Instrument of Government* will not do your work.' [2]

The case against a uni-cameral legislature was never put with more telling effect. 'By the proceedings of this Parliament you see they stand in need of a check or balancing power.' The appeal to recent experience was irresistible. More horrid arbitrariness had never been displayed by any government. The lawyers were especially emphatic in their demand for some bulwark against the caprice and tyranny of a single elected chamber:

'The other House', said Thurloe, 'is to be called by writ, in the nature of the Lords' House; but is not to consist of the old

[1] Firth, *Last Years of the Protectorate*, i. 155.
[2] *Ap*. Firth, *op. cit.*, i. 137–8.

Lords, but of such as have never been against the Parliament, but are to be men fearing God and of good conversation, and such as his Highness shall be fully satisfied in, both as to their interest, affection, and integrity to the good cause. And we judge here that this House thus constituted will be a great security and bulwark to the honest interest and to the good people that have been engaged therein; and will not be so uncertain as the House of Commons, which depends upon the election of the people. Those that sit in the other House are to be for life, and as any die his place is to be filled up with the consent of the House itself, and not otherwise; so that if that House be but made good at first, it is likely to continue so for ever, as far as man can provide.' [1]

The preference of the lawyers for a bi-cameral legislature is, however, only according to expectation. They frankly favoured a return as speedy as possible to the old order, if not to the old dynasty.` More remarkable is the acquiescence of the soldiers. But they too had come to realize both the inconvenience—to use no harsher term—caused by the sovereignty of a single chamber, and the insufficiency of paper restrictions imposed by the *Instrument of Government*. A freely elected House of Commons meant the restoration of the 'King of the Scots'.

'On reflection, therefore, they were not sorry', as Sir Charles Firth pertinently remarks, 'to see a sort of Senate established as a check to the popularly elected Lower House, thinking that it would serve to maintain the principles for which they had fought against the reactionary tendencies of the nation in general. They were so much convinced of this that in 1659 the necessity of "a select Senate" became one of the chief planks in the political platform of the army.' [2]

On 8 May Cromwell communicated to the House his final decision not to 'undertake the government with the title of King'. After much debate the *Petition* was amended in accordance with the Protector's views, and in its amended form was definitely accepted on 25 May. On 26 June Cromwell was installed with solemn pomp as

<hr>

[1] *Ap.* Firth, i. 41.   [2] *Op. cit.*, i. 142, 3.

Protector, and on 29 January 1658 he met his remodelled Parliament for the first time.

According to the terms of the *Petition*, the 'other House' was to consist of not more than seventy and not less than forty members, 'being such as shall be nominated by your Highness and approved by this House'. But after much debate the approval of 'this' House was waived and the Protector was authorized to summon whom he would. The task of selection was no easy one, but Cromwell took enormous pains to perform it faithfully. 'The difficulty proves great,' wrote Thurloe, 'between those who are fit, and not willing to serve, and those who are willing and expect it, and are not fit.' At last sixty-three names were selected and writs were issued, according to the ancient form, bidding them, 'all excuses being set aside,' to be 'personally present at Westminster . . . there to treat, confer, and give your advice with us, and with the great men and nobles'. Of the sixty-three summoned, only forty-two responded; among them being Richard, son of the Protector,[1] his three sons-in-law, Fauconberg, Claypole, and Fleetwood, and his brothers-in-law, Desborough and John Jones. Of the seven English peers summoned, only two consented to serve, one being Cromwell's son-in-law, Lord Fauconberg, the other Lord Eure, a peer of no standing or repute. Lord Saye, staunch Puritan though he was, refused to countenance any Second Chamber save the real House of Lords.

'The chiefest remedy and prop to uphold this frame and building and keep it standing and steady is (and experience hath showed it to be) the Peers of England, and their powers and privileges in the House of Lords; they have been at the beam keeping both scales, King and people, in an even posture, without encroachments one upon the other to the hurt and damage of both. Long experience hath made it manifest that they have preserved the just rights and liberties of the people against the tyrannical usurpation of kings; and have also as steps and stairs upheld the Crown from falling upon the floor,

---

[1] Henry also was summoned, but was detained by his duties in Ireland.

by the insolency of the multitude, from the throne of government.'

That being so, he thought it unworthy that any ancient peer of England should so far play the traitor to his House and order as to be 'made a party, and indeed a stalking-horse and vizard, to the design of this nominated Chamber'.[1] His sons John and Nathaniel Fiennes had no such scruples, and obeyed the Protector's summons. The latter indeed was one of the most enthusiastic apologists for the 'other House'.

But the Protector had still to reckon with the bitter and pedantic republicans in the House of Commons. Sir Arthur Haslerig, who had refused a place in the 'other' House, was foremost among the querulous critics of the new constitutional experiment. The Protector insisted upon the critical condition of affairs at home and abroad; but to no exhortations would the Commons give heed. Once again they insisted on questioning 'fundamentals', and debating the powers, position, and title to be assigned to the 'other' House. A week of this 'foolery' sufficed to exhaust the Protector's patience, and on 4 February he dissolved Parliament with some passion: 'Let God be judge between you and me.' 'Amen,' responded some of the irreconcilable republicans. Thus ended in confusion and failure the constitutional experiments of the Commonwealth and the Protectorate. *Republican opposition*

That Cromwell was genuinely anxious to restore the authority of the civil power and to re-establish parliamentary institutions is unquestionable. That he signally failed is obvious. *Reasons for Cromwell's failure*

To ascribe his failure entirely to the abolition of the monarchy and of the House of Lords would be uncandid, though it cannot be doubted that the absence of these balancing elements rendered Cromwell's task wellnigh insuperable. Nor can it be ascribed wholly to the personality or to the peculiarities of Cromwell himself. It is true that he never gave any indication of special capacity for

[1] *Ap.* Firth, *op. cit.*, ii. 14.

the task of constitutional reconstruction; it is truer still that he was unfitted alike by temperament and training for the role of a 'constitutional' ruler in the modern sense. He was quite as determined as Strafford or Charles I to retain in his own hands the control of the Executive, and he refused to assign to his Parliaments anything more than a legislative authority to be exercised under the strait limitations of a written and a rigid constitution. On the other hand, it is hardly matter for surprise that a Parliament which imagined that it had brought a Stuart sovereign to the dust should be reluctant to accept so limited a sphere of action and authority. The Protectorate Parliaments were, as already indicated, determined to exercise not merely legislative, but constituent powers; not only to make laws, but to revise and define the Constitution itself. The claim, though reasonable enough in theory, was inconvenient and inopportune. If the sword was ever to be sheathed, if civil government was ever to be restored, it was absolutely necessary, as Cromwell pointed out with homely good sense, to start somewhere, to agree on certain preliminary fundamentals. Parliament refused to see the necessity, and insisted upon throwing the whole Constitution into the melting-pot on each successive occasion.

The problem of Sovereignty again   The point at issue was precisely what it had been under the Stuart Kings: Where does *Sovereignty* reside? Does it reside in a Constitution, or in Parliament, or in the People? It is difficult to maintain that there was much moral authority behind either of the written Constitutions —the *Instrument of Government* or the *Petition and Advice*. On the other hand, to admit the sovereignty of the people in any genuine and effective sense—to summon a constituent assembly freely elected by the constituencies— would have been, beyond all question, to pave the way for a Stuart restoration. Must *Sovereignty*, then, be vested in a Parliament, either uni-cameral or bi-cameral, elected on a notoriously restricted franchise and with manifest disregard for 'popular' rights? The dilemma was in fact complete, the problem insoluble. The more so since it was impossible to avow the naked truth that the real sovereignty in England during the interregnum was vested neither in People, nor in Parliament, nor in paper Constitutions, but in the sword. Cromwell's authority, anxious as he was to ignore or disguise the fact, rested upon the fidelity of his unconquerable Ironsides. His parliamentary experiments, though undertaken in all good faith, were in consequence foredoomed to failure. The failure is, however, unusually instructive. It is a striking illustration of the truths, too often neglected by Englishmen, that parliamentary government is not for all peoples, nor for all times; that it postulates certain conditions; that its success depends on presuppositions by no means invariably fulfilled; that if it is to work smoothly there must be a tolerable measure of agreement upon 'fundamentals'; that on 'circumstantials' men and parties may indulge in wide difference of opinion; but that on general principles of government they must be in accord. Further, and finally, it would seem to suggest the conclusion that parliamentary institutions, at any rate in England, are workable only with a legislature genuinely bi-cameral in structure, and under the aegis of a constitutional but hereditary monarchy.

For ten years the English people submitted sullenly, but in the main silently, to a military autocracy thinly disguised under the veil of a parliamentary Commonwealth, or a Protectorate limited by a written Constitution. On the death of the great Protector, himself the leader and general of an irresistible army, the sword and the robe at once came into sharp and open conflict. The people after a short period of confusion got the opportunity—the first they had enjoyed since 1640—of giving expression to their true political sentiment. They used it, as we shall see, by recalling the Stuarts.

XV. THE RESTORATION

THE reign of Charles II, though legally dated from 30 January 1649, was not actually effective until May 1660. But the restoration of the hereditary monarchy had become inevitable, if not from the day on which Charles I was executed, at least from that on which Oliver Cromwell passed away.

Richard Cromwell On Oliver's death[1] the Council immediately proclaimed Richard, his eldest surviving son, Protector, in accordance with the terms of the most recent of the written Constitutions. 'Who knoweth', said the old Protector, 'whether he may beget a wise man or a fool.' He did both. Henry Cromwell proved himself competent both as soldier and administrator. Richard never gave any sign of ability to control a situation admittedly difficult if not impossible. A man of pleasure according to Ludlow; a well-meaning, easy-going country gentleman, as others, less prejudiced than Ludlow, describe him; to us a somewhat obscure figure who on his virtual deposition betook himself to Paris where he sojourned for twenty years under the name of John Clarke, but returned to England in 1680, living in retirement as a quiet country gentleman, until his death at the age of 86 in 1712.

Position of parties The eighteen months which intervened between the death of the Great Protector and the return of Charles II possess little constitutional significance, and the events of that period may therefore be very briefly summarized.

The death of Oliver let loose the strife of parties which his personality had temporarily held in check. 'Those men', according to Ludlow, 'who had been sharers with him in the Usurped Authority were exceedingly troubled whilst all other Parties rejoiced.' The new Protector was supported by London, by a large body of Presbyterians, and by about a half the members of the two Houses of Parliament; in particular by the men who had wanted

[1] 3 September 1658.

Oliver to found an hereditary monarchy. Among these Whitelocke, Thurloe, Maynard, and St. John were prominent.

The 'honest' Republicans or 'Commonwealth men', as Ludlow now calls them, held meetings at the house of Sir Henry Vane and decided to stand for the Parliament which Richard had immediately summoned. The writs were issued, however, not to the new constituencies created by the written Constitutions of the Protectorate, but to the old constituencies which had returned members to the Long Parliament. It was hoped in this way to secure a more amenable body. The Upper House was, however, retained as was the representation from Scotland and Ireland.

The grandees of the army, now known as the Wallingford House Party, formèd a third group. Led by men like Fleetwood and Desborough, their immediate object was to separate the offices of Protector and General and to confer the latter office on Fleetwood.

General Lambert, an arch-intriguer, did not act (except perhaps temporarily) with his colleagues at Wallingford House and aimed at getting the Protectorship for himself. But he was almost completely isolated.

Finally, there were the Royalists who, following Clarendon's sagacious advice, stood for Parliament and 'found themselves much more numerous than they expected'.

The army, encouraged by the conflict between parties in Parliament, lost no time in drafting and presenting their demands. The office of Protector was to be separated from that of General, which was to be given to Fleetwood; the General was to have the appointment of all officers; and the army was in effect to be a self-governing entity, independent of Parliament. Parliament replied to these insolent demands by prohibiting the meeting of any General Council of Officers during the sitting of Parliament without the consent of the Protector and Parliament, and by requiring that every officer should pledge himself in writing not to disturb the proceedings of Parliament.

Dissolu-
tion of
Parlia-
ment

Interpreting these votes as a declaration of war upon the army, the officers forthwith compelled the Protector to dissolve Parliament (22 April 1659), promising him in return their own support. 'This', says Whitelocke, 'was the beginning of Richard's fall set on foot by his relations.' 'From that minute', writes Clarendon, 'no one resorted to him, nor was the name of Protector heard of but in derision.'

Restora-
tion of
the Rump

In the army, itself, however, there were divisions. While the grandees would have liked to retain a Protector 'in the nature of a Duke of Venice', the lower officers were in favour of a Republic. There was some talk of another 'Sanhedrim', a repetition of the experiment of the Bare-bones Parliament, but on 7 May the army, supported by the 'honest' republicans, reinstated the Rump of the Long Parliament. The members excluded by Pride were not summoned, but about 120 members of the Rump still survived, though the maximum attendance was 76.[1] The army, however, had misgivings as to the wisdom of restoring an omnipotent and uni-cameral Parliament, and on 13 May they presented a list of their demands to Parliament. These included a regularly elected House of Commons and 'a select Senate co-ordinate in power of able and faithful persons eminent for Godliness and such as continue adhering to their Cause'.[2] Ludlow, on behalf of the Republicans, opposed the revival of a Second Chamber 'co-ordinate with the authority of the people's repre-sentative and not chosen by the people', save as a tem-porary expedient to meet the difficulties of the moment, 'to prevent [the people] from destroying themselves and not to enslave them to any faction or party'.[3] The objection of the army to a uni-cameral Parliament was shared by some of the more thoughtful Republicans, led by James Harrington, the author of *Oceana* (1656) and of many political pamphlets published during these months.

---

[1] Firth, Introduction to vol. iv of the *Clarke Papers*, but cf. also his *House of Lords*, p. 260.
[2] *Old Parliamentary History*, xxi. 404.　　　[3] *Memoirs*, ii. 648.

'A Parliament,' wrote Harrington, 'consisting of a single
assembly and invested with the whole power of the
Government, was so new a thing that neither ancient nor
modern prudence can show any avowed example of the
like.' On 25 May Richard Cromwell made a formal submission to Parliament and soon afterwards abdicated and
departed from Whitehall. He asked only that his own and
his father's debts incurred in the service of the State, and
amounting to some £30,000, might be paid. Parliament
agreed to do so, but the promise was not fulfilled.

In the course of the summer Scotland was disturbed by
rumours of the activity of Stuart emissaries, and several
Royalist risings occurred in England, notably in Lancashire
and Cheshire. Monk dealt promptly with Scotland, and
Lambert at Northwich defeated and dispersed a considerable force collected by Sir George Booth. It was evident
that the Stuart embers were smouldering, and that it was
not the moment to impair the efficiency or discipline of the
army, which alone stood between the country and a Stuart
restoration. Parliament, however, appeared even more
anxious to reassert the supremacy of the Civil power than
to save the Republic. They were willing, indeed, to retain
Fleetwood as Commander-in-Chief, but many officers supposed to be too favourable to the House of Cromwell were
cashiered. The breach between the army and the Rump
widened daily; and on 13 October 1659 Lambert, treading
in the footsteps of the man to whose place he aspired, a
second time expelled the Rump. A contemporary pamphlet depicted the situation with precision:

'Do the men in the Parliament House signify any more than
the man that stands upon the clock in Westminster Abbey with
the hammer in his hand, and when the iron wheel bids him
strike, he strikes: hath it not been so between the army and the
Parliament, as it is called?'

The question was pertinent. Nevertheless there were Monk
many who shared the misgivings of Monk, who now assumes
the leading role in the exciting drama about to be enacted.
George Monk, who after the Restoration became first

Duke of Albemarle, had already proved himself a fine soldier and a more than competent sailor. He was greatly trusted by Cromwell, though in 1649 he had been censured by Parliament for the surrender of Dundalk. His wise and strong administration in Scotland had, moreover, given promise of the statesmanship he was now to display in a larger sphere. On hearing of the second expulsion of the Rump he wrote to remonstrate with Lambert:

'It is much upon my spiritt that this poore Commonwealth can never be happy if the army make itself a divided interest from the rest of the nation which must bring us into such a slavery as will not be long indured; and at least when all meanes faile, if ever we are settled the Parliament must do it.' (3 November 1659).[1]

A few weeks later he wrote to Dr. John Owen, Dean of Christ Church, a still more significant letter in which, while repudiating any intention of espousing the Royalist cause, he said: 'I am enjoyed in conscience and honour to see my country freed (as much as in mee lies) from that intolerable slavery of a sword government,' and he added that the unhappy divisions among patriots would certainly encourage Stuart hopes. 'Neither can I see,' he concluded, 'any legall foundations for a free State unless this Parliament sitts down againe, or some other legally called.'[2]

Committee of Public Safety When this letter was written Monk had already begun preparations for a march on London, and on 8 December, at the head of 7,000 men, he crossed the Tweed at Coldstream. Meanwhile, the army had set up a Committee of Public Safety, and a small sub-Committee was set up 'to prepare such a form of government as may best suit and comport with a free state and commonwealth, without a Single Person Kingship or House of Peers'. On this advisory Committee Whitelocke, Ludlow, and Vane consented to serve with Fleetwood and two other soldiers. Ludlow made the interesting suggestion that in order to preserve certain fundamentals, 'inviolable by any authority whatsoever', there should be an independent body of

---

[1] *Clarke Papers*, iv. 87. [2] *Ibid.* iv. 153.

twenty-one persons of known integrity, who were to be styled 'Conservators of Liberty', and whose function should be to decide whether a 'fundamental' had or had not been violated.

In this suggestion the curious may perhaps detect an anticipation of the function now performed by the Supreme Court of the United States. In the latter case there is, indeed, an appeal to the people of the constituent States as represented by their several Legislatures, by whose action the Federal Constitution may itself be amended. No such device was (or under the circumstances of the moment could be) admitted into any of the written Constitutions of the English Commonwealth, but Ludlow's suggestion does at least indicate a perception of the difficulty inherent in Rigid Constitutions, in the absence of specific machinery for effecting revision.

For the moment nothing came of the deliberations of the Constitutional Committee. The disposition of events was in other hands. Monk was marching south; Lambert at the head of 10,000 men was dispatched to bar his way. He got as far as Yorkshire, but Fairfax had come to an agreement with Monk, and on the appearance of their old General in the field Lambert's force melted away like snow at the first touch of spring. Lambert himself slunk away but was imprisoned (3 December). Monk marched on the capital unopposed. On 26 December the twice-expelled Rump was recalled; on 3 February Monk entered London. *Monk's march on London*

Monk's intentions were unknown—perhaps even to himself; but (he was declared Lieutenant-General of the Commonwealth and placed himself under the orders of Parliament.) The Commonwealth men were in high spirits: 'All is our own, he will be honest.' The city, meanwhile, had declared for a 'free' Parliament, and though Monk, at the bidding of the Rump, destroyed the gates of the city (9 February), he was impressed by the demonstrations he witnessed, and the very next day returned to the city, summoned the Common Council, and joined them in a demand for a full and free Parliament. *A 'free' Parliament*

Dissolu-
tion of
Long
Parlia-
ment
On the 23rd February the members excluded by Pride were, under pressure from Monk, restored after an exile of eleven years to their seats in Parliament. Their readmission gave the Presbyterians a majority. Parliament thereupon appointed Monk General of all the land forces of the three Kingdoms and Joint Commander of the Navy; appointed a new Council of State; and having summoned a new Parliament, to be 'freely' elected and to meet on 25 April, dissolved itself (16 March). Thus, at long last, the Parliament elected in 1640 was legally ended.

Monk's
position
What next? Everything depended on Monk, but Monk had not yet declared himself in favour of a Stuart restoration. Nor is it even now certain when he actually decided to promote it.[1] Ludlow declares that at the time of the return of the secluded members Monk protested to Sir Arthur Haslerig and other 'honest' Republicans that he would 'oppose to the utmost the setting up of Charles Stuart, a single person over the House of Peers'.[1] Clarendon also asserts that Monk 'had not to this hour (February) entertained any purpose or thought to serve him' [Charles Stuart], and that he decided to restore him only when he perceived that there was no alternative. He thus became the glorious instrument of things 'which he had neither the wisdom to foresee, nor courage to attempt, nor understanding to contrive'.[2] But neither Ludlow nor Clarendon is an unprejudiced witness. The probability is that when he began to move south Monk had not got beyond a decision to summon a 'free' Parliament. What he saw on his march through England convinced him that a Parliament, freely elected, would inevitably recall the Stuarts, and he resolved, not unwisely, to anticipate their decision.

Declara-
tion of
Breda
A trustworthy agent, Sir John Greenvil, was dispatched, with verbal instructions, carefully learnt by heart, to Brussels, where Charles Stuart was residing. Charles was required to promise an amnesty and liberty of conscience; to confirm the sales of Crown lands and to remove from Brussels to Dutch territory. Hyde advised compliance and

[1] *Memoirs*, ii. 849.   [2] *History*, vii. 445 and 461.

on 4 April Charles issued the Declaration of Breda.
Declaring that he desired that his subjects might enjoy
what by law was theirs, as he hoped to enjoy his own, he
promised amnesty and oblivion for all not excepted by
Parliament, an Act to secure a liberty to tender consciences, and a parliamentary settlement of land grants
and purchases.

Parliament met on 25 April with a full complement of
elected members in the Commons, but in the House of
Lords only ten peers. On 1 May both Houses resolved that
'according to the ancient and fundamental laws of this
Kingdom the Government is and ought to be by King,
Lords and Commons'. An invitation was forthwith dispatched to Breda; on the 25th Charles landed at Dover
where he was met by Monk, and thence made a triumphal
progress to the capital which he entered on 29 May. To
the general enthusiasm there was one notable exception.
The stern republicans, still the strongest element in the
army which had been Cromwell's and by no means unrepresented among the civilians, stood sullen and silent
amid the cheering crowds.

The 'Convention' Parliament

There was some ground perhaps for Dryden's satire:

> 'Crowds err not, though to both extremes they run;
>   To kill the father, and recall the son.'

But there was also sound political philosophy as well as
satire in *The Medal*:

> 'Such impious axioms foolishly they show,
> For in some soils republics will not grow:
> Our temperate isle will no extremes sustain,
> Of popular sway, or arbitrary reign:
> But slides, between them both, into the best,
> Secure in freedom, in a monarch blest.'

That the restoration of Charles II was generally popular
cannot be gainsaid. Nor is there much obscurity as to the
reasons. Perhaps the most pervasive was the conviction
gradually formed among all classes that unless the nation
was prepared to accept a succession of Praetorian rulers
there was no alternative, except a restoration of the

General popularity of the Restoration

monarchy. As the years passed after the execution of Charles I, people perceived more and more clearly that they had but exchanged a monarchy for a military dictatorship. However anxious, genuinely anxious, Cromwell might be to share legislative (though not executive) authority with Parliament, his power rested essentially on the devotion of his army. Disguise it as he might, his rule was the rule of the sword, and it left bitter memories. So persistent indeed was the popular dread of a military dictatorship that half a century after Cromwell's death his 'shadow fell darkly across the path of Marlborough's ambition'.[1] That the victor of Blenheim could, in Queen Anne's day, have re-established a military dictatorship, is incredible; but it is the more significant that the fear of it should have contributed to his downfall.

A second reason is to be found in the perturbation produced among the commercial classes by the prolongation of a period of uncertainty and unsettlement. The barometer of trade is peculiarly susceptible to such influences, and the barometer, despite the development of colonial plantations, was falling. Heavy taxation further depressed trade, and the merchants, largely Presbyterian in religious persuasion, became more and more impatient of military rule and more and more anxious for a 'settlement'.

The great mass of the people, though staunch in their adherence to the Protestant faith, were not enamoured of Puritanism in power. The rule of the saints meant, as we have seen, not merely the suppression of vice but a violent disturbance of habits, deeply ingrained among the people, and the prohibition of many forms of amusement which to us seem innocent. Under the grim rule of the Puritans the tradition of a 'Merrie England' was fast fading, and the licence of the Restoration was the price paid for a denial, in the previous decade, of reasonable liberty.

All these considerations undoubtedly had weight, but the two outstanding reasons for the Stuart restoration were

[1] The striking phrase is Lecky's.

the growing attachment of the country to Parliament as an institution, and the deepening conviction that without an hereditary monarchy Parliamentary Government was impossible. The former of these two sentiments is rather remarkable. To the Englishman of the nineteenth century the value of Representative Government was axiomatic. We are apt, therefore, to forget that down to the sixteenth century the duty of sending representatives to the House of Commons was regarded as a burden imposed on localities rather than a privilege enjoyed by them. The Tudor period was marked, as we have seen, by a striking change of sentiment. Stuart opposition to Parliament intensified popular feeling in its favour. The military dictatorship of Cromwell clinched the matter; warm regard was converted into almost fanatical devotion.

Parallel with this development, paradoxical as it may at first sight appear, was the growth of an attachment to the principle of hereditary kingship. These truths, not hidden from Englishmen, have been emphasized by a great German commentator on English History:

'The English Restoration', wrote Leopold von Ranke, 'was essentially a parliamentary revolution. The chief reason for recalling Charles II was the impossibility of establishing parliamentary government without a King. . . . The right of hereditary succession . . . was once more hailed as the keystone of that ideal arch, which is called the Constitution of the realm.[1]

These sentences supply some of the clues wherewith to unravel the complicated tangle of the period which follows. There were at least two others: a general suspicion of all foreigners, particularly of the French, and a cordial attachment to the Established Episcopal Church. Three out of the four sentiments were responsible for the Restoration itself; three out of four accounted for the rapid cooling of enthusiasm between 1660 and 1681; the attempt of the Whigs to exclude the Duke of York from the succession aroused afresh the sentiment of attachment to the hereditary principle and brought to an abrupt close their brief ascendancy; finally, James II, as we shall see, contrived,

The clues to the period 1660–88

with perverse ingenuity, simultaneously to violate all four sentiments.

Charles II   The restored King was faced by some difficult problems: but his intellectual endowments were much above the average. He was in the best (and in the worst) sense a 'man of the world'; he had high courage, perfect manners and had learnt much in the school of adversity. He came back to England determined to exact compensation for the buffetings of fortune, if not to be avenged on individuals. His oft quoted resolution 'never to go on his travels again' supplies one of the clues to his somewhat shifty conduct. His complacent conviction that no one would ever kill him to put his brother on the throne supplies another. On his landing at Dover he was presented by the Mayor with a 'very rich Bible', and he declared that 'he loved it above all things in the world'. But he never gave any proof that his attachment to Protestantism, or indeed to any creed, was more than tepid, and the wit was not far wrong who declared that 'he oscillated in contented suspense between Roman Catholicism and atheism'. Morally, he was much inferior to his father: intellectually he was much the ablest of the Stuart Kings; but he was incurably indolent. His fondness for women was notorious, but Lord Sheffield declared that 'sauntering was the true Sultana Queen of His Majesty's affections'. Yet perhaps in his case, as in Lord Melbourne's, laziness and indifference were a pose rather than a reality.

Settlement of the Kingdom   From the angle of the present book the interest of the period between the Restoration and the Revolution is concentrated on five points: (i) the definition of the relation between Church and State; (ii) the control of Parliament over national finance; (iii) the problem of ministerial responsibility and of the relations between the Legislature and the Executive; (iv) the rise of the Party system; and (v) the statutory guarantee of personal liberty by the passing of the *Habeas Corpus Act*, and the definition of the relations between the Judiciary on the one side and the Executive and Legislature on the other. Before, however, we can deal with these fundamentally important questions, some of the confusion caused by the revolutionary years must be cleared up.

The Declaration of Breda had promised a general amnesty, subject to any exceptions made by Parliament. Thirteen regicides, including Harrison and Hugh Peters, were executed, and about a score were imprisoned, some of them for life. Ludlow escaped to Switzerland and died at Vevey thirty years later; Sir Henry Vane was put on his trial for treason and executed in 1662. The bodies of John Pym, of the historian Thomas May, of Blake and Popham who had conferred fresh lustre on the English navy, of Cromwell's mother and his daughter Lady Claypole were torn out of their graves in the Abbey and thrown into a pit near the cloisters. The bodies of Cromwell, Ireton, and Bradshaw were not only disinterred but hung on gibbets at Tyburn, within a stone's throw of the present Marble Arch. The executions of the regicides in Whitehall, and even the horrid spectacle of the hanging of the dead bodies of Cromwell, Ireton, and Bradshaw were witnessed apparently with satisfaction and rejoicing by the mob. A more sensitive age has condemned the whole proceeding; but though we may regard with horror the desecration of the dead, it must be confessed that, in view of all that had happened in the preceding twenty years, the vengeance exacted by the Convention Parliament was on a moderate scale. Charles II and Clarendon would, if they could, have restricted it within even narrower limits. *Amnesty and Oblivion*

Nor were they willing to associate the restoration of the Monarchy with any violent disturbance of the existing distribution of landed property. The civil war, and the revolutionary régime which followed it, witnessed inevitably an immense change in the ownership of land. Much land had been confiscated; much more had been sold to meet the fiscal demands of successive governments. Royalists whose lands had been confiscated recovered them; but no compensation was awarded to those who had sold, nor *Land Settlement* were the purchasers of private estates disturbed. Those who had been rash enough to purchase land belonging to the Crown or the Church were evicted without compensation.

The Crown and the Church emerged without loss, but all other parties were dissatisfied, particularly the Cavaliers who complained with intelligible bitterness that the Statute was an Act of Indemnity for the King's enemies, of Oblivion for the King's friends.

Public Finance Much more satisfactory was the settlement arrived at in regard to the revenues of the Crown. In more ways than one, the modern system of national finance may be said to date from this period, though, *more Anglicano*, the transition from the medieval to the modern was very gradual.

Hitherto the national revenue had been Royal revenue and the expenses of Government had been defrayed by the King. In early days the revenue had been wholly obtained from the land itself, or from obligations imposed on the ownership of land: from Crown lands ('Royal Demesne'), or from the incidents of feudal tenure: payments on succession ('reliefs'), or the proceeds of wardship of minors, the marriage of heiresses, pre-emption, purveyance and the like.[1]

The Long Parliament, by a resolution of both Houses (1645), converted all tenures in chivalry into free and common soccage, and an Act of 1656 confirmed these resolutions. Neither the resolutions nor the Statute retained any legal validity after 1660, but the revenue derived from such sources was insignificant, while the incidents themselves were vexatious.

No sovereign, therefore, would have been foolish enough to revive these unpopular and unprofitable prerogatives. Least of all one who, like Charles II, was exceedingly anxious to regain the good will of his people. Accordingly, by the Act 12, Charles II, c. 24, feudal tenure was abolished and with it all the incidents attaching thereto.

[1] For these incidents cf. Stubbs, *C.H.*, ii. C. xvii; Maitland, *C.H.*, p. 183 and on the whole subject of the financial settlement of 1660, Dowell, *History of Taxation*, ii. 20 seq.

In compensation the King was to receive £100,000 a year. But this, though historically interesting, was a relatively small matter. Much more important were the additional sources of revenue: parliamentary grants of various kinds, customs and excise. Owing in part to the fall in the value of silver, in part to the rapid growth in the expenses of administration, the revenue was under the early Stuarts totally inadequate.[1] An attempt was, as we have seen, made in the *Great Contract* to strike a bargain between the Crown and Parliament, but it proved abortive. In 1660 a Committee was appointed to 'consider of settling such a revenue on His Majesty as may maintain the splendour and grandeur of his kingly office and preserve the Crown from want and from being undervalued by his neighbours'. The Committee reported that during the years 1637 to 1641 the revenue of Charles I had averaged £900,000 a year, but that of this amount £200,000 had either been raised by illegal means or was no longer available. It recommended that the revenue should for the future be fixed at £1,200,000 a year. The sum thus fixed proved wholly inadequate, while the sources of revenue designed to produce it fell short of it by nearly 50 per cent.

During the revolutionary period Parliament raised large sums, partly by means of an Excise duty—a new device borrowed from the Dutch, and partly by monthly assessments on property. The Restoration Parliament was not too proud to borrow the financial expedients of its irregular predecessor. The custom duties were consolidated: the old distinction between customs and 'impositions', old and new customs, were abolished and the duties were classified in four categories: (i) tunnage on wine; (ii) poundage on imported goods; (iii) poundage on exports; (iv) a duty on woollen cloth. These consolidated customs were granted to Charles II and his successor for life.

An *Excise* duty was also imposed on beer, cider, and spirits produced at home, and also on the sale of certain

Sources of revenue

---

[1] *Supra*, c. pp. 32 seq.

imported commodities, which, having already paid customs duties, were in effect taxed twice over.

The assessment of the old 'subsidy'—a charge of 4s. in the £ on land and 2s. 8d. in the £ on personalty—was so bad that in 1663 one subsidy from the laity and clergy produced only about £70,000. The 'subsidy', the successor of the older 'Tenths and Fifteenths', was abolished, and in place of it direct taxation in three forms was imposed: a poll tax; a tax of 2s. for every hearth or stove ('Hearth money') and the 'assessment'. The profits of the Post Office, first established as a State service under James I and extended under Charles I, had gone originally to the Postmaster, who 'farmed' them under the State. The Statute 12, Charles II, c. 35 first gave legislative sanction to the new institution and in 1663 the revenue, therefrom, estimated at £21,000 a year, was settled on James, Duke of York, and his heirs male in perpetuity. On his accession to the throne this revenue, by that time increased to £65,000 a year, was vested in the Crown and merged in the hereditary revenue.

Appro-priation This period also witnessed a considerable step forward in the principle of appropriation, though not until the time of the younger Pitt did it approach its modern development. The modern 'Estimate' appropriates every penny of supply granted to the Crown with meticulous minuteness, while it is the function of the Controller and Auditor-General, and of the Public Accounts Committee, to see that the intentions of the House of Commons have been precisely fulfilled. But down to the Restoration the application of the principle of appropriation had been spasmodic and embryonic. As long as the expenditure of the King did not exceed his income, no questions were asked by Parliament. Parliament was, in fine, much more concerned to prevent illegal taxation than to find out how the proceeds of taxation had been spent. But from Charles II onwards, Parliament showed itself increasingly alive to the principle of appropriation. In 1665 a large sum was voted for the Dutch war, and the Bill contained a clause to the effect that the money should be applied to that purpose only. This followed a precedent set in 1624 when money was voted for the relief of the Palatinate, and was in turn followed, though by no means invariably, in other cases. It was dropped by the parliament of James II, but after the Revolution became the regular practice. Another change, not less significant, dates from the same period, and marks the beginning of the Civil List. Parliament voted to William and Mary a revenue of £1,200,000 a year, £700,000 of it being appropriated to the support of the Royal household, the personal expenses of the Sovereigns, the payment of civil offices, &c., and the remaining £500,000 to the more general expenses of administration. This principle was carried still further in succeeding reigns, the Civil List being progressively diminished and concurrently relieved of all charges save those which are strictly personal to the Sovereign. The Crown has also surrendered all claim to the hereditary revenues which now bring in to the State a sum far in excess of all the expenses of the Monarchy.[1] The revenue granted to Charles II was evidently intended only to maintain a peace establishment. Parliament made a special grant to pay off the great army of the Commonwealth. Fifteen regiments of horse and twenty-two of foot were rapidly demobilized, and only two regiments, one of horse and one of foot, were retained for the King's guard, with a third regiment, brought from Dunkirk. These regiments, numbering about 5,000 men, formed the nucleus of the modern standing army.

Not, however, until after the Revolution was the position of this standing army, which under James II numbered nearly 9,000 men, regularized. The Bill of Rights had declared the raising or keeping a standing army in time of peace, without the consent of Parliament, to be against law. But in 1689 the Mutiny Act was passed to secure the discipline of (and by subsequent amendment to provide pay and quarters for) the Army. Enacted in the

The Army

[1] The Civil List of King George V was fixed at £470,000 a year: the Crown lands now (1929) produce over £1,000,000 a year. Grants to other members of the Royal Family amount to £106,000, but even so the margin is an ample one.

first instance only for seven months the Statute has been annually[1] re-enacted and has thus, incidentally, secured the regular meeting of Parliament. The Militia was not included in the Act until 1807, when for the first time 'all troops in pay under a commissioned officer in any of the Dominions of the Crown or in places in possession of subjects' of the Crown 'were brought under its operation'.[2] A very important and significant clause in the Act provided that nothing in the Act shall be construed to exempt any officer or soldier from the ordinary process of law. This clause contained the clue, as Dicey[3] pointed out, to all our legislation with regard to the standing army. 'A soldier by his contract of enlistment undertakes many obligations in addition to the duties incumbent on a civilian. But he does not escape from any of the duties or liabilities of an ordinary British Subject.[4] Thus, in popular phraseology, a soldier may be shot for refusing, when ordered, to fire on a mob, or executed for obeying. In this characteristic fashion was a compromise reached. A standing army was, they were convinced, a perpetual menace to domestic liberty; without such an army they could not feel secure against external attack; or, as Dicey put it 'the maintenance of national liberty appeared to involve the sacrifice of national independence.'[5] In a Mutiny Act passed for a strictly limited period, and particularly in the clause to which attention was last called, an escape from the dilemma has been discovered.

The Militia The Militia, it has been said, was expressly excluded from the first *Mutiny Act*. But one of the first acts of the Cavalier Parliament was to pass a Statute (13 Car II, St. I, c. 6, 1661) declaring 'the sole Supreme Government Command and disposition of the Militia and of all forces by sea and land, and of all forts and places of strength, is . . . and ever was . . . the right of His Majesty . . . and that both or either of the houses of Parliament cannot nor

[1] It is now known as the 'Army and Air Force (Annual) Act'.
[2] Robertson, *Statutes and Documents*, p. 60.
[3] *Law of the Constitution*, Lecture vii.
[4] *Op. cit.*, p. 308.   [5] *Ibid.*, p. 305.

ought to pretend to the same.' Subsequent Acts passed
in 1662 and 1663 determined the establishment of the
Militia as a constitutional force. The Lords-lieutenant,
appointed by the King, were to nominate the officers and
generally to control the forces. Liability to service came
to rest on the possession of landed property, and the
Militia, therefore, fitted in precisely to the scheme of the
territorial oligarchy by which England was governed, in
the main with eminent success, for a century and a half,
The officers of the Militia were local gentry, and the ranks
were largely supplied by their tenants. In fact it was a
county force, locally officered, and locally manned.

Convenience has led us to anticipate the sequence of
events. The 'Convention' Parliament was dissolved on
29 December 1660, and its successor, destined to continue
in being for eighteen years, met in May 1661. The House
of Commons was elected on the same basis, as regards
franchise and constituency, as the Long Parliament of
1640. It consisted therefore, of 507 members for England
and Wales. Scotland and Ireland were not represented,
but Charles II subsequently gave representation to the
city and county of Durham and to the borough of Newark,[1]
thus bringing the number of the House of Commons up to
513, at which figure it remained until after the Union with
Scotland. Elected at a moment of limitless enthusiasm for
the restored Monarchy the vast majority of the members
were ardent Royalists and devoted to the Episcopal Church.
They proved themselves, indeed, in Macaulay's famous
phrase 'more zealous for royalty than the King, more
zealous for Episcopacy than the Bishops'. Yet there was
from the first a minority of some fifty or sixty; and this
opposition increased as years went on.

If, however, the Restoration can be accurately described
as a Parliamentary restoration, it was, even more markedly,
a restoration of the aristocracy. Not only did the House

The Cavalier or 'Pension' Parliament, 1661-79

The House of Lords

[1] Newark (1677) was the last parliamentary borough enfranchised by
Royal prerogative, and even in the Cavalier Parliament, the exercise of
it did not pass unquestioned.

348   THE RESTORATION

of Commons include now and for nearly two centuries to
come, a large number of cadets of noble houses and country
gentlemen, but the House of Lords itself was restored in
all its former prerogatives; though not with its full complement of members. King Charles I having given his assent
(14 February 1641) to the exclusion of the Bishops from
the House of Lords, a Statute was required to restore them.
It was passed in 1661. One hundred and forty-seven lay peers
were entitled to sit in this Parliament and were summoned
to it.[1] The Peers thus recovered all their legal and social
privileges, but they had, in the opinion of a high authority,
lost something of their political prestige. 'There was', says
Sir Charles Firth, 'less respect and more criticism, and
much of the divinity that used to hedge a peer had
vanished.'[2] Moreover, the House of Commons had
increased greatly in self confidence, and the result
was a notable increase of friction between the two
Houses.

Separate taxation of the Clergy ends

Another change of high historical significance, though
little heeded at the time, was effected in 1663. The clerical
'Estate', in so far as an 'Estate' implies separate taxation
disappeared. During the Commonwealth no distinction, as
regards taxation, was made between clergy and laity, and
when, after the Restoration, tenths, fifteenths, and subsidies were swept away, the clergy gave up their right to
tax themselves separately in their Convocations. The
change was effected by a verbal and informal understanding between Lord Chancellor Clarendon and Archbishop
Sheldon, whose commemorative buildings still confront
each other in Broad Street at Oxford. Thenceforward, the
clergy were qualified to act as parliamentary electors, but
not, by a curious and characteristic inconsistency, to be
elected as members of the House of Commons. Disquali-
fication, as so often, has survived the extinction of the
privilege which originally justified it. Thus the clergy, like

[1] About 20 more than in 1640. It included all creations (which had
not in the meantime become extinct) since that date: and two peerages
(Albemarle and Sandwich) created since 1660; Firth, *Lords*, p. 291.
[2] *Ibid.*, p. 292.

the 'Barons', were for the first time brought, in a fiscal sense, into the national system.

This was the moment chosen by the Commons for the reassertion of their claims to exclusive, or at least pre-eminent, control over taxation. The whole burden of maintaining the national services, in peace and war, now fell—apart from the 'hereditary' revenues of the Crown—as a common charge upon the nation at large. It was natural that the Commons should regard with jealousy and suspicion any attempt to tax the electors whom they represented. A pretext for a quarrel soon arose. In 1661 the Lords passed and sent down to the Commons a Bill for 'paving, repairing, and cleansing the streets and highways of Westminster'. The Commons in high dudgeon rejected the Bill, on the ground that 'it went to lay a charge upon the people', and 'that no Bill ought to begin in the Lords' House which lays any charge or tax upon any of the Commons'. To this assertion the Lords demurred, as being 'against the inherent Privileges of the House of Peers, as by several Precedents wherein Bills have begun in the Lords' House, *videlicet* 5to Elizabethae, a Bill for the Poor, and 31 Eliz. for Repair of Dover Haven, and divers other Acts, does appear'. The Commons thereupon passed a Bill of their own, and sent it up to the Lords. This time it was for the Lords to protest: but eventually

> 'The Lords, out of their tender and dutiful Respects to His Majesty, who is much incommodated by the Neglect of those Highways and Sewers mentioned in the Bill, have for this Time in that respect alone, given Way to the Bill now in Agitation, which came from the House of Commons, with a Proviso of their Lordships; *videlicet*, "Provided always that nothing in the passing of this Bill, nor any thing therein contained, shall extend to the Prejudice of the Privileges of both or either of the Houses of Parliament, or any of them; but that all the Privileges of the said Houses, or either of them, shall be and remain, and be construed to be and remain, as they were before the passing of this Act, any thing therein contained to the contrary notwithstanding; with this Protestation that this Act

Disputes between the two Houses

shall not be drawn into Example to their Prejudice for the future".'[1]

The Commons refused to accept the Bill with the insertion of this proviso; matters came to a deadlock, and the proposed legislation had to be abandoned.

A similar Bill of a more general nature was, however, passed in the following year; a similar impasse was threatened, but on this occasion the Lords, after formal protest from several of their members, gave way.[2]

The Lords and Finance This was only the beginning. In 1671, and again in 1678, the Lords attempted to amend Bills of Supply sent up to them by the House of Commons—proceedings which evoked the two famous resolutions which are the *loci classici* of the constitutional lawyer. By that of 1671 the Commons affirmed that 'in all aids given to the King by the Commons, the rate or tax ought not to be altered by the Lords'.[3] That of 1678 asserted

'That all aids and supplies, and aids to His Majesty in Parliament are the sole gift of the Commons; and that all Bills for the granting of any such aids or supplies ought to begin with the Commons; and that it is the undoubted and sole right of the Commons to direct, limit, and appoint, in such Bills, the ends, purposes, considerations, conditions, limitations, and qualifications of such Grants which ought not to be changed or altered by the House of Lords.'[4]

On both occasions the Lords in the end gave way, but not without the following emphatic protest:

'Resolved, *Nemine contradicente*, that the Power exercised by the House of Peers, in making the Amendments and Abatements in the Bill, instituted, "An Act for an additional Imposition on several Foreign Commodities, and for the Encouragement of several Commodities and Manufactures of this Kingdom," both as to the Matter, Measure, and Time, concerning the Rates and Impositions on Merchandize, is a fundamental, inherent, and undoubted right of the House of Peers, from which they cannot depart.'[5]

What then is the general principle affirmed in these

---

[1] *L. J.* xi. 328*a*.　　　[2] *L. J.* xi. 467–9.　　　[3] *C. J.* ix. 235.
[4] Cp. *C. J.* ix. 509.　　　　　[5] *L. J.* xii. 498*b*.

historic resolutions? It will be observed that the Lords'
right of concurrence in taxation was not questioned; but,
under the resolutions, they cannot legally *impose* a charge
upon the people; hence they cannot 'alter or amend' a tax
proposed by the Commons, though they may refuse to
concur in its imposition, and, therefore, may reject it. In
course of time, however, and partly, perhaps, in consequence of the ambiguity of the wording of the resolution
of 3 July 1678, confusion has arisen between a tax or grant,
and the aggregation of taxes contained in a modern Finance
Bill. That confusion was at last ended by the *Parliament
Act* of 1911 under which the Lords were deprived of the
right either to amend or to veto 'money bills'.[1]

If the Parliament of 1661 was more royalist than the
King it was also more Episcopal than the Bishops. Called
upon to confirm, as a legal precaution, the Acts of the
Convention, Parliament was with difficulty persuaded by
Clarendon to include in that confirmation the *Act of
Indemnity*. But they showed their temper by requiring all
members to receive the Sacrament of the Lord's Supper
according to the rites of the Church of England; by ordering the Covenant to be burnt by the common hangman,
and by an attempt to exclude Presbyterians and other
Dissenters from offices in local government.

The Ecclesiastical settlement

Under the *Corporation Act* of 1661 all office bearers
in Municipal Corporations were required to receive the
Sacrament, in the same manner as Members of Parliament, to renounce the Covenant, and to swear to their
belief in the doctrine of passive obedience. The Act was
not formally repealed until 1828, though Dissenters had
been in practice relieved from disabilities by the passing
(from 1727 onwards) of annual Acts of Parliament.

The 'Clarendon Code'

The *Conventicle Act* 1664 was designed to suppress
'seditious' Conventicles. A Conventicle was defined as a
place where more than five persons, exclusive of the members of a household, assembled for worship, and made such
assembling a crime punishable by fine, imprisonment, and,

---

[1] Cf. Marriott, *Second Chambers*, c. xii.

for a third offence, by transportation. The *Five Mile Act*
(1665) forbade any minister of religion to teach in a school
or come within five miles of any Corporate town or
Parliamentary Borough unless he subscribed the Act of
Uniformity, swore to the doctrines of passive obedience,
and pledged himself not to attempt any alteration in the
Government of Church and State. This Act was regarded
with the deeper resentment by the ejected ministers and
other Dissenters in view of the noble services performed
by them during the recent visitation of the plague, in
tending the sick and filling vacant or deserted pulpits.

These Acts are a curious commentary on the noteworthy
clause in the Declaration of Breda. It ran as follows:

'And because the passion and uncharitableness of the times
have produced several opinions in religion, by which men are
engaged in parties and animosities against each other (which,
when they shall hereafter unite in a freedom of conversation,
will be composed or better understood), we do declare a liberty
to tender consciences, and that no man shall be disquieted or
called in question for differences of opinion in matter of
religion, which do not disturb the peace of the Kingdom; and
that we shall be ready to consent to such an Act of Parliament,
as, upon mature deliberation, shall be offered to us, for the full
granting that indulgence.'

Of the suggested Act of Indulgence more will be heard
presently. 'Passion and uncharitableness' were reflected
in the legislation already outlined. The (miscalled) 'Clarendon Code' was, however, altogether overshadowed in permanent significance by the *Act of Uniformity* passed in
1662.

The Pro-   That Act defined afresh, and thus far finally, the rela-
blem of   tions of Church and State, and still remains the Great
Church
and State governing Statute of the Church of England. Of the many
problems presented for solution to the Englishmen of the
seventeenth century, the ecclesiastical problem was not
the least important nor the least obstinate. Moreover, the
alternative methods of solution raised in an acute form the

problem of personal liberty with which this work is primarily concerned.

'A liberty for tender consciences' was a phrase constantly on the lips of disputants in all parties. Had any party the faintest conception of what it meant? On one point only all the main parties were agreed: religion was the business of the State. The 'Church' was only the State in its ecclesiastical aspect. But if Church and State were in this sense identical, what was to be the doctrine, the discipline, the form of government of the national Church? Was it to be Roman or Anglican (Arminian) or Puritan? Was it to be governed by Bishops, or Presbyters? Was it to look for definition of doctrine to Trent or Augsburg, Zurich or Geneva? Or was it to be content with the characteristically English compromise embodied in Elizabethan legislation? If, on the other hand, the old unity of Church and State were dissolved, if diversity of creed, worship and government was to take the place of uniformity, the problem would assume another and entirely novel aspect. Were all Churches and creeds to be, in relation to the State, in a position of complete equality, mutually tolerant of each other? Or was the State to associate itself with one form of ecclesiastical organization; and, if so, with which? And what were to be the relations of the State and the State Church to other tolerated religious bodies?

Such, in brief, were the ecclesiastical problems bequeathed by the sixteenth century to the seventeenth. The sixty years which had passed since the accession of the Stuarts had failed to solve them. The utmost for which the Roman Catholics could hope was toleration. But each of the great Protestant organizations had had its turn of ascendancy: the Anglicans or Arminians from 1603 to 1640, or technically until the acceptance of the Covenant in 1643; the Presbyterians from that date until the complete ascendancy of the Army in 1647; the Independents from the latter date until the Restoration.

None of them had taken advantage of their term of power to solve the root problem. None had attempted

3679   A a

a settlement on the basis either of comprehension or of toleration even for all sections of Protestants. Episcopalians have been persistently blamed, particularly by the Whig historians of the nineteenth century, for missing a great opportunity in 1661-2. Candour compels the confession that if comprehension were a practicable policy the Presbyterians were not less to blame for rejecting it. The 2,000 Puritan Ministers who resigned their benefices in 1662 did but balance the 2,000 Episcopalian clergymen who were ejected from their livings in the period of Presbyterian ascendancy (1643-7). In the meantime the Independents, represented by Cromwell, had had their chance and had lost it. Cromwell stood stoutly and consistently for the general principle of liberty of conscience. But the comprehensive Protestant State Church adumbrated in the Constitutions of the Protectorate was one from which 'Prelatists' and, of course, 'Papists' were to be excluded. The hope of comprehension was in truth killed, not at the Savoy Conference in 1661, but when the Long Parliament had refused to heed the wise words of Falkland. Falkland was indeed the 'apostle of moderation'; and his fate was that of all 'centre' parties in times of revolution.

'His ideas', as Principal Tulloch truly says, 'were born out of due time; and the extremes first of destruction and then of reaction, were destined to run their course. In all times of excitement this is more or less likely to be the case. The voice of reason is unheard among the clamours of party, and Falkland dies broken hearted when a Cromwell and a Clarendon take their turn of success.'[1]

The Savoy Conference Clarendon's turn had come. But neither Clarendon nor Charles II can be held responsible for the failure to bring about comprehension in 1661. A Bill was introduced in the Convention Parliament to give the force of law to a proposal that Presbyters should be joined with Bishops in the exercise of Church discipline and that the ceremonies of which Presbyterians had, ever since the Hampton Court Conferences, been complaining should not be en-

[1] *Rational Theology in England in the Seventeenth Century*, pp. 168-9.

forced. But, even in a Parliament which contained so large
a proportion of Presbyterians, the compromise was rejected
in the House of Commons by a majority of twenty-six.

Nevertheless, the King and Clarendon persisted in their
desire for the meeting of a Conference to devise, if possible,
some scheme for the union of Episcopalians and Presbyterians. Twenty-one Episcopalian divines and an equal
number of Presbyterians accordingly met in April 1661
at the Bishop of London's lodgings in the Savoy. They
were authorized to revise the Book of Common Prayer,
making, 'if occasion be', 'such reasonable and necessary
alterations, corrections, and amendments therein as . . .
shall be agreed upon to be needful or expedient for the
giving satisfaction to tender consciences and the restoring
and continuance of peace and unity in the Churches', and
to report thereon to the King. The temper on both sides
was wholly uncompromising. The Presbyterians demanded
that ceremonies, such as the use of the surplice, the sign
of the cross, kneeling at the Lord's Supper, the observance
of Lent and Saints' days, and other things of like nature,
should not be obligatory. No agreement, however, could
be reached and the Conference broke up with a report to
the King, 'That the Church's welfare, that unity and peace
and His Majesty's satisfaction were ends upon which they
were all agreed, but as to the means they could not come
to any harmony.' Evidently it was too late for comprehension. Was it too soon for toleration?

Convocation, meanwhile, was busy on its own scheme
of Prayer Book revision. Juxon, Sheldon, and Cosin the
learned Bishop of Durham were among its members, and
the noble Liturgy of to-day—the product of their labours—
was embodied, without amendment, in the Act of Uniformity, which received the Royal assent on 19 May 1662.
Though there were many slight and a few substantial
alterations the revised Prayer Book was substantially the
same as the Book of 1559. The 'Black Rubric' of 1552
was reintroduced at the end of the Communion Service, but
'significantly altered so as to deny not the real and

The Act of Uni- formity

essential presence but only the *corporal* presence in the Sacrament of Christ's natural flesh and blood'.[1] The other changes were mostly, though not obtrusively, in an anti-Puritan direction. The Prayer Book was accepted by Parliament without any (save drafting) amendments, and its use was enjoined upon all ministers and parishioners, who were required, under penalties, to attend the Parish Church; Episcopal ordination was for the first time made a *sine qua non* for the care of souls or other ecclesiastical promotion; and every clerical dignity or person in Holy Orders, every University or College officer, every schoolmaster and private tutor was, before the ensuing Feast-day of St. Bartholomew, and on pain of deprivation, to subscribe a specified 'Declaration'. The Declaration included a promise of conformity to the new Liturgy, an abjuration of the Solemn League and Covenant, and an undertaking not to attempt any alteration of government in Church and State, or on any pretence whatever to take up arms against the King.

Ejection of Puritan Ministers
In consequence of the passing of this Act some 2,000 Puritan Ministers were ejected from their benefices. Unfortunately, unlike the ejected Ministers of 1643–7, they received no compensation. Conscience, however, would not have permitted them to remain within the pale of the Established Church. Many pious and devoted men were thus lost to the Ministry, but the differences of principle proved then, as they have invariably proved at every subsequent attempt at comprehension, too wide and deep to be bridged over.

With the passing of the *Act of Uniformity* the work of restoration may be said to have been completed. The Crown, the Houses of Lords and Commons, the Church and the Convocations were all restored to the positions they had severally filled in the State prior to the outbreak of revolution. Yet the preceding sixty years had left their

---

[1] Patterson, *Church of England*, p. 359. Cf. for text of *Act of Uniformity*, Gee and Hardy, *Documents*, pp. 600–19, and generally Cardwell, *Prayer Book Conferences*.

mark on the English Polity. The twenty-eight years of
the restored Stuart Monarchy did indeed temporarily
obscure, if they did not permanently obliterate, the results
accomplished by the Puritan Revolution. Those results
cannot, therefore, be accurately measured, nor their value
estimated, until the curtain has been rung down on the
Revolution of 1688.

Nevertheless, it may be convenient at this point to
register certain results which had been definitely and in-
controvertibly attained. Sovereignty had unmistakably
passed from the King to the King-in-Parliament, though
it was not yet clear how that Sovereignty was to be
exercised. The idea of an absolute Monarchy in England
had been dissipated for ever. It is by no means certain,
that, despite all the metaphysical homilies of James I,
either he or his successor had any fixed purpose of exercising
the prerogatives of an absolute monarch. But the philosophy proclaimed by James I was strange to English ears,
and sufficed to engender apprehensions of an absolutism
which the crowned philosopher had no serious intention of
practising. But if the Stuarts did not aim at absolute
Monarchy they had no intention of abdicating the functions which as *personal* rulers their predecessors had performed. The Puritan Revolution made even personal
Monarchy impossible. The rule of Cromwell enforced the
lesson which the Stuarts had taught. The Puritan Revolution also proved that the mass of the English people were
as devoted to the Episcopal Church as they were to the
hereditary Monarchy. Most of all it proved that parliamentary government was impossible without a King.

Three problems, however, remained in detail unsolved.
The Established Church was to remain pre-eminent in its
legal connexion with the State. But how was its supremacy
to be reconciled with the existence of other religious bodies
and with the civil liberties of the citizens adhering to them?
John (Viscount) Morley held that 'perhaps the heaviest
charge against' the Puritan rebellion and the gravest set
off against its indubitable gains' was that 'by arresting

Results
of the
'Puritan
Revolu-
tion'.

Unsolved
Problems

and diverting the liberal movement in progress within the Church when the political outbreak first began [it] had for ever made a real comprehension impossible'. Be that as it may, comprehension proved to be impracticable, and the problem remained: how was toleration—the only alternative—to be achieved?

A second problem was presented by the relations of England, Scotland, and Ireland. Cromwell had temporarily solved it, but his solution was rejected at the Restoration. It remained, therefore, to perplex his successors.

The third outstanding problem was to devise machinery for enabling King and Parliament henceforward to be partners in Sovereignty, to carry on with mutual satisfaction the actual, day to day, business of the State.

These problems post-Restoration England had to face and if possible to solve.

XVI. CHARLES II AND HIS MINISTERS

DURING the first seven years after the Restoration the Claren- King's principal adviser was Sir Edward Hyde, Earl of don Clarendon. From the moment when Pym proposed the *Grand Remonstrance*, Clarendon had given his entire allegiance to Charles I and had served him faithfully to the end. Most of the State Papers and Declarations issued, after November 1641, in the King's name, were indited by his brilliant pen. In 1645 he became the leading member of Prince Charles's Council in the West, and followed him to Scilly and to Jersey, where the famous *History of the Rebellion* was begun. From 1651 onwards he was chief adviser to Charles II, and retained that position after the Restoration as head of a secret committee of six. He had become Lord Chancellor in 1658, was raised to the peerage as Baron Hyde in 1660, and created Earl of Clarendon and Viscount Cornbury in the following year. But though Lord Chancellor he was not a Prime Minister. Until the accession of George I the Sovereign was in fact as well as name head of the Executive.

As the first exultant enthusiasm of the Restoration began to wane, Clarendon had to bear the brunt of the unpopularity which the administration gradually incurred. Too devoted to the Monarchy to be acceptable to Parliament, he was too loyal to constitutional principles to be a favourite at Court. Unfairly charged by the Protestant Dissenters with responsibility for the intolerant policy of the Cavalier Parliament, he was too firm in his attachment to the English Church to please the King's Roman Catholic friends. The virtue of his private life was a reproach to the profligacy of the Court; his adherence to the principle of the Indemnity Act offended the Cavaliers. His foreign policy alienated good patriots, his domestic administration made him no friends. In fine, the platform on which he stood was too narrow for stability. Consequently, his overthrow was easily accomplished by a temporary combination among his enemies. He was rudely dismissed by the King in August 1667, was impeached by Parliament, and fled the country never to return. But his remains found a resting place, and properly, among England's Great in the Abbey.

Fall of Clarendon, 1667 Though the King's ingratitude, the profligacy of his accusers, and his own high character may excite pity for a fallen minister, Clarendon's errors and faults were neither few nor venial. Yet the grounds on which he was impeached were almost grotesque in their exaggeration and misdirection: that he had sought to govern England by a standing army to the retention of which he was notoriously opposed, and without Parliament; that he had imprisoned English subjects illegally and overseas; that he had enriched himself by the sale of offices and by other corrupt means; that he had introduced arbitrary government in the 'Plantations'; that he had advised the sale of Dunkirk to France and had otherwise deluded the King and the nation in regard to foreign affairs—it is a curious farrago of truth and falsehood, of sense and nonsense. The impeachment, however, was abortive, and as it possesses little constitutional significance need not detain us. The real reasons for Clarendon's fall are to be found in the alienation of the King's good-will, in the hatred he had excited among courtiers and courtesans; in the growth of a real opposition in parliament, and above all, in the desire to find a scape-goat for the humiliations suffered in the course of the Dutch war and in the sphere of foreign policy.[1]

The Cabal Ministry, 1667–73 Clarendon's place in the Council Chamber was taken by a group of men, known as the 'Cabal Ministry'. The Cabal was not in fact a Ministry, but a group of Ministers, who acted as the personal advisers of a personal Monarch. It is due, indeed, to the accident of an anagram that the 'Cabal' has been held to possess significance as marking a stage in the development of the Cabinet system. Apart from that, the years 1667–73 are remarkable chiefly for the development of the Franco-phil and pro-Catholic policy of

[1] See *infra*.

the King, and the consequent consolidation of the parliamentary opposition.

Charles II had taken the precaution of repealing the Triennial Act of 1641, on the supposition that the Act limited the duration of Parliament to three years. But in the repealing Statute (1664) a proviso was inserted, 'with an inconsistency not unusual in our Statutes', that the meeting of Parliament should not in future be intermitted more than three years at most. The prolonged duration of the Cavalier Parliament was, however, less favourable to the King than he had anticipated. Not only had he reason to recall his father's aphorism that 'Parliaments like cats, grow curst with age', but in fact the Parliament of 1673 was vastly different in personnel from that which had been elected in 1661. Owing to the advanced age of many members of the House of Lords, and of cavaliers returned to the House of Commons in 1661, to rapid successions to the peerage and some new creations,[1] to the great mortality in the Plague (1665) and in the Great Fire of London (1666), and, consequent on all these causes, the unusual number of by-elections, no fewer than 263 seats changed hands in a period of twelve years.[2]

Growing opposition of Parliament

The new members, drawn in larger proportions from the commercial and less from the landed classes, more interested in financial and less in religious issues than those whom they replaced, found a leader whose talents were as eminent as his conduct was vacillating and tortuous. Anthony Ashley Cooper, created first Earl of Shaftesbury in 1672, was returned as a lad of eighteen to the Long Parliament. He followed the King's fortunes until 1644 when, just in time to avoid the imputation of prudential tergiversation, he went over to the side of Parliament and took command of their forces in his own county of Dorset:

'A beardless chief, a rebel ere a man,
So young his hatred to his prince began.'[3]

---

[1] 18 members were added to the Peerage between 1660 and 1685.
[2] W. C. Abbott, 'Long Parliament of Charles II', *ap. E.H.R.* xxi.
21–56 and 254–85.   [3] Dryden, *Medal*, l. 27.

In the Protectorate parliaments he joined Sir Henry Vane in leading the opposition to the 'usurper'; he promised to co-operate with Monk in 1659 and was justly imprisoned as a suspect; but, on his release, he served on the Council of State and actively promoted the recall of Charles II, by whom he was rewarded with offices and honours. He served as Chancellor of the Exchequer from 1661 to 1672, as Lord Chancellor 1672–3, and as President of the newly formed Board of Trade and Plantations from 1672 until 1676. An acute commentator has said that the whole interest of the reign of Charles II 'centres in two opposite and pre-eminent chiefs, Shaftesbury and the King. It is a game of chess played by two masterly hands to whom all the rest are no better than rooks and pawns'.[1] But if Shaftesbury was clever, Charles was much cleverer, and really outplayed his minister at every point of the game. Like the King, but for opposite reasons, he ardently supported a policy of indulgence, but was opposed to Roman Catholicism, and, unlike Clifford and Arlington, was kept in ignorance of those clauses in the Secret Treaty of Dover which promised its restoration. He must, however, share responsibility for the Franco-phil policy of his master and in particular for the rupture of the famous Triple Alliance of 1668. As Dryden has it:

> 'Thus framed for ill, he loosed our triple hold;
> Advice unsafe, precipitous, and bold.'

On the other hand, he may share the credit for the steps which, as we have seen, were taken by Parliament in 1666 and 1671 towards stricter control over natural expenditure, though his financial virtues were more than balanced by the criminal act of repudiation (1672), when notice was given that the principal of loans due in that year would not be repaid.

Charles II and the Roman Catholics It was, however, the ecclesiastical policy of the King which finally broke up the Cabal. If Charles II had any religious convictions he inherited them from his mother

---

[1] Brewer, *Studies*, p. 189.

and not from his father. But his inclination towards Roman Catholicism was political rather than spiritual. Of his Cabal ministers Clifford was a professing Catholic, Arlington had Catholic sympathies, Buckingham, like Shaftesbury, was inclined towards a French alliance and towards a policy of toleration at home, though, like Shaftesbury, he was not cognizant of the Catholic clauses of the Treaty of Dover. Lauderdale was the principal agent of Charles's policy in Scotland.

Before the issue of the *Declaration of Indulgence* Charles had already made two attempts to secure toleration for Nonconformists and Roman Catholics. In May 1662, directly after the passing of the *Act of Uniformity*, he proposed to suspend its operation for three months, but yielded to the strong opposition of the Bishops and the lawyers. In December of the same year he actually issued a Declaration of Indulgence, in which he promised to exercise his 'Dispensing Power' on behalf of the Non-conformists if Parliament would pass an authorizing Act. Parliament, however, very definitely declined to do so. By March 1672 the King had grown bolder and waited for no leave. *(Declaration of Indulgence)*

Premising that 'the sad experience of twelve years' had proved that 'there is very little fruit of . . . the many and frequent ways of coercion that we have used for reducing all erring or dissenting persons and for composing the unhappy differences in matters of religion which we found among our subjects on our return', he proceeded, in virtue of 'that supreme power in ecclesiastical matters which is not only inherent in us' but has been recognized by Statute, to proclaim the immediate suspension of the penal laws against whatever sort of nonconformists or recusants; to give free opportunities (under due regulation) for public worship to the former, and liberty of private worship to the latter; while at the same time confirming in all respects the pre-eminent position of the Established Church.

But such confirmation availed nothing to lull the *(The Test Act 1673)* suspicions of the Anglican Parliament. Nor were the Non-conformists willing to accept privileges for themselves at the price of toleration for Roman Catholicism. Parliament compelled the King to withdraw the *Declaration* and countered his move by passing the *Test Act*, rendering it obligatory upon all holders of office, civil or military under the Crown, to take the Sacrament of the Lord's Supper according to the usage of the Church of England and to subscribe a declaration against Transubstantiation. The House of Commons also passed a resolution against the legality of the suspending power claimed by the King in matters Ecclesiastical.

The *Test Act* broke up the Cabal. Clifford the Lord Treasurer, a man who was said by Clarendon to know 'no more about the Constitution of England than he did of China',[1] retired with Arlington from office. The Duke of York also resigned his position as Lord High Admiral. Shaftesbury executed one more *volte-face* and, with Buckingham, gave his full adherence to the party in Parliament soon afterwards known as the Whigs. Lauderdale continued to rule Scotland. The triumph of the Parliamentary opposition was completed when the Commons, by a threatened refusal of supplies, compelled the King to withdraw from the French alliance, to conclude a separate peace with the Dutch, and to reinstate Sir William Temple as ambassador at The Hague (1674).

Danby's Ministry, 1673–9   The increasingly independent temper of Parliament was further manifested during the ministry of Danby. Sir Thomas Osborne, known to history as the Earl of Danby, and to the peerage as Marquis of Carmarthen and Duke of Leeds, was a Yorkshire squire who was elected as member for the City of York in 1665 and was first introduced to the King's notice by Buckingham. He was made treasurer of the Navy in 1671 and on the resignation of Clifford became Lord High Treasurer and took the first place in the Councils of the King.

Danby was eminently representative of the sentiments

[1] *Autobiography*, p. 193.

which, as already explained, were dominant in English politics between the Restoration and the Revolution, and for that, as well as for other reasons, his tenure of office was a period of high significance; but in a curiously contradictory sense. A loyal servant of a personal monarchy Danby was also, like Clarendon, strongly attached to Parliament. The Minister of Charles II, he was bitterly opposed to the two objects nearest to the King's heart, Roman Catholicism and the French alliance. In all these matters he was in closest sympathy with the Parliament by which he was impeached and disgraced. Paradox could hardly go further. But there is yet another point, which may partially resolve it.

At no period of the reign was the influence of Parliament more consistently exercised and more publicly demonstrated; at no period were its members or their constituencies more open to corruption. The history of these years thus anticipates the rule of Walpole and the reign of George III. At once independent in temper and oligarchical in composition, Parliament was rendered amenable to the influence of the Executive by pensions, places, and the power of the purse. *Independence and Corruption of Parliament*

'In the purchase of votes, the wholesale bribery of constituencies, the pressure on corporations, the use of Court and ministerial influence, of government servants, even of soldiers, the corruption of election officers, the suborning of sheriffs, and various methods of family and financial pressure on electors, we observe a skill and resource generally ascribed only to a much later and more sophisticated age of political corruption.'

So writes an American historian;[1] and he is right.

The war against the Dutch, a war in which as Sir William Temple said, 'the nations had fought without being angry' was, as we have seen, brought to a close in February 1674, and in the same month Parliament passed resolutions

---

[1] Professor W. C. Abbott to whose admirable articles in *E.H.R.* xxi. 257, any commentator on the constitutional history of this period must acknowledge a heavy debt.

against a standing army. In the following year the House of Commons gave further proof of its independent spirit. Danby had proposed and carried through the House of Lords a Bill imposing upon all placemen and all members of both Houses the obligation to take an oath against any attempt to alter the government of Church or State, and declaring all resistance to the King unlawful. The House of Commons resisted the Bill so strongly that Danby dropped it. Louis XIV, alarmed by the temper of the English Parliament, thereupon, induced his royal brother to prorogue Parliament for fifteen months in return for a pension of 500,000 crowns a year. Not until February 1677 did Parliament meet again. When it did, four Peers, Shaftesbury, Buckingham, Salisbury, and Wharton, raised the constitutional point whether so prolonged a proroga-tion did not *ipso facto* involve a dissolution. But the *Mutiny Act* was still in the future; the constitutional point was not sound, and the King retorted by sending the Peers to the Tower. Shaftesbury remained there for a year.

Closing of the Coffee Houses   Having temporarily silenced Parliament, the King turned his attention to the Coffee Houses. The Coffee House had since the Restoration almost attained the dignity of a Political Institution. Interest in public affairs had inevit-ably been stimulated, in unprecedented measure, during the preceding decades, and in days of strict licensing laws, when parliamentary debates were not published and there was a dearth of newspapers, only the coffee house could satisfy curiosity and afford opportunity for discussion. So general and popular had these 'clubs' become that Charles's attempt to close them soon proved itself a failure. Nor was the experiment of suspending the sittings of Parliament more successful.

When it reassembled Parliament was indeed persuaded to vote a subsidy for the navy, but it stipulated that the money should be paid not into the Treasury but to parlia-mentary receivers, and urged that the forces of the Crown should be employed not against the Dutch but against

France. An army of 20,000 to 30,000 men was collected, but so suspicious was Parliament as to its use or destination that supplies were refused and the dismissal of the army was demanded. But if Parliament mistrusted Charles so did Louis XIV, who used his influence for the disbandment of the army and the further prorogation of Parliament. The price of prorogation was 2,000,000 livres.

Meanwhile, an event of outstanding importance had occurred. In November 1677 the Princess Mary, eldest daughter of the Duke of York and Anne Hyde the daughter of Clarendon, was married to William, Prince of Orange. Momentous in its ultimate consequences, the marriage was an immediate and brilliant triumph for Danby and the Anti-French and Anti-Catholic party. Louis XIV withdrew his subsidy from the English King, who countered by summoning Parliament for February 1678, two months short of the period for which it had been prorogued. *Marriage of Princess Mary to the Prince of Orange, Nov. 1677*

Almost the first act of Parliament was to demand the dismissal of the force which the King had collected, avowedly for an attack on France. How far the demand was due to the bribes lavished by the French King upon the Opposition, how far to the mistrust of Parliament as to its purpose, remains uncertain. But negotiations had already begun for the Treaty ultimately signed at Nimeguen (10 August 1678), between France, Spain, and the Dutch. During the negotiations a second Secret Treaty was concluded between Charles II and Louis XIV. In return for a subsidy of 6,000 livres Charles agreed to dissolve Parliament, to disband the army, and to give no help to the Dutch if they continued the war. *Secret Treaty with France, May 1678*

Public attention was, however, diverted by one of those ebullitions against Popery which during the last three centuries have periodically troubled the usually placid surface of a singularly tolerant society. Readers of Dickens's vivid story *Barnaby Rudge* will not need to be reminded how at such moments peace loving and kindly folk are roused to *The Popish Plot* a fury which expends itself in deeds of unbelievable ferocity.[1]

On 13 August 1678 Charles II received an anonymous letter warning him not to expose his person heedlessly 'for that his death was determined on'. The writer of the letter was discovered in one Titus Oates, an unfrocked clergyman of the Church of England who had become a Roman Catholic, and had been expelled from more than one Jesuit College on the continent, having insinuated himself into them in order to equip himself for his nefarious design. On 28 September Oates was brought before the Privy Council, and shortly afterwards the body of Sir Edmund Berry Godfrey, a prominent magistrate before whom Oates had made his depositions, was found, apparently murdered, on Primrose Hill.

A wild panic ensued. Oates's story was that the English and continental Papists were conspiring to murder Charles II and to extirpate Protestantism in England. Coleman, the secretary to the Duke of York, and three Romish priests, were tried and executed; a pension of £1,200 a year, and lodgings in Whitehall and a special guard were assigned to Oates, whose good fortune naturally stimulated a crowd of imitators. Their industry and ingenuity were rewarded by a large number of arrests, trials, and convictions. For some months the popularity of Chief Justice Scroggs, whose methods afforded a model and a precedent for those of Judge Jeffreys, was second only to that of Titus Oates. Their names are now linked together in the reprobation of posterity. Hallam and Macaulay and their disciples were apt, perhaps, to minimize the gravity of the actual situation, but Macaulay admits that, though the greater part of the plot was a pure fabrication, there was some excuse for the credulity of the people, even if there were none for the mendacity of the witnesses. 'A State trial', he declared, 'was merely a murder preceded by the uttering of certain gibberish and the performance of certain

[1] For the Popish Plot see Christie, *Life of Shaftesbury*, vol. ii, and John Pollock, *Popish Plot*.

mummeries'. The description was true not only of the
State trials of 1678. As to the plot itself, the contemporary satirist got nearer to the truth, may be, than any
chronicler:

'From hence began that plot, the nation's curse,
Bad in itself, but represented worse;
Raised in extremes, and in extremes decried
With oaths affirmed, with dying vows denied;
Not weighed or winnowed by the multitude;
But swallowed in the mass unchewed and crude.
Some truth there was, but dashed and brewed with lies
To please the fools, and puzzle all the wise.
Succeeding times did equal folly call,
Believing nothing, or believing all.' [1]

But poets are not required to produce precise evidence for
their conclusions.

Whatever be the truth about the plot itself there is no
obscurity about the effect of its reverberations. The plot
dashed the last hopes of toleration. Parliament, summoned in haste, addressed the King with a request for the
dismissal of the Duke of York from his counsels and
passed an Act which, by imposing a strict test, prevented
Papists from sitting in either House. An exception in
favour of the Duke of York was, however, carried by a
majority of two. The Commons then proceeded to make
a scapegoat of Danby. Louis XIV, having made peace
with his continental enemies, had for the moment no
further use for Charles II, but he was not the less anxious
to procure the disgrace of a statesman whose presence at
the King's elbow might again prove inconvenient to himself. Montagu who, until 1675, had been English ambassador in Paris, was also anxious to be avenged on the minister
responsible for his dismissal. He revealed enough of
Danby's correspondence with France to furnish ammuni-
tion to the Opposition in Parliament, and on this and other
grounds Danby was impeached. Danby, however, received

Results of the Plot

---

[1] Dryden, *Absalom and Achitophel*, l. 108.

a pardon under the Great Seal, and his master, to stay further proceedings, dissolved Parliament (January 1679).

The new Parliament met in March. The preceding election, the first General Election since 1661, had naturally aroused unprecedented excitement in the constituencies; the triumph of the Opposition, or 'country party', was complete; and most of the members (in Macaulay's phrase) 'came up to Westminster in a mood little differing from that of their predecessors who had sent Strafford and Laud to the Tower'.

The Dissolution had not served the interests of Danby or his master. The King did indeed reject the Speaker chosen by the House of Commons, but the latter at once resumed proceedings against Danby. Not only had he betrayed his country to France; he had tried to subvert the Constitution, to maintain a standing army, to get rid of Parliament, to subvert the Protestant religion and introduce Popery: he had tried to hush up the Popish plot and had 'wasted the King's treasure'.[1] Charges more grotesque could hardly have been devised. Danby was pre-eminently a Parliament man; virtually nominated to office by Parliament in 1673, he resigned it on the election of a hostile Parliament in 1679, having, throughout his tenure of office, relied on Parliament for support in a policy of financial reform, and in the pursuit of a truly national policy at home and abroad. He pleaded the King's pardon under the Great Seal, but the Commons denied the plea and demanded justice from the Lords. Though the trial was not proceeded with, Danby was committed to the Tower. So low had his fortunes fallen that Oates was emboldened to accuse him of complicity in the murder of Godfrey, but the ridiculous charge was not brought to an issue. Danby was restored to his place in the House of
Constitu-
tional
signifi-
cance of
his Im-
peach-
ment
Lords in 1685; joined the Opposition, and was among the signatories to the invitation to William of Orange in 1688.

The impeachment of Danby, though not carried through, is commonly regarded as an event of high constitutional

[1] Robertson, *Statutes, &c.*, pp. 418–19.

significance. It did in fact decide that neither the King's pardon nor a dissolution of Parliament can bar an impeachment; it raised the question of the right of spiritual Peers to vote in capital cases, and that of the responsibility of ministers for the acts of the Crown during their tenure of office whether those acts were or were not approved by them, and even if they were done in obedience to the direct command of the Sovereign. But the significance of Danby's impeachment is limited to these points. It went far towards clinching the principle that no minister can shelter himself behind the throne by pleading obedience to the orders of his Sovereign. The minister is, 'answerable for the justice, the honesty, the utility of all measures emanating from the Crown as well as for their legality'.[1] But Danby was not the head of a Cabinet, nor even a member of a Cabinet in the modern sense, and neither his ministry nor his impeachment advanced, in any substantial degree, the evolution of the Cabinet system.

The King's fortunes reached the nadir in 1679. Not content with impeaching Danby, unappeased by the retirement from England of the Duke of York, the Country party introduced a Bill for the exclusion of the Duke from the throne. Contemporary accounts describe the King's mood as one almost of despair.[2] But he once more proved his astuteness and resource. He decided to adopt a scheme for a reconstituted Privy Council. The invention of the new scheme is generally attributed to Sir William Temple, by whose name it is commonly known.[3]

The Privy Council of 1679

For some time past there had been a growing suspicion that the Privy Council, a Constitutional body known to the law, was being superseded by secret committees or Cabals which were unknown to the law and owed no responsibility to any one. In 1667 (24 June) Pepys reports gossip about

[1] Hallam: *Constitutional History*, ii. 411.
[2] I never saw any man more sensible of the miserable condition of his affairs than I found His Majesty', writes Temple of this period (*Works*, ii. 506–7).
[3] On the whole matter cf. an exceedingly illuminating article by E. R. Turner, *E.H.R.* xxx. 251.

the way in which the Council was kept in ignorance as to public affairs, and in 1673 Sir William Coventry published a pamphlet, the title of which is a sufficient index to its contents, *England's Appeal from the Private Cabal at White-Hall to the Great Council of the Nation.*[1] Suspicion and discontent waxed rapidly in the next few years, and on 20 October 1679 the King made a formal announcement to his Privy Council of a 'Resolution He hath taken in a matter of Great Importance to his Crowne and Government'. He thanked the Council for all the good advice which they had given him, but declared that, owing to the unwieldy size to which the Council had grown, he had been driven to employ a small number in a 'foreign committee', 'and sometimes the advices of some few'.[2] But he disliked the development as much as did Parliament, and he proposed therefore to constitute a new and smaller Privy Council and thereafter to govern his Kingdom by their constant advice, together with the frequent use of Parliament which 'he takes to be the true Auncient Constitution of this State and Government'.

The new Council was to consist, in addition to the Princes of the blood, of a Lord President, a Secretary of Scotland and thirty ordinary Councillors, fifteen of whom were to be officials of the Crown and to be 'Privy Councillors by their places, ten to be Peers and five commoners', 'whose knowne abilityes, Interest, and Esteeme in the Nation shall render them all without suspition'. The new experiment was forthwith announced to Parliament by the King himself, 'I have made choice', he said, 'of such Persons as are worthy and able to advise me; and am resolved in all my weighty and important affairs, next to the Advice of My Great Council in Parliament (which I shall very often consult with) to be advised by this Privy Council'. Shaftesbury became President of the new Council, and Russell, with other prominent members of the Opposition, was admitted to it. But the scheme quickly broke down: the

---

[1] Meaning by this phrase the Privy Council not (as more properly) Parliament.   [2] Temple, *Memoirs*, iii. 45.

tendency towards a small advisory Committee or Cabinet was too strong to be arrested by a revived Privy Council, however diminished in numbers, and the King, despite his promises, admitted to his inner Councils only four members, Temple himself, Essex, Sunderland, and Halifax the 'Trimmer'. Shaftesbury and Russell again went into opposition, and pushed on the Exclusion Bill, which received a second reading in the House of Commons. Thereupon the King prorogued and then dissolved Parliament. Not, however, before it had put upon the Statute book one of the most famous Acts in the history of English law. The scope of the Habeas Corpus Act has, however, already been described.[1]

A new Parliament was elected in the early autumn of 1679. But so crushing was the defeat of the Court Party that Parliament was prorogued before it met; Charles turned once more to Louis XIV for help. The French King promised him a pension of 1,000,000 livres a year, on condition that during that time Parliament was not permitted to assemble. Charles found it impossible to fulfil the condition for more than twelve months, and after seven successive prorogations the fourth Parliament of the reign met in October 1780. *The Definition of Parties*

The months intervening between its election and its assembling were remarkable for an agitation which has left a permanent mark upon the development of the English Constitution. Petitions poured in to the King from all parts of the country begging him to permit the elected Parliament to meet. These were countered by petitions expressing abhorrence of the idea of tampering with the hereditary succession and excluding the Duke of York from the throne. The parties thus arrayed in opposition to each other became known as 'Petitioners' (or Addressers) and 'Abhorrers', and later on were nicknamed 'Whigs' and 'Tories' respectively.[2] The nicknames, as so often happens, *Whigs and Tories*

---

[1] *Supra*, pp. 111 seq. and c. iv. *passim*.
[2] The 'Whigs' were the strictest sect of Scottish Covenanters; the 'Tories' were the wildest party among the Irish outlaws.

stuck; and consequently it became a tradition among
Constitutional historians to ascribe to the struggle of
these months the origin of the two historic English parties.[1]
No precise date can, however, be assigned to a process of
evolution. Undoubtedly the struggles of the period now
under review did much to define the attitude of parties,
but there is something to be said for the contention of a
learned Austrian jurist who discerns the origin of English
parties in the divisions which manifested themselves in
Parliament after the passing of the Elizabethan *Act of
Uniformity*.[2] That date, however, is not more satisfactory
than the conventional date. The true genesis of the party
system is to be found in the prolonged and acrimonious
debates of the first sessions of the Long Parliament of
Charles I. It was then that the two historic parties began
to define their respective positions. Roundheads and
Cavaliers were the predecessors in title of Whigs and
Tories, Liberals and Conservatives. An embryonic socialist
party arose somewhat later under the name of Levellers.
The Liberal Party descends in unbroken succession from
the Puritans, who in 1640 ranged themselves under Pym
and Hampden against the Court and the Laudian Bishops;
the true predecessors of modern Conservatives may be
discovered in the devoted adherents of the Established
Church who were reluctantly compelled, in consequence
of the increasing violence of the Puritans, to espouse the
cause of the Stuart Monarchy. The first 'party' division,
in the modern sense, was taken on the *Grand Remonstrance*
when Pym, as we have seen, carried his motion by 159 votes
to 148. Falkland, accepting the responsibility of his
opposition, albeit unsuccessful to the motion, took office
as Secretary of State. In that debate and division the
modern party system was born.[3]

Parties   Parties were even more distinctly defined after the
under
Charles II   [1] e.g. Hallam.
            [2] Dr. Joseph Redlich, *Parliamentary Procedure*, i. 33.
            [3] Gardiner prefers the division of 8th of February 1642 on the abolition
of Episcopy (*Hist.* ix. 281). There is not much between us, but the
Division of 22 Nov. was on the more strictly political issue.

Restoration. The Parliament of 1661 contained, at first, an immense preponderance of Tories—Cavaliers devoted to Church and King; but the 'Opposition' was larger than has been commonly supposed, and was, as already indicated, rapidly reinforced by an unusual number of by-elections.[1] In 1679 the Tories were almost wiped out, and the ascendancy of the Whigs remained unchallenged until they committed the blunder of pressing forward, in defiance of public sentiment, the Exclusion Bill.

A more significant point remains to be noted. The rise of the Party system was coincident with the development of Parliamentary Government. In the long history of the English Parliament no period was more truly critical than the first two decades of the reign of Charles II. Those years really decided the question whether Parliament should or should not become the predominant partner in the joint-Sovereignty of King-in-Parliament; and to some extent the form which Parliamentary Government should take. Then also it first became manifest that, without a system of organized Parties, Parliamentary Government is an impossibility. Some years were to elapse before the scheme of a Parliamentary Executive was completely developed, but, throughout the whole reign of Charles II, things were moving steadily in that direction. The overthrow of Clarendon, the appointment and dismissal of Danby, and most of all the constant intrusion of Parliament into the once sacred domain of Foreign Affairs, are some among the many indications of a consistent tendency. When, in 1677, the House of Commons demanded, as the price of Supply, an alliance with the Dutch against Louis XIV, Charles angrily replied in words reminiscent of Queen Elizabeth:

'You have intrenched upon so undoubted a right of the Crown that I am confident it will appear in no age (when the

Parlia-mentary Govern-ment

---

[1] 56 is the number usually assigned to the Presbyterians, but Mr. W. C. Abbott gives reasons for putting it higher. In the division on the burning of the Solemn League and Covenant (1661) the Opposition mustered 103 against 228. On the Indemnity Bill, 129 against 209 and on the Corporation Bill 136 against 185 (*op. cit.*).

sword was not drawn) that the prerogative of making peace and war hath been so dangerously invaded', and added, 'that should he assent to the demands of the House no Prince in Europe would any longer believe that the Sovereignty in England rests in the Crown.'[1]

The plain truth was that the Sovereignty of England no longer rested absolutely in the Crown, but in the Crown-in-Parliament. An acute American commentator is, therefore, accurate in saying that 'the prerogative suffered greater permanent loss during [this] reign than in almost any similar period in English History'.[2]

The Exclusion Bill

Thus far Charles II might seem to have been playing the game of the Opposition. They now played his. During the last eighteen years the nation had proved its increasing reliance upon the principle of Parliamentary Government, its loyalty to the Established Church, its dread of Roman Catholicism and its detestation of French interference in English affairs. The Whigs now gave it the opportunity of demonstrating its devotion to the principle of hereditary Monarchy.

When Parliament met in October 1680 the House of Commons affirmed the historic right of the subjects of England to petition for a Parliament, and then immediately proceeded to pass the Exclusion Bill. The temper of the time is succinctly indicated in the Preamble. 'Whereas', it runs, 'James, Duke of York, is notoriously known to have been perverted from the Protestant to the Popish Religion whereby not only great encouragement hath been given to the Popish party to enter into and carry on most devilish and horrid plots and conspiracies for the destruction of His Majesty's sacred person and government, and for the extirpation of the true Protestant Religion, but also if the said Duke should succeed to the Imperial Crown of this Realm, nothing is more manifest than that a total change of Religion within these Kingdoms would ensue;

---

[1] ap. Tanner, *English Constitutional Conflicts*, p. 237.
[2] W. C. Abbott, ap. *E.H.R.* xxi. 284.

For the prevention whereof Be it therefore enacted' that the Duke should be excluded from the throne and the Crown should descend as if the said Duke were 'naturally dead'. In the House of Lords, the Bill, after four days' debate was rejected on the first reading by 63 votes to 30.

King Charles sailed into comparatively smooth waters for the brief remainder of his earthly voyage, and King James succeeded without opposition to his inheritance. It has been the fashion among English historians to acclaim this result as a triumph achieved by the patience and astuteness of Charles II, but the American commentator, already quoted, questions this view and ascribes the re-action in the King's favour less to his adroitness than to the fact that the moderate men in Parliament had obtained everything for which during the long years they had been fighting—the control of finance, the final guarantee of personal liberty in the Habeas Corpus Act, the exclusion of Papists from public life, the practical toleration of Protestant Nonconformists, and an increasing measure of control over the Executive. The two views are not mutually exclusive. Parliament had undoubtedly achieved much; but the King, thanks in the main to his own ability and adroitness, had not been compelled to go on his travels again; he had freely indulged his own perverted tastes without undue interference from his own conscience or that of his subjects, and above all he had maintained the sanctity of the hereditary succession. He had not, however, got toleration for his Roman Catholic friends, nor had he superseded Parliament. The question of his Foreign policy will receive attention at a later stage.

Triumph of the King

Despite the rejection of the Bill by the Lords and the King's emphatic declaration that he would never assent to Exclusion, the Commons persisted. They refused sup-plies; Parliament was dissolved (January 1681) but when the fifth Parliament of the reign opened in the more loyal atmosphere of Oxford, the Whigs, many of whom came armed to the House, returned to the attack. The King made a final effort at compromise. He would banish the

Duke of York and assent to a Regency under the Prince of Orange. But the Whigs refused to accept anything short of total Exclusion. The King was quick to realize their blunder. Parliament was promptly dissolved, and did not meet again during the remnant of the reign.

Attack on City Corporations   The King's triumph appeared to be complete. Shaftesbury was charged with high treason, but the Grand Jury in London refused to find a true Bill. Shaftesbury himself withdrew to the continent, where he died in January 1683. The King revenged himself on the Whig Corporation of London by the withdrawal of its Charter. Under the same writ of *Quo Warranto* the charters of many other corporate towns were subjected to similar scrutiny and their governing bodies were similarly reconstituted in the Royalist interest.

The Rye House Plot   The reaction in the King's favour was still further emphasized in 1683 by the discovery of a plot for his assassination at the Rye House in Hertfordshire. How far the Whig leaders were actually involved in the conspiracy to murder the King remains uncertain, but among those who were arrested, were Russell, Essex, and Algernon Sidney. Essex was found dead, probably having died by his own hand, in the Tower; Russell and Sidney, despite the absence of a second witness, essential to a conviction for treason, were convicted and executed. The conviction may have been irregular but of the substantial guilt of the two men there can, despite the efforts of Whig apologists, be little doubt. Algernon Sidney, a rebel by nature and a republican by conviction, had conspired with Louis XIV against his own King; William (Lord) Russell had held communications of a treasonable nature with the Prince of Orange.

Death of Charles II   The horror excited by the conspiracy was reflected in a decree passed by the University of Oxford condemning the doctrine that resistance to a King can under any circumstances be lawful (21 July 1683). Halifax was now alone among the Councillors of the King in urging adherence to legality. No parliament, however, was summoned, and

Charles felt strong enough to recall his brother, restore him to his place at the Admiralty and readmit him to the Council. Halifax so far prevailed as to secure the dismissal from the Treasury of Lawrence Hyde, now raised to the peerage as Earl of Rochester. Rochester was the leading supporter of his brother-in-law, the Duke of York. His removal was therefore of sinister import for the Duke. But it mattered little; for at this juncture Charles II unexpectedly died, having on his death-bed declared his adhesion to the Catholic faith, and his Catholic brother succeeded without question to the throne.

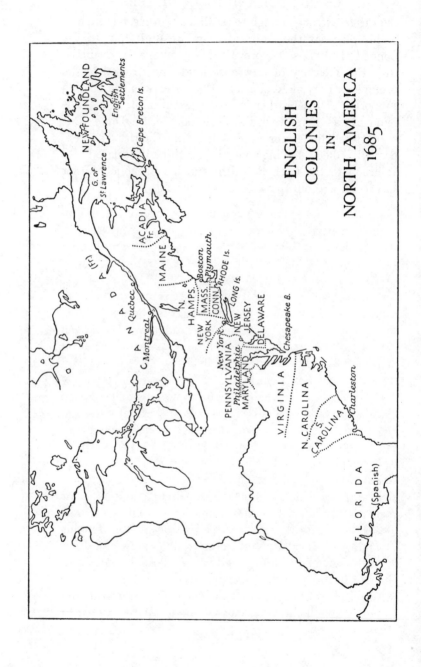

ENGLISH
COLONIES
IN
NORTH AMERICA
1685

NEWFOUNDLAND

English
Settlements

Cape Breton Is.

G. of
St Lawrence

ACADIA
Fr.

MAINE

(Fr.)

C A N A D A

Quebec

Montreal

N.
HAMPS.

Boston

MASS.

Plymouth

CONN.

RHODE Is.

NEW
YORK

LONG Is.

New York

NEW
JERSEY

DELAWARE

PENNSYLVANIA

Philadelphia

MARYLAND

Chesapeake B.

V I R G I N I A

N. CAROLINA

S.
CAROLINA

Charleston

F L O R I D A
(Spanish)

XVII. THE COLONIES AND DEPENDENCIES
1603–1688

NOT only in relation to insular England was the seventeenth century a critical period. A work whose keynote is the development of the idea of Liberty among the English people must not therefore ignore the origins of the Oversea Empire. The Colonies and Liberty

The connexion between the movements at home and overseas is plainly indicated by an incident related by Clarendon. As members hurried out of the House of Commons after the fateful division on the Grand Remonstrance Falkland happened to encounter Cromwell, and asked him ironically 'whether there had been a debate?' to which he answered 'that he would take his word another time' and whispered him in the ear with some asseveration, that if the remonstrance had been rejected he would have sold all he had the next morning and never have seen England more', and he knew there were many other honest men of the same resolution'. 'So near', adds Clarendon, 'was the poor Kingdom at that time to its deliverance.'[1]

Had Cromwell carried out his intention and migrated to New England he would have found there many friends. During the previous decade there had been an exodus of Puritans to the new colony of Massachusetts. Puritans were not, however, the pioneers of the British Empire in North America. That distinction belongs to the commercial company which founded the colony of Virginia. Nor was the Virginia Company the first of its kind as it was founded (1606) in conscious imitation of the famous Company of London Merchants trading with the East Indies, a company which had received its Patent from Queen Elizabeth on 31 December 1600.

Tardily had the eyes of Englishmen turned towards the distant lands in the far East and the far West. Down to The Geographical Renaissance

[1] *History*, ii. 43.

the end of the fifteenth century the English were not
pre-eminently a seafaring race; still less were they a
'nation of shop-keepers'. Not until the reign of Henry VIII
did England possess a regular navy; such foreign wares as
she bought were carried, like her own meagre exports, in
foreign bottoms. She had, in brief, neither ships nor shops.
Her people lived on the primary products of the land,
though from the fifteenth century onwards she did an
increasing trade in raw wool with the Low Countries, from
which in return she bought the finished cloth. Commercially, politically, no less than geographically, England was
an appendage of the European Continent.

Trade
Routes
The great geographical discoveries of the late fifteenth
century shifted the world's centre of gravity. For many
centuries civilization had centred in the countries bordering
on the Mediterranean. But in 1453 the Ottoman Turks
completed their conquest of the Balkan peninsula by the
capture of Constantinople, and in the period that followed
they made themselves masters of the whole of the Levant
and the Eastern Mediterranean, including all the great
emporia of medieval trade. If their conquests did not
actually block the old trade routes, their occupation of
Constantinople, Alexandria, and the coasts of Syria and
Palestine, rendered trade between Asia and the nations
of Western Europe exceedingly difficult and precarious.
The geographical discoveries at the end of the fifteenth
century were a direct consequence of this situation. The
Portuguese had for some time been feeling their way along
the Western Coast of Africa. In 1498 their great naviga-
tor Vasco da Gama actually rounded the Cape of Good
Hope and for the first time a European expedition found
its way by sea into the oceans of the East. Meanwhile,
Venetian navigators sojourning in Spain and England,
anxious like the Portuguese to turn the flank of the Ottoman
Empire, had led Spanish and English expeditions on a
similar enterprise. Columbus and the Cabots, in their
quest for a new sea route to the East, stumbled across the
West Indies and North America. Thus England became

for the first time the geographical centre of the world—a position from which she can never be dislodged.

That was the beginning of England's overseas empire and overseas trade. But at the end of the fifteenth century she was not in a position, economically, socially, or politically, to take advantage of the opportunity offered to her by the discoveries of the Cabots and their contemporaries. Commercially backward, politically exhausted by the faction fights of the Roses, economically anaemic and underpopulated, England did not possess the vigour essential to the success of overseas enterprise. Nor, indeed, had she the necessary ships. The Tudor régime, as we have already seen in another connexion, wrought an amazing change. The Reformation released us from the restrictions imposed upon Catholic nations by the Bull of Alexander VI. Stories of the vast wealth accruing to Spain and Portugal from their Empires in South America, and to Portugal from her Empire in India, stimulated the latent spirit of adventure in Englishmen. There were tales also (still to be read in Hakluyt's collection of *Voyages*) of the cruelties inflicted on English sailors and merchants by the Inquisition. Half in the temper of buccaneers, half in the spirit of crusaders, the Elizabethan sea-dogs went forth, with the Bible in one hand and the cutlass in the other, to revenge the wrongs done to their countrymen and to carry the light of Protestant Christianity to the benighted victims of Catholicism.[1]

From these roots English colonization sprang. The spirit of adventure and lust for gain lured Englishmen to Virginia, as they had lured them to the far East; zeal for the purity of the Protestant faith drove them to New England.

The adventurers of the Elizabethan era had pointed the way. Hawkins, Frobisher, and Drake had taught Englishmen how to fight at sea; Raleigh and Gilbert had made valiant attempts to plant Englishmen on the soil of North

Colonization in North America

---

[1] I need hardly say that I attempt in these words to reproduce the temper of that day and do not reflect the spirit of our own.

America. But the Elizabethan temper, apt for adventure, was too volatile for the more tedious work of plantation. Consequently, despite all the splendid enterprises of the sea-dogs, there was not, when Elizabeth died, a single Englishman living under the English flag in any English land overseas.[1] In 1606, however, two companies originating in London and Plymouth respectively, obtained Charters from James I entitling them to plant settlements on the Coast of North America between the thirty-fourth and forty-fifth degrees of north latitude.

Virginia

On the first day of the following year their ships sailed from England for Virginia, with 143 intending emigrants on board. They landed at Chesapeake Bay and founded a settlement to which they gave the name of Jamestown. But the young colony encountered all manner of difficulties: disease and famine, troubles with the natives, quarrels among the colonists; and the expedition of 1607 would have added one more to the series of failures in Virginia but for the energy and pluck of one man—Captain John Smith. Smith saved the infant colony chiefly by demanding from the Council at home the supply of a better and different type of settlers. 'I entreat you', he wrote, 'rather send but thirty carpenters, husbandmen, gardeners, fishermen, blacksmiths, masons, diggers up of tree roots, well provided, than a thousand of such as we have here.'[2] The Council responded; the company was reorganized; a new Charter (1609) transferred practical control from the Crown to the stockholders; Lord Salisbury, Francis Bacon, and many leading men interested themselves in the colony, and Lord Delaware was sent out as Governor. Delaware was disgusted, on his arrival, by the state of affairs in the colony, but, given an immediate supply of food and a better class of settlers, he did not despair of success. For the land itself was a fair one. 'Heaven and earth', wrote Smith, 'seemed never to have agreed better to frame a place for man's

[1] Except, of course, in Ireland.
[2] Echoing the language of Bacon, or did Bacon echo Smith's? Cf. *Essay on Plantation.*

commodious and delightful habitation.' But it is men not skies that make colonies.

'It is not', wrote Delaware to the Council, 'men of such distempered bodies and infected minds whom no example either of goodness or punishment can deter from their habitual impieties or terrify from a shameful death that must be carpenters and workers in this so glorious a building. But to delude and mock the business no longer, as a necessary quantity of provisions for a year must be carefully sent, so likewise must there be the same care for men of quality and painstaking men of arts and practices chosen out and sent into the business.'

The position slowly improved and the year 1619 witnessed the birth of representative institutions in the new world:

'That they might have a hand in the governinge of them-selves', runs the *Briefe Declaration*, 'yet was graunted that a General Assemblie should be helde yearly once, whereat were to be present the Governor and Counsell with two burgesses from each plantation freely to be elected by the inhabitants thereof, this Assemblie to have power to make and ordaine whatsoever lawes and orders should by them be thought good and profitable for our subsistence.'

The year thus rendered memorable by the meeting of the first Colonial Assembly was memorable also for the landing in Virginia of some twenty African slaves from a Dutch ship. Then was sown the seed which germinated two centuries later. But Virginia was now fairly on its feet. By 1650 the Colony contained 15,000 people of English blood. After the execution of King Charles large numbers of Cavaliers found new homes in Virginia; by 1670 the Colony numbered 40,000 souls, and before the close of the century close on 100,000.

One of the statesmen most keenly interested in the Maryland Virginia enterprise was Sir George Calvert, the first Lord Baltimore. Compelled, by his reception into the Roman Catholic Church, to withdraw from public life in England, Baltimore established in 1623 a small settlement in New-foundland. But, encountering difficulties from French

3679   C C

privateers and still more from his Puritan neighbours in New England, he migrated to Virginia. There, however, he found the Anglican Establishment too strict for him and in 1632 he obtained from Charles I a grant of land in the northern part of Virginia. He died in that same year but in 1633, his son established Maryland as a separate Colony. This was the first of the 'Proprietary' group of colonies. The Charter granted to Baltimore by Charles I is for more than one reason interesting. The Proprietor was established in almost complete independence, and the country was to be held by him by tenure of fealty from, and on payment of quit-rents to, the Crown. The Proprietor was, however, instructed to make laws for his Colony with the advice and approbation of the majority of the freemen or their deputies. When it was inconvenient to summon a representative Assembly, Ordinances, having the force of law, might be issued by the Proprietor, provided such Ordinances did not prejudicially affect the lives or property of his subjects. Security was taken for the protection of members of the Church of England, and King Charles agreed, on behalf of himself and his heirs, never to lay any tax, imposition or customs duty on the colonists.

Maryland had its troubles, like other Colonies, but it was honourably distinguished among them. Established primarily for the reception of Roman Catholics who enjoyed no toleration in the Protestant States of the old world, Maryland was the first colony in the new world to embody in a formal Statute the principle, already in practice adopted, of complete toleration for all Christians.

'Whereas', ran the Act of 1649, 'the inforcing of the conscience in matters of religion hath frequently fallen out to bee of dangerous consequence in those commonwealths where it has beene practised, and for the more quiet and peaceable government of this province and the better to preserve mutuall love and unity amongst the inhabitants here "it is enacted that no person" professing to believe in Jesus Christ shall from henceforth be any waies troubled, molested or discountenanced for, or in respect of, his or her religion nor in the free exercise thereof

within this province, . . . nor any way compelled to the beleefe
or exercise of any other religion, against his or her consent.'

Admirable in itself the Toleration Act might be impugned
from the standpoint of the once dominant creed, for, by the
end of the century Maryland had ceased to be a preserve
of Roman Catholicism. It had indeed almost disappeared
from the Colony.

To the same geographical group as Virginia and Mary- The
land belonged Georgia and the two Carolinas. The latter Carolinas
Colonies were granted by Charles II, in 1663, to a body of
eight proprietors, among whom were Clarendon, Monk (by
then Duke of Albemarle), Shaftesbury and Sir George
Carteret. No colony had yet been established under
auspices so distinguished. Its 'fundamental Constitution'
was drafted by Shaftesbury with the assistance of John
Locke. But the Constitution-making of philosophers
rarely prospers. The Carolina Constitution formed no
exception to this rule. It vested the government in a
territorial aristocracy with the eight hereditary proprietors
at its head. Minute regulations were drawn up as to the
Executive and Judicial powers which were vested in the
proprietors: legislation was confided to a Parliament
consisting of the Proprietors, the nobles, and representatives of the freeholders. Provision was made for the
Establishment of the Church of England, but all creeds
were, on certain conditions, to enjoy complete toleration.
The Constitution possesses a speculative interest, but it
never worked, and was rescinded in 1693.

The tale of the Southern Colonies was completed, though Georgia
not until 1732, by the establishment, to the South of the
Carolinas, of Georgia. Georgia was much the latest in
date of the original thirteen colonies on the Atlantic seaboard, and was unique in origin and characteristics.
Its foundation was due to the philanthropic zeal of a
member of the House of Commons, General Oglethorpe.
Commemorated in Pope's couplet,

'One driven by strong benevolence of soul
Shall fly like Oglethorpe from poll to poll,'

Oglethorpe persuaded the House of Commons to vote £10,000 towards the expense of establishing an asylum for debtors and other distressed persons.

'Not the depraved,' writes its chronicler, 'not felons but the honestly unfortunate were to be the beneficiaries of this benevolent and patriotic scheme. . . . Robert Southey did but re-echo the general sentiment when he affirmed that no colony was ever projected or established upon principles more honourable to its founders.'

Oglethorpe himself went out with a batch of 116 emigrants in 1732 and settled at Savannah, a town which they established on the southern bank of the river of that name. The original settlers were reinforced by a number of Moravians and other German Protestants in 1733, and among the early visitors to the infant Colony were the Wesleys and Whitefield. The importation of spirits and slaves was prohibited, but both in time found their way into the Colony, where economic and climatic conditions made some form of slave labour almost indispensable. The trustees surrendered their charter to the Crown in 1752 and a constitution of the usual type was then adopted.

The
Southern
Group
Virginia, the Carolinas, Maryland, and Georgia had from the first, and long retained, outstanding characteristics which differentiated them from the New England Colonies. Their pervading sentiment was royalist and aristocratic. Anglicanism was the dominant creed. Spacious mansions housed the proprietors of the large plantations which were worked by slaves or semi-servile labour. The cultivation of tobacco, the chief product, and cotton, lends itself to, if it does not economically demand, the utilization of slave labourers working in gangs. There were no towns and few villages; the 'Plantation' was the unit of the industrial and the political system, as slavery formed the basis of the whole economic structure. The 'Southerners' had the virtues as well as the defects of aristocracies. Self reliant, self respecting, self contained and exclusive, they produce leaders of men. Hence it was to Virginia and its neighbours that, when the time of stress and trial came, the rebellious

Colonies looked for generals, statesmen, and administrators. But he who would know intimately the life of the Southern Colonies in their early days will go for information to Thackeray.[1]

The strength of a country largely depends on the variety of elements which go to make up its population. England obtained that variety from successive invasions and conquests. The American Colonies derived similar strength from the diversity of elements of which they were built. New England was planted by men very different in outlook, social, religious and political, from the lordly proprietors of the southern Colonies. In temper if not in fact its founders were rebels against authority in Church and State. A little band of these Brownists or Independents had sought refuge from the rigours of the Elizabethan régime in Holland. Even Calvinistic Holland however, proved too narrow for their large ideas of religious liberty, and in 1620 some of them decided to seek a new home across the Atlantic. New England

The story of the Pilgrim Fathers is one of the most familiar in English history and need not be retold. The parting of the Pilgrims from their saintly pastor John Robinson, the sailing of the *Mayflower* from Plymouth, the landing of the little band on the bleak shores of Massachusetts Bay, their struggles, their sufferings, and their valiant conquest of every obstacle—all this has been told in touching verse and noble prose. The motive of this fresh migration was purely religious. The Pilgrim Fathers

'It concerneth New England always to remember that they were originally a plantation of religions, not a plantation of trade. And if any man among us make religion as twelve and the world as thirteen, such an one hath not the spirit of a true New Englandman.'

So spake Higginson in his 'Election' sermon of 1663.

'When the Founders of these Colonies came over, it was a time of general tyranny both in Church and State throughout

---

[1] *The Virginians.* Not less vivid or accurate is Miss Johnstone's delightful romance, *By Order of the Company.*

their mother island, under which the British kingdoms loudly groaned; as the united voice declared both of their Lords and Commons in several Parliaments both of England and of Scotland, the only national representatives and the most proper witnesses of the national oppressions.'

So Prince of Boston wrote in 1736.

New Plymouth   The germ of the New England Colonies was New Plymouth where the Pilgrim Fathers first settled in 1620. The settlers were drawn from the humbler classes at home; they had crossed the ocean not in quest of gold, but to find an asylum in the wilderness, where they could worship God after their own fashion—a liberty denied them in Holland not less than in England. The migration was on a small scale; the progress of the Colony was slow, so slow that at the end of ten years it contained only three hundred souls. But if the Pilgrims suffered they won through. 'Let it not be grievous unto you', wrote one of their friends from England, 'that you have been instruments to break the ice for others. The honour shall be yours till the world's end.'

Massachusetts   The great Puritan exodus took place a few years later when, after the dissolution of the third Parliament of Charles I in 1629, things were looking hopeless for Puritans and Parliamentarians in the old country. It was then that a number of leading members of the Puritan party, country gentlemen of the type of the Pyms and Cromwells, wealthy merchants and other men of substance, obtained from Charles I a Charter to enable them to establish a Colony on Massachusetts Bay. In 1630 John Winthrop, a country gentleman of considerable estate, sailed in command of an expedition comprising seventeen ships with 1,000–1,500 emigrants on board. Boston was the site selected for their settlement and, despite some privation and suffering not comparable, however, to those of Virginia or New Plymouth, the new Colony rapidly progressed and became the parent of others.

'We here enjoy', wrote Governor Winthrop, 'God and Jesus Christ and is not this enough? I thank God I like so well to be here as I do not repent my coming. I would not have altered my course though I had foreseen all these afflictions. I never had more content of mind.'

The English Crown looked with little favour on the growth of a 'rebel' settlement. Efforts were made, in vain, to arrest emigration and even to revoke the Charter. But the Colony went on its way unheeding. Yet, it had its religious difficulties. No more than the old country could it solve the religious problem. The founders meant to make the new Commonwealth a body politic of Saints. But this meant, in effect, a connexion between State and Church as close as that in Geneva, much closer than that in England. Consequently, the government of the Colony soon found itself in conflict with those who, like the young Pastor Roger Williams, had crossed the Atlantic to enjoy liberty of conscience, who held that 'in soul matters there should be no weapons but soul weapons'. Holding these views, Williams, a man not merely of deep spirituality but of culture and education[1], soon found himself in difficulties; he was imprisoned and later on was sentenced, with unconscious irony, to deportation to England. He escaped, however, and founded an exile settlement on his own lines at Providence, which was later (1644) incorporated in Rhode Island. Rhode Island, founded like Providence in protest against the religious exclusiveness of Massachusetts, was the home of Mrs. Hutchinson and her friends. Other offshoots of Massachusetts were Connecticut (1635), Newhaven (1638), and New Hampshire (1641). Maine, on the other hand, was a Proprietary Colony granted by Charter (1639) to Sir Ferdinando Gorges. Settled by emigrants from England it had little in common with its Puritan neighbours and was, like Providence and Rhode Island, expressly excluded from the New England Federation formed in 1643 by Massachusetts, Plymouth, Connecticut, and Newhaven.

This Federation, a forerunner of the greater union of 1788, was due partly to dread of interference from home,

Religious Difficulties

[1] Educated at Charterhouse and Pembroke College, Cambridge.

and partly to fear of the native Indians, of the French Settlements on the north, and of the Dutch who had established themselves to the south at New Amsterdam and elsewhere on the banks of the Hudson. The last danger was eliminated when in 1664 the Dutch Colony passed by a bloodless conquest into the hands of an English proprietor, the Duke of York. But we anticipate events.

The Civil War and the Colonies
The English Civil War had its repercussions in the Colonies. Parliament had never admitted the exclusive jurisdiction of the Crown over colonial affairs, and, after the execution of Charles I, the Rump took prompt measures to assert its authority. The Puritan Colonies had, naturally, no scruple in accepting the jurisdiction of the Commonwealth. But it was otherwise with Virginia. The mansions of the planters were filled with royalist refugees from the homeland, Sir William Berkeley, the Governor, was an ardent adherent to the same cause, and, on the death of Charles I, the Virginia Assembly promptly recognized his son as King, passed an Act declaring it high treason to speak disrespectfully of the late King, to defend his execution or question the title of Charles II to the Crown. Barbados took a similar line.

The English Parliament was, however, in no mood to allow its authority to be thus set at naught. An Ordinance was promptly (1650) passed prohibiting trade with Barbados, Antigua, Virginia, and Somers Islands and in 1651 a Fleet was dispatched under Sir George Ayscue to reduce the recalcitrant colonies to obedience. The work was quickly accomplished, and in the same year an Ordinance of the highest significance was passed.

The Navigation Act 1651
The policy embodied in the Navigation Acts was not indeed new. It had been pursued, with a varying degree of persistency, ever since the fourteenth century. The object at which it aimed was twofold: to increase the Navy and to encourage English trade. The Ordinance of 1651 was aimed not against our own Colonies, but against the Dutch, who, in the words of Thomas Mun, 'undermine, hurt and eclipse us daily in our Navigation and Trade'. Colonial

shipping was in fact explicitly protected. No goods were to be exported to the Colonies or imported thence into England except in English or Colonial built ships, the property of English subjects, having English commanders and a crew, three-fourths of whom were English. Whether or no the authors of the Ordinance contemplated war with the Dutch, war did in fact ensue. Nor can it be denied, even by the sternest critics of a measure avowedly protective, that the carrying trade, hitherto almost monopolized by the Dutch, was after, if not in consequence of, its enactment, gradually transferred to England. Adam Smith, while insisting that the Act was detrimental to English trade with foreigners, and admitting that some of its provisions 'may have proceeded from national animosity', nevertheless maintains that 'they are as wise as if they had all been dictated by the most deliberate wisdom'. In other words, though economic theory might condemn it, the Act was abundantly justified by its political results. Commercial and naval supremacy passed from Holland to England.

The first naval war between the two Powers was fought wholly at sea and with alternating fortunes, but the Peace by which in 1654 it was brought to a close was entirely favourable to England: the Navigation Act was to stand, the English flag to be saluted, and compensation paid for the Amboyna massacre. *First Dutch War 1652–4*

Before the Peace was concluded Cromwell had expelled the Rump and become the Head of the State. Nor has any ruler of England ever been more jealous of England's repute among the nations, or more successful in promoting her greatness as an Imperial Power. As compared with his predecessors, he had indeed everything in his favour. The master of legions which had never known defeat; served by capable commanders at sea, and unencumbered by any dynastic connexions, he could speak with his enemies in the gate as no Stuart or even Tudor Sovereign could dare speak. His policy, as we have seen, was inspired by two motives; zeal for the Protestant faith and *Cromwell's policy* devotion to the imperial and commercial interests of England. Spain was the inevitable enemy; France, consequently, the natural ally. Jamaica and Dunkirk were the fruits of his victories.

Foreign policy of the later Stuarts   The later Stuarts, as Seeley has observed, always had before their minds the brilliant success achieved by Cromwell in the sphere of foreign affairs: and they did their utmost to 'appropriate for the Monarchy the advantage derived from religious toleration and a standing army'.[1] Unlike Cromwell, however, they could not disentangle themselves from dynastic complications.

The Portuguese marriage   The marriage of Charles II with a Portuguese princess, Catherine of Braganza, is ascribed by a brilliant historian to 'a shrewd combination of English designs on the trade of tropical Empires with French designs on the sovereignty of European Provinces'.[2] The alliance thus concluded has remained one of the few constant factors in European, indeed in world politics. Seeley justly described the marriage treaty as 'one of the great events of English history'. It carried on the Stuart tradition that 'England, though a Protestant nation, should have a Catholic Queen'. It committed England to active participation in continental affairs, and virtually pledged her to continued co-operation with France against Spain. But the Anglo-French alliance was no longer, as under Cromwell, an alliance of equals. Cromwell had, at his disposal, great military resources; Charles had not: and consequently became the pensioner of Louis XIV. By allying himself with France Cromwell abated not one jot of his Protestant fervour. Charles's inclinations were towards Catholicism. Like Cromwell, however, Charles II was keenly interested in Colonial development, and English interests in the extra-European sphere suffered, at his hands, no diminution. Dunkirk indeed was sold to France, but Catherine of Braganza brought her husband the rich dowry of Tangier and Bombay—not to mention a considerable sum in hard cash.

[1] *Growth of British Policy*, ii. 107 seq.
[2] Trevelyan, *England under the Stuarts*, p. 351.

Passing into English hands half a century before the capture of Gibraltar (1704), Tangier was an important naval base for a Power which aspired to influence in the Mediterranean. Its occupation for that purpose was one more welcome indication that the continuity of Cromwell's Imperial policy would remain unbroken under Charles II.

Much more important, however, was the acquisition of the island of Bombay. Destined to become the great western port of British India, and a great industrial centre, Bombay was the third of the 'factories' to be established on the continent of Hindustan by the East India Company. Like their Dutch rivals the English merchants had originally sought trade in the spice islands. But the position of the Dutch was in every respect stronger than our own; the English merchants were gradually edged out from the islands, and after the massacre of Amboyna (1623), they abandoned the unequal struggle and, fortunately, betook themselves to the mainland. *The English in India*

In India the Portuguese had for more than a century been the dominant European Power. Their Empire, though decadent, was still imposing, and the advent of the English merchants was unwelcome to them. In the year 1608, however, English merchants by permission of the Mogul Emperor established a factory at Surat, and though warned off from Goa, the Portuguese capital, gradually established a considerable trade. The capture (1622) of the Portuguese island of Ormuz in the Persian Gulf afforded further security to English trade, and by 1639 the Company had set up factories at Balasore and Masulipatam and had begun the fortification of Fort St. George at Madras. A factory was set up at Hugli in Bengal in 1650, and at Calcutta in 1690. The acquisition of Bombay was, therefore, both timely and significant, and its sale by Charles II to the Company marked one of the red-letter days in the romantic history of British Dominion in India.

Not only in India was Charles II attentive to the interests of English trade. He had, indeed, every reason *Trade Policy* to cherish it. When impeached by his enemies Clarendon asserted that

'soon after the Restoration he used all the endeavour he could to bring His Majesty to have a great esteem for his Plantations, and to encourage the improvement of them, and that he was confirmed in his opinion and desire by the entries at the Custom House, by which he found what a great revenue accrued to the King from these plantations; inasmuch as the receipts from them had repaired the decrease of the Customs which the late troubles had brought upon the ports of trade.'[1]

Naviga-
tion Act
1660
Clarendon's endeavour bore immediate fruit in the re-enactment and amendment of the Navigation Act. The scope of the earlier Ordinance was now greatly extended. The former Act was intended to encourage English shipping; the Act of 1660 was designed to protect the products of English industry. On the one hand it prohibited the importation into England, or the exportation from any English plantation in Africa, Asia, or America, of any commodity except in English built and English manned ships. On the other hand it prohibited altogether the export from the Colonies of certain enumerated commodities except to England or an English Plantation. An Explanatory Act of 1662 made it clear that by 'English' was intended 'all of His Majesty's subjects of England, Ireland and His Plantations'.

Mercan-
tilism
These Navigation Acts, their numerous successors, and the policy they embodied, have become the field of interminable controversy, political and economic. They were passed at a time when the supremacy of the Mercantilist School was unchallenged; when the doctrine of 'Power' was held of more account than that of wealth; when Great Nation-States were being built up on a basis of Economic self-sufficiency. A century later the whole doctrine of the Mercantilist School was bitterly assailed by Adam Smith. As to the Navigation Acts themselves he drew a very proper distinction between the political motives which he

[1] *Life of Lord Clarendon*, vol. iii. Quoted *ap*. Egerton, *Colonial Policy*, p. 68.

approved, and the economic results which he condemned. Published in the same year (1776) as the Declaration of American Independence *The Wealth of Nations* bears on the surface many traces of the controversy between the Home Government and the American Colonies. To attack the commercial policy of England as 'a manifest violation of the most sacred rights of mankind' was perhaps a pardonable exaggeration in one who was at once a strong Free Trader and an ardent Imperialist. Burke, however, while attacking the policy of taxation of the Colonies, approved that of commercial restriction; and later critics, in America not less than in England, have inclined towards the views of Burke rather than to those of Adam Smith.

This much, however, is clear: that in their origin the Navigation laws were completely in harmony with the accepted doctrine, political and economic of that day; that they were directly instrumental in transferring commercial supremacy in general and particularly the carrying trade from Holland to England; and, not least important, that they inflicted no hardship whatsoever upon the Colonies. Sir William Ashley goes much further.[1] He maintains that these laws gave an immense impulse to the ship-building industry in New England, and that, prior to 1760, the restriction of colonial exports to an English *entrepôt* was no economic disadvantage to the Colonies, while the political connexion with England was wholly to their advantage. Nor is Sir William Ashley without support from eminent American Economists. That in the largest sense English 'Liberty' was advanced by the economic legislation of this period can hardly, indeed, be questioned by any one acquainted with the facts.

Nor was Charles II's solicitude for the promotion of Imperial interests expressed only in legislation. Colonial affairs, so far as they claimed attention at all, were at first dealt with by the Privy Council. In 1634, however, Charles I set up a commission, consisting of the Archbishops of Canterbury and York, the Lord Keeper, the

Administration of Colonial Affairs

[1] *Surveys Historic and Economic*, pp. 309 seq.

Lord Treasurer and some other officers of State 'for making laws and orders for the Government of English Colonies, &c.' Parliament in 1643 replaced this by a Special Commission which, though unofficial, was as strong in personnel as Parliament could make it, including, as it did, Pym and Cromwell, Lords Pembroke, Manchester, and Saye and Sele, Sir Henry Vane the younger and Sir Benjamin Rudyard.

Board of Trade and Plantations   The Committee of the Privy Council for Plantation affairs was restored in 1660, but two years later a Standing Committee on Trade and Plantations was set up to assist the work of the Great Trading Companies and, in particular, their trade with the Plantations. This Committee—the ancestor of the Board of Trade—was to consist of forty 'understanding able persons', some of whom were to be merchants representing the East India and other Trading Companies, others were to represent the 'unincorporated trades for Spain, France, Portugal, Italy, and the West India Plantations', while the Board was to be 'dignified also with the presence and assistance of some of His Majesty's Privy Council'. The Board was to take a special care for the strict application of the Navigation Act, to encourage and control emigration to the Plantations, to keep themselves informed of the state of the Plantations, of their government and their trade, and to inquire into any grievances of which they might complain.

Of this Committee Shaftesbury was President, and John Locke was for a short time (1673–4) Secretary. After the fall of Shaftesbury, however, the Joint Committee was abolished and its functions were transferred to a Committee of the Privy Council consisting of the Lord Treasurer, the Privy Seal, and seventeen other members. This Committee continued to control colonial affairs until after the Revolution when a new Board of Trade was set up (1696).

The Middle Colonies   Meanwhile, important developments were taking place in North America. Down to the reign of Charles II the New England Colonies were separated from the southern group by the Dutch Settlement of the New Netherlands.

The Dutch were essentially traders rather than colonizers, but their settlement occupied a strong strategical position on the Hudson and was a source of considerable inconvenience, not to say of danger, to the growing English Settlements in Connecticut and Newhaven. To the south of the New Netherlands the Swedes had planted a settlement on the estuary of the Delaware River; but in 1655 this settlement was conquered and absorbed by the Dutch who were thus in possession of the whole coast-line between Connecticut and Maryland.

Cromwell was planning an expedition for the conquest of the New Netherlands when the conclusion of peace between England and Holland (1654) intervened to give the Dutch Colony a ten years' respite. The project was resumed, however, by Charles II who in 1664 dispatched a small fleet under the command of Colonel Nicholls to the Hudson River. Nicholls, with four ships and less than five hundred soldiers aboard, appeared before New Amsterdam in August of that year and demanded the surrender of the Colony. The Dutch settlers promptly yielded, and the New Netherlands, including New Sweden, passed quietly into the hands of the English who now held the whole coast from the Kennebeck to the Savannah.

The territories thus easily acquired were handed over by the King to his brother the Duke of York after whom the Colony, and its capital New Amsterdam, were renamed. New Sweden was, after some vicissitudes, constituted a separate Colony (1703) and renamed Delaware. The lands between the Hudson and the Delaware had in 1664 been handed over by the Duke of York to Lord Berkeley and Sir George Carteret, and in compliment to the latter, who had held Jersey for the King during the Civil War, were christened New Jersey. *New York*

Delaware and New Jersey

Of the Middle Colonies the most interesting and important was Pennsylvania. Its founder was William Penn, a son of the admiral who conquered Jamaica and a leading member of the Society of Friends. Penn was sent down from Christ Church for refusal to conform to the eccle- *Pennsylvania* siastical discipline of the University and, after a brief period of naval service, attached himself definitely to the Quakers. At war both with Anglicans and Calvinists, Penn soon became involved in serious difficulties with the secular arm. Committed to the Tower for publishing his *Sandy Foundation Shaken* he repeated his offence in his famous *No Cross No Crown*, and obtained his release only through the intervention of his tolerant patron the Duke of York. But his unremitting efforts to lighten the hardships suffered by his Quaker co-religionists led to his being repeatedly imprisoned, and at last he decided to seek a refuge for himself and his friends in the new world. In 1682 he obtained from the Duke of York the grant of a tract of land 47,000 square miles in extent, on the western bank of the River Delaware, bounded by Maryland on the south, by New York and Delaware on the east, and stretching up to the great lakes on the north. The Crown thus conveniently discharged a debt of £16,000 due to Admiral Penn and by him bequeathed to his son. Penn himself sailed with a band of one hundred companions for his Colony in 1682. The name of the new Settlement was due to the fancy of the King who insisted that the name of a great sailor and a loyal servant of the Crown should be prefixed to the 'Sylvania' originally selected for it. Penn went to the new world with no hope of material gain, but to initiate a 'holy experiment' in government. By the 'Great Law of Pennsylvania', promulgated on the arrival of the Proprietor, it was ordained that the Constitution, framed by him in conjuction with Algernon Sidney, should be based on the principles of pure democracy. The government was to be 'for the support of power in reverence with the people and to secure the people from the abuse of power. For liberty without obedience is confusion, and obedience without liberty is slavery'. All forms of religious worship consistent with monotheism and religious liberty were to be tolerated. In every way Pennsylvania started under the happiest auspices: the original English settlers were quickly and largely reinforced by immigrants not only from the homeland but from Scandinavia, Holland, and Germany, and from the first the friendliest relations were maintained with the native tribes.

With the establishment of Pennsylvania the tale of the thirteen original Colonies is complete.[1] Except for the Dutch Colonies, the conquest of which was bloodless, all the Colonies on the Atlantic seaboard were the product not of conquest but of peaceful settlement. Many motives contributed to their establishment; their founders differed widely in temperament, in opinions political and religious, and in social status, and these differences were reflected in the structure, the constitution, and the economic life of their settlements. Hence the extraordinary but most fortunate variety of type exhibited by the Colonies, and by them transmitted to the great nation of which they were destined to be the nucleus.

Before that nation emerged the Colonies were to suffer many vicissitudes of fortune. France, strongly planted on the St. Lawrence and the Mississippi, threatened not merely their independence but their existence. Rescued from that peril by the armies and fleets of Great Britain, they then became involved in the quarrel with the home-government which led to the War of Independence. Having wrested their independence from the motherland they had to meet the grave peril of disruption within their own borders. Courageously encountered, that peril also was dissipated; a great nation sprung from the loins of Britain was born.

The origins of that nation belong to the period when England herself was engaged in her desperate struggle for liberty. Consequently no work which essays to tell the story of the one can ignore the other. The two stories are, indeed, inextricably interwoven. The ecclesiastical policy of the first two Stuarts; the assertive Protestanism and Imperialism of Cromwell; the mercantilist prepossessions of Charles II—all these had their reactions in the field of

[1] Georgia was chronologically the latest but has been dealt with *supra.*

D d

colonial policy. Nor did the attack of the later Stuarts upon local liberties at home lack its counterpart in the colonies. Charles II made more than one attempt to 'dispose the people [of New England] to an entire submission and obedience to the King's Government'. The colonists were accused of persistent evasion of the Acts of Navigation and Trade; of direct trading with various European countries, and non-payment of the duties claimed by the mother country; of coining money in colonial mints, and of denying to members of the Church of England the rights of citizenship. The charges were unfortunately true, and, as no satisfaction could be obtained, the Charter of Massachusetts was, by a writ of *Quo Warranto*, withdrawn (1684).

James II carried his brother's policy much further. In 1686 Sir Edmund Andros was sent over to abolish local autonomy and to consolidate thé whole of the territory from Maine to the Delaware under a single autocratic government. Episcopal services were held in the principal towns, often in the Congregational Churches; the writ of habeas corpus was suspended; arbitrary taxes were levied; a strict press censorship was established; land grants were annulled and common lands enclosed—in fine all the familiar machinery of a despotic administration was introduced. The Puritans of New England were not the men tamely to submit, and civil war was averted only by the news that King James had 'abdicated'; that a revolution had been accomplished in England, and that William and Mary had been proclaimed King and Queen.

The Stuart régime in New England collapsed like a house of cards: Andros was deposed; the charters were restored, and the *status quo ante* completely re-established.

We now return to the homeland.

XVIII. THE REVOLUTION OF 1688

THE fervid enthusiasm with which the restored Stuarts Charles II and the Whigs were welcomed evaporated, as we have seen, very rapidly. Nor are the reasons far to seek. The English people were deeply attached to the Established Church; they had learnt to believe in Parliamentary Government; and they were profoundly suspicious of the influence exerted by foreigners upon English affairs. The King, on the other hand, showed increasing contempt for Parliament, an increasing inclination towards Roman Catholicism, and a disposition, not unnatural, to attach himself to the cause of France. As a consequence, his popularity quickly waned. But just when his fortunes were at the lowest his opponents, by a colossal blunder, played into his hands. The Bill for the exclusion of the Duke of York from the sucession deeply affronted the dominant sentiment in favour of the hereditary Monarchy.

Charles was quick to take advantage of the tactical blunder of the Whigs. In the last years of the reign he proved himself to be in the judgement of a highly competent critic, 'one of the greatest politicians who ever succeeded in the struggle for power in England'.[1] So complete indeed was his victory that, on his sudden demise, not a finger was raised to obstruct the succession of the Duke of York, despite the Duke's unconcealed devotion to Roman Catholicism.

The two brothers were curiously contrasted in character, James II temperament, and endowments. Charles II was a brilliant opportunist, witty and ingratiating, averse from business and devoted to pleasure. James II proved himself to be, in some senses, a man of principle; but though punctual and precise in the conduct of State business he was markedly inferior to his brother in ability and adroitness. As loose in morals as Charles, James had none of the

[1] Trevelyan, *England under the Stuarts*, p. 350.

D d 2

affability which went far to conceal, if not to redeem, his brother's callousness and cruelty.

In his first interview with the Council James declared that, though he had been represented as fond of arbitrary power, they should find the contrary; he promised to maintain the Government in State and Church as by law established; he knew the members of the Church of England to be good and loyal subjects, and he undertook, therefore, to support and defend their Church; he would never yield the just rights and prerogatives of the Crown, but promised that the property and person of every subject should be secure. The speech did something to allay the natural apprehensions of his Protestant subjects, but the first acts of the reign went far to discount his words.

The King and Parliament The collection of taxes voted to the late King only for his life was regarded, and rightly, as an affront to the principle of Parliamentary control. Parliament, however, showed magnaminity in voting to the new King not only the revenue of his predecessor, but, in addition, taxes on sugar and tobacco. James thus found himself in possession of an uncontrolled income of two millions a year.

With singular perversity James contrived, in the short space of three years, to violate all four of the dominant sentiments enumerated above, and simultaneously to alienate every class and every interest in the Community.

Judge Jeffreys The King found in the Lord Chief Justice of the Common Pleas a fitting instrument for a régime of brutality. Jeffreys had already distinguished himself in the prosecution of Lord Russell and in the trial of Algernon Sidney, not to mention his service to the Crown in obtaining a writ of *Quo Warranto* against the City of London (1682). One of the first acts of James II was to bring to trial Titus Oates and Dangerfield, the villains of the Popish Plot. Tried by Jeffreys, Oates was convicted and sentenced to heavy fines and imprisonment for life, to be flogged by the Common hangman, and, if he survived the floggings, to be set in the pillory four times a year. Oates did survive the floggings, though inflicted with the utmost severity, and lived to have his sentence reversed and his pension restored after the Revolution. Dangerfield, sentenced to similar punishment, was killed in a street brawl. Another victim of Jeffrey's brutality was the saintly Divine, Richard Baxter. Indicted for libel he was convicted and sentenced by Jeffreys to a heavy fine, and in default of payment was imprisoned for eighteen months.

These punishments were, however, only a foretaste of those which awaited the defeated followers of Monmouth. The ill-fated son of Charles II and Lucy Walters, had returned to Holland after the discovery of the Rye House Plot, but on the accession of James was expelled by Prince William of Orange. He landed at Lyme Regis (11 June) and, joined by the peasants of Dorset and Somerset, made his way to Taunton. As 'head and captain-general of the Protestant forces of the Kingdom' he asserted 'a legitimate and legal right to the Crown'. At Taunton he was proclaimed King, but only to meet with disaster and defeat at Sedgemoor (6 July). He fled from the field but was captured, and, after abject submission, met the fate which he deserved. To his deluded and devoted followers, however, a wise King might have shown some clemency. Not so; those who escaped military execution, at the hands of Colonel Kirke, on the morrow of the battle, were either hanged or transported to Barbados by Judge Jeffreys. Memories of that 'Bloody Assize' are not, even now, extinct in the West. *The Monmouth Rebellion*

Jeffreys was not the only judge, by excess of zeal in the King's cause, to do grave disservice to the cause of hereditary Monarchy. The King had resolved to pack both the army and the judicial bench with Roman Catholics. Parliament, having refused to repeal the Test Act, was prorogued, but the King nevertheless proceeded to carry out his policy of 'Thorough'. The Court of High Commission, with Jeffreys and Sunderland as its chief members, was set up in July 1686, and an attempt was made to undermine the Protestantism of the Established Church. The task proved too much even for Jeffreys. *The King and the Judges*

The Army presented a less difficult problem. Sir Edward Hales, a professed Roman Catholic, was convicted at the Rochester Assizes for having acted as a Colonel of Foot, without taking the oaths of Supremacy and Allegiance prescribed by the Test Act of 1673. The case afterwards came before the Court of King's Bench, on a collusive action brought by one Godden for the recovery of the reward (£500) due under the Statute to an informer. Hales pleaded the King's pardon and dispensation in bar of the action, and the full Bench of twelve judges decided, with only one dissentient, in favour of the plea. The language of the judgement went, if anything, further than that of the most obsequious of the judges before the Great Rebellion. 'There is no law whatsoever', said Lord Chief Justice Herbert, 'but may be dispensed with by the supreme lawgiver; as the laws of God may be dispensed with by God himself'; while formal judgement of the Court affirmed that 'It is an inseparable prerogative in the Kings of England to dispense with penal laws in particular cases, and upon particular necessary reasons, and that of those reasons and those necessities the King himself is sole judge'.[1]

Imme- Encouraged by this judgement, and still more by the
diate grounds on which it was based, the King hurried on his
antece- plans for the complete restoration of Roman Catholicism.
dents of
the Revo- As a preliminary precaution, a camp of 13,000 men under
lution Catholic officers was formed near the capital, at Hounslow. Dr. Massey, a Roman Catholic, was appointed to the Deanery of Christ Church, Oxford, and the Royal Chapel in Whitehall was opened to all who might wish to take part in the celebration of the Mass. Rochester, on a refusal to change his religion, was dismissed from the office of Lord Treasurer, and the Treasury was put in commission. The King's brother-in-law Hyde, second Earl of Clarendon, was dismissed from the Lord Lieutenancy of Ireland and replaced by Richard Talbot, lately created Earl of Tyrconnel (1687). Tyrconnel, as we shall see, was charged with

[1] Robertson, *Statutes and Cases*, pp. 245–8.

the duty of restoring Roman Catholic ascendancy in Ireland, and raising an Irish army for the support of the King in England.

A still more significant step was taken when in April 1687 the King issued, in virtue of the Royal Prerogative, a *Declaration of Indulgence* suspending, at one stroke, all the penal laws against both Roman Catholics and Protestant Nonconformists (April 1687). To this sinister and insidious act of toleration the King was incited by one whose motives were above suspicion. The King meditated an assault upon the Established Constitution in State and Church. William Penn was fighting, now as always, for liberty of conscience.

Declaration of Indulgence

Nor were the immediate results wholly disappointing to Penn. A distinguished historian dates from this year 'the beginning of religious freedom in England'. 'The prisons', says Mr. Trevelyan, 'were opened to thousands of the best men in England and everywhere public worship was freely resumed by congregations who have never since been forced to close their doors.'[1] Schools were opened in London by Jesuits and other Roman Catholic Orders; Roman Catholic peers were admitted to the Privy Council, and a Papal Nuncio was received in London. At the same time the pulpits of the Anglican Church were tuned to the pitch required by the High Commission.

Then came the attack on the Universities. Dr. Peachell, Vice-Chancellor of Cambridge, was summoned before the Ecclesiastical Commission and suspended from office and deprived of his emoluments as Master of Magdalene College, for refusing to grant a Degree to one Francis, a Benedictine monk who declined to take the oaths required by the University. The Fellows of Magdalen College, Oxford, for refusing to elect to the Presidentship the King's Papist nominee, were deprived of their Fellowships, and replaced by Papists.

Attack on the Universities

This was an attack not merely upon the Established Church but upon the whole principle of property. The

[1] Trevelyan, *op. cit.*, p. 437.

University of Oxford was pre-eminent in its loyalty to the Stuart Monarchy. It had but recently passed a formal Decree against the lawfulness of resistance. But its loyalty could not save it from the vengeance of a Romanizing autocrat. Every Protestant landowner in the country took alarm.

Attack on Lords-Lieutenant

Their alarm was intensified by the King's affront to the Lords-Lieutenant. The King, having secured, by the writs of *Quo Warranto*, the subserviency of the Borough constituencies and the remodelling of the Corporations in the Catholic interest, now attempted the more difficult task of undermining the independence of the counties. The Lords-Lieutenant were instructed to furnish a list of Papists and Nonconformists suitable for election as members of Parliament. Many of them refused and were dismissed.

Reissue of Declaration of Indulgence

The cup of offence was now nearly full. In April 1688 the King issued the *Declaration of Indulgence* in a revised and enlarged form. Not only were all Tests abolished, but no one was to be employed either in civil or military office who refused concurrence in their abolition. On 4 May the clergy of all denominations were ordered to read the Declaration from their pulpits on two successive Sundays (20 and 27 May).

The Seven Bishops

The Order was regarded as an outrageous attack upon the liberties of the Church and was almost universally disobeyed. Archbishop Sancroft and six of his suffragans prayed to be excused from publishing a Declaration which contained 'such a dispensing power as Parliament hath declared illegal'. Being subsequently informed that a criminal information for libel would be exhibited against them in the Court of King's Bench, they claimed their privilege as Peers. They were then committed to the Tower, but their passage to it by water was one long triumphal procession, the river being lined on both sides with boats crowded with sympathizers. Brought to trial before the Lord Chief Justice on a charge of writing and publishing a 'false, feigned, malicious, pernicious and seditious libel' on 29 June, they were, on the following day, acquitted on all the charges.

The acquittal of the Bishops sounded the death-knell of the Stuart monarchy. The verdict was received with wild and general enthusiasm. All parties and every interest, save the Roman Catholics, were now combined in opposition to the Crown. Counties and boroughs, squires and merchants, Anglicans and Nonconformists—three years had sufficed to alienate them all.

Only one more cause of offence could the King have discovered. His resource did not fail him. He could still affront the principle of hereditary Monarchy. The birth of a son (10 June) to Mary of Modena, the King's second wife, sealed his fate. Whigs and Tories, Anglicans and Nonconformists, declared, and perhaps believed, that the Jesuits had plotted to foist a supposititious child upon the country, and to exclude the rightful Protestant heirs from the succession. *Birth of an heir*

The same principle which had secured the throne to James II was now turned to his undoing. As to the legitimacy of the child there can be no reasonable doubt: but the suspicion sufficed. The Protestants now decided to take action. So long as the Protestant daughters of Anne Hyde were next in succession to the Crown, action might have been postponed; James, no longer young, might have been permitted to wear the Crown till his death; but a succession of Papist sovereigns was not to be thought of.

On the day when the seven Bishops were acquitted (30 June) a letter was dispatched to William, Prince of Orange, asking him to bring over an army to secure the liberties of the English people. It was signed by the Earls of Devonshire, Shrewsbury, Danby, Compton the suspended Bishop of London, Lord Lumley, Henry, brother of Algernon, Sidney, and Admiral Edward Russell. The invitation was a strong measure, but all parties concurred in it. *Invitation to William of Orange*

Louis XIV, more alive than his cousin to movements in

Holland warned James in August of the designs of the Prince of Orange and offered him the assistance of a French Fleet. The offer was contemptuously declined. James was as proud as he was obstinate. In October the bomb-shell fell.

William of Orange issued a Declaration, enumerating the illegal acts of James, questioning the legitimacy of the 'Pretended Prince', and disclaiming all ideas of conquest or violence, announced his intention of coming to England with a force sufficient to secure the freedom of Parliament, by whose decision he would abide. The drama of Monk was re-enacted.

Landing of William of Orange

On 5 November, William landed at Torbay and marched unopposed on Exeter. During October James, at last realizing the situation, made an eleventh hour effort to retrace his steps; reinstated Compton (in the see of London), and other dignitaries, including the Fellows of Magdalen College; abolished the Ecclesiastical Commission and restored its Charter to the City of London. But the concessions came too late. Nor were they adequate. James clung —obstinately or loyally—to his Church; he would not surrender the dispensing power, nor summon a free Parliament. Nevertheless, his throne was not overthrown; it collapsed. His friends, his kinsmen, even his daughter Anne deserted him; his enemies encompassed him on every side. Of the deserters the most conspicuous and the most base was his former page John Churchill, now Lieutenant-General and peer of the realm.

Flight of James

Yet, even now, James might have saved, if not the Monarchy as the Stuarts understood it, at least a constitutional Crown, had he accepted the terms which William was constrained by his English friends to offer. He preferred to flee the Kingdom and appeal for help to France.

His flight greatly simplified a situation which would otherwise have been exceedingly complex. Deeply as James had offended English Churchmen and Tory squires, it is doubtful whether they would have assented to his forcible dethronement, so deeply had the doctrine of

Passive Obedience taken root. His abdication absolved them from their allegiance; yet, even so, many of them were unwilling to renounce it.

Nor was the King's abdication without its dangers for the Kingdom. Legal authority disappeared with the King. Rioting took place in London. Popish chapels were burnt and foreign embassies were pillaged. The capture of the King by some fishermen near Sheerness and his return, under escort to Whitehall, deepened the confusion: but a Committee, including some peers, the Lord Mayor and Aldermen, was set up at the Guildhall and took measures for the safety of the capital. The King, permitted to withdraw to Rochester, again fled, and a Convention was hastily got together. It consisted of the House of Lords, the Lord Mayor, Aldermen and fifty of the Common Council of London, together with all members of the House of Commons who had sat in any of the Parliaments of the previous reign; it requested Prince William to administer the Government provisionally and to summon a Parliament for the following month (January 1689).

The Kingless Parliament, more strictly styled a Convention, met on 22 January. But as to the next step to be taken there was no unanimity. The Tories, of all shades of opinion, shrank from any action inconsistent with their dogma of Passive Obedience. James, it is true, had fled, but even if he had ceased to reign the throne was not vacant; his heir reigned in his stead. The high Tories were anxious that James should be recalled, though under conditions which would guarantee the liberties of the people and the security of the Established Church. Archbishop Sancroft and a considerable group of Tories wished to assume the insanity of the King and appoint a Regent. Danby, followed by another though smaller section of the party, would have treated the King's flight as equivalent to abdication, and have proceeded to proclaim the Princess Mary, as the legitimate heiress, as Queen. The doubts as to the legitimacy of the infant Prince could not, under the circumstances, be dispelled, the Princess Mary

The Convention

was, therefore, next in succession and should be proclaimed.

None of these proposed solutions satisfied the Whigs. They maintained that James had broken the mutual contract between King and people—expressed on the one side by the coronation oath and on the other by the oath of allegiance—that he had thereby fortified the Crown: that the throne was therefore vacant, and that it was the right of the nation to elect a new King, and to impose upon him such conditions as might ensure the country against misgovernment.

The Whig view substantially prevailed, and on 28 and 29 January the House of Commons adopted two historic resolutions:

(1) 'That King James II having endeavoured to subvert the constitution of the kingdom by breaking the original contract between King and People, and having by the advice of Jesuits and other wicked persons violated the fundamental laws and withdrawn himself out of the kingdom has abdicated the government and that the throne is thereby vacant. (2) That it hath been found by experience inconsistent with the safety and welfare of this Protestant kingdom to be governed by a Popish prince.'

The Lords promptly assented to the second resolution but demurred to the first. Was the throne 'vacant'? If not, a regency was the obvious expedient. But after a spirited debate the plan of a regency was defeated, though by the narrow majority of 151 votes to 149. Debate then arose on the reference to an 'original contract'—a phrase which contained, accordingly to Macaulay, the 'quintessence of Whiggism'. Had there ever been such a contract? If so, what did it imply? Was it in truth the 'quintessence of Whiggism'? As interpreted by Locke it was; but his interpretation was posterior to the Resolution of 1689.[1] The theory of the Social Contract, adumbrated by Richard Hooker, had first been elaborated by Thomas Hobbes of Malmesbury. But by him it had been formulated as a

[1] Treatise on Civil Government, 1690-1.

basis for his theory of absolute Monarchy. John Locke, borrowing the doctrine from Hobbes, drew from it a practical conclusion in favour of limited Monarchy. Later on Rousseau based on it his doctrine of the Sovereignty of the people. Neither Hobbes, Locke, or Rousseau had any historical justification for the theory on which they built their several and contradictory philosophical superstructures. The sociological researches of Sir Henry Maine have clearly demonstrated the baselessness of the theory of the Social Contract as an explanation of the origin of political Society. But a dogma, though historically worthless, may nevertheless be philosophically valuable, and, in even greater degree, politically convenient. Such was the curious and paradoxical fate of the Social Contract Theory. It served the purpose of the hour in January 1689, and throughout the greater part of the eighteenth century it provided a philosophical apology for the principles proclaimed and the policy pursued by the Whig party.

Despite general acceptance of the 'Social Contract' theory, an effort was, nevertheless, made, in the Convention, to save some remnant of the hereditary principle by offering the Crown to the Princess Mary, with Prince William as regent. This characteristically illogical compromise was defeated by the Princess who declined to reign except in conjunction with her husband; the Prince refused to play the gentleman usher to his wife. Finally, the Resolutions were adopted in their original form, and on 13 February it was agreed to offer the throne conjointly to William and Mary, by whom it was accepted.

The offer was, however, accompanied by a Declaration of the 'true ancient and indubitable rights of the people of this realm'. Accepted by William, the Declaration was embodied in a Bill which became law as William and Mary *Sess. 2, Cap. 2, 1869.*

The Bill of Rights is one of the outstanding Acts which in the aggregate form the Charter of English Constitutional Liberty. Declaratory in form, it reaffirmed the theory of the 'abdication' of James and the consequent 'vacancy' of the throne; it declared that the 'late King' had endeavoured 'to subvert and extirpate the Protestant religion and the Lawes and Liberties of this Kingdome'; and it catalogued his chief offences. It then proceeded to declare illegal (i) the pretended power of suspending laws without consent of Parliament; (ii) the Dispensing power *as it hath been assumed and exercised of late*; (iii) the Ecclesiastical Commissions and other like Courts; (iv) levying of money by 'Pretence of Prerogative' and without consent of Parliament; (v) the maintenance of a standing army without consent of Parliament; (vi) all Grants and Promises of Fines and Forfeitures before the conviction of the suspected person, and (vii) the punishment of subjects for exercising their legal right of petitioning the King. Conversely it declared it to be lawful to petition, and for Protestants to carry arms It further declared that the election of members of Parliament ought to be free; that freedom of speech in Parliament ought not to be questioned in any Court or Place out of Parliament; that Jurors should be properly empanelled; that excessive bail ought not to be required nor excessive Fines imposed nor cruel and unusual punishments inflicted; and, finally, that 'for the Redresse of all grievances and for the amending, strengthening and preserving of the Lawes, Parlyaments ought to be held frequently'. The Bill also prescribed new forms of the oaths of allegiance and supremacy.

It was further declared that William and Mary having on these terms accepted the Crown, the existing Parliament should continue to sit as a legal Parliament and 'with their Majesty's Royal Concurrence make affectual provision for the Religion, Lawes and Liberties of this Kingdom'.

An Act had been already passed for removing and preventing all Questions and Disputes concerning the Assembling and Sitting of the Convention Parliament and its Acts, which were to be valid 'notwithstanding any want of writ or writs of summons or any defect of form or default whatsoever'; and Parliament now proceeded to pass the

Mutiny Act,[1] and Acts prescribing an amended form of the Coronation Oath and the Oaths of Supremacy and Allegiance.

Thus was the 'glorious' Revolution of 1688 accomplished; without the shedding of blood, and with relatively little disturbance of the normal life of the nation.

The Revolution of 1688, like all similar movements in English history, was essentially 'conservative' or in Macaulay's phrase 'defensive'. This is the characteristic on which Burke particularly insists. Burke poured indignant scorn upon the English Radicals of 1789 who, in sympathy with the French Revolution, attempted to establish a parallel between that movement and the English Revolution of 1688. There was between them no analogy. The eminent nonconformist divine, to whom Burke in his *Reflections* replied, had argued that by the Revolution of 1688 the English people had acquired three fundamental rights: (1) to choose their own governors; (2) to cashier them for misconduct; and (3) to frame a government for themselves. Rightly interpreted Dr. Price's propositions were true; but not as Dr. Price interpreted them. Burke was right in denying the doctrine of Elective Kingship and in maintaining that the choice of William and Mary represented 'a small and temporary deviation from the strict order of a regular hereditary succession'. Assuming the illegitimacy of the infant born in 1688, it was hardly so much as that. The Resolutions of 1689, so far from affirming any general right to 'cashier our governors for misconduct', were in Burke's opinion almost 'too guarded'; but the 'spirit of caution' then so clearly predominant did at least prove the anxiety of the great men who influenced the conduct of affairs at that juncture to make the Revolution 'a parent of Settlement and not a nursery of future revolutions'.

Macaulay so far concurs with Burke as to declare that 'the highest eulogy which can be pronounced on the Revolution of 1688 is this, that it was our last revolution'.

Characteristics of the English Revolution

(a) Conservative

---

[1] Cf. *supra*.

But he is much less concerned than Burke to establish its 'conservative' character. On the contrary, he emphasizes the fact that the dynasty was changed and changed by the deliberate act of the people as represented in Parliament.

'It was', he writes, 'even more necessary to England at that time that her king should be a usurper than that he should be a hero. There could be no security for good government without a change of dynasty. The reverence for hereditary right and the doctrine of passive obedience had taken such a hold on the mind of the Tories that if James had been restored to power on any conditions their attachment to him would in all probability have revived, as the indignation which recent oppression had produced faded from their minds. It had become indispensable to have a sovereign whose title to the throne was bound up with the title of the nation to its liberties.'

(b) Parlia-
mentary
Whether Burke be right in regarding the Revolution as essentially 'Conservative' in character, or Macaulay in emphasizing the radical nature of the change effected thereby, it possessed one feature as to which there can be no controversy. The movement of 1688, like that of 1660, was pre-eminently a parliamentary movement. Regarded by some as embodying the triumph of 'Whig' principles; by others as testifying to the innate conservatism of the English character, the success of the Revolution is a striking illustration of the virtues of Representative Government. 'By far its most momentous scenes were', as Mr. H. D. Traill justly observed, 'enacted within the four walls of the meeting places of deliberative assemblies and find their chronicle in the dry records of votes and resolutions.'[1] The Revolution was not, in the strict sense a 'democratic' movement. Its work was not confirmed by plebiscite or Referendum. It was rather 'aristocratic' in the sense that throughout the critical days the nation was led, and was seemingly content to be led, by the best and wisest among them. That the nation acquiesced in the decisions at which the leaders arrived is clear; but the

[1] *William III*, p. 39.

movement was never a popular movement either in the strict or the common use of the word.

Such popularity as it did command was, indeed, singularly evanescent. For this there were several reasons. Perhaps the strongest was the shock which, despite all the precautions taken by Archbishop Sancroft and other leaders of the Tory party in Parliament, was inevitably given to the principle of Passive Obedience. That principle had taken a firm hold on the minds of English Churchmen. The consequences which had ensued to the Church from the temporary divergence from the strait path under Charles II had not been forgotten. The sin of apostasy had been heavily punished. *(c) Popularity Short-lived*

Apart from the inconvenient consequences of disobedience, the doctrine of non-resistance commended itself to the conscience of the nation and to the intelligence of its leaders. All that was best in the nation, as well as a good deal that was worse, was in complete accord with the philosophy proclaimed by Thomas Hobbes of Malmesbury, if not with that of Filmer. The more permanent elements which go to the formation of public opinion were during the period between 1660 and 1688 on the whole inimical to liberty. The Revolution was in fact, as Mr. Lecky insisted, due to temporary, almost accidental, causes.

Nor was the shock to Anglican and Tory sentiments diminished by the decision of Parliament to impose on all the clergy the obligation to take the oath of allegiance. That they had, in the main, passively accepted the new régime ought to have been enough; that they should be compelled to abjure their former loyalties was at once an outrage and · a blunder. The only result of it was to create a schism in the Anglican Church and to give to the less intelligent, though not less devoted, section of the clergy a prominence they would not otherwise have received. The blunder was indeed repeated by the revolutionists in France. But we like to think that the *Civil Constitution of the Clergy* was more characteristic of French logic, than was the Oaths Act of English common sense. *The Non-Jurors*

The Tolera-tion Act The King personally intervened to soften the asperities of his Whig supporters and at the same time to induce the churchmen to relax the provisions of the Test Act. William of Orange was not, indeed, interested in the ecclesiastical prepossessions of his new subjects, and would gladly have concurred in a measure of comprehension which would have admitted Protestants of every type to all the privileges and duties of citizenship. But the Whigs could not forgive the Tory Churchmen for their part in resisting the Exclusion Bill. The Tories were not prepared to forgo the monopoly of office secured to Churchmen by the Test Act. The clergy, therefore, were compelled to choose between their benefices and their consciences. Six Bishops and about four hundred clergy refused the oath and were accordingly deprived of their benefices. A Toleration Bill became law, but it only relieved those who had taken the new oaths of supremacy and allegiance from penalties for non-attendance at Church. Limited as the 'toleration' thus secured might be, it was a step towards religious equality, and the Indemnity Bills which were regularly passed from 1727 onwards gave the Protestant Nonconformists virtual though not nominal equality long before the Test Act was formally repealed.

Character of Wil-liam III Another reason for the short-lived popularity of the Revolution was to be found in the character of the new King and in the rapid development of differences between him and his English sponsors. His cold manners, his austere temper, and his indifferent health militated against general popularity. Few English Sovereigns have had, indeed, less personal hold upon the affections of their subjects. But there was much more in it than this. It soon became clear that the motives which had inspired the invitation to William of Orange were far different from those which had actuated his acceptance.

Diver-gence of views between William and the Whigs To put it briefly and bluntly, William had been invited to England in order to save English liberty from the assaults of an autocratically minded Sovereign; William came to England in order to save the liberties of Europe at large and Holland in particular from the assault of a

King who sought to establish a French domination over Europe. As Sir Henry Maine has expressed it, perhaps with some exaggeration, 'William III was merely a foreign politician and general who submitted to the eccentricities of his subjects for the sake of using their wealth and arms in foreign war'. This judgement though severe is not essentially inaccurate. As to the personal character of William, Bishop Burnet showed perhaps most understanding:

'His strength lay rather in a true discerning and sound judgement than in imagination or invention. His designs were always great and good; but it was thought he trusted too much to that, and that he did not descend enough to the humours of his people to make himself and his notions more acceptable to them. This in a government that has so much of freedom in it as ours, was more necessary than he was inclined to believe. His reservedness grew on him so that it disgusted most of those who served him. But he had observed the errors of too much talking more than those of too much silence.'

But whether the reasons were personal or political the fact cannot be ignored that, despite his high intelligence, his greatness as a soldier, his statesmanlike outlook upon European affairs, and not least the immense service he rendered to this country at an anxious crisis in its domestic history, William III never evoked anything more than cold respect from his English subjects and sank to the tomb unregretted by them.

Nevertheless, though the popularity of the Revolution was evanescent, and though the King responsible for its orderly and peaceful accomplishment was little liked, the results attained were great and enduring. Never again could the figment of the Divine Right of Monarchy be with any assurance maintained. The English Monarchy did not become elective; but its character was fundamentally altered. We claimed no right to cashier our Kings; but we did gradually establish the effective right of choosing and cashiering our rulers. Without any infringement of the formal prerogatives of the Crown, or any inroad upon the

Results of the Revolution

personal dignity of the Sovereign, we were enabled to secure all the advantages of a republican form of Government without sacrificing the great and solid advantages inherent in Monarchy. In this sense Dr. S. R. Gardiner is right when he says:

'The Revolution was more than a mere change of sovereigns. It was the rejection of the ideas of the minority of 1641 which had been adopted as sufficient at the Restoration in favour of the idea of the supremacy of Parliament. Pym's political ideas were at last to be realized. The name and title of the King were to remain as they had been before. But it was to be clearly understood that if a serious difficulty ensued the King was to give way to Parliament and more especially to the House of Commons, by which the nation was more directly represented. Up to the Revolution England was under a Monarchy surrounded by certain constitutional checks, intended to prevent the will of the monarch from degenerating into arbitrary wilfulness . . .'

So far Gardiner's words will command general assent. The Revolution or its subsequent results were a triumphant vindication of the prescience of Pym. But Gardiner is surely guilty of a very unusual exaggeration when he adds. 'After the Revolution England became practically a Republic in which the Crown possessed various constitutional powers intended to prevent the will of the representatives of the people from degenerating into arbitrary wilfulness.'

Had Gardiner lived another twenty years and seen the growing importance of the Monarchy in relation to the British Commonwealth of Nations, to say nothing of its conspicuous services in the assuagement of class bitterness at home, he would almost certainly have reconsidered his statement. General Smuts was nearer to the truth when he affirmed that 'you cannot make a Republic of the British Commonwealth of Nations'. The Monarchy, valuable as a domestic Institution, is indispensable to the Empire.

Nevertheless, the Revolution did mark an important change. Henceforward Sovereignty was vested in the

King-in-Parliament. The exclusive control over national taxation and expenditure; the control of the armed forces of the Crown through the annual Mutiny Act; above all, the control over the Executive gradually established by the evolution of the cabinet did undoubtedly combine to invest Parliament, and in particular the House of Commons, with a new importance in the Polity.

Another change social as well as political dates from the Revolution. The Government of England between 1688 and 1832 may, with propriety, be described as an Aristocracy, though Seeley and others contend that as the century advanced, Aristocracy was degenerating into Oligarchy. Whichever appellation be more precisely accurate the Government was certainly in the hands of the few. In the earlier part of the period the 'few' were almost invariably large landed proprietors. But gradually, though very gradually, the exclusive influence of the landed interest diminished. The 'monied interest'—closely connected with ecclesiastical nonconformity—began to challenge the supremacy of the land. The 'nabobs', men enriched by trade with India, purchased boroughs and they or their nominees began to jostle in the House of Commons, the nominees of the great landlords, the Pelhams, Russells, Cavendishes, Bentincks, and the rest.

The rule of an Aristocracy

'The State is become under ancient and known forms a new and undefinable monster; composed of a King without monarchical splendour, a Senate of Nobles without aristocratical independency, and a Senate of Commons without democratical freedom.'

So Bolingbroke wrote in his *Dissertation on Parties* (1733). But Bolingbroke wrote as a disappointed politician. Disraeli reviewing, a century later, the same situation wrote:

'It could no longer be concealed that by virtue of a plausible phrase power had been transferred from the Crown to a Parliament, the members of which were appointed by an extremely limited and exclusive class, who owned no responsibility to the country, who debated and voted in secret and who were regularly paid by the small knot of great families that by this machinery secured the permanent possession of the King's treasury. Whiggism was putrescent in the nostrils of the nation.' There was an element of truth in the indictment, but Disraeli, like Bolingbroke, wrote as a keen partisan. Impartial history has decided that the Aristocratic régime of the eighteenth century, though by no means exempt from the characteristic defects of Aristocracy, secured to England better domestic government than any other régime in contemporary Europe, and brought the country, on the whole with triumphal success,[1] through a difficult and critical period in world history.

Freedom of Opinion   Finally, it must be observed that in three important directions the bounds of English freedom were widened in the period initiated by the Revolution. Of the growth of religious toleration something has been said already. Closely related to it was the increased liberty accorded to the expression of opinion.

'Give me', wrote Milton, 'the liberty to know, to utter and to argue, freely according to conscience, above all other liberties.'[2] That liberty was consistently denied to their subjects by the Stuart Kings. Until the Reformation a vigorous censorship over the expression of opinion was exercised by the Church. After the Reformation the censorship became part of the Royal Prerogative, and to no part of it did the Stuarts cling more tenaciously.

'Political discussion', writes Erskine May, 'was silenced by the licenser, the Star Chamber, the dungeon, the pillory, mutilation and branding. Nothing marked more deeply the tyrannical spirit of the two first Stuarts than their barbarous persecution of authors, printers and the importers of prohibited books: nothing illustrated more signally the love of freedom, than the heroic courage and constancy with which these persecutions were borne.'[3]

Parliament, when in the ascendant, showed little more liberality than the Crown. But some of the machinery of repression, notably the Prerogative Courts, had been

---

[1] The responsibility for the War of American Secession cannot be ascribed to the Aristocracy.

[2] *Areopagitica.*   [3] *Constitutional History*, ii. 239 seq.

destroyed. So the censorship was less effective, and between 1640 and 1660 upwards of 30,000 political pamphlets and newspapers were issued from the press.

The Licensing Act of 1662 placed the entire control of printing in the hands of the Crown, and the later Stuarts exercised their powers with not less severity than their predecessors. Authors and printers were hanged, quartered, mutilated, pilloried, flogged, fined, and imprisoned according to the temper of the judges.[1]

The Revolution brought immediate relief from intoler- able tyranny in this important sphere, and after Parliament refused, in 1695, to renew the Licensing Act, the Press entered upon an era of freedom limited only by the uncertainties of the law of libel.

Of all directions in which the Revolution opened up new paths to freedom the most important, from the angle of the present work, perhaps from any angle, was the emancipation of the Judiciary from the control of the Executive. The *Act of Settlement*, as we have already seen,[2] contained a clause declaring that ' Judges Commissions be made *quamdiu se bene gesserint* and their salaries ascertained and established, but upon the Address of both Houses of Parliament it may be lawful to remove them'. In this respect Parliament has not stepped into the shoes of the Crown. The Stuarts, as we have seen, constantly dismissed Judges who displeased them. Since the Act of Settlement the Judges have been practically irremovable, and have fulfilled their supremely important functions fearlessly, to the immense advantage of the cause of personal and political liberty.

An acute German critic of English institutions has characterized England as a law-State. ' The Parliamentary Government of England is a Government', wrote Rudolph von Gneist, 'according to law and through law.' Conspicuously true as the observation is, it has been true only since the Revolution emancipated the Judges from dependence upon the Executive.

Marginal notes: Licensing Act lapsed 1695

Independence of the Judiciary

[1] May, *op. cit.*   [2] *Supra*, c. iv

XIX. THE THREE KINGDOMS

The Revolution in Scotland and Ireland

THE Revolution of 1688 is an outstanding event in
Scottish and Irish, no less than in English history. But it
varied greatly in the three Kingdoms in circumstances, in
proximate antecedents, and in ultimate results. Accomplished in England without bloodshed and within the four
walls of Parliament, it is associated in Irish history with
the sieges of Derry and Limerick, and the battle of the
Boyne; in Scottish history with stormy scenes in the
capital, with Dundee's victory at Killiecrankie, and with
the massacre of Glencoe. Yet sharply contrasted as were
the scenes which marked the climax of the great drama of
the Stuart Monarchy, the fortunes of the three Kingdoms
were throughout the whole of that drama closely interwoven.

Personal
union of
England
and
Scotland

By the accession of James I to the English throne, England
and Scotland were brought into personal, though not into
organic or legislative, union. The Crowns were united in
one person; the two Kingdoms remained distinct and
independent. Yet the union of the Crowns meant a great
deal to the King. James spoke from bitter experience
when he declared that 'Presbyterianism agreeth as well
with Monarchy as God and the Devil'. The position of
'God's silly vassal in Scotland' was indeed humiliating,
and James himself frequently confided to his intimates
that 'he never looked upon himself to be more than King
of Scotland in name, till he came to be King of England,
but *now one Kingdom would help him to govern the other
or he had studied Kingcraft to very little purpose*'. The
italicized words give us the clue to Stuart policy in both
countries. To James and Charles the union of the Crowns
meant the opportunity of playing off one Kingdom against
the other. With what disastrous results they attempted to
play a game appropriate to men of mean stature we have
already seen.

The conflict which the Kings provoked wears, however, a very different aspect in the two countries. In England the King was confronted by a Parliament which was truly representative of a people who had already attained a remarkable degree of national solidarity. Nobles, squires, and burgesses were united in repelling the assaults of the King upon 'rights' which were the common heritage of all classes. Contrast between the two Kingdoms

In Scotland no such solidarity existed. It is true that when her independence was threatened by the Plantagenets Scotland showed that she possessed a sense of nationality strong enough to repel all attempts at forcible union with her southern neighbour. But in the absence of external attack the fissiparous forces incidental to a feudal society reasserted themselves. Between the nobility still feudal, the Church, and the boroughs, there was no real cohesion. Consequently the centre of opposition to the Crown was found not in the Scottish Estates, or Parliament, but in the hierarchical organization of the Presbyterian Church.

To describe the English Reformation as a political movement is to give a false impression. The influence of Parliament, composed mainly of lay-men, was throughout predominant. In Scotland the Reformation was primarily an ecclesiastical movement. In England it issued in the domination of the State over the Church. In Scotland the Church dominated the State. Milton spoke more than a half-truth when he said 'New Presbyter is but old Priest writ large'. Consequently, in England resistance to the Crown was led by Parliament; in Scotland the Monarchy found its most powerful opponent in a Church organized on the Genevan model.

Even before his accession to the English throne James I had made strenuous efforts to impose Episcopacy upon the Scottish Church. But in Scotland 'Bishops were always looked upon with a frown', and though James forced many of the clergy to recognize Episcopacy in 1584 his success was short-lived, and in 1592 the Scottish Estates abolished Episcopacy and established Presbyterianism by James VI and the Scottish Church law. James, thwarted by Parliament, then attempted to introduce Episcopacy by packing the General Assembly; but again he found the forces opposed to him too strong, and realized that persistence might cost him his Crown.

Episco-
pacy in
Scotland
As King of England, ruling his northern Kingdom from London, James was, however, in a very different position. In 1604 he forbade the meeting of the General Assembly, and Ministers who defied his order were arrested, their leaders were tried for, and convicted of, high treason, and the sentence of death was commuted only for one of transportation for life. Bitter persecution was the lot of any who attempted to withstand the will of a King safely entrenched in England, and by a series of measures (1609–12) Episcopacy was established in its entirety in Scotland. Three Scottish Bishops were summoned to England to receive Consecration at the hands of those who were in direct succession to the apostles, and in turn imparted a like authority to their brethren in Scotland. The edifice of Scottish Episcopacy was crowned by the establishment by Royal Prerogative of two Courts of High Commission for the chastisement of offenders against the laws of the Church.

The
Articles
of Perth
1618
In 1617 James visited his northern Kingdom to make personal investigation into the progress of his policy, and to complete the assimilation of the two churches. Laud, lately promoted to the Deanery of Gloucester, was in attendance on the King. Special emphasis was laid on five points: kneeling at Communion, private Communion for the sick, private Baptism in special cases, observance of the great Christian festivals, and Episcopal Confirmation.

Even the Scottish Episcopalians disliked and resisted these innovations, but they were accepted by a pseudo General Assembly which met at Perth in 1618, and in 1621 were enacted by the Scottish Parliament, though by a small majority, as the law of the land. Between 1618 and 1638 the General Assembly never met.

Attempt-
ed Union
Meanwhile James had made more than one attempt to bring about complete legislative union between his two

Kingdoms. Hardly was he seated on the English throne when (1604) he confided to Parliament his anxiety to leave at his death 'one worship of God, one Kingdom entirely governed, one uniformity of law'. Cecil warned him against undue haste, and Parliament refused to prejudge their decision by assenting to his assumption of the title of King of Great Britain. Twenty-eight Commissioners, selected in equal numbers from the two Houses were, however, appointed to confer on the whole matter with a similar body appointed by the Scots. The Commissioners, in addition to several minor recommendations, expressed themselves in favour of a large measure of free-trade and of the naturalization of Scotsmen born since the King's accession to the English throne. The question was settled in favour of the *post-nati* by a judicial decision, but the proposal of a commercial union was hotly resisted and, despite the powerful advocacy of Bacon, was finally rejected. Only the minor recommendations of the Commissioners were accepted.

Charles I took no steps to promote legislative or commercial union, but his anxiety to see complete religious uniformity achieved was greater even than that of his father. It was very near also to the heart of Laud who in 1633 became Archbishop of Canterbury.

Charles I and Scotland

From 1638 to 1660 the affairs of the two Kingdoms are, as preceding chapters have demonstrated, inextricably intermingled. The first and second Bishops' Wars; the 'Incident'; the Solemn League and Covenant; the Second Civil War; the crowning of Charles II; and the legislative and commercial union effected by Cromwell—all these things are as much part of the history of England as of Scotland and further reference to them is, therefore, unnecessary.

By the Restoration of Charles II Scotland may be said, for a second time, to have given a King to England. Scottish pride was gratified and Scottish hopes rose unwarrantably high. Great was their disappointment. For bad as the second Stuart rule proved in England it was

Scotland after the Restoration

infinitely worse in Scotland. The Restoration in Scotland meant not, as in England, the revival of a Parliamentary Monarchy, but the inauguration of despotism more un-limited than any that Scotland had known. A Parliament was indeed restored to Edinburgh, but merely to be the obse-quious instrument of the Crown; all the Acts and Proceed-ings of all the Parliaments since 1633 were by a Rescissory Act annulled; the Lords of the Articles, as constituted under James VI, were revived; a standing army of 22,000 men was established; Presbyterianism was proscribed; more than a third of the ministers were ejected from their benefices; the General Assembly was suspended, and Episcopacy was revived in its most tyrannical form. 'Whoso shall com-pare', writes a Scottish historian, 'this set of bishops with the old bishops established in the year 1612 shall find that these were but a sort of pigmies compared with our new bishops.' Among these, the most tyrannical and the least scrupulous was James Sharp who in 1661 became Arch-bishop of St. Andrews and Primate of Scotland. Until his murder in 1679 the Government of Scotland was virtually vested in his hands and those of the Earl of Lauderdale. Their legal instruments were the Privy Council and the revised Court of High Commission.

They encountered a spirit at least equal to their own. The Presbyterians, especially in the south-western Low-lands, showed no sign of bowing the knee to Prelacy. Denied access to their Churches they betook themselves to field meetings or conventicles. The King's troops, recruited mainly from the Highlands, were quartered upon them: heavy fines were exacted and many suffered torture and death. But nothing could break the indomitable spirit either of the clergy or the people. The conflict between the Government and the Covenanters reached a climax in 1679 with the murder of Archbishop Sharp (3 May), with the defeat of Graham of Claverhouse at Drumclog (1 June) and Monmouth's bloody victory over the Conventiclers at Bothwell Brigg (22 June).

At this juncture the Duke of York arrived in Scotland as

High Commissioner. He soon showed that his little finger was thicker than the loins of Lauderdale.[1] Hallam, most judicial of historians, has given it as his opinion that 'no part of modern history for so long a period can be compared for the wickedness of Government to the Scots administration of this reign'.[2] Strong as the statement is, it does not lack justification. A policy of bitter persecution, steadily enforced, 'produced a dark fanaticism which believed the revenge of its own wrongs to be the execution of divine justice; and as this acquired new strength by every successive aggravation of tyranny it is literally possible that a continuance of the Stuart Government might have led to something very like an extermination of the people in the western counties of Scotland'.[3] Even Sir Walter Scott, Tory as he was, declares that 'consciences which at first were only scrupulous became confirmed in their opinions instead of giving way to the terrors of authority'.[4]

Duke of York as High Commissioner

Terrible, indeed, was authority in those dark days. Nor was there aught in Scotland, as there was in England, to restrain its excesses. A packed and obsequious Legislature, a servile Judiciary, and an Executive entirely controlled by the Crown, combined to establish a tyranny in State and Church rarely surpassed for ingenuity or ferocity. Only people of passionate conviction dared to oppose its decrees. Thus one fanatical leader succeeded another and each led his devoted followers into insurrections which could only end in tortures, executions, or exile. From one of these intrepid leaders, Richard Cameron, the insurgents came to be known as Cameronians.

In July 1681 the new Royal Commissioner summoned a Parliament, the first that had met for nine years, and extorted from it two significant Statutes. The *Act of Succession* declared that 'no difference in religion . . . can

Parliament of 1681

---

[1] Lauderdale did not actually become High Commissioner in succession to Lord Middleton till 1668 but as Secretary to the Scottish Privy Council he exercised great influence over policy.

[2] *Constitutional History*, iii. 328.   [3] *Ibid.*

[4] *Old Mortality*, p. 35. The narrative of Scott's masterpiece opens on 5 May 1979.

alter or divert the right of succession and lineal descent of the Crown'. The *Test Act* compelled all holders of office in Church or State to make a declaration affirming the doctrine of passive obedience and promising never to attempt any alteration in the government of either Church or State.

The extreme Cameronians were ready with their retort. Hunted 'like partridges on the mountains' they at last in their *Apologetical Declaration* took the offensive against their oppressors. Agents of the Government rash enough to hunt them down were warned that they did so at peril of their lives. It is small wonder that those who refused to abjure this Declaration were handed over to military execution. Nothing, however, could crush the spirit of men who were convinced that they were fighting under the standard of the Cross against apostasy and idolatry.

Reign of James II The accession of James II to the throne of both Kingdoms rendered even more desperate the plight of the Scottish Presbyterians. The new King omitted to take the Coronation oath binding the Scottish Kings to defend the Protestant religion. Nevertheless, the Scottish Estates gave further proof of their servility by an increased grant of revenue to the King for life, and by passing Acts which made it high treason to take the Covenant, and made attendance at a conventicle punishable by confiscation and death.

Yet there was a limit to their subservience. Enjoined by the new King to repeal the Penal Laws against 'his innocent subjects, those of the Roman Catholic Religion' they would only promise to 'go as great lengths therein, as their consciences would allow', not doubting 'that His Majesty will be careful to secure the Protestant Religion established by law.' Their hesitation was enough for the fanatical autocrat in Whitehall. His request to Parliament had been 'merely an act of courtesy'. As it was not reciprocated, Parliament should be dismissed. The Royal Prerogative availed to secure toleration for Roman Catholics. But at this the Privy Council took alarm. So did the Bishops.

James so far yielded as to include Presbyterians as well as Roman Catholics in his Proclamation of Indulgence. The more moderate Presbyterians availed themselves of its terms to bring home their exiled ministers; the Cameronians would have no truck with a Papist.

Meanwhile the failure of Monmouth's rebellion in England had had its counterpart in Argyll's abortive rising in Scotland. Argyll shared Monmouth's fate. But the long tyranny was nearly overpast. In Scotland as in England the crisis was precipitated by the birth of the Prince of Wales (30 June). On 10 October William of Orange offered to come and deliver the people of Scotland from the tyranny under which they groaned. As in England so in Scotland the partisans of James made little effort to avert the impending doom. The Stuart Monarchy collapsed: and with it the Episcopalian Church Polity.

The Scottish Estates met as a Convention on 14 March 1689, issued (11 April) a Claim of Right and offered the Crown of Scotland to William and Mary. The Estates claimed the right to depose a ruler who had violated the laws of the Kingdom; they adduced fifteen illegal and unconstitutional acts of James, they declared that on these grounds he had forfeited the Crown, and the throne being vacant was offered to William and Mary. The succession was settled upon the heirs of Mary, the Princess Anne and her heirs, and in default on the heirs of William. Three Commissioners representative of the earls, barons, and burghs respectively were appointed to convey the offer of the Crown to William and Mary who formally accepted it and took the customary oath. William did, indeed, demur to that clause of the oath which pledged him to 'root out all heretics and enemies to the true worship of God', refusing to 'lay himself under any obligation to be a persecutor'; but the explanations offered by the Commissioners appeared satisfactory and William gave way. *The Convention*

Scotland, however, was not England; the Highland clans were more interested in the feud between Campbells and Macdonalds than in the conflict between Papists, Prelatists, *Killiecrankie*

and Presbyterians. The fall of Argyll, chief of the Campbells, had delighted the Macdonalds and other clans opposed to the Campbells. To them the advent of
William meant the restoration of Campbell supremacy.
When the Stuart régime collapsed Graham of Claverhouse,
raised to the peerage as Earl of Dundee by James just
before he abdicated, fled into the Highlands to avoid arrest
and roused the clans to resistance. Some 3,000 clansmen
responded to his call and with them he occupied Blair
Castle, commanding the entrance to the pass of Killiecrankie. General Mackay, with a force about equal in
numbers but much superior in equipment, was sent to
disperse them. The Highlanders attacked Mackay's tired
troops in the pass and they were flung back in headlong
rout; but their defeat was more than discounted by the
death, from a chance shot in battle, of the gallant Dundee.
Mackay soon rallied his forces and dispersed such Highlanders as kept the field after the death of their Chief.

Glencoe   Though the clansmen dispersed, the Highlands as a whole
were far from being reconciled to the new Government.
A free pardon and a considerable bribe—amounting in the
aggregate to £10,000 to £15,000—was offered to all chiefs
who took the oath of allegiance and disarmed their clans
before 31 December 1691. By the day appointed all the
chiefs with one exception had come in, and the clansmen
had brought in their arms to the newly built stronghold
of Fort William. Only the Macdonalds of Glencoe delayed.

Even they were prepared to come in, but William, kept
in ignorance of their intended submission, gave Dalrymple
an order for the extirpation of 'that sept of thieves'.
Under circumstances of revolting treachery and by gross
abuse of hospitality the order was literally obeyed. A
company of Campbells entrusted with the execution of the
order marched to Glencoe where the Macdonalds, un-
suspicious of their mission, entertained them hospitably.
Suddenly and without warning the Campbells fell upon
their hosts, put forty of them to the sword, and the rest
of the clan with their women folk and children fled into

the mountains and there perished miserably. After some years delay the Scottish Parliament investigated the circumstances of the 'massacre'. Dalrymple's resignation was accepted by William; Lord Breadalbane, jointly responsible with Dalrymple for the atrocious crime, was committed to prison on a charge of high treason, but the prosecution was subsequently dropped.

Glencoe left a stain on the memory of William, but the crime achieved its purpose. The Highlands gave the new Sovereigns no further trouble.

The mutual jealousy of the two Kingdoms remained, however, unabated. England was jealous for its trade; Scotland for the independence of its Church and its laws. Yet no statesman, on either side of the border, could ignore the inconvenience, to put it no higher, of the existing arrangement. William, like his great-grandfather, was particularly anxious to bring about the organic union of the two Kingdoms, and in deference to his wishes, though after his death, commissioners met to treat for a union (1702), but failed to find a basis of agreement. *The Union*

The obstacles to Union were, indeed, far from negligible: but the passing of the Act of Security by the Scottish Estates in 1704 brought home to all sober-minded statesmen the danger of further delay. That measure represented an agreement, in a sense hostile to the English connexion, between all parties in Scotland. The Protestants insisted that no sovereign of England should, after the death of Queen Anne, be recognized as Sovereign of Scotland unless satisfactory guarrantees were given for the religion, trade, and laws of the Scottish Kingdom. The Jacobites and Roman Catholics procured the exclusion of the descendants of the Princess Sophia of Hanover from the succession to the throne. This meant, in effect, that on the death of the reigning Queen the Scottish Crown would descend to the Pretender. That in turn meant a renewal of war between the two Kingdoms.

The idea was insupportable: but not until 1706 were negotiations so far advanced as to permit the reappointment of Commissioners to draw up a treaty of Union. Despite the opposition of the extreme Jacobites and extreme Presbyterians, terms were at last agreed and Bills giving effect to them were passed through both Parliaments.

The principal articles of the Union were as follows:

(1) That the two kingdoms should upon the first day of May next ensuing and for ever after be united into one kingdom by the name of Great Britain; (2) That the succession to the Monarchy of Great Britain should be vested in the Princess Sophia of Hanover and the heirs of her body being Protestants; (3) That there should be one Common Parliament in which sixteen Scotch peers, to be elected by their own body, and forty-five representatives of the counties and boroughs should sit; (4) That Scotland should have perfect equality of trade and navigation with England; (5) That the two countries should have a common mint, common coinage, common weights and measures, and equal excise duties; but Scotland in all other matters was to retain her own laws and forms of judicial procedure; (6) The English Parliament voted £398,085 10s. to indemnify the Scotch for loss consequent on change of coinage, &c.: the public debts of Scotland were paid and £2,000 a year was voted for the encouragement of Scotch industries; lastly, and not least, the Presbyterian Church of Scotland was to be preserved as an Establishment.

The Royal assent to the English Bill was given (1707) in words of unusual emphasis and feeling.

'I desire', said the Queen, 'and expect from my subjects of both nations that from henceforth they act with all possible respect and kindness to one another, that so it may appear to all the world they have hearts disposed to become one people.'

That the Union has proved, for both countries, an unqualified success is a commonplace of historical criticism. The fears of Scotland have been entirely dissipated. She has lost nothing of her independence and has gained enormously in wealth. Nor has England suffered. On the contrary, Scottish brains and character have contributed not a little to the expanding trade and the widening political influence of Britain throughout the world.

The best contemporary account of the Union was written by Defoe. From his rival Swift it evoked a satirical comment:

> 'The Queen has lately lost a part
> Of her "entirely-English" heart,
> For want of which, by way of botch,
> She pieced it up again with Scotch.
> Blest Revolution! which creates
> Divided hearts, united states!
> See how the double nation lies,
> Like a rich coat with skirts of frieze:
> As if a man, in making posies,
> Should bundle thistles up with roses.'

Swift's satire was not confined to Scotland. With much better reason, and with far greater effect, he employed it against English ascendancy in Ireland.

If for Scotland the Revolution meant the advent of a new period of prosperity, and the opening of fresh avenues to greatness for her sons, with no real loss of independence, to Ireland it brought a century of unrest and discontent, issuing ultimately in the achievement of a legislative Union which may have mitigated existing sores but certainly opened fresh ones. *The Revolution in Ireland*

The Restoration of the Stuarts was hailed in Ireland with an enthusiasm greater even, if it were possible, than that displayed in England and Scotland. The great mass of the inhabitants had, as we have seen, united in acceptance of Charles II as King as soon as Charles I was dead, and the events of the intervening years had done nothing to alienate their affections from the Stuarts though much to exacerbate their feelings towards the Puritan and Parliamentary party in England.

The situation in Ireland in 1660 was, none the less, one of difficulty and embarrassment. Successive rebellions followed by confiscations, confiscations followed by schemes of colonization and land settlement, had resulted in con- *The situation in 1660* fusion almost indescribable. The whole land of Ireland had been granted and regranted times without number to this party temporarily ascendant, now to that. Mutually conflicting claims had now to be liquidated. To go no farther back than the outbreak of the rebellion, there were at least three parties who could assert valid claims to the land: first, the 'original' proprietors of the soil, that is to say those persons—some Protestants but mostly Catholics —who had been in possession before the rebellion of 1641; secondly, the 'adventurers' who had lent money to the English Parliament for the reduction of Ireland, on the security of debentures redeemable in Irish land; and thirdly, the Cromwellian soldiers who had received grants of land in Ireland in lieu of pay.

Land Settlement under Charles II

At the Restoration most of the land in the three Provinces of Ulster, Munster, and Leinster was in the hands of the 'adventurers' and soldiers. But in November 1660 the King issued a Declaration on which the subsequent *Act of Settlement* was based. The scheme was reasonably fair, but its details need not, for reasons given by Ormonde, detain us.

'If', wrote Ormonde, 'the adventurers and soldiers must be satisfied to the extent of what they suppose intended them by the Declaration; and if all that accepted and constantly adhered to the Prince in 1648 be restored, as the same Declaration seems also to intend, . . . there must be new discoveries made of a new Ireland, for the old will not serve to satisfy these engagements. It remains, then, to determine which party must suffer in the default of means to satisfy all.' [1]

There could not be much doubt. The King's Declaration had been made in all good faith, in the mistaken belief that there was land enough to satisfy all legitimate claims.

'But now', writes Ormonde's biographer, 'that he was sensible of that mistake, and it appeared that one interest or another must suffer for want of reprises, he thought it must be for the good of the Kingdom, advantage of the Crown and security of the Government that the loss should fall on the Irish. This was

[1] Carter, *Life of Ormonde*, ii. 240.

the opinion of his Council; and a contrary conduct would have been matter of discontent to the Parliament of England which he desired to preserve in good humour for the advantage of his affairs and the ease of his Government.'

The Act of Settlement (1662) was, therefore, followed by an Act of Explanation (1665), and in the event, the Catholics who before the Rebellion had held at least two-thirds of the good land of Ireland had now to be satisfied with about one-third.[1] The Irish proprietary became predominantly Protestant.

Nevertheless, though the 'Settlement' was naturally resented by the old proprietors, Ireland enjoyed between the Restoration and the Revolution an exceptional measure of prosperity.

Prosperity of Ireland 1660–88

'Lands', writes a contemporary witness, 'were everywhere improved, and rents advanced to near double what they had been a few years before. The Kingdom abounded with money; trade flourished, even to the envy of our neighbours; cities, especially Dublin, increased exceedingly; gentlemen's seats were built or building everywhere; and parks, enclosures, and other ornaments were carefully promoted insomuch that many places of the Kingdom equalled the improvements of England. . . . And the King's revenue increased proportionately to the Kingdom's advance in wealth and was everyday growing. It amounted to more than three hundred thousand pounds per annum—a sum sufficient to defray all the expenses of the crown, and to return yearly a considerable sum to England to which this nation had formerly been a constant expense.'[2]

Archbishop King was a strong partisan who owed his ecclesiastical preferments to the Protestant interest, but his glowing account of Ireland's prosperity at this period is amply confirmed by other contemporary writers and by modern research.

'Before the days of coal and steam the unlimited waterpower of Ireland gave her natural advantages in the race of manufactures which, if she had received fair play, would have

---

[1] Petty, *Political Anatomy of Ireland.*
[2] Archbishop (of Dublin) King (1650–1729). Quoted by Dunbar Ingram, *Two Chapters of Irish History*, p. 13.

attracted thither thousands of skilled immigrants. . . . This [fair play] was precisely what the reconstituted government of England refused to allow her. By the parties now and for another century in the ascendant there Ireland was regarded as a colony to be administered not for her own benefit but for the convenience of the mother country.'[1]

Though admitted to the benefit of the first Navigation Act of 1660 Ireland was excluded from the Second (1663). Her incipient shipping interest, for the development of which her harbours gave her many advantages, was gradually destroyed. She was forbidden to export her cattle and agricultural produce to England. Later on, the woollen trade, successfully revived by Cromwell, was also suppressed in deference to the jealousy of English manufacturers.[2] For the moment, however, Ireland was exceptionally prosperous, and from the desert of the eighteenth century Irishmen looked back to the reign of Charles II as to a green oasis.

Meanwhile, the legislative union was dissolved, the Irish Parliament restored, and the Protestant Episcopal Church re-established. So complete, indeed, was the restoration of Protestant ascendancy that out of 260 members returned to the House of Commons in 1661 there was but one Roman Catholic.

Irish policy of James II

The accession of James II marked yet another complete revolution in Ireland's wheel of fortune, or misfortune. The efforts of James II to Catholicize England were necessarily tentative. His task in Ireland was naturally easier; there was no need for caution or concealment. His steps, therefore, were rapid and bold. The Protestants were, on one pretext or another, deprived of arms; the Oath of Supremacy was quietly set aside, and the Army, the Commission of the Peace, and virtually all offices were opened to Catholics; the Privy Council was remodelled in the same interest; all the Protestant judges, except three, were dismissed and their places were taken by Catholics. Finally, Clarendon who had accepted office as Lord

[1] e.g. Froude, English in Ireland, i. 181.   [2] Under William III.

Deputy on the understanding that the Restoration settlement was to be maintained in its entirety was recalled, and
'Lying Dick'—Colonel Richard Talbot, now raised to the
peerage as the Earl of Tyrconnel, was appointed in his
place.

'All power', wrote Clarendon to his brother Rochester, 'is in
the hands of the conquered nation, and the English who did
conquer are left naked and deprived even of the arms which
by the patents of plantation, they are obliged to have in readiness for the King's service.'

Many Puritans of the best type had, even in the previous
reign, emigrated to New England. They were now reinforced not only by a large number of Presbyterians and
other Protestant nonconformists but by Episcopalians.

So things developed apace in Ireland until James, a
fugitive from England, landed at Kinsale (12 March 1689).

The arrival of James on the Irish coast announced the James II
approach of yet another crisis in the relations of the two in Ireland
Kingdoms.

It is important to observe its precise character. In
virtue of the decisions of the Parliament at Westminster
James II had ceased to be King of England; William and
Mary reigned in his stead. Had he *ipso facto* ceased to be
King of Ireland? Despite the dissolution of the Legislative
Union accomplished by Cromwell, despite the re-establish-
ment of the Parliament at Dublin, the relations between
England and Ireland were not constitutionally parallel
with those between England and Scotland. Only the
Crown united Scotland and England. Scotland had never
been conquered by England except by the regicide and
rebel who had also, in a sense, conquered England.
Ireland had been conquered, if tardily, by England; the
Irish Parliament had by the *Statute of Drogheda* (1494)
popularly known as *Poynings' Law*—been made dependent
on the English Privy Council, and the Anglican Church
had been established. Ireland, in fine, was regarded as an
English 'colony', Scotland was not.

James II had prepared the ground for himself and his Irish
Catholics

co-religionists in Ireland. It was more than natural that
the Irish Catholics should proceed to cultivate it, and should
clutch at the opportunity provided for them by the English
Revolution and by the arrival of their legitimate King on
Irish soil. Religious zeal, the desire for revenge, the hope of
reinstatement, the prospect of material advantage—all
combined to predispose them in favour of James. The
memories of the Puritan ascendancy were still intensely
bitter; the 'curse of Cromwell' was on the land and the
people; even the Restoration had meant disappointment
and disillusionment for the mass of the Irish Catholics.
The turn of fortune's wheel had now given them their
chance; it were surely madness not to seize it.

Irish
Parlia-
ment of
1689

On the 7th May the Lords and Commons of Ireland met
in Dublin. It was a moot point whether since they had not
been summoned by the 'King of England' they were
technically a Parliament. But, plainly, they were as much
a Parliament as the Convention which in England had
deposed James and enthroned William and Mary. Anyway,
they were so regarded by King James. All those who had
fled from Ireland were summoned to return to the assistance of their King. But the summons was disregarded,
and of the members returned in 1689 only six were Protestants. The Legislation of 1689 reflected the Catholic
complexion of the Parliament not less faithfully than the
Legislation of Charles II reflected the Protestant complexion of the Restoration Parliament. Poynings' Law was
repealed; Catholicism was virtually re-established as the
religion of the Irish State, though there was to be toleration for Protestants who were, moreover, permitted to
pay their dues to their own clergy. As regards the land
an attempt was made to restore the *status quo ante* 1641:
the Acts of Settlement and Explanation were repealed, but
full compensation was to be paid to all who had purchased
land on the security of those Acts; all who gave in their
adherence to William and Mary were to be summarily
deprived of their property; and a sweeping Act of Attainder
was passed. Some 2,000 landowners were declared guilty

of High Treason unless by a given date they could establish their innocence before an Irish Court.

The work of this Parliament has been very variously judged. Macaulay and other Whig writers have thundered forth denunciation of Acts which were undeniably arbitrary and confiscatory in character. Were they more arbitrary and confiscatory than the Acts of the Protestant Parliament of the Restoration? The task of stone throwing in Ireland must be left to those who are without sin. The Catholics were not; nor were the Protestants. Froude brings, perhaps, less cant than most writers to the consideration of a cruel dilemma.

'The question at issue', he writes, 'was whether England had or had not the right to govern Ireland, and the right depended on the relative strength of the two countries. If the Irish could succeed in driving the invaders out by force history would see only legitimate retribution in the proceedings of James's Parliament. . . . It remained to be seen whether the sword would ratify the Statute roll.'[1]

It did not. War had broken out between England and France. With Louis XIV James II was in alliance. Naturally, therefore, the campaign opened on Irish soil. The story of that campaign has been told once for all by a master, and may be read in the twelfth, sixteenth, and seventeenth chapters of Macaulay's *History*. The terrified Protestants had taken refuge in the northern towns of Enniskillen and Londonderry. Of the latter Macaulay writes in one of the finest passages in English prose:

The
Orange
Conques

'Thirty thousand Protestants of both sexes and every age were crowded behind the bulwarks of the City of Refuge. There at length, on the verge of the ocean, hunted to the last asylum and baited into a mood in which men may be destroyed but will not easily be subjugated, the imperial race turned desperately to bay.'

Londonderry was besieged by the Catholic army under Hamilton, but so fierce were the sallies of the brave defenders that the siege had been turned into a blockade.

[1] *Op. cit.*, i. 211, 213.

Hamilton hoped to starve the town into submission and only two days' food remained when on 30 July the English fleet, ordered to relieve the town at any cost, broke the boom across the Foyle. Derry was saved; the Catholic army withdrew and their retreat was turned into a rout by the men of Enniskillen who, under Colonel Wolseley, fell on them at Newtown Butler and drove them south in headlong flight.

Battle of the Boyne 1 July 1690   Ireland, as a whole, however, was held for James. William dare not take the offensive against France leaving the ally of France unconquered in his rear. In June 1690, therefore, he crossed to Belfast, and on 1 July inflicted on James, reinforced though he was by French troops, a crushing defeat on the Boyne. James fled south and took ship at Kinsale for France and Ireland saw no more of him. William entered Dublin in triumph. From Dublin he advanced and gradually conquered the country up to the gates of Limerick where the Irish army, under Sarsfield, made a stand. So stubborn was Sarsfield's resistance that William raised the siege and returned to England (6 September).

Campaign of 1691   In the autumn of 1690 Marlborough took over a force of some 5,000 men to the south of Ireland, and being joined by the Dutch troops, released from the siege of Limerick, quickly reduced Cork and Kinsale. The army was then put under the command of the Dutch General Ginkel and went into winter quarters. The Protestants now held the Provinces of Ulster and Leinster, and, besides Londonderry and Enniskillen, garrisoned the towns of Dublin, Belfast, Dundalk, Drogheda, Waterford, Cork, and Kinsale.

Early in June 1691 Ginkel moved north from Mullingar and encountered the Irish army holding a strong position at Athlone.

Athlone, commanding the passage of the Shannon, had been selected by St. Ruth a French general of ability; but to his astonishment and chagrin it was taken by Ginkel on 30 June, and on 12 July the Dutch general inflicted a crushing defeat upon the Irish at Aughrim where St. Ruth was killed. This battle decided the campaign. Galway was taken and Ginkel then advanced for a second time on Limerick. Cut off from all hope of succour by an English squadron which occupied the Shannon, Limerick capitulated, on honourable terms (3 October).

The surrender of Limerick completed the Orange Conquest of Ireland. More than that, it marked the failure of an attempt to make Ireland, restored to Papal obedience, a dependency of France. Tyrconnel had by a secret treaty with Louis XIV engaged, in case of failure of heirs to James II, to hand over Ireland to the French King and to rule it as a dependency of France. The chance did not come to him. Before Ginkel appeared before Limerick, Tyrconnel, the main agent of James's policy in Ireland, had been carried off by an attack of apoplexy.

Limerick capitulated on the faith of two treaties, a military treaty being signed by Ginkel and a civil treaty by the Lords Justices. By the former the Irish officers and soldiers were to be permitted to withdraw to France and to enter the service of Louis XIV, on condition that, if they elected to do so, they would renounce for ever the birth-right of Irishmen and would be perpetually excluded from their country. The vast majority of the troops, 10,000 in all, exercised this option and earned for themselves great distinction as the Irish Brigade. In the course of the next fifty years they were followed by nearly half a million of their proscribed co-religionists of all classes. Consequently, as Macaulay writes, *Treaties of Limerick*

'scattered over all Europe were to be found brave Irish Generals dexterous Irish Diplomatists, Irish Counts, Irish Barons, Irish Knights of St. Lewis, and of St. Leopold, of the White Eagle and of the Golden Fleece, who if they had remained in the House of Bondage could not have been ensigns of marching regiments, or freemen of petty corporations.'

The Civil Treaty stipulated that Irish Roman Catholics should enjoy such privileges 'in the exercise of their religion as are consistent with the laws of Ireland, or as they did enjoy in the reign of King Charles II; and their Majesties, as soon as their affairs will permit them to summon a Parliament in this Kingdom, will endeavour to procure the said Roman Catholics such further security as may preserve them from any disturbance upon account of the said religion'.[1]

The Irish Parliament was summoned to meet in Dublin in 1695, but refused to ratify the treaty. The refusal was deeply resented by the Irish Catholics who gave to Limerick the name, justly conferred, of 'The City of the violated treaty'. Shamelessly violated the Treaty was, and its violation was a fitting prelude to the period of Whig ascendancy in Ireland (1691–1782). During that period the Dublin Parliament was completely subordinated to that of Westminster; Irish trade was crushed in the supposed interests of English competitors; worst of all, the Irish Catholics, constituting some four-fifths of the entire population of Ireland were cruelly proscribed and subjected to the provisions of the Penal Code, a code built up by a series of enactments and truly described by Burke as 'well digested and well disposed in all its parts; a machine of wise and elaborate contrivance, and as well fitted for the oppression, impoverishment, and degradation of a people and the debasement in them of human nature itself, as ever proceeded from the perverted ingenuity of man.'

Contrast between Scotland and Ireland

The contrast between the effects of the Revolution upon Scotland and Ireland is too painful to be drawn out in detail. Thanks to the precautions taken for the continued establishment of the Scottish Kirk, to the enjoyment of commercial equality with England, to the destruction of feudal privileges, to the jealous regard for the sanctity of Scottish law, and not least to an admirable system of popular education, Scotland entered in the eighteenth century upon a period of unprecedented prosperity.

Had the English Parliament of Queen Anne acceded

[1] Full text of the Treaties in Ingram, *op. cit.*, pp. 143–54.

to Ireland's request for a union of the Parliaments, the darkest chapter in the volume of Irish history need never have been written. As things were, Ireland suffered all the disadvantages of legislative subordination and reaped none of the benefits of union. Crushed under the Penal Laws, denied access to their altars and shut out from the schools, excluded from partnership in the expanding trade of England, and ruled by an oligarchy opposed to them in creed and half alien in blood, the mass of the Irish people could only nourish a deepening hatred of their conquerors and couple in their curses the names of Dutch William and English Cromwell. Paradoxically, however, the demand for reform ultimately came not from the oppressed Irish but from their immediate oppressors—the English colonists in Ireland. But whatever the source, the demand was not heeded, until after the English colonists in America had wrested from England their independence. It was while she still reeled under the shock of American secession that England conceded legislative independence (the 'Grattan Constitution') to Ireland.

XX. ENGLAND AND EUROPE

Four crises of European Liberty LIBERTY is a term admittedly difficult to define, but, in respect of nations, it indubitably involves independence. Four times in the course of the last four centuries has England been compelled to defend her independence against a great Continental Power. In each case she has 'saved herself by her exertions'; in each case she has 'saved Europe by her example'. At the end of the sixteenth century she resisted the assault of the Austro-Spanish Hapsburgs represented by Philip II of Spain. At the end of the seventeenth she resisted a similar assault by Louis XIV of France. At the end of the eighteenth she repelled the attack of Napoleon, bent on the conquest of England as a prelude to the domination of the World. At the beginning of the twentieth century she sustained the Coalition which Germany's bid for world-power had called tardily and reluctantly into being.

It is the second of the great crises with which this narrative is concerned.

The Crisis of 1688 The English Revolution of 1688 marked, as we have seen, the apex of the Constitutional conflict of the seventeenth century in England. But not that only. The fruits of the victory might never have been garnered had England not temporarily accepted the leadership of a great continental statesman who watched the development of the crises from a European and not from an insular standpoint. It is easy to affirm that William of Orange regarded the European situation primarily from the point of view of Dutch independence. He did; but it happened that the interests of the United Provinces, and incidentally the interests of England, coincided with those of Europe at large.

Louis XIV The Treaty of Westphalia (1648), supplemented by the Treaty of the Pyrenees (1659), gave to France a position of pre-eminence in Europe. It was the Austro-Spanish

Hapsburgs who in the sixteenth century had threatened the European equilibrium; it was France who threatened it in the latter half of the seventeenth.

Louis XIV was the heir to the work of the Cardinals, as William II of Germany inherited the estate accumulated by Bismarck. Louis XIV, however, like the Kaiser, was not content with his inheritance. It was his ambition to dominate the loosely federated States of Germany and to erase the Pyrenees. In a word he aimed not merely at achieving security for France, but at dominating Europe.

He might well have attained his ambition had he not, with the insolence begotten of autocracy, thought it incumbent upon him to chastise the republicans of Holland for venturing to thwart his plans; had not the republic thrown up a great statesman and a great soldier in the person of William of Orange; and had not the dynastic connexion of William and the Stuarts pointed him out to the English Protestants as a suitable champion of their cause against a Catholic King.

Thus did the crisis in English domestic politics become inextricably involved in the crisis which threatened the liberties of Europe.

The later Stuarts were the least 'English' of all the Kings who ever governed England. Of their four grand- parents one was a Scot, one a Dane, the third a Frenchman, and the fourth an Italian. Their mother was French. The demands made upon his purse by mistresses and bastards kept Charles II perpetually short of money; Louis XIV was always ready and indeed anxious to supply his necessities—for a consideration. Critics of a later generation, wise after the event, were, as we have seen, quick to upbraid Cromwell for his failure to gauge the situation, and for upsetting the European equilibrium by allying himself with France against Spain. Cromwell, however, allied himself with Mazarin on equal terms. Charles II was not the ally but the pensioner of Louis XIV.

From the moment that his designs upon the Spanish Netherlands were thwarted, albeit partially, by the triple

Charles II and Louis XIV

alliance of England, Holland, and Sweden (1668) Louis XIV recognized the importance of securing at least the friendly neutrality of the insular Kingdom.

The Treaty of Dover (1670) was the first-fruit of the secret negotiations between Louis XIV and his cousin of England. In return for a pension Charles was to aid Louis to achieve his continental ambitions, including, should events fall out favourably, the throne of Spain and its vast dependencies. So it came that when in 1672 Louis XIV delivered his assault upon Holland his army included an English contingent. But, as we have seen, Parliament in 1674 insisted on peace with Holland, though the English contingent remained under the command of Turenne. Not indeed until the last months of the war did the English Parliament succeed in withdrawing the English troops from France and sending them to the assistance of the hard pressed Dutchmen. Even then the action of Parliament was partly neutralized by two further secret treaties (1676 and 1678) negotiated between the two Kings.

William of Orange In 1677 William of Orange had, as we have seen, become the husband of Princess Mary of England, and in the following year Louis having concluded peace with Holland and having no further use, momentarily, for Charles, disclosed to the Opposition the secret treaty negotiated in 1678 with his cousin.

The English Parliament greatly alarmed by the revelation of the intrigues between the two Kings pressed on the Bill for the Exclusion of a Popish Prince from the English throne. The effects of this tactical blunder have been already discussed in another connexion. Meanwhile Louis XIV was steadily pushing the French frontier towards the Rhine. By the Treaty of Nimeguen (1678) he retained Franche-Comté, and on his north-eastern frontier secured a strong line of fortresses stretching from Dunkirk to the Meuse. In 1681 he seized, by a legal subterfuge, the great fortress of Strasburg. In 1684 he besieged and captured Luxemburg, and by the Treaty of Ratisbon, concluded in

that year, obtained control of other important fortresses
on his eastern and north-eastern frontiers.

Hitherto the victorious advance of Louis XIV had been
virtually unchecked. Every indication seemed to point
to the establishment of a French domination over Europe,
not less menacing than that of the Hapsburgs in the
sixteenth century. But in 1688 the Revolution brought
William and Mary to the throne of England. William
accepted the Crown not with the idea of replacing the
Monarchy by a 'Venetian Oligarchy', but mainly with the
object of meeting the threatened supremacy of France by
throwing the whole weight of England into the opposite
scale. The English Revolution and Louis XIV

William achieved his purpose; but not without difficulty.
The outlook of his English friends was curiously, though
characteristically, insular. Their anxiety was for the Protestant Church and the Parliamentary Constitution. They
feared the Pope more than they feared Louis XIV. The
more enlightened of them were convinced that the time
had come for giving effect to the ideas adumbrated by
Pym in the early days of the Long Parliament. The
development of those ideas was temporarily arrested by
the Civil War, followed by the military dictatorship of
Cromwell; but they were based on the logic of constitu-
tional evolution, and their ultimate triumph was assured. William and English Parties

The change of Sovereigns in 1689 afforded a convenient
opportunity for registering a definite constitutional advance. The control over the Executive was to pass from
the King to Parliament. But William was no more disposed
than Cromwell or Charles I to part with a control which
was essential to the fulfilment of the hopes which had
brought him to England.

Personal characteristics increased the tension between
the King and the Whig leaders. William's habits were
those of a recluse; he had as little small talk as Wellington,
and his manners were not more ingratiating than those of
Peel; he neither appealed to the populace nor conciliated
his councillors; above all: he had no mind to be the leader William and the Whigs

of a Party. If he could not lead the English nation into the European crusade he preferred to return to The Hague.

Yet, anxious as he was to be the leader not of a party but of the nation, he was persuaded by the Earl of Sunderland to confide the executive offices exclusively to Whigs, who were thus able between 1693 and 1697 to form a strictly party ministry. Somers, already a great lawyer and soon to establish his repute as a great statesman, became Lord Keeper of the Privy Seal; Lord Shrewsbury and Thomas Wharton were appointed Secretaries of State; Russell, despite his correspondence with James, was rewarded for his great naval victory at La Hogue (1692) by the First Lordship of the Admiralty, while Charles Montagu gave for the first time eminent distinction to the office of Chancellor of the Exchequer. To find in the formation of this Whig *Junto* the origin of the modern Cabinet is greatly to exaggerate its significance. Nevertheless, it does mark an important stage in its evolution.

The French War As so often happened, it was the exigencies of war and the pressure of foreign affairs which hastened constitutional evolution at home. The war against Louis XIV had been going none too well for William and his allies of the League of Augsburg. William's victory at the Boyne (1 July 1690) was dimmed in English eyes by the humiliating defeat inflicted by the French upon the English fleet off Beachy Head (10 July). In May 1692 that defeat was more than avenged by Russell's great victory at La Hogue, but three months later William himself suffered defeat at Steinkirke and a year·later at Neerwinden and Landen (July 1693). In 1694 an English expedition against Brest was repulsed with heavy loss, but the English fleet retorted by the bombardment of the channel ports—Dunkirk, Calais, Dieppe, and Havre. Russell rendered admirable service to the allied cause by his successful operations in the Mediterranean, and in August 1695 William won a resounding triumph by recapturing the great fortress of Namur.

Peace of Ryswick Crowned with the laurels of this victory William returned to England, dissolved Parliament, and was rewarded by the election of a House of Commons, preponderatingly Whig in complexion and pledged to a vigorous prosecution of the war. But Louis XIV was tiring of the struggle, or perhaps wanted his hands free to prepare for a greater one. In May 1697 a congress met at Ryswick and terms of peace were agreed. France restored all the conquests she had made since 1678, acknowledged William as King of England and the Princess Anne as his successor.

The Treaty was highly popular in England and was rightly regarded as a great personal triumph for William; but it did not avail to avert a drastic reduction of the army nor the dismissal of William's Dutch guards who were sent back to Holland in the following year. William was deeply chagrined and contemplated retirement to The Hague; but the European situation was menacing, and England might again be brought to realize the interdependence of her liberties and those of Europe at large. Once again William 'submitted to the eccentricities of his [English] subjects for the sake of using their wealth and arms' in the war, the imminent renewal of which he clearly foresaw.

The Treaty of Ryswick merely provided a breathing space for the combatants. Charles II of Spain, always feeble in body and mind, was known to be approaching his end. He had been twice married, but was childless. Who was to succeed to his dominions? Though greatly diminished since the days of Spain's grandeur those dominions were still vast, including as they did, besides Spain itself, the Spanish Netherlands (later known as Belgium), the Duchy of Milan, the Kingdom of Naples and Sicily, and a great transatlantic Empire in the West Indies and South America. Evidently the disposition of such an inheritance was a matter of interest far beyond the confines of Spain itself. *The Spanish Succession*

Who were the claimants? Charles had two sisters: the elder, Maria Theresa was the wife of Louis XIV, the younger Margaret had married the Emperor Leopold I. The Infanta Maria Theresa had on her marriage renounced for herself and her posterity all claim on the Spanish inheritance, and the renunciation had been duly ratified by the Cortes. But Louis XIV himself had a claim derived from his mother Anne, a daughter of Philip III of Spain and aunt therefore to the dying king. The Emperor Leopold was also a grandson of Philip III and in the direct male line.[1] His wife Margaret had, like her sister, renounced her claims, but as the renunciation had not been ratified it was regarded as invalid. As it was clearly against the common interest of Europe that the crown of Spain should be united either with that of France or that of the Empire Louis renounced his claims in favour of his second grandson Philip of Anjou; Leopold renounced his in favour of his daughter's son Joseph the Electoral Prince of Bavaria, and on the latter's death (1699) in favour of his second son the Archduke Charles.

The Partition Treaties
In 1699, however, Louis XIV arrived at an agreement with William III for the partition of the inheritance. The bulk of the inheritance—Spain, the Indies, and the Netherlands—was to go to the Electoral Prince Joseph, as the least influential of the claimants; the Archduke Charles was to have Lombardy (the Milanese); the two Sicilies, and the cis-Pyrenaean Province of Guipuzcoa were assigned to France. Such were the terms of the First Partition

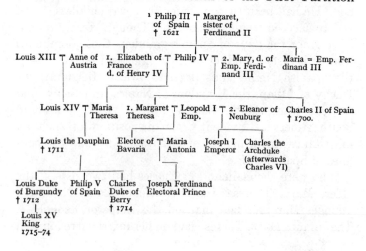

[1] Philip III of Spain † 1621 ⊤ Margaret, sister of Ferdinand II

Louis XIII ⊤ Anne of Austria | 1. Elizabeth of France d. of Henry IV ⊤ Philip IV ⊤ 2. Mary, d. of Emp. Ferdinand III | Maria = Emp. Ferdinand III

Louis XIV ⊤ Maria Theresa | 1. Margaret Theresa ⊤ Leopold I Emp. ⊤ 2. Eleanor of Neuburg | Charles II of Spain † 1700.

Louis the Dauphin † 1711 | Elector of Bavaria ⊤ Maria Antonia | Joseph I Emperor | Charles the Archduke (afterwards Charles VI)

Louis Duke of Burgundy † 1712 | Philip V of Spain | Charles Duke of Berry † 1714 | Joseph Ferdinand Electoral Prince

Louis XV King 1715–74

Treaty (1698). But the Electoral Prince Joseph died in 1699; the work had to begin afresh and by the Second Partition Treaty (1700) Spain, the Indies, and the Netherlands were assigned to the Austrian Archduke Charles, while France, in addition to her former share, was to get the Milanese which were to be subsequently exchanged for Lorraine.

The terms of the Partition Treaties aroused great indignation in England, partly by reason of the fact that William, acting as his own Foreign Secretary, had negotiated them on his own sole responsibility, but not less because the proposed aggrandizement of France in the Mediterranean seemed to the English merchants to be gravely menacing to their interests.

The matter possesses, indeed, only an academic interest for Louis XIV had not the slightest intention of allowing the bulk of the Spanish inheritance to pass to the rival house. He meant to secure the whole of it for his grandson, and so virtually to 'erase the Pyrenees from the map of Europe'. The miserable King of Spain was accordingly tormented on his death-bed by the intrigues of rival diplomatists and the contradictory counsels of competing confessors. In the end he was pursuaded not to break up the splendid Empire he had inherited but secretly to execute a will leaving the whole of his possessions to Philip Count of Anjou.

Charles died on 1 November 1700. The terms of his will were revealed. Louis XIV promptly accepted the splendid inheritance for his grandson. William had been tricked: his laborious handiwork was shattered. *Triumph of Louis XIV*

Bitter as was his indignation against Louis, it was still more bitter against the English people who actually preferred the will to the Partition Treaties. Whether the Spanish throne was occupied by an Austrian or a Bourbon cadet was to them a matter of indifference: that the command of the Mediterranean should pass to France was, on the contrary, a matter of deep concern. The chagrin of William was matched only by his astonishment. 'The blindness of the people here', he wrote to the Pensionary Heinsius in Holland, 'is incredible. For though the affair is not yet public, yet it was no sooner said that the King of Spain's will was in favour of the Duke of Anjou than it was the general opinion that it was better for England that France should accept the will than fulfil the Treaty of Partition.'

In face of this prevalent opinion William was powerless. He could do no other than recognize the Count of Anjou as King of Spain. Moreover, his personal popularity had touched the nadir. Parliament had bitterly resented the large grants of forfeited Irish lands which the King had made to his Dutch friends and his mistress, and had insisted on passing an Act of Resumption (1700). Bentinck, now Lord Portland, Russell (now Lord Oxford), Charles Montagu (now Lord Halifax), and Somers were impeached, though the charges against Somers were dropped.

Louis's Blunders

William's fortunes were clearly at their lowest, when they were almost miraculously restored by two colossal blunders on the part of his great antagonist. Louis XIV had the folly and effrontery to occupy the fortresses of the Spanish Netherlands with French troops. Worse still: when on 16 September 1701 James II died at St. Germains Louis XIV promptly recognized the Prince of Wales as *de jure* King of England.

England and the Low Countries

The English people were touched on their two tenderest spots. For countless generations the Netherlands have been the pivot of England's diplomacy. It is a tradition of English foreign policy that under no circumstances may the Low Countries be absorbed by, or pass under the exclusive influence of, a great continental power. The crises of 1588, of 1793 and of 1914—to name no others— attest the strength and persistence of this tradition. To throw French troops into fortresses which belonged to Spain was at once an intimation to the world that the Pyrenees had been erased and a challenge to the cherished and consistent traditions of English diplomacy.[1]

[1] For a detailed account of the relations between England and the Low Countries. Cf. Marriott, *European Commonwealth*, c. viii.

The menace to Belgian independence was bad enough; the offensive intrusion into English domestic politics was worse. Nothing better calculated to arouse English indignation against France could have been devised by the clumsiest of diplomatists than the action of Louis in recognizing the *de jure* right of the 'Old Pretender', still a very youthful Prince of Wales, to the English throne. William could have asked for no more opportune or effective assistance. The reaction in English opinion was instantaneous. A petition was presented to Parliament from Kent imploring the House of Commons to 'drop their disputes, have regard to the voice of the people and change their loyal addresses into bills of supply'.

The King, quick to trim his sails to catch the passing breeze, dismissed the Tory ministers who had been virtually imposed upon him by the House of Commons, and dissolved Parliament. The country gave the new House a definite mandate in favour of William's foreign policy. A bill was hastily passed for attainting the Pretender. This was followed by a measure to maintain the Protestant succession and to impose an oath to that effect upon all who held office in Church or State.

The Act of Settlement had become law in the previous session (1701). By the enactment of that great statute[1] the coping stone was put on the constitutional edifice of the Revolution. The succession to the throne was settled after the deaths of King William and the Princess Ann, and in default of issue of them, upon the 'Princess Sophia, Electress and Duchess Dowager of Hanover, Daughter of the most excellent Princess Elizabeth, Queen of Bohemia, Daughter of our late Sovereign Lord King James, and upon the heirs of her body being Protestants'. Securities were provided that future Sovereigns should 'join in communion with the Church of England as by law established' and should not marry a Papist. No Sovereign was to leave England without consent of Parliament, and without the same consent no war was henceforth to be

[1] 12 & 13 William III, c. 2.

undertaken in defence of the continental possessions of the Sovereign. No alien was to sit in Parliament or in the Privy Council or to hold office or lands from the Crown. The independence of the Judicial Bench was (as already noticed) to be secured by the provision that Judges were henceforward to hold office during good behaviour and to be removable only on an address to the Crown from both Houses of Parliament. Questions such as those which had arisen in the case of Danby were set at rest by the declaration that a pardon under the Great Seal was not pleadable in bar of an impeachment. Finally, an attempt was made to arrest recent constitutional developments by providing that all matters properly cognizable in the Privy Council should be transacted there, and that all resolutions taken thereupon should be signed by such of the Privy Council as advise and consent to the same. It was also enacted that no person holding an office or place of profit under the Crown or in receipt of a Crown pension should sit in the House of Commons. The last provision was modified in the next reign, the preceding one, in reference to the Privy Council, was repealed. Had these clauses been allowed to stand the evolution of the Cabinet system would have been summarily arrested; the close correspondence between the Legislature and the Executive, perhaps the most characteristic feature of the English Polity, would never have been established, and instead of the mutual and collective responsibility of a small Cabinet we should have substituted the personal responsibility of individual Privy Councillors. Opinions may legitimately differ as to the respective merits of Departmentalism and Cabinet Government; nor is this the place to discuss them; but it is clear that the Act of Settlement, reflecting as it did the fears and jealousies engendered by recent events, would, if unamended, have effectually frustrated the experiment of Cabinet Government and have prevented such merits as it may possess from being manifested to the world.

Death of
William
III

Nevertheless the Act of Settlement, though its main

provisions were dictated by the circumstances of the day, stands out as a great and characteristic feature of our constitutional edifice. The responsibility of Ministers, the independence of the Judiciary, and the Protestant entail of the Crown:—these are among the 'Fundamentals' of a Constitution which in a technical sense has consistently repudiated that distinction between 'fundamentals' and 'circumstantials' on which Cromwell so emphatically insisted.

'The Act of Settlement', in Hallam's stately words, 'was the seal of our constitutional laws, the complement of the Revolution itself and the Bill of Rights, the last great Statute which restrains the power of the Crown and manifests in any conspicuous degree, a jealousy of Parliament on behalf of its own and the subjects privileges. The battle had been fought and gained. . . .'[1]

Within twelve months from the passing of the Act of Settlement William was dead. His mind was vigorous but his body was frail, and a fall from his horse precipitated an illness which resulted in death (8 March 1702).

William died more happy than he had lived. His life had been spent in a prolonged duel with Louis XIV of France. The acceptance of the English Crown was but an incident in the fight. The results which he had achieved by coming to England had disappointed the expectations of both parties to the bargain. To William the English Revolution meant one thing; to the English people or the oligarchy which acted on their behalf it meant another. Yet disparate as were the motives which had inspired the action of William and his English sponsors, the policy of the one was the complement and completion of the policy of the others. The domestic liberties of Englishmen were necessarily insecure so long as the independence of England was threatened by a foreign Power. The menace to the liberties of Europe could not have been averted, as the sequel was to show, but for the cordial co-operation of England. Bolingbroke and Swift may well have been right

[1] *Constitutional History*, iii. 198.

in their contention that the war of the Spanish Succession was unduly and unnecessarily prolonged in order to serve the personal and party ends of the Whigs and of the great soldier who threw in his lot with that party. 'It will not', wrote Bolingbroke, 'because it cannot be denied that all the ends of the Grand Alliance might have been obtained by a peace in 1706.' Nevertheless Bolingbroke himself is the first to admit that the interests of England, no less than of Europe, demanded our active intervention in the war, and our cordial co-operation with our continental allies.

'It is my deliberate conviction,' wrote Bolingbroke, 'after more than twenty years of recollection, re-examination and reflexion, that before this change of policy (in 1707) the war was wise and just, because necessary to maintain that equality among the powers of Europe on which the public peace and common prosperity depend.' [1]

That passage is a complete vindication at once of the men responsible for the transference of the Crown and of the policy of the European statesman to whom it was transferred. Before England could secure her own liberties it was essential to repel the attempt of a great continental Power to establish an hegemony over Europe. Before she could save Europe by her example, she had to save herself by her exertions. In the history of European, no less than of English, liberty the seventeenth century was, therefore, in the largest sense, critical.

[1] *Letters on the Study of History*, Letter viii.

EPILOGUE

THE Bill of Rights and the Act of Settlement marked the close of the conflict between Crown and Parliament, the climax of the struggle for political and personal liberty. The liberties of Englishmen were definitely established on a twofold basis: Responsible Government secured by the doctrine of Parliamentary Sovereignty, and the Rule of Law. But although the constitutional conflict of the seventeenth century had issued in a decisive victory for Parliament, in the refutation of political theories which struck at the root of the liberty of the subject, it was not yet clear by what precise method Parliament would effectively exercise control over the Executive, or by what procedure the Courts of Law would safeguard the liberties of the individual citizen. Victory was implicit in the Revolution Settlement of 1688, but time was needed to harvest its fruits. The points left over for settlement were, however, matters not of principle but of mechanism, and a people who had successfully vindicated their fundamental liberties could safely be trusted to devise appropriate machinery for securing them in detail. A solution of the problem of the Executive was in fact found in the evolution of the Cabinet system; the problem of personal liberty was solved by the steady application of certain fixed principles to the decision of individual cases by an unbroken succession of great lawyers.

To the victory achieved in the seventeenth century Scotland contributed not a little, and in the enjoyment of its fruits Scotland, thanks to the Legislative Union, generously shared. Had it not been for the short-sightedness of the Whig leaders and the jealousy of their commercial supporters, Ireland might, by adopting a similar measure, have shared in them as well. But the Legislative Union with Ireland was unhappily postponed for a century; nor was it, when attained, like the Scottish Union, the outcome of free discussion and friendly adjustment between two independent parliaments. It was imposed on Ireland at a moment when it could be plausibly represented as a penal measure inflicted for the crime of rebellion and it was not accompanied, as in the case of Scotland, by any guarantee for the creed passionately professed by the vast majority of the Irish people.

The Colonies   The seventeenth century was critical not only for England, Scotland, and Ireland, but also, as we have seen, for Englishmen beyond the seas. During that same period Englishmen of all parties, classes, and creeds had carried the seeds of liberty across the Atlantic and had there planted virgin fields from which a liberal harvest was subsequently garnered. The connexion between the insular and the colonial struggle was eloquently demonstrated by a great poet of the Victorian era:

> 'O thou, that sendest out the man
>   To rule by land and sea,
> Strong mother of a Lion-line,
> Be proud of those strong sons of thine
>   Who wrench'd their rights from thee!
>
> What wonder, if in noble heat
>   Those men thine arms withstood,
> Retaught the lessons thou hadst taught,
> And in thy spirit with thee fought—
>   Who sprang from English blood!
>
> .   .   .   .
>
> Whatever harmonies of law
>   The growing world assume,
> Thy work is thine—The single note
> From that deep chord which Hampden smote
>   Will vibrate to the doom.'[1]

Politics and History   Tennyson, like his contemporaries of the Victorian era, looked back with complacent satisfaction upon the work accomplished by their forefathers in the seventeenth

---

[1] Tennyson, *England and America in 1782.*

century. The Eliots and Hampdens, the Pyms and Cokes, had fought a good fight; nor was the guerdon of victory ultimately withheld. But the problems of Politics though presenting themselves in Protean forms are in their essence eternal. Obtruding themselves from the moment when individuals are aggregated in an organized society they cease to clamour for solution only when society is dissolved in anarchy. It is, therefore, less surprising than would at first sight appear that the Lord Chief Justice[1] of to-day should deem it an imperative duty to buckle on again the armour which Chief Justice Coke once wore; that the latest of Bacon's successors[2] on the Woolsack should think it wise to allay apprehensions widely entertained by appointing a committee to consider afresh problems which the seventeenth century was thought to have solved.

Old problems in new forms

The Imperial Parliament is not, as some think, obsolescent, nor are the Judges of to-day less vigilant or less zealous in defence of Liberty than were their predecessors. But Parliament is suffering from overpressure of business; it has been tardy in adapting its procedure and machinery to the altered conditions of the twentieth century; and consequently much of its legislative work is slipshod.

The same insidious disease is attacking the Local Authorities.

Similar results ensue from similar causes. More and more power is inevitably delegated to expert officials. The professional is ousting the amateur. Legislation is passing from Westminster to Whitehall. The work of local administration is increasingly committed to increasingly efficient clerks, secretaries, and directors. County and City Councils are more and more in the hands of their clerks; Education Committees are really directed by their Directors; Watch Committees look to the Chief Constable; Sanitary Committees to the Medical Officer of Health, and so on.

The tendency may be inevitable and, therefore, irresistible. But no one who attempts a scientific analysis of contemporary affairs, who would fain discover whether we

---

[1] Lord Hewart of Bury.   [2] Lord Sankey.

are on the right road or are gliding down the easy descent to the Avernus, can regard these tendencies without concern and even apprehension. On the English citizen-ruler of to-day a responsibility has been imposed heavier than any that ever rested on Roman Caesar, on Feudal Prince, on a King who claimed to be the State, on modern President or Premier. He can discharge it faithfully only if he discerns aright the signs of the times. Some help at any rate towards a clearer vision may be afforded by a careful study of the past. History, it has been truly said, is past Politics; Politics is present History. History is proverbially said to repeat itself. There is a sense in which the proverb is true; another in which it is profoundly misleading. Consequently we must not look to history, as Lord Bryce once sagely remarked, to furnish 'precepts or recipes which can be directly applied to a political problem, as a reported case can be applied by judges to a lawsuit brought before them'.

Nevertheless, the study of History may be and should be invaluable not only to the student of Politics but to the citizen charged with political responsibility. More particularly should he obtain help and guidance from the study of a period in which the English people were faced with problems which, if not identical, were precisely parallel with those which confront them to-day. The problems were presented to the seventeenth century, perhaps, in a cruder and more elementary form. They are on that account the easier to discern, if they were equally difficult to solve. The phenomena of to-day are infinitely more complex, the disease which is attacking our institutions is more insidious; the appropriate remedies are, therefore, less obvious. But we may discover them the more quickly, if we study the symptoms as presented in a less complicated case.

With an ardent desire to contribute to an accurate diagnosis of the disease, and to the discovery of remedies, in the hope that, if discovered, they may be timely applied, the foregoing pages have been penned.

APPENDIX I

A SHORT LIST OF AUTHORITIES
A. CONTEMPORARY

Bacon, F. (Viscount St. Albans): *Works* (ed. J. Spedding). 1857–9.
—— *The Life and Letters of* (ed. J. Spedding). 7 vols. 1868–74.
Baillie, R.: *Letters and Journals* (ed. D. Laing). 3 vols. 1841.
Bruce (ed.): *Notes of Proceedings in the Long Parliament, by R. Verney.*
Calendar of State Papers (Colonial, 1574–). 1860, &c.
—— (Domestic):
————— Edward VI–James I. 12 vols. 1856, &c.
————— Charles I. 23 vols. 1858, &c.
————— Commonwealth. 13 vols. 1875, &c.
————— Charles II. 1860, &c.
————— William and Mary. 1895, &c.
Carte, T. (ed.): *Ormonde Papers.* Original Letters and Papers. 1641–60. 2 vols. 1739.
Clarendon, Edward, Earl of: *A History of the Rebellion.* 7 vols. 1839.
—— *Life* (Autobiography). 2 vols. Oxford, 1857.
Cobbett W. (ed.): *Parliamentary History.* 1806, &c.
—— *State Trials.* 1809, &c.
Cromwell, O.: *Letters and Speeches* (ed. Carlyle). 5 vols. 1871. (Later edition ed. S. C. Lomas, 1904; and of the *Speeches*, ed. C. L. Stainer, 1901).
Davis, Sir J.: *A Discoverie of the True Causes why Ireland was Never Conquered.* 1612.
D'Ewes, Sir S.: *Autobiography* (ed. I. O. Halliwell-Phillipps). 2 vols. 1845.
Dryden, John: *Poems* (ed. 1871).
Firth, Sir C. H. (ed.): *Clarke Papers.* 4 vols. 1891, &c.
—— *Scotland and the Commonwealth.* 1894.
—— *Scotland and the Protectorate.* 1898.
—— and Rait (ed.): *Acts and Ordinances of the Interregnum* 1642–60. 1911.
Gardiner, S. R. (ed.): *Cases in the Courts of Star Chamber and High Commission.* 1886.
—— *Constitutional Documents.* 1889.
Gee and Hardy (ed.): *Documents Illustrative of English Church History.* 1896.
Irish Calendar of State Papers (Ireland) (especially for Chichester's State Papers, which are of great value). 1860, &c.
Journals of the House of Commons (quoted as C. J.).

Journals of the House of Lords (quoted as L. J.).
Ludlow, E.: *Memoirs.* 3 vols. Vevay, 1698.
May, T.: *History of the Long Parliament.* Oxford, 1854.
Nalson, T.: *Impartial Collection of the Great Affairs of State.* 1639–49. 2 vols. 1682.
Prothero, G. W. (ed.): *Select Statutes and Documents.* 1894.
Robertson (ed.): *Select Statutes, Cases, and Documents.* 1904.
Rushworth, T.: *Historical Collections.* 7 vols. 1659.
Strafford, Thomas, Earl of: *Letters and Despatches* (ed. W. Knowles). 2 vols. 1739.
Terry (ed.): *The Cromwellian Union.* 1902.
Whitelock, B.: *Memorials.* 1732.

B. MODERN

Allen, C. K.: *Law in the Making.* 2nd edition, 1930.
Beer, G. L.: *Origins of the British Colonial System.* 1908.
—— *The Old Colonial System.* 1912.
Bright, J. F.: *English History (Personal Monarchy).* 1876.
Carte, T.: *Life of James, Duke of Ormonde.* 3 vols. 1736.
Christie, W. D.: *Life of Earl of Shaftesbury.* 2 vols. 1871.
Corbett, Sir J. S.: *England in the Mediterranean.* 2 vols. 1904.
Dicey, A. V.: *The Law of the Constitution.* 1885.
Doyle, J. A.: *The English in America.* 3 vols. 1882 and 1887.
—— *The Middle Colonies,* 1907.
Egerton, H. E.: *Short History of British Colonial Policy.* 1905.
—— *Origin and Growth of the English Colonies.* 1903.
Feiling, K.: *A History of the Tory Party 1646–1714.* 1924.
Figgis, J. N.: *The Divine Right of Kings.* 1914.
Firth, Sir C. H.: *The Last Years of the Protectorate.* 2 vols. 1909.
—— *Cromwell.* 1900.
—— *Cromwell's Army* (largely based on the Clarke Papers). 1902.
—— *The House of Lords During the Civil War.* 1910.
Forster, J.: *Sir J. Eliot.* 2 vols. 1872.
—— *Arrest of the Five Members.* 1860.
Frere, W. H.: *The English Church.* 1558–1625. 1904.
Gardiner, S. R.: *History of England.* 1603–42. 10 vols. 1883.
—— *History of the Civil War.* 4 vols. 1886.
—— *Oliver Cromwell.* 1899.
—— *History of the Commwealth and Protectorate.* 4 vols. 1903.
Gooch, G. P.: *English Democratic Ideas in Seventeenth Century.* 1898.
Green, J. R.: *Short History of the English People* 1875.
Hale, E.: *The Fall of the Stuarts.* 1877.
Hallam, H.: *Constitutional History* (ed. 1869).
Harrison, F.: *Cromwell.* 1889.
Hewart, Lord: *The New Despotism.* 1929.

Hunter, Sir W. W.: *History of British India.* 2 vols. 1899, &c.
Hutton, W. H.: *The English Church* 1625–1714. 1903.
—— *Laud.* 1895.
Jenks, E.: *Constitutional Experiments of the Commonwealth.* 1890.
Kermack, W. R.: *The Expansion of Britain.* 1925.
Lucas, Sir C. P.: *Historical Geography of the British Colonies.* 1887.
Macaulay, Lord: *History of England.* 4 vols. (ed. 1869).
Marriott, J. A. R.: *Life and Times of Lucius Cary, Lord Falkland.* 1907.
—— *English Political Instituions.* 1910.
—— *The Mechanism of the State.* 2 vols. 1927.
Marsden, J. B.: *History of the Puritans.* 2 vols. 1854.
Masson, D.: *Life of Milton.* 1859–80.
Morley, John (Viscount): *Cromwell.* 1900.
Mozley, T.: *Essays Historical and Theological.*
Neal, D.: *History of the Puritans.* 5 vols. 1822.
Oppenheim, I. M.: *Royal Navy and Merchant Shipping.* 1896.
Patterson, W. M.: *History of the English Church.* 1909.
Pattison, M.: *Milton,* 1879.
Payne, E. J.: *Colonies and Colonial Federations.* 1904.
Pollard, A. F.: *Factors in Modern History.* 1907.
Port, F. J.: *Administrative Law.* 1929.
Ranke, L. von: *History of England.* (E.T.). 1875.
Robinson, Gleeson: *Public Authorities and Legal Liability.* 1925.
Robson, W. A.: *Justice and Administrative Law.* 1928.
Sankey, Lord Justice: *Principles and Practice of the Law To-day.* 1928.
Scott, W. R.: *Joint Stock Companies.* 3 vols. 1910, &c.
Seeley, Sir J. R.: *Growth of British Policy.* 1895.
—— *Expansion of England.* 1884.
Shaw, W. A.: *History of the English Church* 1640–60. 2 vols. 1900.
Smith, V. A.: *History of India.* 1919.
Tanner, J. R.: *English Constitutional Conflicts of the Seventeenth Century.* 1828.
Trail, H. D.: *Strafford.* 1889.
—— *William III.* 1888.
Trevelyan, G. M.: *History of England under the Stuarts.* 1904.
Tullock, J.: *Rational Theology and Christian Philosophy in England in the Seventeenth Century.* 2 vols. 1874.
Wakeman, H. O.: *The Church and the Puritans.* (n. d.)
Williamson, J. A.: *A Short History of British Expansion.* 2 vols. 1930.
—— *Europe Overseas.* 1925.
Woodward, W. H.: *The Expansion of the British Empire.* 1899.

Bagwell, R.: *Ireland under the Stuarts* 1603–90. 3 vols. 1909 &c.
Ball, J. T.: *Irish Legislative Systems.* 1888.

Buchan, J.: *Montrose*. 1929.

Firth (ed.): *Scotland and the Commonwealth*.

Froude, J. A.: *English in Ireland*. 3 vols. 1872.

Hamilton, Lord E.: *The Irish Rebellion of* 1641. 1920.

Hickson, M. A.: *Ireland in the Seventeenth Century*. 2 vols. 1884.

Hume Brown, P.: *History of Scotland*. vol. ii. 1902.

Ingram, T. D.: *Irish History from Elizabeth to* 1800. 2 vols. 1900.

—— *Two Chapters of Irish History*. 1888.

Killen, W. D.: *The Ecclesiastical History of Ireland*. 2 vols. 1875.

Lecky, W. E. H.: *History of England*. (Chapters vi and vii).

Morris Mowbray: *Montrose*. 1892.

Prendergast, J. P.: *Cromwellian Settlement of Ireland*. 1865.

—— *Ireland* 1660–90. 1887.

Rait, R. S.: *Relations between England and Scotland*. 1901.

—— *The Scottish Parliament*. 1901.

Reid, J. S.: *History of the Presbyterian Church in Ireland*. 3 vols. 1867.

INDEX

INDEX

NO